HOUSING ACT 1

Updated as of March 26, 2018

THE LAW LIBRARY

TABLE OF CONTENTS

Introductory Text	5
Part I Rented Accommodation	5
Interpretation of Part I.	55
Part II Housing Associations	56
Determinations under Part II.	70
Interpretation of Part II and amendments of Housing Associations Act 1985.	72
Part III Housing Action Trust Areas	74
Interpretation of Part III.	99
Part IV	100
Right conferred by Part IV.	100
Interpretation of Part IV.	100
Part V Miscellaneous and General	101
Schedules	117
Schedule 1. Tenancies Which Cannot be Assured Tenancies	117
Schedule 2. Grounds for Possession of Dwelling-houses let on Assured Tenancies	127
Schedule 3. Assured Tenancies: Non-Shortholds	137
Schedule 4. Agricultural Worker Conditions	139
Schedule 5. Statutory Tenants: Succession	142
Schedule 6. Amendments of Housing Associations Act 1985	144
Schedule 7. Housing Action Trusts: Constitution	149
Schedule 8. Housing Action Trusts: Finance Etc.	152
Schedule 9. Orders Vesting Land in Housing Action Trusts	156
Schedule 10. Housing Action Trusts: Land	158
Schedule 11. Provisions Applicable to Certain Disposals of Houses	173
Schedule 12. Amendments of Landlord and Tenant Act 1987	179
Schedule 13. Appointment etc. of Rent Officers	180
Schedule 14. Repair Notices: Amendments of Housing Act 1985, Part VI	182
Schedule 15. Schedule to be Inserted in the Housing (Scotland) Act 1987	183
Schedule 16. Minor and Consequential Amendments	185
Schedule 17. Enactments Repealed	204
Open Government Licence v3.0	205

Introductory Text

Housing Act 1988

1988 CHAPTER 50

An Act to make further provision with respect to dwelling-houses let on tenancies or occupied under licences; to amend the Rent Act 1977 and the Rent (Agriculture) Act 1976; to establish a body, Housing for Wales, having functions relating to housing associations; to amend the Housing Associations Act 1985 and to repeal and re-enact with amendments certain provisions of Part II of that Act; to make provision for the establishment of housing action trusts for areas designated by the Secretary of State; to confer on persons approved for the purpose the right to acquire from public sector landlords certain dwelling-houses occupied by secure tenants; to make further provision about rent officers, the administration of housing benefit and rent allowance subsidy, the right to buy, repair notices and certain disposals of land and the application of capital money arising thereon; to make provision consequential upon the Housing (Scotland) Act 1988; and for connected purposes.

[15th November 1988]

X1. Be it enacted by the Queen's most Excellent Majesty, by and with the advice and consent of the Lords Spiritual and Temporal, and Commons, in this present Parliament assembled, and by the authority of the same, as follows:—

Editorial Information

X1. The text of ss. 1–45, 115–121, 138–141, Schs. 1–4, 13, 14, Sch. 17 paras. 1–17, 21–26, 29–36, 67–76, 81–88, 90, 98–100, 114, Sch. 18 was taken from S.I.F. Group 75:1. (Landlord and Tenant: General, England and Wales); the text of ss. 46–114, 121–141, Schs. 5–12, 15–18 was taken from S.I.F. Group 61 (Housing); provisions omitted from S.I.F. have been dealt with as referred to in other commentary

Modifications etc. (not altering text)

C1. Act restricted (26.7.1993) by 1993 c. 23, s. 4. (5), Sch. 1 para. 6. (1)(b); S.I. 1993/1655, art. 2
C2. Act excluded (10.11.1993) by 1993 c. 28, s. 169, Sch. 20 Pt. II para.8; S.I. 1993/2762, art. 3
Act excluded (1.10.1998) by 1975 c. 70, Sch. 4 Pt. IV para. 16 (as inserted (1.10.1998) by 1998 c. 38, s. 127, Sch. 13 para. 3 (with ss. 137. (1), 139. (2), 141. (1), 143. (2)); S.I. 1998/2244, art. 4
Act excluded (25.11.1999 for the purposes of regional development agencies established on that date, otherwise 3.7.2000) by 1998 c. 45, s. 23, Sch. 6 para. 5; S.I. 1998/2952, art. 2. (2); S.I. 2000/1173, art. 2
C3. Act: certain functions of a Minister of the Crown in so far as exercisable in relation to Wales transferred to the National Assembly for Wales (1.7.1999) by S.I. 1999/672, art. 2, Sch. 1

Part I Rented Accommodation

Part I Rented Accommodation

Modifications etc. (not altering text)

C1. Part I (ss. 1–45) modified by S.I. 1990/776, arts. 2. (2), 5. (2)(b) and excluded by Town and Country Planning Act 1990 (c. 8, SIF 123:1), s. 242

C2. Part I (ss. 1–45) applied by National Health Service and Community Care Act 1990 (c. 19, SIF 113:2), s. 60. (2), Sch. 8, para. 19. (3)

C3. Part I (ss. 1-45) definition applied (1.12.1991) by Water Industry Act 1991 (c. 56, SIF 130), ss. 167. (3), 223. (2), Sch. 11 para. 10 (with ss. 82. (3), 186. (1), 222. (1), Sch. 14 para. 6)

C4. Pt. I (ss. 1-45) definition applied (1.12.1991) by Water Resources Act 1991 (c. 57, SIF 130), ss. 168. (3), 225. (2), Sch. 19 para. 10 (with ss. 15. (6), 179, 222. (3), 224. (1), Sch. 22 para. 1, Sch. 23 para. 6)

C5. Pt. I (ss. 1-45) restricted (1.11.1993) by 1993 c. 28, s. 59. (2)(c)(iii); S.I. 1993/2134, arts. 2, 5

Pt. I (ss. 1-45) excluded (3.3.1997) by 1985 c. 68, s. 348. D(5) (as inserted (3.3.1997) by 1996 c. 52, s. 67. (1) (with s. 70); S.I. 1997/350, art. 2

Pt. I (ss. 1-45) modified (1.10.1996) by 1996 c. 27, s. 30. (4)(b); S.I. 1996/2402, art. 3 (subject to transitional provisions in Sch.)

C6. Pt. 1 excluded (6.4.2006 for E. and 16.6.2006 for W.) by Housing 2004 (c. 34), {ss. 33}, 270. (3); S.I. 2006/1060, art. 2. (1)(a) (with Sch.); S.I. 2006/1535, art. 2. (a) (with Sch.)

chapter I Assured Tenancies

1 Assured tenancies.

(1) A tenancy under which a dwelling-house is let as a separate dwelling is for the purposes of this Act an assured tenancy if and so long as—

(a) the tenant or, as the case may be, each of the joint tenants is an individual; and

(b) the tenant or, as the case may be, at least one of the joint tenants occupies the dwelling-house as his only or principal home; and

(c) the tenancy is not one which, by virtue of subsection (2) or subsection (6) below, cannot be an assured tenancy.

[F1. (1. A)Subsection (1) has effect subject to section 15. A (loss of assured tenancy status).]

(2) Subject to subsection (3) below, if and so long as a tenancy falls within any paragraph in Part I of Schedule 1 to this Act, it cannot be an assured tenancy; and in that Schedule—

(a) "tenancy" means a tenancy under which a dwelling-house is let as a separate dwelling;

(b) Part II has effect for determining the rateable value of a dwelling-house for the purposes of Part I; and

(c) Part III has effect for supplementing paragraph 10 in Part I.

[F2. (2. A)The Secretary of State may by order replace any amount referred to in paragraphs 2 and 3. A of Schedule 1 to this Act by such amount as is specified in the order; and such an order shall be made by statutory instrument which shall be subject to annulment in pursuance of a resolution of either House of Parliament.]

(3) Except as provided in Chapter V below, at the commencement of this Act, a tenancy—

(a) under which a dwelling-house was then let as a separate dwelling, and

(b) which immediately before that commencement was an assured tenancy for the purposes of sections 56 to 58 of the M1. Housing Act 1980 (tenancies granted by approved bodies),

shall become an assured tenancy for the purposes of this Act.

(4) In relation to an assured tenancy falling within subsection (3) above—

(a) Part I of Schedule 1 to this Act shall have effect, subject to subsection (5) below, as if it consisted only of paragraphs 11 and 12; and

(b) sections 56 to 58 of the Housing Act 1980 (and Schedule 5 to that Act) shall not apply after the commencement of this Act.

(5) In any case where—

(a) immediately before the commencement of this Act the landlord under a tenancy is a fully mutual housing association, and

(b) at the commencement of this Act the tenancy becomes an assured tenancy by virtue of subsection (3) above,

then, so long as that association remains the landlord under that tenancy (and under any statutory periodic tenancy which arises on the coming to an end of that tenancy), paragraph 12 of Schedule 1 to this Act shall have effect in relation to that tenancy with the omission of sub-paragraph (1)(h).

F3. (6). . . . .

F3. (7). . . . .

Amendments (Textual)

F1. S. 1. (1. A) inserted (15.10.2013 for E., 5.11.2013 for W.) by Prevention of Social Housing Fraud Act 2013 (c. 3), s. 12, Sch. para. 4; S.I. 2013/2622, art. 2; S.I. 2013/2861, art. 2

F2. S. 1. (2. A) inserted by S.I. 1990/434, reg. 2, Sch. para. 27

F3. S. 1. (6)(7) repealed (20.1.1997) by 1996 c. 52, s. 227, Sch. 19 Pt. VIII; S.I. 1996/2959, art. 2 (subject to transitional provisions in Sch. para. 1)

Modifications etc. (not altering text)

C7. S. 1. (2) excluded (6.4.2006 for E. and 16.6.2006 for W.) by Housing Act 2004 (c. 34), ss. 132, 270, Sch. 7 para. 18. (6)(b); S.I. 2006/1060, art. 2. (1)(a) (with Sch.); S.I. 2006/1535, art. 2. (a) (with Sch.)

C8. S. 1. (2) excluded (6.4.2006 for E. and 16.6.2006 for W.) by Housing Act 2004 (c. 34), ss. 132, 270, Sch. 7 para. 12. (5)(b) (with Sch. 7 para. 12. (9)); S.I. 2006/1060, art. 2. (1)(a) (with Sch.); S.I. 2006/1535, art. 2. (a) (with Sch.)

C9. S. 1. (2) excluded (6.4.2006 for E. and 16.6.2006 for W.) by Housing Act 2004 (c. 34), ss. 132, 270, Sch. 7 para. 4. (5)(b); S.I. 2006/1060 {art. 2. (1)(a)} (with Sch.); S.I. 2006/1535, art. 2. (a) (with Sch.)

C10. S. 1. (2) excluded (16.6.2006 for W. and 6.4.2006 for E.) by Housing Act 2004 (c. 34), ss. 124. (8), 270 (with s. 124. (9)(10)); S.I. 2006/1535, art. 2. (a) (with Sch.); S.I. 2006/1060, art. 2

Marginal Citations

M1 1980 c. 51.

2 Letting of a dwelling-house together with other land.

(1) If, under a tenancy, a dwelling-house is let together with other land, then, for the purposes of this Part of this Act,—

(a) if and so long as the main purpose of the letting is the provision of a home for the tenant or, where there are joint tenants, at least one of them, the other land shall be treated as part of the dwelling-house; and

(b) if and so long as the main purpose of the letting is not as mentioned in paragraph (a) above, the tenancy shall be treated as not being one under which a dwelling-house is let as a separate dwelling.

(2) Nothing in subsection (1) above affects any question whether a tenancy is precluded from being an assured tenancy by virtue of any provision of Schedule 1 to this Act.

3 Tenant sharing accommodation with persons other than landlord.

(1) Where a tenant has the exclusive occupation of any accommodation (in this section referred to as "the separate accommodation") and—

(a) the terms as between the tenant and his landlord on which he holds the separate accommodation include the use of other accommodation (in this section referred to as "the shared accommodation") in common with another person or other persons, not being or including the landlord, and

(b) by reason only of the circumstances mentioned in paragraph (a) above, the separate accommodation would not, apart from this section, be a dwelling-house let on an assured tenancy, the separate accommodation shall be deemed to be a dwelling-house let on an assured tenancy and the following provisions of this section shall have effect.

(2) For the avoidance of doubt it is hereby declared that where, for the purpose of determining the rateable value of the separate accommodation, it is necessary to make an apportionment under Part II of Schedule 1 to this Act, regard is to be had to the circumstances mentioned in subsection (1)(a) above.

(3) While the tenant is in possession of the separate accommodation, any term of the tenancy

terminating or modifying, or providing for the termination or modification of, his right to the use of any of the shared accommodation which is living accommodation shall be of no effect.

(4) Where the terms of the tenancy are such that, at any time during the tenancy, the persons in common with whom the tenant is entitled to the use of the shared accommodation could be varied or their number could be increased, nothing in subsection (3) above shall prevent those terms from having effect so far as they relate to any such variation or increase.

(5) In this section "living accommodation" means accommodation of such a nature that the fact that it constitutes or is included in the shared accommodation is sufficient, apart from this section, to prevent the tenancy from constituting an assured tenancy of a dwelling-house.

4 Certain sublettings not to exclude any part of sub-lessor's premises from assured tenancy.

(1) Where the tenant of a dwelling-house has sub-let a part but not the whole of the dwelling-house, then, as against his landlord or any superior landlord, no part of the dwelling-house shall be treated as excluded from being a dwelling-house let on an assured tenancy by reason only that the terms on which any person claiming under the tenant holds any part of the dwelling-house include the use of accommodation in common with other persons.

(2) Nothing in this section affects the rights against, and liabilities to, each other of the tenant and any person claiming under him, or of any two such persons.

Security of tenure

5 Security of tenure.
[F4. (1)An assured tenancy cannot be brought to an end by the landlord except by—
    (a) obtaining—
(i) an order of the court for possession of the dwelling-house under section 7 or 21, and
(ii) the execution of the order,
    (b) obtaining an order of the court under section 6. A (demotion order), F5...
    (c) in the case of a fixed term tenancy which contains power for the landlord to determine the tenancy in certain circumstances, by the exercise of that power[F6, or
    (d) in the case of an assured tenancy—
(i) which is a residential tenancy agreement within the meaning of Chapter 1 of Part 3 of the Immigration Act 2014, and
(ii) in relation to which the condition in section 33. D(2) of that Act is met,
giving a notice in accordance with that section,]
and, accordingly, the service by the landlord of a notice to quit is of no effect in relation to a periodic assured tenancy.
(1. A)Where an order of the court for possession of the dwelling-house is obtained, the tenancy ends when the order is executed.]
(2) If an assured tenancy which is a fixed term tenancy comes to an end otherwise than by virtue of—
    (a) an order of the court [F7of the kind mentioned in subsection (1)(a) or (b) or any other order of the court], F8...
    (b) a surrender or other action on the part of the tenant[F9, or
    (c) the giving of a notice under section 33. D of the Immigration Act 2014,]
then, subject to section 7 and Chapter II below, the tenant shall be entitled to remain in possession of the dwelling-house let under that tenancy and, subject to subsection (4) below, his right to possession shall depend upon a periodic tenancy arising by virtue of this section.
(3) The periodic tenancy referred to in subsection (2) above is one—
    (a) taking effect in possession immediately on the coming to an end of the fixed term tenancy;
    (b) deemed to have been granted by the person who was the landlord under the fixed term tenancy immediately before it came to an end to the person who was then the tenant under that tenancy;
    (c) under which the premises which are let are the same dwelling-house as was let under the

fixed term tenancy;

(d) under which the periods of the tenancy are the same as those for which rent was last payable under the fixed term tenancy; and

(e) under which, subject to the following provisions of this Part of this Act, the other terms are the same as those of the fixed term tenancy immediately before it came to an end, except that any term which makes provision for determination by the landlord or the tenant shall not have effect while the tenancy remains an assured tenancy.

(4) The periodic tenancy referred to in subsection (2) above shall not arise if, on the coming to an end of the fixed term tenancy, the tenant is entitled, by virtue of the grant of another tenancy, to possession of the same or substantially the same dwelling-house as was let to him under the fixed term tenancy.

(5) If, on or before the date on which a tenancy is entered into or is deemed to have been granted as mentioned in subsection (3)(b) above, the person who is to be the tenant under that tenancy—

(a) enters into an obligation to do any act which (apart from this subsection) will cause the tenancy to come to an end at a time when it is an assured tenancy, or

(b) executes, signs or gives any surrender, notice to quit or other document which (apart from this subsection) has the effect of bringing the tenancy to an end at a time when it is an assured tenancy,

the obligation referred to in paragraph (a) above shall not be enforceable or, as the case may be, the surrender, notice to quit or other document referred to in paragraph (b) above shall be of no effect.

[F10. (5. A) Nothing in subsection (5) affects any right of pre-emption—

(a) which is exercisable by the landlord under a tenancy in circumstances where the tenant indicates his intention to dispose of the whole of his interest under the tenancy, and

(b) in pursuance of which the landlord would be required to pay, in respect of the acquisition of that interest, an amount representing its market value.

" Dispose " means dispose by assignment or surrender, and " acquisition " has a corresponding meaning.]

(6) If, by virtue of any provision of this Part of this Act, Part I of Schedule 1 to this Act has effect in relation to a fixed term tenancy as if it consisted only of paragraphs 11 and 12, that Part shall have the like effect in relation to any periodic tenancy which arises by virtue of this section on the coming to an end of the fixed term tenancy.

(7) Any reference in this Part of this Act to a statutory periodic tenancy is a reference to a periodic tenancy arising by virtue of this section.

Amendments (Textual)

F4. S. 5. (1)(1. A) substituted (20.5.2009) for s. 5. (1) by Housing and Regeneration Act 2008 (c. 17), ss. 299, 325, Sch. 11 para. 6. (2) (with Sch. 11 para. 14); S.I. 2009/1261, {arts. 2, 3}

F5. Word in s. 5. (1)(b) omitted (1.11.2016 for specified purposes, 1.12.2016 in so far as not already in force) by virtue of Immigration Act 2016 (c. 19), ss. 40. (6)(a), 94. (1) (with s. 40. (7)); S.I. 2016/1037, regs. 2. (b), 5. (d)

F6. S. 5. (1)(d) and word inserted (1.11.2016 for specified purposes, 1.12.2016 in so far as not already in force) by Immigration Act 2016 (c. 19), ss. 40. (6)(a), 94. (1) (with s. 40. (7)); S.I. 2016/1037, regs. 2. (b), 5. (d)

F7. Words in s. 5. (2)(a) inserted (20.5.2009) by Housing and Regeneration Act 2008 (c. 17), ss. 299, 325, Sch. 11 para. 6. (3) (with Sch. 11 para. 14); S.I. 2009/1261, {arts. 2, 3}

F8. Word in s. 5. (2)(a) omitted (1.11.2016 for specified purposes, 1.12.2016 in so far as not already in force) by virtue of Immigration Act 2016 (c. 19), ss. 40. (6)(b), 94. (1) (with s. 40. (7)); S.I. 2016/1037, regs. 2. (b), 5. (d)

F9. S. 5. (2)(c) and word inserted (1.11.2016 for specified purposes, 1.12.2016 in so far as not already in force) by Immigration Act 2016 (c. 19), ss. 40. (6)(b), 94. (1) (with s. 40. (7)); S.I. 2016/1037, regs. 2. (b), 5. (d)

F10. S. 5. (5. A) inserted (18.1.2005) by Housing Act 2004 (c. 34), ss. 222. (1)(2), 270. (3)(a)

6 Fixing of terms of statutory periodic tenancy.

(1) In this section, in relation to a statutory periodic tenancy,—
　(a) "the former tenancy" means the fixed term tenancy on the coming to an end of which the statutory periodic tenancy arises; and
　(b) "the implied terms" means the terms of the tenancy which have effect by virtue of section 5.(3)(e) above, other than terms as to the amount of the rent;
but nothing in the following provisions of this section applies to a statutory periodic tenancy at a time when, by virtue of paragraph 11 or paragraph 12 in Part 1 of Schedule 1 to this Act, it cannot be an assured tenancy.
(2) Not later than the first anniversary of the day on which the former tenancy came to an end, the landlord may serve on the tenant, or the tenant may serve on the landlord, a notice in the prescribed form proposing terms of the statutory periodic tenancy different from the implied terms and, if the landlord or the tenant considers it appropriate, proposing an adjustment of the amount of the rent to take account of the proposed terms.
(3) Where a notice has been served under subsection (2) above,—
　(a) within the period of three months beginning on the date on which the notice was served on him, the landlord or the tenant, as the case may be, may, by an application in the prescribed form, refer the notice to [F11the appropriate tribunal] under subsection (4) below; and
　(b) if the notice is not so referred, then, with effect from such date, not falling within the period referred to in paragraph (a) above, as may be specified in the notice, the terms proposed in the notice shall become terms of the tenancy in substitution for any of the implied terms dealing with the same subject matter and the amount of the rent shall be varied in accordance with any adjustment so proposed.
(4) Where a notice under subsection (2) above is referred to [F12the appropriate tribunal], the [F13appropriate tribunal] shall consider the terms proposed in the notice and shall determine whether those terms, or some other terms (dealing with the same subject matter as the proposed terms), are such as, in [F14the appropriate tribunal's] opinion, might reasonably be expected to be found in an assured periodic tenancy of the dwelling-house concerned, being a tenancy—
　(a) which begins on the coming to an end of the former tenancy; and
　(b) which is granted by a willing landlord on terms which, except in so far as they relate to the subject matter of the proposed terms, are those of the statutory periodic tenancy at the time of [F14the appropriate tribunal's] consideration.
(5) Whether or not a notice under subsection (2) above proposes an adjustment of the amount of the rent under the statutory periodic tenancy, where [F15the appropriate tribunal] determine any terms under subsection (4) above, they shall, if they consider it appropriate, specify such an adjustment to take account of the terms so determined.
(6) In making a determination under subsection (4) above, or specifying an adjustment of an amount of rent under subsection (5) above, there shall be disregarded any effect on the terms or the amount of the rent attributable to the granting of a tenancy to a sitting tenant.
(7) Where a notice under subsection (2) above is referred to [F16the appropriate tribunal], then, unless the landlord and the tenant otherwise agree, with effect from such date as the [F17appropriate tribunal] may direct—
　(a) the terms determined by the [F17appropriate tribunal] shall become terms of the statutory periodic tenancy in substitution for any of the implied terms dealing with the same subject matter; and
　(b) the amount of the rent under the statutory periodic tenancy shall be altered to accord with any adjustment specified by the [F17appropriate tribunal];
but for the purposes of paragraph (b) above the [F17appropriate tribunal] shall not direct a date earlier than the date specified, in accordance with subsection (3)(b) above, in the notice referred to them.
(8) Nothing in this section requires [F18the appropriate tribunal] to continue with a determination under subsection (4) above if the landlord and tenant give notice in writing that they no longer require such a determination or if the tenancy has come to an end.
Amendments (Textual)

F11. Words in s. 6. (3)(a) substituted (1.7.2013) by The Transfer of Tribunal Functions Order 2013 (S.I. 2013/1036), art. 1, Sch. 1 para. 81. (a) (with Sch. 3)

F12. Words in s. 6. (4) substituted (1.7.2013) by The Transfer of Tribunal Functions Order 2013 (S.I. 2013/1036), art. 1, Sch. 1 para. 81. (b)(i) (with Sch. 3)

F13. Words in s. 6. (4) substituted (1.7.2013) by The Transfer of Tribunal Functions Order 2013 (S.I. 2013/1036), art. 1, Sch. 1 para. 81. (b)(ii) (with Sch. 3)

F14. Words in s. 6. (4) substituted (1.7.2013) by The Transfer of Tribunal Functions Order 2013 (S.I. 2013/1036), art. 1, Sch. 1 para. 81. (b)(iii) (with Sch. 3)

F15. Words in s. 6. (5) substituted (1.7.2013) by The Transfer of Tribunal Functions Order 2013 (S.I. 2013/1036), art. 1, Sch. 1 para. 81. (c) (with Sch. 3)

F16. Words in s. 6. (7) substituted (1.7.2013) by The Transfer of Tribunal Functions Order 2013 (S.I. 2013/1036), art. 1, Sch. 1 para. 81. (d)(i) (with Sch. 3)

F17. Words in s. 6. (7) substituted (1.7.2013) by The Transfer of Tribunal Functions Order 2013 (S.I. 2013/1036), art. 1, Sch. 1 para. 81. (d)(ii) (with Sch. 3)

F18. Words in s. 6. (8) substituted (1.7.2013) by The Transfer of Tribunal Functions Order 2013 (S.I. 2013/1036), art. 1, Sch. 1 para. 81. (e) (with Sch. 3)

[F19 6. A Demotion because of anti-social behaviour

(1) This section applies to an assured tenancy if[F20—

(a) the landlord is a non-profit registered provider of social housing,

(b) the landlord is a profit-making registered provider of social housing and the dwelling-house let on the tenancy is social housing within the meaning of Part 2 of the Housing and Regeneration Act 2008, or

(c)]

the landlord is a registered social landlord.

(2) The landlord may apply to [F21the county court] for a demotion order.

(3) A demotion order has the following effect—

(a) the assured tenancy is terminated with effect from the date specified in the order;

(b) if the tenant remains in occupation of the dwelling-house after that date a demoted tenancy is created with effect from that date;

(c) it is a term of the demoted tenancy that any arrears of rent payable at the termination of the assured tenancy become payable under the demoted tenancy;

(d) it is also a term of the demoted tenancy that any rent paid in advance or overpaid at the termination of the assured tenancy is credited to the tenant's liability to pay rent under the demoted tenancy.

(4) The court must not make a demotion order unless it is satisfied—

[F22. (a)that the tenant or a person residing in or visiting the dwelling-house has engaged or has threatened to engage in—

(i) conduct that is capable of causing nuisance or annoyance to some person (who need not be a particular identified person) and that directly or indirectly relates to or affects the landlord's housing management functions, or

(ii) conduct that consists of or involves using housing accommodation owned or managed by the landlord for an unlawful purpose, and]

(b) that it is reasonable to make the order.

(5) The court must not entertain proceedings for a demotion order unless—

(a) the landlord has served on the tenant a notice under subsection (6), or

(b) the court thinks it is just and equitable to dispense with the requirement of the notice.

(6) The notice must—

(a) give particulars of the conduct in respect of which the order is sought;

(b) state that the proceedings will not begin before the date specified in the notice;

(c) state that the proceedings will not begin after the end of the period of twelve months beginning with the date of service of the notice.

(7) The date specified for the purposes of subsection (6)(b) must not be before the end of the period of two weeks beginning with the date of service of the notice.

(8) Each of the following has effect in respect of a demoted tenancy at the time it is created by virtue of an order under this section as it has effect in relation to the assured tenancy at the time it is terminated by virtue of the order—
  (a) the parties to the tenancy;
  (b) the period of the tenancy;
  (c) the amount of the rent;
  (d) the dates on which the rent is payable.
(9) Subsection (8)(b) does not apply if the assured tenancy was for a fixed term and in such a case the demoted tenancy is a weekly periodic tenancy.
(10) If the landlord of the demoted tenancy serves on the tenant a statement of any other express terms of the assured tenancy which are to apply to the demoted tenancy such terms are also terms of the demoted tenancy.
[F23. (10. A)In subsection (4)(a)(ii) "housing accommodation" includes—
  (a) flats, lodging-houses and hostels;
  (b) any yard, garden, outhouses and appurtenances belonging to the accommodation or usually enjoyed with it;
  (c) any common areas used in connection with the accommodation.]
(11) For the purposes of this section a demoted tenancy is a tenancy to which section 20. B of the Housing Act 1988 applies.]
Amendments (Textual)
F19. S. 6. A inserted (30.6.2004 for E. and 30.4.2005 for W.) by Anti-Social Behaviour Act 2003 (c. 38), s. 14. (4); S.I. 2004/1502, art. 2. (a)(iii) (with savings in Sch.); S.I. 2005/1225, art. 2. (b)
F20. Words in s. 6. A(1) inserted (1.4.2010) by The Housing and Regeneration Act 2008 (Consequential Provisions) Order 2010 (S.I. 2010/866), art. 1. (2), Sch. 2 para. 64 (with art. 6, Sch. 3)
F21. Words in s. 6. A(2) substituted (22.4.2014) by Crime and Courts Act 2013 (c. 22), s. 61. (3), Sch. 9 para. 52; S.I. 2014/954, art. 2. (c) (with art. 3) (with transitional provisions and savings in S.I. 2014/956, arts. 3-11)
F22. S. 6. A(4)(a) substituted (23.3.2015) by Anti-social Behaviour, Crime and Policing Act 2014 (c. 12), s. 185. (1), Sch. 11 para. 17. (2) (with ss. 21, 33, 42, 58, 75, 93); S.I. 2015/373, art. 4. (f)(iv)
F23. S. 6. A(10. A) inserted (23.3.2015) by Anti-social Behaviour, Crime and Policing Act 2014 (c. 12), s. 185. (1), Sch. 11 para. 17. (3) (with ss. 21, 33, 42, 58, 75, 93); S.I. 2015/373, art. 4. (f)(iv)
7 Orders for possession.
(1) The court shall not make an order for possession of a dwelling-house let on an assured tenancy except on one or more of the grounds set out in Schedule 2 to this Act; but nothing in this Part of this Act relates to proceedings for possession of such a dwelling-house which are brought by a mortgagee, within the meaning of the M2. Law of Property Act 1925, who has lent money on the security of the assured tenancy.
(2) The following provisions of this section have effect, subject to section 8 below, in relation to proceedings for the recovery of possession of a dwelling-house let on an assured tenancy.
(3) If the court is satisfied that any of the grounds in Part I of Schedule 2 to this Act is established then, subject to [F24subsections (5. A) and (6)] [F25and section 10. A] below [F26. (and to any available defence based on the tenant's Convention rights, within the meaning of the Human Rights Act 1998)], the court shall make an order for possession.
(4) If the court is satisfied that any of the grounds in Part II of Schedule 2 to this Act is established, then, subject to [F27subsections (5. A) and (6)] below, the court may make an order for possession if it considers it reasonable to do so.
(5) Part III of Schedule 2 to this Act shall have effect for supplementing Ground 9 in that Schedule and Part IV of that Schedule shall have effect in relation to notices given as mentioned in Grounds 1 to 5 of that Schedule.
[F28. (5. A)The court shall not make an order for possession of a dwellinghouse let on an assured

periodic tenancy arising under Schedule 10 to the Local Government and Housing Act 1989 on any of the following grounds, that is to say,—

(a) Grounds 1, 2 [F29, 5 [F30, 7. A and 7. B]] in Part I of Schedule 2 to this Act;

(b) Ground 16 in Part II of that Schedule; and

(c) if the assured periodic tenancy arose on the termination of a former 1954 Act tenancy, within the meaning of the said Schedule 10, Ground 6 in Part I of Schedule 2 to this Act.]

(6) The court shall not make an order for possession of a dwelling-house to take effect at a time when it is let on an assured fixed term tenancy unless—

(a) the ground for possession is Ground 2[F31, Ground 7. A] [F32 , Ground 7. B] or Ground 8 in Part I of Schedule 2 to this Act or any of the grounds in Part II of that Schedule, other than Ground 9 or Ground 16; and

(b) the terms of the tenancy make provision for it to be brought to an end on the ground in question (whether that provision takes the form of a provision for re-entry, for forfeiture, for determination by notice or otherwise).

[F33. (6. A)In the case of a dwelling-house in England, subsection (6)(a) has effect as if it also referred to Ground 7 in Part 1 of Schedule 2 to this Act.]

[F34. (6. B)The requirement in subsection (6)(b) that would otherwise apply to an order for possession of a dwelling-house let on an assured fixed term tenancy does not apply where the ground for possession is Ground 7. B in Part 1 of Schedule 2 to this Act.]

(7) Subject to the preceding provisions of this section, the court may make an order for possession of a dwelling-house on grounds relating to a fixed term tenancy which has come to an end; and where an order is made in such circumstances, any statutory periodic tenancy which has arisen on the ending of the fixed term tenancy shall end (without any notice and regardless of the period) [F35in accordance with section 5. (1. A)].

Amendments (Textual)

F24. Words substituted by Local Government and Housing Act 1989 (c. 42, SIF 75:1), s. 194, Sch. 11 para. 101

F25. Words in s. 7. (3) inserted (1.12.2016) by Immigration Act 2016 (c. 19), ss. 41. (3)(a), 94. (1) (with s. 41. (7)); S.I. 2016/1037, reg. 5. (e)

F26. Words in s. 7. (3) inserted (20.10.2014 for E., 21.10.2014 for W.) by Anti-social Behaviour, Crime and Policing Act 2014 (c. 12), s. 185. (1)(2)(c)(3)(c), Sch. 11 para. 18. (2) (with ss. 21, 33, 42, 58, 75, 93); S.I. 2014/2590, art. 2. (h); S.I. 2014/2830, art. 2. (g)(x)

F27. Words substituted by Local Government and Housing Act 1989 (c. 42, SIF 75:1), s. 194, Sch. 11 para. 101. (2)

F28. S. 7. (5. A) inserted by Local Government and Housing Act 1989 (c. 42, SIF 75:1), s. 194, Sch. 11 para. 101. (3)

F29. Words in s. 7. (5. A)(a) substituted (20.10.2014 for E., 21.10.2014 for W.) by Anti-social Behaviour, Crime and Policing Act 2014 (c. 12), s. 185. (1)(2)(c)(3)(c), Sch. 11 para. 18. (3) (with ss. 21, 33, 42, 58, 75, 93); S.I. 2014/2590, art. 2. (h); S.I. 2014/2830, art. 2. (g)(x)

F30. Words in s. 7. (5. A)(a) substituted (1.12.2016) by Immigration Act 2016 (c. 19), ss. 41. (3)(b), 94. (1) (with s. 41. (7)); S.I. 2016/1037, reg. 5. (e)

F31. Words in s. 7. (6)(a) inserted (20.10.2014 for E., 21.10.2014 for W.) by Anti-social Behaviour, Crime and Policing Act 2014 (c. 12), s. 185. (1)(2)(c)(3)(c), Sch. 11 para. 18. (4) (with ss. 21, 33, 42, 58, 75, 93); S.I. 2014/2590, art. 2. (h); S.I. 2014/2830, art. 2. (g)(x)

F32. Words in s. 7. (6)(a) inserted (1.12.2016) by Immigration Act 2016 (c. 19), ss. 41. (3)(c), 94. (1) (with s. 41. (7)); S.I. 2016/1037, reg. 5. (e)

F33. S. 7. (6. A) inserted (1.4.2012) by Localism Act 2011 (c. 20), ss. 162. (4), 240. (2); S.I. 2012/628, art. 6. (b) (with arts. 9 11 14 15 17)

F34. S. 7. (6. B) inserted (1.12.2016) by Immigration Act 2016 (c. 19), ss. 41. (3)(d), 94. (1) (with s. 41. (7)); S.I. 2016/1037, reg. 5. (e)

F35. Words in s. 7. (7) substituted (20.5.2009) by Housing and Regeneration Act 2008 (c. 17), ss. 299, 325, Sch. 11 para. 7 (with Sch. 11 para. 14); S.I. 2009/1261, {arts. 2, 3}

Marginal Citations

M2 1925 c. 20.

8 Notice of proceedings for possession.

(1) The court shall not entertain proceedings for possession of a dwelling-house let on an assured tenancy unless—

(a) the landlord or, in the case of joint landlords, at least one of them has served on the tenant a notice in accordance with this section and the proceedings are begun within the time limits stated in the notice in accordance with [F36subsections (3) to (4. B)] below; or

(b) the court considers it just and equitable to dispense with the requirement of such a notice.

(2) The court shall not make an order for possession on any of the grounds in Schedule 2 to this Act unless that ground and particulars of it are specified in the notice under this section; but the grounds specified in such a notice may be altered or added to with the leave of the court.

(3) A notice under this section is one in the prescribed form informing the tenant that—

(a) the landlord intends to begin proceedings for possession of the dwelling-house on one or more of the grounds specified in the notice; and

(b) those proceedings will not begin earlier than a date specified in the notice [F37in accordance with [F38subsections (3. A)] to (4. B) below]; and

(c) those proceedings will not begin later than twelve months from the date of service of the notice.

[F39. (3. A)If a notice under this section specifies in accordance with subsection (3)(a) Ground 7. A in Schedule 2 to this Act (whether with or without other grounds), the date specified in the notice as mentioned in subsection (3)(b) is not to be earlier than—

(a) in the case of a periodic tenancy, the earliest date on which, apart from section 5. (1), the tenancy could be brought to an end by a notice to quit given by the landlord on the same date as the date of service of the notice under this section;

(b) in the case of a fixed term tenancy, one month after the date on which the notice was served.]

[F40. (4)If a notice under this section specifies in accordance with subsection (3)(a) above Ground 14 in Schedule 2 to this Act [F41. (whether without other grounds or with any ground other than Ground 7. A)], the date specified in the notice as mentioned in subsection (3)(b) above shall not be earlier than the date of the service of the notice.

(4. A)If a notice under this section specifies in accordance with subsection (3)(a) above, any of Grounds 1, 2, 5 to 7, 9 and 16 in Schedule 2 to this Act (whether without other grounds or with any ground other than Ground [F427. A or] 14), the date specified in the notice as mentioned in subsection (3)(b) above shall not be earlier than—

(a) two months from the date of service of the notice; and

(b) if the tenancy is a periodic tenancy, the earliest date on which, apart from section 5. (1) above, the tenancy could be brought to an end by a notice to quit given by the landlord on the same date as the date of service of the notice under this section.

(4. B)In any other case, the date specified in the notice as mentioned in subsection (3)(b) above shall not be earlier than the expiry of the period of two weeks from the date of the service of the notice.]

[F43. (4. C)A notice under this section that specifies in accordance with subsection (3)(a) Ground 7. A in Schedule 2 to this Act (whether with or without other grounds) must be served on the tenant within the time period specified in subsection (4. D), (4. E) or (4. F).

(4. D)Where the landlord proposes to rely on condition 1, 3 or 5 in Ground 7. A, the notice must be served on the tenant within—

(a) the period of 12 months beginning with the day of the conviction, or

(b) if there is an appeal against the conviction, the period of 12 months beginning with the day on which the appeal is finally determined or abandoned.

(4. E)Where the landlord proposes to rely on condition 2 in Ground 7. A, the notice must be served on the tenant within—

(a) the period of 12 months beginning with the day on which the court has made the finding, or

(b) if there is an appeal against the finding, the period of 12 months beginning with the day on

which the appeal is finally determined, abandoned or withdrawn.
(4. F)Where the landlord proposes to rely on condition 4 in Ground 7. A, the notice must be served on the tenant within—
   (a) the period of 3 months beginning with the day on which the closure order was made, or
   (b) if there is an appeal against the making of the order, the period of 3 months beginning with the day on which the appeal is finally determined, abandoned or withdrawn.]
(5) The court may not exercise the power conferred by subsection (1)(b) above if the landlord seeks to recover possession on Ground [F447. A [F45 , 7. B] or] 8 in Schedule 2 to this Act.
(6) Where a notice under this section—
   (a) is served at a time when the dwelling-house is let on a fixed term tenancy, or
   (b) is served after a fixed term tenancy has come to an end but relates (in whole or in part) to events occurring during that tenancy,
the notice shall have effect notwithstanding that the tenant becomes or has become tenant under a statutory periodic tenancy arising on the coming to an end of the fixed term tenancy.

Amendments (Textual)

F36. Words in s. 8. (1)(a) substituted (28.2.1997) by 1996 c. 52, s. 151. (2); S.I. 1997/225, art. 1 (with Sch.)

F37. Words in s. 8. (3)(b) substituted (28.2.1997) by 1996 c. 52, s. 151. (3); S.I. 1997/225, art. 1 (with Sch.)

F38. Words in s. 8. (3)(b) substituted (20.10.2014 for E., 21.10.2014 for W.) by Anti-social Behaviour, Crime and Policing Act 2014 (c. 12), ss. 97. (2)(a), 185. (1), (2)(c), (3)(a) (with ss. 21, 33, 42, 58, 75, 93); S.I. 2014/2590, art. 2. (d) (with art. 5); S.I. 2014/2830, art. 2. (d) (with art. 3)

F39. S. 8. (3. A) inserted (20.10.2014 for E., 21.10.2014 for W.) by Anti-social Behaviour, Crime and Policing Act 2014 (c. 12), ss. 97. (2)(b), 185. (1), (2)(c), (3)(a) (with ss. 21, 33, 42, 58, 75, 93); S.I. 2014/2590, art. 2. (d) (with art. 5); S.I. 2014/2830, art. 2. (d) (with art. 3)

F40. S. 8: subsections (4)-(4. B) substituted for subsection (4) (28.2.1997) by 1996 c. 52, s. 151. (4); S.I. 1997/225, art. 2 (with Sch.)

F41. Words in s. 8. (4) substituted (20.10.2014 for E., 21.10.2014 for W.) by Anti-social Behaviour, Crime and Policing Act 2014 (c. 12), ss. 97. (2)(c), 185. (1), (2)(c), (3)(a) (with ss. 21, 33, 42, 58, 75, 93); S.I. 2014/2590, art. 2. (d) (with art. 5); S.I. 2014/2830, art. 2. (d) (with art. 3)

F42. Words in s. 8. (4. A) inserted (20.10.2014 for E., 21.10.2014 for W.) by Anti-social Behaviour, Crime and Policing Act 2014 (c. 12), ss. 97. (2)(d), 185. (1), (2)(c), (3)(a) (with ss. 21, 33, 42, 58, 75, 93); S.I. 2014/2590, art. 2. (d) (with art. 5); S.I. 2014/2830, art. 2. (d) (with art. 3)

F43. S. 8. (4. C)-(4. F) inserted (20.10.2014 for E., 21.10.2014 for W.) by Anti-social Behaviour, Crime and Policing Act 2014 (c. 12), ss. 97. (2)(e), 185. (1), (2)(c), (3)(a) (with ss. 21, 33, 42, 58, 75, 93); S.I. 2014/2590, art. 2. (d) (with art. 5); S.I. 2014/2830, art. 2. (d) (with art. 3)

F44. Words in s. 8. (5) inserted (20.10.2014 for E., 21.10.2014 for W.) by Anti-social Behaviour, Crime and Policing Act 2014 (c. 12), ss. 97. (2)(f), 185. (1), (2)(c), (3)(a) (with ss. 21, 33, 42, 58, 75, 93); S.I. 2014/2590, art. 2. (d) (with art. 5); S.I. 2014/2830, art. 2. (d) (with art. 3)

F45. Word in s. 8. (5) inserted (1.12.2016) by Immigration Act 2016 (c. 19), ss. 41. (4), 94. (1) (with s. 41. (7)); S.I. 2016/1037, reg. 5. (e)

[F468. A Additional notice requirements: ground of domestic violence.
(1) Where the ground specified in a notice under section 8 (whether with or without other grounds) is Ground 14. A in Schedule 2 to this Act and the partner who has left the dwelling-house as mentioned in that ground is not a tenant of the dwelling-house, the court shall not entertain proceedings for possession of the dwelling-house unless—
   (a) the landlord or, in the case of joint landlords, at least one of them has served on the partner who has left a copy of the notice or has taken all reasonable steps to serve a copy of the notice on that partner, or
   (b) the court considers it just and equitable to dispense with such requirements as to service.
(2) Where Ground 14. A in Schedule 2 to this Act is added to a notice under section 8 with the leave of the court after proceedings for possession are begun and the partner who has left the dwelling-house as mentioned in that ground is not a party to the proceedings, the court shall not

continue to entertain the proceedings unless—
(a) the landlord or, in the case of joint landlords, at least one of them has served a notice under subsection (3) below on the partner who has left or has taken all reasonable steps to serve such a notice on that partner, or
(b) the court considers it just and equitable to dispense with the requirement of such a notice.
(3) A notice under this subsection shall—
(a) state that proceedings for the possession of the dwelling-house have begun,
(b) specify the ground or grounds on which possession is being sought, and
(c) give particulars of the ground or grounds.]

Amendments (Textual)
F46. S. 8. A inserted (28.2.1997) by 1996 c. 52, s. 150; S.I. 1997/225, art. 2 (with Sch.)

9 Extended discretion of court in possession claims.
(1) Subject to subsection (6) below, the court may adjourn for such period or periods as it thinks fit proceedings for possession of a dwelling-house let on an assured tenancy.
(2) On the making of an order for possession of a dwelling-house let on an assured tenancy or at any time before the execution of such an order, the court, subject to subsection (6) below, may—
(a) stay or suspend execution of the order, or
(b) postpone the date of possession,
for such period or periods as the court thinks just.
(3) On any such adjournment as is referred to in subsection (1) above or on any such stay, suspension or postponement as is referred to in subsection (2) above, the court, unless it considers that to do so would cause exceptional hardship to the tenant or would otherwise be unreasonable, shall impose conditions with regard to payment by the tenant of arrears of rent (if any) and rent F47. . . and may impose such other conditions as it thinks fit.
(4) If any such conditions as are referred to in subsection (3) above are complied with, the court may, if it thinks fit, discharge or rescind any such order as is referred to in subsection (2) above.
(5) F48. . . . .
(5. A)F48. . . . .
(6) This section does not apply if the court is satisfied that the landlord is entitled to possession of the dwelling-house—
(a) on any of the grounds in Part I of Schedule 2 to this Act; or
(b) by virtue of subsection (1) or subsection (4) of section 21 below.

Amendments (Textual)
F47. Words in s. 9. (3) omitted (20.5.2009) by virtue of and repealed (prosp.) by Housing and Regeneration Act 2008 (c. 17), ss. 299, 321. (1), 325, Sch. 11 para. 8. (2), Sch. 16 (with Sch. 11 para. 14); S.I. 2009/1261, {arts. 2, 3}
F48. S. 9. (5)(5. A) omitted (20.5.2009) by virtue of and repealed (prosp.) by Housing and Regeneration Act 2008 (c. 17), ss. 299, 321. (1), 325, Sch. 11 para. 8. (4), Sch. 16 (with Sch. 11 para. 14); S.I. 2009/1261, {arts. 2, 3}

[F499. AProceedings for possession [F50on non-absolute grounds]: anti-social behaviour
(1) This section applies if the court is considering under section 7. (4) whether it is reasonable to make an order for possession on ground 14 set out in Part 2 of Schedule 2 (conduct of tenant or other person).
(2) The court must consider, in particular—
(a) the effect that the nuisance or annoyance has had on persons other than the person against whom the order is sought;
(b) any continuing effect the nuisance or annoyance is likely to have on such persons;
(c) the effect that the nuisance or annoyance would be likely to have on such persons if the conduct is repeated.]

Amendments (Textual)
F49. S. 9. A inserted (30.6.2004 for E. and 30.9.2004 for W.) by Anti-Social Behaviour Act 2003 (c. 38), s. 16. (2); S.I. 2004/1502, art. 2. (a)(v) (with Sch.) and S.I. 2004/2557, art. 2. (a)(iii) (with Sch.)

F50. Words in s. 9. A heading inserted (20.10.2014 for E., 21.10.2014 for W.) by Anti-social Behaviour, Crime and Policing Act 2014 (c. 12), s. 185. (1)(2)(c)(3)(c), Sch. 11 para. 19 (with ss. 21, 33, 42, 58, 75, 93); S.I. 2014/2590, art. 2. (h); S.I. 2014/2830, art. 2. (g)(xi)

10 Special provisions applicable to shared accommodation.

(1) This section applies in a case falling within subsection (1) of section 3 above and expressions used in this section have the same meaning as in that section.

(2) Without prejudice to the enforcement of any order made under subsection (3) below, while the tenant is in possession of the separate accommodation, no order shall be made for possession of any of the shared accommodation, whether on the application of the immediate landlord of the tenant or on the application of any person under whom that landlord derives title, unless a like order has been made, or is made at the same time, in respect of the separate accommodation; and the provisions of section 6 above shall have effect accordingly.

(3) On the application of the landlord, the court may make such order as it thinks just either—

   (a) terminating the right of the tenant to use the whole or any part of the shared accommodation other than living accommodation; or

   (b) modifying his right to use the whole or any part of the shared accommodation, whether by varying the persons or increasing the number of persons entitled to the use of that accommodation or otherwise.

(4) No order shall be made under subsection (3) above so as to effect any termination or modification of the rights of the tenant which, apart from section 3. (3) above, could not be effected by or under the terms of the tenancy.

[F51 10. APower to order transfer of tenancy in certain cases

(1) This section applies on an application for an order for possession of a dwelling-house let on an assured tenancy if the court is satisfied that—

   (a) Ground 7. B in Schedule 2 is established,

   (b) no other ground in that Schedule is established, or one or more grounds in Part 2 of that Schedule are established but it is not reasonable to make an order for possession on that ground or those grounds,

   (c) the tenancy is a joint tenancy, and

   (d) one or more of the tenants is a qualifying tenant.

(2) In subsection (1)(d) "qualifying tenant" means a person who (within the meaning of Ground 7. B) is not disqualified as a result of the person's immigration status from occupying the dwelling-house under the tenancy.

(3) The court may, instead of making an order for possession, order that the tenant's interest under the tenancy is to be transferred so that it is held—

   (a) if there is one qualifying tenant, by the qualifying tenant as sole tenant, or

   (b) if there is more than one qualifying tenant, by all of them as joint tenants.

(4) The effect of an order under this section is that, from the time the order takes effect, the qualifying tenant or tenants—

   (a) are entitled to performance of the landlord's covenants under the tenancy, and

   (b) are liable to perform the tenant's covenants under the tenancy.

(5) The effect of an order under this section is that, from the time it takes effect, any other person who was a tenant under the tenancy before the order took effect—

   (a) ceases to be entitled to performance of the landlord's covenants under the tenancy, or

   (b) ceases to be liable to perform the tenant's covenants under the tenancy.

(6) Subsection (5) does not remove any right or liability of the person which accrued before the order took effect.

(7) An order under this section does not operate to create a new tenancy as between the landlord and the qualifying tenant or tenants.

(8) In particular, if the tenancy is a fixed term tenancy, the term comes to an end at the same time as if the order had not been made.]

Amendments (Textual)

F51. S. 10. A inserted (1.12.2016) by Immigration Act 2016 (c. 19), ss. 41. (5), 94. (1) (with s. 41.

(7))]; S.I. 2016/1037, reg. 5. (e)
11 Payment of removal expenses in certain cases.
(1) Where a court makes an order for possession of a dwelling-house let on an assured tenancy on Ground 6 or Ground 9 in Schedule 2 to this Act (but not on any other ground), the landlord shall pay to the tenant a sum equal to the reasonable expenses likely to be incurred by the tenant in removing from the dwelling-house.
(2) Any question as to the amount of the sum referred to in subsection (1) above shall be determined by agreement between the landlord and the tenant or, in default of agreement, by the court.
(3) Any sum payable to a tenant by virtue of this section shall be recoverable as a civil debt due from the landlord.
12 Compensation for misrepresentation or concealment.
Where a landlord obtains an order for possession of a dwelling-house let on an assured tenancy on one or more of the grounds in Schedule 2 to this Act and it is subsequently made to appear to the court that the order was obtained by misrepresentation or concealment of material facts, the court may order the landlord to pay to the former tenant such sum as appears sufficient as compensation for damage or loss sustained by that tenant as a result of the order.

Rent and other terms

13 Increases of rent under assured periodic tenancies.
(1) This section applies to—
   (a) a statutory periodic tenancy other than one which, by virtue of paragraph 11 or paragraph 12 in Part I of Schedule 1 to this Act, cannot for the time being be an assured tenancy; and
   (b) any other periodic tenancy which is an assured tenancy, other than one in relation to which there is a provision, for the time being binding on the tenant, under which the rent for a particular period of the tenancy will or may be greater than the rent for an earlier period.
(2) For the purpose of securing an increase in the rent under a tenancy to which this section applies, the landlord may serve on the tenant a notice in the prescribed form proposing a new rent to take effect at the beginning of a new period of the tenancy specified in the notice, being a period beginning not earlier than—
   (a) the minimum period after the date of the service of the notice; and
   (b) except in the case of a statutory periodic [F52 tenancy—
(i) in the case of an assured agricultural occupancy, the first anniversary of the date on which the first period of the tenancy began;
(ii) in any other case, on the date that falls 52 weeks after the date on which the first period of the tenancy began; and]
   (c) if the rent under the tenancy has previously been increased by virtue of a notice under this subsection or a determination under section 14 [F53 below—
(i) in the case of an assured agricultural occupancy, the first anniversary of the date on which the increased rent took effect;
(ii) in any other case, the appropriate date]
(3) The minimum period referred to in subsection (2) above is—
   (a) in the case of a yearly tenancy, six months;
   (b) in the case of a tenancy where the period is less than a month, one month; and
   (c) in any other case, a period equal to the period of the tenancy.
[F54. (3. A)The appropriate date referred to in subsection (2)(c)(ii) above is—
   (a) in a case to which subsection (3. B) below applies, the date that falls 53 weeks after the date on which the increased rent took effect;
   (b) in any other case, the date that falls 52 weeks after the date on which the increased rent took effect.
(3. B)This subsection applies where—

(a) the rent under the tenancy has been increased by virtue of a notice under this section or a determination under section 14 below on at least one occasion after the coming into force of the Regulatory Reform (Assured Periodic Tenancies)(Rent Increases) Order 2003; and

(b) the fifty-third week after the date on which the last such increase took effect begins more than six days before the anniversary of the date on which the first such increase took effect.]

(4) Where a notice is served under subsection (2) above, a new rent specified in the notice shall take effect as mentioned in the notice unless, before the beginning of the new period specified in the notice,—

(a) the tenant by an application in the prescribed form refers the notice to [F55the appropriate tribunal]; or

(b) the landlord and the tenant agree on a variation of the rent which is different from that proposed in the notice or agree that the rent should not be varied.

(5) Nothing in this section (or in section 14 below) affects the right of the landlord and the tenant under an assured tenancy to vary by agreement any term of the tenancy (including a term relating to rent).

Amendments (Textual)

F52. Words in s. 13. (2)(b) substituted (11.2.2003) by The Regulatory Reform (Assured Periodic Tenancies) (Rent Increases) Order 2003 (S.I. 2003/259), art. 2. (a)(i)

F53. Words in s. 13. (2)(c) substituted (11.2.2003) by The Regulatory Reform (Assured Periodic Tenancies) (Rent Increases) Order 2003 (S.I. 2003/259), art. 2. (a)(ii)

F54. S. 13. (3. A)(3. B) inserted (11.2.2003) by The Regulatory Reform (Assured Periodic Tenancies) (Rent Increases) Order 2003 (S.I. 2003/259), art. 2. (b)

F55. Words in s. 13. (4)(a) substituted (1.7.2013) by The Transfer of Tribunal Functions Order 2013 (S.I. 2013/1036), art. 1, Sch. 1 para. 82 (with Sch. 3)

14 Determination of rent by [F56tribunal].

(1) Where, under subsection (4)(a) of section 13 above, a tenant refers to [F57the appropriate tribunal] a notice under subsection (2) of that section, the [F58appropriate tribunal] shall determine the rent at which, subject to subsections (2) and (4) below, the [F58appropriate tribunal] consider that the dwelling-house concerned might reasonably be expected to be let in the open market by a willing landlord under an assured tenancy—

(a) which is a periodic tenancy having the same periods as those of the tenancy to which the notice relates;

(b) which begins at the beginning of the new period specified in the notice;

(c) the terms of which (other than relating to the amount of the rent) are the same as those of the tenancy to which the notice relates; and

(d) in respect of which the same notices, if any, have been given under any of Grounds 1 to 5 of Schedule 2 to this Act, as have been given (or have effect as if given) in relation to the tenancy to which the notice relates.

(2) In making a determination under this section, there shall be disregarded—

(a) any effect on the rent attributable to the granting of a tenancy to a sitting tenant;

(b) any increase in the value of the dwelling-house attributable to a relevant improvement carried out by a person who at the time it was carried out was the tenant, if the improvement—
(i) was carried out otherwise than in pursuance of an obligation to his immediate landlord, or
(ii) was carried out pursuant to an obligation to his immediate landlord being an obligation which did not relate to the specific improvement concerned but arose by reference to consent given to the carrying out of that improvement; and

(c) any reduction in the value of the dwelling-house attributable to a failure by the tenant to comply with any terms of the tenancy.

(3) For the purposes of subsection (2)(b) above, in relation to a notice which is referred by a tenant as mentioned in subsection (1) above, an improvement is a relevant improvement if either it was carried out during the tenancy to which the notice relates or the following conditions are satisfied, namely—

(a) that it was carried out not more than twenty-one years before the date of service of the notice; and

(b) that, at all times during the period beginning when the improvement was carried out and ending on the date of service of the notice, the dwelling-house has been let under an assured tenancy; and

(c) that, on the coming to an end of an assured tenancy at any time during that period, the tenant (or, in the case of joint tenants, at least one of them) did not quit.

F59 [(3. A)In making a determination under this section in any case where under Part I of the Local Government Finance Act 1992 the landlord or a superior landlord is liable to pay council tax in respect of a hereditament ("the relevant hereditament") of which the dwelling-house forms part. the [F60appropriate tribunal] shall have regard to the amount of council tax which, as at the date on which the notice under section 13. (2) above was served, was set by the billing authority—

(a) for the financial year in which that notice was served, and

(b) for the category of dwellings within which the relevant hereditament fell on that date, but any discount or other reduction affecting the amount of council tax payable shall be disregarded.

(3. B)In subsection (3. A) above—

(a) "hereditament" means a dwelling within the meaning of Part I of the Local Government Finance Act 1992,

(b) "billing authority" has the same meaning as in that Part of that Act, and

(c) "category of dwellings" has the same meaning as in section 30. (1) and (2) of that Act.]

(4) In this section "rent" does not include any service charge, within the meaning of section 18 of the M3. Landlord and Tenant Act 1985, but, subject to that, includes any sums payable by the tenant to the landlord on account of the use of furniture [F61, in respect of council tax] or for any of the matters referred to in subsection (1)(a) of that section, whether or not those sums are separate from the sums payable for the occupation of the dwelling-house concerned or are payable under separate agreements.

(5) Where any rates in respect of the dwelling-house concerned are borne by the landlord or a superior landlord, the [F62appropriate tribunal] shall make their determination under this section as if the rates were not so borne.

(6) In any case where—

(a) [F63the appropriate tribunal] have before them at the same time the reference of a notice under section 6. (2) above relating to a tenancy (in this subsection referred to as "the section 6 reference") and the reference of a notice under section 13. (2) above relating to the same tenancy (in this subsection referred to as "the section 13 reference"), and

(b) the date specified in the notice under section 6. (2) above is not later than the first day of the new period specified in the notice under section 13. (2) above, and

(c) the [F64appropriate tribunal] propose to hear the two references together,

the [F64appropriate tribunal] shall make a determination in relation to the section 6 reference before making their determination in relation to the section 13 reference and, accordingly, in such a case the reference in subsection(1)(c) above to the terms of the tenancy to which the notice relates shall be construed as a reference to those terms as varied by virtue of the determination made in relation to the section 6 reference.

(7) Where a notice under section 13. (2) above has been referred to [F65the appropriate tribunal], then, unless the landlord and the tenant otherwise agree, the rent determined by [F66the appropriate tribunal] (subject, in a case where subsection (5) above applies, to the addition of the appropriate amount in respect of rates) shall be the rent under the tenancy with effect from the beginning of the new period specified in the notice or, if it appears to [F67the appropriate tribunal] that that would cause undue hardship to the tenant, with effect from such later date (not being later than the date the rent is determined) as [F66the appropriate tribunal] may direct.

(8) Nothing in this section requires [F68the appropriate tribunal] to continue with their determination of a rent for a dwelling-house if the landlord and tenant give notice in writing that they no longer require such a determination or if the tenancy has come to an end.

[F69. (9)This section shall apply in relation to an assured shorthold tenancy as if in subsection (1)

the reference to an assured tenancy were a reference to an assured shorthold tenancy.]
Amendments (Textual)
F56. Word in s. 14 heading substituted (1.7.2013) by The Transfer of Tribunal Functions Order 2013 (S.I. 2013/1036), art. 1, Sch. 1 para. 83. (a) (with Sch. 3)
F57. Words in s. 14. (1) substituted (1.7.2013) by The Transfer of Tribunal Functions Order 2013 (S.I. 2013/1036), art. 1, Sch. 1 para. 83. (b)(i) (with Sch. 3)
F58. Words in s. 14. (1) substituted (1.7.2013) by The Transfer of Tribunal Functions Order 2013 (S.I. 2013/1036), art. 1, Sch. 1 para. 83. (b)(ii) (with Sch. 3)
F59. S. 14. (3. A)(3. B) inserted (1.4.1993) by S.I. 1993/651, art. 2. (1), Sch. 1 para. 17. (2)
F60. Words in s. 14. (3. A) substituted (1.7.2013) by The Transfer of Tribunal Functions Order 2013 (S.I. 2013/1036), art. 1, Sch. 1 para. 83. (c) (with Sch. 3)
F61. Words in s. 14. (4) inserted (1.4.1993) by S.I. 1993/651, art. 2. (1), Sch. 1 para. 17. (3)
F62. Words in s. 14. (5) substituted (1.7.2013) by The Transfer of Tribunal Functions Order 2013 (S.I. 2013/1036), art. 1, Sch. 1 para. 83. (d) (with Sch. 3)
F63. Words in s. 14. (6) substituted (1.7.2013) by The Transfer of Tribunal Functions Order 2013 (S.I. 2013/1036), art. 1, Sch. 1 para. 83. (e)(i) (with Sch. 3)
F64. Words in s. 14. (6) substituted (1.7.2013) by The Transfer of Tribunal Functions Order 2013 (S.I. 2013/1036), art. 1, Sch. 1 para. 83. (e)(ii) (with Sch. 3)
F65. Words in s. 14. (7) substituted (1.7.2013) by The Transfer of Tribunal Functions Order 2013 (S.I. 2013/1036), art. 1, Sch. 1 para. 83. (f)(i) (with Sch. 3)
F66. Words in s. 14. (7) substituted (1.7.2013) by The Transfer of Tribunal Functions Order 2013 (S.I. 2013/1036), art. 1, Sch. 1 para. 83. (f)(ii) (with Sch. 3)
F67. Words in s. 14. (7) substituted (1.7.2013) by The Transfer of Tribunal Functions Order 2013 (S.I. 2013/1036), art. 1, Sch. 1 para. 83. (f)(iii) (with Sch. 3)
F68. Words in s. 14. (8) substituted (1.7.2013) by The Transfer of Tribunal Functions Order 2013 (S.I. 2013/1036), art. 1, Sch. 1 para. 83. (g) (with Sch. 3)
F69. S. 14. (9) inserted (28.2.1997) by 1996 c. 52, s. 104, Sch. 8 para. 2. (2); S.I. 1997/225, art. 2 (with Sch.)
Modifications etc. (not altering text)
C11. S. 14. (2)(4)(5) applied with modifications by Local Government and Housing Act 1989 (c. 42, SIF 75:1), s. 186, Sch. 10 paras. 6. (4)(5), 7, 11. (6), 12. (2)(3), 21, 22
Marginal Citations
M31985 c. 70.
[F7014. A Interim increase before 1st April 1994 of rent under assured periodic tenancies in certain cases where landlord liable for council tax
(1) In any case where—

(a) under Part I of the Local Government Finance Act 1992 the landlord of a dwelling-house let under an assured tenancy to which section 13 above applies or a superior landlord is liable to pay council tax in respect of a dwelling (within the meaning of that Part of that Act) which includes that dwelling-house,

(b) under the terms of the tenancy (or an agreement collateral to the tenancy) the tenant is liable to make payments to the landlord in respect of council tax,

(c) the case falls within subsection (2) or subsection (3) below, and

(d) no previous notice under this subsection has been served in relation to the dwelling-house, the landlord may serve on the tenant a notice in the prescribed form proposing an increased rent to take account of the tenant's liability to make payments to the landlord in respect of council tax, such increased rent to take effect at the beginning of a new period of the tenancy specified in the notice being a period beginning not earlier than one month after the date on which the notice was served.

(2) The case falls within this subsection if—

(a) the rent under the tenancy has previously been increased by virtue of a notice under section 13. (2) above or a determination under section 14 above, and

(b) the first anniversary of the date on which the increased rent took effect has not yet occurred.

(3) The case falls within this subsection if a notice has been served under section 13. (2) above before 1st April 1993 but no increased rent has taken effect before that date.
(4) No notice may be served under subsection (1) above after 31st March 1994.
(5) Where a notice is served under subsection (1) above, the new rent specified in the notice shall take effect as mentioned in the notice unless, before the beginning of the new period specified in the notice—

(a) the tenant by an application in the prescribed form refers the notice to [F71the appropriate tribunal], or

(b) the landlord and the tenant agree on a variation of the rent which is different from that proposed in the notice or agree that the rent should not be varied.
(6) Nothing in this section (or in section 14. B below) affects the right of the landlord and the tenant under an assured tenancy to vary by agreement any term of the tenancy (including a term relating to rent).]

Amendments (Textual)
F70. Ss. 14. A, 14. B inserted (1.4.1993) by S.I. 1993/651, art. 2. (2), Sch. 2 para. 8
F71. Words in s. 14. A(5)(a) substituted (1.7.2013) by The Transfer of Tribunal Functions Order 2013 (S.I. 2013/1036), art. 1, Sch. 1 para. 84 (with Sch. 3)

F7314. B Interim determination of rent by [F72the appropriate tribunal]
(1) Where, under subsection (5)(a) of section 14. A above, a tenant refers to [F74the appropriate tribunal] a notice under subsection (1) of that section, the [F75appropriate tribunal] shall determine the amount by which, having regard to the provisions of section 14. (3. A) above, the existing rent might reasonably be increased to take account of the tenant's liability to make payments to the landlord in respect of council tax.
(2) Where a notice under section 14. A(1) above has been referred to [F76the appropriate tribunal], then, unless the landlord and the tenant otherwise agree, the existing rent shall be increased by the amount determined by the [F77appropriate tribunal] with effect from the beginning of the new period specified in the notice or, if it appears to the [F77appropriate tribunal] that that would cause undue hardship to the tenant, with effect from such later date (not being later than the date the increase is determined) as the [F77appropriate tribunal] may direct.
(3) In any case where—

(a) [F78the appropriate tribunal] have before them at the same time the reference of a notice under section 13. (2) above relating to a tenancy (in this subsection referred to as "the section 13 reference") and the reference of a notice under section 14. A(1) above relating to the same tenancy (in this subsection referred to as "the section 14. A reference"); and

(b) the [F79appropriate tribunal] propose to hear the two references together,

the [F79appropriate tribunal] shall make a determination in relation to the section 13 reference before making their determination in relation to the section 14. A reference, and if in such a case the date specified in the notice under section 13. (2) above is later than the date specified in the notice under section 14. A(1) above, the rent determined under the section 14. A reference shall not take effect until the date specified in the notice under section 13. (2).
(4) In this section "rent" has the same meaning as in section 14 above; and section 14. (4) above applies to a determination under this section as it applies to a determination under that section.

Amendments (Textual)
F72. Words in s. 14. B heading substituted (1.7.2013) by The Transfer of Tribunal Functions Order 2013 (S.I. 2013/1036), art. 1, Sch. 1 para. 85. (a) (with Sch. 3)
F73. Ss. 14. A, 14. B inserted (1.4.1993) by S.I. 1993/651, art. 2. (2), Sch. 2 para. 8
F74. Words in s. 14. B(1) substituted (1.7.2013) by The Transfer of Tribunal Functions Order 2013 (S.I. 2013/1036), art. 1, Sch. 1 para. 85. (b)(i) (with Sch. 3)
F75. Words in s. 14. B(1) substituted (1.7.2013) by The Transfer of Tribunal Functions Order 2013 (S.I. 2013/1036), art. 1, Sch. 1 para. 85. (b)(ii) (with Sch. 3)
F76. Words in s. 14. B(2) substituted (1.7.2013) by The Transfer of Tribunal Functions Order 2013 (S.I. 2013/1036), art. 1, Sch. 1 para. 85. (c)(i) (with Sch. 3)
F77. Words in s. 14. B(2) substituted (1.7.2013) by The Transfer of Tribunal Functions Order

2013 (S.I. 2013/1036), art. 1, Sch. 1 para. 85. (c)(ii) (with Sch. 3)
F78. Words in s. 14. B(3) substituted (1.7.2013) by The Transfer of Tribunal Functions Order 2013 (S.I. 2013/1036), art. 1, Sch. 1 para. 85. (d)(i) (with Sch. 3)
F79. Words in s. 14. B(3) substituted (1.7.2013) by The Transfer of Tribunal Functions Order 2013 (S.I. 2013/1036), art. 1, Sch. 1 para. 85. (d)(ii) (with Sch. 3)

15 Limited prohibition on assignment etc. without consent.

(1) Subject to subsection (3) below, it shall be an implied term of every assured tenancy which is a periodic tenancy that, except with the consent of the landlord, the tenant shall not—

(a) assign the tenancy (in whole or in part); or

(b) sub-let or part with possession of the whole or any part of the dwelling-house let on the tenancy.

(2) Section 19 of the M4. Landlord and Tenant Act 1927 (consents to assign not to be unreasonably withheld etc.) shall not apply to a term which is implied into an assured tenancy by subsection (1) above.

(3) In the case of a periodic tenancy which is not a statutory periodic tenancy [F80or an assured periodic tenancy arising under Schedule 10 to the Local Government and Housing Act 1989] subsection (1) above does not apply if—

(a) there is a provision (whether contained in the tenancy or not) under which the tenant is prohibited (whether absolutely or conditionally) from assigning or sub-letting or parting with possession or is permitted (whether absolutely or conditionally) to assign, sub-let or part with possession; or

(b) a premium is required to be paid on the grant or renewal of the tenancy.

(4) In subsection (3)(b) above "premium" includes—

(a) any fine or other like sum;

(b) any other pecuniary consideration in addition to rent; and

(c) any sum paid by way of deposit, other than one which does not exceed one-sixth of the annual rent payable under the tenancy immediately after the grant or renewal in question.

Amendments (Textual)
F80. Words inserted by Local Government and Housing Act 1989 (c. 42, SIF 75:1), s. 194, Sch. 11 para. 102

Marginal Citations
M41927 c. 36.

[F8115. ALoss of assured tenancy status

(1) Subsection (2) applies if, in breach of an express or implied term of the tenancy, a tenant of a dwelling-house let under an assured tenancy to which this section applies—

(a) parts with possession of the dwelling-house, or

(b) sub-lets the whole of the dwelling-house (or sub-lets first part of it and then the remainder).

(2) The tenancy ceases to be an assured tenancy and cannot subsequently become an assured tenancy.

(3) This section applies to an assured tenancy—

(a) under which the landlord is a private registered provider of social housing or a registered social landlord, and

(b) which is not a shared ownership lease.

(4) In this section "registered social landlord" has the same meaning as in Part 1 of the Housing Act 1996.

(5) In this section "shared ownership lease" means a lease of a dwelling-house—

(a) granted on payment of a premium calculated by reference to a percentage of the value of the dwelling-house or of the cost of providing it, or

(b) under which the lessee (or the lessee's personal representatives) will or may be entitled to a sum calculated by reference, directly or indirectly, to the value of the dwelling-house.]

Amendments (Textual)
F81. S. 15. A inserted (15.10.2013 for E., 5.11.2013 for W.) by Prevention of Social Housing Fraud Act 2013 (c. 3), ss. 6, 12; S.I. 2013/2622, art. 2; S.I. 2013/2861, art. 2

16 Access for repairs.
It shall be an implied term of every assured tenancy that the tenant shall afford to the landlord access to the dwelling-house let on the tenancy and all reasonable facilities for executing therein any repairs which the landlord is entitled to execute.

Miscellaneous

17 Succession to [F82assured tenancy].
(1) [F83. Subject to subsection (1. D),] In any case where—
   (a) the sole tenant under an assured periodic tenancy dies, and
   (b) immediately before the death, the tenant's spouse [F84or civil partner] was occupying the dwelling-house as his or her only or principal home, and
   F85. (c). . . . .
then, on the death, the tenancy vests by virtue of this section in the spouse [F84or civil partner] (and, accordingly, does not devolve under the tenant's will or intestacy).
[F86. (1. A)Subject to subsection (1. D), in any case where—
   (a) there is an assured periodic tenancy of a dwelling-house in England under which—
(i) the landlord is a private registered provider of social housing, and
(ii) the tenant is a sole tenant,
   (b) the tenant under the tenancy dies,
   (c) immediately before the death, the dwelling-house was not occupied by a spouse or civil partner of the tenant as his or her only or principal home,
   (d) an express term of the tenancy makes provision for a person other than such a spouse or civil partner of the tenant to succeed to the tenancy, and
   (e) there is a person whose succession is in accordance with that term,
then, on the death, the tenancy vests by virtue of this section in that person (and, accordingly, does not devolve under the tenant's will or intestacy).
(1. B)Subject to subsection (1. D), in any case where—
   (a) there is an assured tenancy of a dwelling-house in England for a fixed term of not less than two years under which—
(i) the landlord is a private registered provider of social housing, and
(ii) the tenant is a sole tenant,
   (b) the tenant under the tenancy dies, and
   (c) immediately before the death, the tenant's spouse or civil partner was occupying the dwelling-house as his or her only or principal home,
then, on the death, the tenancy vests by virtue of this section in the spouse or civil partner (and, accordingly, does not devolve under the tenant's will or intestacy).
(1. C)Subject to subsection (1. D), in any case where—
   (a) there is an assured tenancy of a dwelling-house in England for a fixed term of not less than two years under which—
(i) the landlord is a private registered provider of social housing, and
(ii) the tenant is a sole tenant,
   (b) the tenant under the tenancy dies,
   (c) immediately before the death, the dwelling-house was not occupied by a spouse or civil partner of the tenant as his or her only or principal home,
   (d) an express term of the tenancy makes provision for a person other than such a spouse or civil partner of the tenant to succeed to the tenancy, and
   (e) there is a person whose succession is in accordance with that term,
then, on the death, the tenancy vests by virtue of this section in that person (and accordingly does not devolve under the tenant's will or intestacy).
(1. D)Subsection (1), (1. A), (1. B) or (1. C) does not apply if the tenant was himself a successor as defined in subsection (2) or subsection (3).

(1. E) In such a case, on the death, the tenancy vests by virtue of this section in a person ("P") (and, accordingly, does not devolve under the tenant's will or intestacy) if, and only if—

(a) (in a case within subsection (1)) the tenancy is of a dwelling-house in England under which the landlord is a private registered provider of social housing,

(b) an express term of the tenancy makes provision for a person to succeed a successor to the tenancy, and

(c) P's succession is in accordance with that term.]

(2) For the purposes of this section, a tenant is a successor in relation to a tenancy if—

(a) the tenancy became vested in him either by virtue of this section or under the will or intestacy of a previous tenant; or

(b) at some time before the tenant's death the tenancy was a joint tenancy held by himself and one or more other persons and, prior to his death, he became the sole tenant by survivorship; or

(c) he became entitled to the tenancy as mentioned in section 39. (5) below.

(3) For the purposes of this section, a tenant is also a successor in relation to a tenancy (in this subsection referred to as "the new tenancy") which was granted to him (alone or jointly with others) if—

(a) at some time before the grant of the new tenancy, he was, by virtue of subsection (2) above, a successor in relation to an earlier tenancy of the same or substantially the same dwelling-house as is let under the new tenancy; and

(b) at all times since he became such a successor he has been a tenant (alone or jointly with others) of the dwelling-house which is let under the new tenancy or of a dwelling-house which is substantially the same as that dwelling-house.

[F87. (4) For the purposes of this section—

(a) a person who was living with the tenant as his or her wife or husband shall be treated as the tenant's spouse, and

(b) a person who was living with the tenant as if they were civil partners shall be treated as the tenant's civil partner.]

(5) If, on the death of the tenant, there is, by virtue of subsection (4) above, more than one person who fulfils the condition in subsection (1)(b) [F88or (1. B)(c)] above, such one of them as may be decided by agreement or, in default of agreement, by the county court [F89shall for the purposes of this section be [F90treated as the tenant's spouse, or if that person is the same sex as the tenant, and falls within subsection (4)(b), as the tenant's civil partner.]] .

[F91. (6) If, on the death of the tenant, there is more than one person in whom the tenancy would otherwise vest by virtue of subsection (1. A), (1. C) or (1. E), the tenancy vests in such one of them as may be agreed between them or, in default of agreement, as is determined by the county court.

(7) This section does not apply to a fixed term assured tenancy that is a lease of a dwelling-house—

(a) granted on payment of a premium calculated by reference to a percentage of the value of the dwelling-house or of the cost of providing it, or

(b) under which the lessee (or the lessee's personal representatives) will or may be entitled to a sum calculated by reference, directly or indirectly, to the value of the dwelling-house.]

Amendments (Textual)

F82. Words in s. 17 heading substituted (1.4.2012) by Localism Act 2011 (c. 20), ss. 161. (2), 240. (2) (with s. 161. (7)); S.I. 2012/628, art. 6. (a) (with arts. 9 11 14 15 17)

F83. Words in s. 17. (1) inserted (1.4.2012) by Localism Act 2011 (c. 20), ss. 161. (3)(a), 240. (2) (with s. 161. (7)); S.I. 2012/628, art. 6. (a) (with arts. 9 11 14 15 17)

F84. Words in s. 17. (1) inserted (5.12.2005) by Civil Partnership Act 2004 (c. 33), ss. 81, 263, Sch. 8 para. 41. (1)(2), S.I. 2005/3175, {art. 2. (1)}, Sch. 1

F85. S. 17. (1)(c) repealed (1.4.2012) by Localism Act 2011 (c. 20), ss. 161. (3)(b), 240. (2), Sch. 25 Pt. 23 (with s. 161. (7)); S.I. 2012/628, art. 6. (a) (with arts. 9 11 14 15 17)

F86. S. 17. (1. A)-(1. E) inserted (1.4.2012) by Localism Act 2011 (c. 20), ss. 161. (4), 240. (2) (with s. 161. (7)); S.I. 2012/628, art. 6. (a) (with arts. 9 11 14 15 17)

F87. Words in s. 17. (4) substituted (5.12.2005) by Civil Partnership Act 2004 (c. 33), ss. 81, 263, Sch. 8 para. 41. (1)(3); S.I. 2005/3175, art. 2. (1), Sch. 1
F88. Words in s. 17. (5) inserted (1.4.2012) by Localism Act 2011 (c. 20), ss. 161. (5), 240. (2) (with s. 161. (7)); S.I. 2012/628, art. 6. (a) (with arts. 9 11 14 15 17)
F89. Words in s. 17. (5) substituted (5.12.2005) by Civil Partnership Act 2004 (c. 33), ss. 81, 263, Sch. 8 para. 41. (1)(4); S.I. 2005/3175, art. 2. (1), Sch. 1
F90. Words in s. 17. (5) substituted (13.3.2014) by The Marriage (Same Sex Couples) Act 2013 (Consequential and Contrary Provisions and Scotland) Order 2014 (S.I. 2014/560), art. 1. (2), Sch. 1 para. 20
F91. S. 17. (6)(7) inserted (1.4.2012) by Localism Act 2011 (c. 20), ss. 161. (6), 240. (2) (with s. 161. (7)); S.I. 2012/628, art. 6. (a) (with arts. 9 11 14 15 17)
Modifications etc. (not altering text)
C12. S. 17 extended (1.10.1997) by 1996 c. 27, ss. 53, 63. (4), Sch. 7 Pt. II para. 7. (4)(6); S.I. 1997/1892, art. 3
18 Provisions as to reversions on assured tenancies.
(1) If at any time—
  (a) a dwelling-house is for the time being lawfully let on an assured tenancy, and
  (b) the landlord under the assured tenancy is himself a tenant under a superior tenancy; and
  (c) the superior tenancy comes to an end,
then, subject to subsection (2) below, the assured tenancy shall continue in existence as a tenancy held of the person whose interest would, apart from the continuance of the assured tenancy, entitle him to actual possession of the dwelling-house at that time.
(2) Subsection (1) above does not apply to an assured tenancy if the interest which, by virtue of that subsection, would become that of the landlord, is such that, by virtue of Schedule 1 to this Act, the tenancy could not be an assured tenancy.
(3) Where, by virtue of any provision of this Part of this Act, an assured tenancy which is a periodic tenancy (including a statutory periodic tenancy) continues beyond the beginning of a reversionary tenancy which was granted (whether before, on or after the commencement of this Act) so as to begin on or after—
  (a) the date on which the previous contractual assured tenancy came to an end, or
  (b) a date on which, apart from any provision of this Part, the periodic tenancy could have been brought to an end by the landlord by notice to quit,
the reversionary tenancy shall have effect as if it had been granted subject to the periodic tenancy.
(4) The reference in subsection (3) above to the previous contractual assured tenancy applies only where the periodic tenancy referred to in that subsection is a statutory periodic tenancy and is a reference to the fixed-term tenancy which immediately preceded the statutory periodic tenancy.
Modifications etc. (not altering text)
C13. S. 18. (1) restricted (1.11.1993) by 1993 c. 28, s. 61, Sch. 14 para. 3. (2)(c); S.I. 1993/2134, arts. 2,5
F9219 Restriction on levy of distress for rent.
. . . .
Amendments (Textual)
F92. S. 19 repealed (6.4.2014) by Tribunals, Courts and Enforcement Act 2007 (c. 15), s. 148, Sch. 14 para. 45, Sch. 23 Pt. 4 (with s. 89); S.I. 2014/768, art. 2. (1)(b)

chapter II Assured Shorthold Tenancies

[F9319. A Assured shorthold tenancies: post-Housing Act 1996 tenancies.

An assured tenancy which—
   (a) is entered into on or after the day on which section 96 of the Housing Act 1996 comes into force (otherwise than pursuant to a contract made before that day), or
   (b) comes into being by virtue of section 5 above on the coming to an end of an assured tenancy within paragraph (a) above,
is an assured shorthold tenancy unless it falls within any paragraph in Schedule 2. A to this Act.]
Amendments (Textual)
F93. S. 19. A inserted (28.2.1997) by 1996 c. 52, s. 96. (1); S.I. 1997/225, art. 2 (with Sch.)

[F9420 Assured shorthold tenancies: pre-Housing Act 1996 tenancies.

(1) Subject to subsection (3) below, an assured tenancy which is not one to which section 19. A above applies is an assured shorthold tenancy if—
   (a) it is a fixed term tenancy granted for a term certain of not less than six months,
   (b) there is no power for the landlord to determine the tenancy at any time earlier than six months from the beginning of the tenancy; and
   (c) a notice in respect of it is served as mentioned in subsection (2) below.]
(2) The notice referred to in subsection (1)(c) above is one which—
   (a) is in such form as may be prescribed;
   (b) is served before the assured tenancy is entered into;
   (c) is served by the person who is to be the landlord under the assured tenancy on the person who is to be the tenant under that tenancy; and
   (d) states that the assured tenancy to which it relates is to be a shorthold tenancy.
(3) Notwithstanding anything in subsection (1) above, where—
   (a) immediately before a tenancy (in this subsection referred to as "the new tenancy") is granted, the person to whom it is granted or, as the case may be, at least one of the persons to whom it is granted was a tenant under an assured tenancy which was not a shorthold tenancy, and
   (b) the new tenancy is granted by the person who, immediately before the beginning of the tenancy, was the landlord under the assured tenancy referred to in paragraph (a) above,
the new tenancy cannot be an assured shorthold tenancy.
(4) Subject to subsection (5) below, if, on the coming to an end of an assured shorthold tenancy (including a tenancy which was an assured shorthold but ceased to be assured before it came to an end), a new tenancy of the same or substantially the same premises comes into being under which the landlord and the tenant are the same as at the coming to an end of the earlier tenancy, then, if and so long as the new tenancy is an assured tenancy, it shall be an assured shorthold tenancy, whether or not it fulfils the conditions in paragraphs (a) to (c) of subsection (1) above.
(5) Subsection (4) above does not apply if, before the new tenancy is entered into (or, in the case of a statutory periodic tenancy, takes effect in possession), the landlord serves notice on the tenant that the new tenancy is not to be a shorthold tenancy.
[F95. (5. A)Subsections (3) and (4) above do not apply where the new tenancy is one to which section 19. A above applies]
(6) In the case of joint landlords—
   (a) the reference in subsection (2)(c) above to the person who is to be the landlord is a reference to at least one of the persons who are to be joint landlords; and
   (b) the reference in subsection (5) above to the landlord is a reference to at least one of the joint landlords.
F96. (7)............................
Amendments (Textual)
F94. S. 20. (1) and side-note substituted (28.2.1997) by 1996 c. 52, s. 104, Sch. 8 para. 2. (3); S.I. 1997/225, art. 2 (with Sch.)
F95. S. 20. (5. A) inserted (28.2.1997) by 1996 c. 52, s. 104, Sch. 8 para. 2. (4); S.I. 1997/225, art.

2 (with Sch.)
F96. S. 20. (7) repealed (28.2.1997) by 1996 c. 52, s. 227, Sch. 19 Pt. IV; S.I. 1997/225, art. 2 (with Sch.)

[F9720. A Post-Housing Act 1996 tenancies: duty of landlord to provide statement as to terms of tenancy.

(1) Subject to subsection (3) below, a tenant under an assured shorthold tenancy to which section 19. A above applies may, by notice in writing, require the landlord under that tenancy to provide him with a written statement of any term of the tenancy which—
   (a) falls within subsection (2) below, and
   (b) is not evidenced in writing.
(2) The following terms of a tenancy fall within this subsection, namely—
   (a) the date on which the tenancy began or, if it is a statutory periodic tenancy or a tenancy to which section 39. (7) below applies, the date on which the tenancy came into being,
   (b) the rent payable under the tenancy and the dates on which that rent is payable,
   (c) any term providing for a review of the rent payable under the tenancy, and
   (d) in the case of a fixed term tenancy, the length of the fixed term.
(3) No notice may be given under subsection (1) above in relation to a term of the tenancy if—
   (a) the landlord under the tenancy has provided a statement of that term in response to an earlier notice under that subsection given by the tenant under the tenancy, and
   (b) the term has not been varied since the provision of the statement referred to in paragraph (a) above.
(4) A landlord who fails, without reasonable excuse, to comply with a notice under subsection (1) above within the period of 28 days beginning with the date on which he received the notice is liable on summary conviction to a fine not exceeding level 4 on the standard scale.
(5) A statement provided for the purposes of subsection (1) above shall not be regarded as conclusive evidence of what was agreed by the parties to the tenancy in question.
(6) Where—
   (a) a term of a statutory periodic tenancy is one which has effect by virtue of section 5. (3)(e) above, or
   (b) a term of a tenancy to which subsection (7) of section 39 below applies is one which has effect by virtue of subsection (6)(e) of that section,
subsection (1) above shall have effect in relation to it as if paragraph (b) related to the term of the tenancy from which it derives.
(7) In subsections (1) and (3) above—
   (a) references to the tenant under the tenancy shall, in the case of joint tenants, be taken to be references to any of the tenants, and
   (b) references to the landlord under the tenancy shall, in the case of joint landlords, be taken to be references to any of the landlords.]
Amendments (Textual)
F97. S. 20. A inserted (28.2.1997) by 1996 c. 52, s. 97; S.I. 1997/225, art. 2 (with Sch.)

[F9820. BDemoted assured shorthold tenancies

(1) An assured tenancy is an assured shorthold tenancy to which this section applies (a demoted assured shorthold tenancy) if—
   (a) the tenancy is created by virtue of an order of the court under section 82. A of the Housing Act 1985 or section 6. A of this Act (a demotion order), and
   (b) the landlord is [F99a private registered provider of social housing or] a registered social landlord.

(2) At the end of the period of one year starting with the day when the demotion order takes effect a demoted assured shorthold tenancy ceases to be an assured shorthold tenancy unless subsection (3) applies[F100, but see section 20. C].

(3) This subsection applies if before the end of the period mentioned in subsection (2) the landlord gives notice of proceedings for possession of the dwelling house.

(4) If subsection (3) applies the tenancy continues to be a demoted assured shorthold tenancy until the end of the period mentioned in subsection (2) or (if later) until one of the following occurs—
 (a) the notice of proceedings for possession is withdrawn;
 (b) the proceedings are determined in favour of the tenant;
 (c) the period of six months beginning with the date on which the notice is given ends and no proceedings for possession have been brought.

(5) Registered social landlord has the same meaning as in Part 1 of the Housing Act 1996.]

Amendments (Textual)

F98. S. 20. B inserted (30.6.2004 for E. and 30.4.2005 for W.) by Anti-Social Behaviour Act 2003 (c. 38), ss. 15, 93; S.I. 2004/1502, art. 2. (a)(iv) (with savings in Sch.); S.I. 2005/1225, art. 2. (c)

F99. Words in s. 20. B(1) inserted (1.4.2010) by The Housing and Regeneration Act 2008 (Consequential Provisions) Order 2010 (S.I. 2010/866), art. 1. (2), Sch. 2 para. 65 (with art. 6, Sch. 3)

F100. Words in s. 20. B(2) inserted (1.4.2012) by Localism Act 2011 (c. 20), ss. 163. (1), 240. (2); S.I. 2012/628, art. 6. (c) (with arts. 9 11 14 15 17)

[F10120. CAssured shorthold tenancies following demoted tenancies

(1) Subsection (2) applies if—
 (a) section 20. B applies to an assured shorthold tenancy of a dwelling-house in England ("the demoted tenancy"),
 (b) the landlord is a private registered provider of social housing,
 (c) the demoted tenancy was created by an order under section 6. A made after the coming into force of section 163. (2) of the Localism Act 2011,
 (d) the assured tenancy that was terminated by that order was an assured shorthold tenancy that, whether or not it was a fixed term tenancy when terminated by the order, was granted for a term certain of not less than two years,
 (e) apart from subsection (2), the demoted tenancy would cease to be an assured shorthold tenancy by virtue of section 20. B(2) or (4), and
 (f) the landlord has served a notice within subsection (3) on the tenant before the demoted tenancy ceases to be an assured shorthold tenancy by virtue of section 20. B(2) or (4).

(2) The demoted tenancy does not cease to be an assured shorthold tenancy by virtue of section 20. B(2) or (4), and at the time when it would otherwise cease to be an assured shorthold tenancy by virtue of section 20. B(2) to (4)—
 (a) it becomes an assured shorthold tenancy which is a fixed term tenancy for a term certain, and
 (b) section 20. B ceases to apply to it.

(3) The notice must—
 (a) state that, on ceasing to be a demoted assured shorthold tenancy, the tenancy will become an assured shorthold tenancy which is a fixed term tenancy for a term certain of the length specified in the notice,
 (b) specify a period of at least two years as the length of the term of the tenancy, and
 (c) set out the other express terms of the tenancy.

(4) Where an assured shorthold tenancy becomes a fixed term tenancy by virtue of subsection (2)—
 (a) the length of its term is that specified in the notice under subsection (3), and

(b) its other express terms are those set out in the notice.]
Amendments (Textual)
F101. S. 20. C inserted (1.4.2012) by Localism Act 2011 (c. 20), ss. 163. (2), 240. (2); S.I. 2012/628, art. 6. (c) (with arts. 9 11 14 15 17)

[F10220. DAssured shorthold tenancies following family intervention tenancies

(1) An assured tenancy that arises by virtue of a notice under paragraph 12. ZA(2) of Schedule 1 in respect of a family intervention tenancy is an assured shorthold tenancy if—
    (a) the landlord under the assured tenancy is a private registered provider of social housing,
    (b) the dwelling-house is in England,
    (c) the family intervention tenancy was granted to a person on the coming to an end of an assured shorthold tenancy under which the person was a tenant, and
    (d) the notice states that the family intervention tenancy is to be regarded as an assured shorthold tenancy.
(2) This section does not apply if the family intervention tenancy was granted before the coming into force of section 163. (3) of the Localism Act 2011.]
Amendments (Textual)
F102. S. 20. D inserted (1.4.2012) by Localism Act 2011 (c. 20), ss. 163. (3), 240. (2); S.I. 2012/628, art. 6. (c) (with arts. 9 11 14 15 17)

21 Recovery of possession on expiry or termination of assured shorthold tenancy.

(1) Without prejudice to any right of the landlord under an assured shorthold tenancy to recover possession of the dwelling-house let on the tenancy in accordance with Chapter I above, on or after the coming to an end of an assured shorthold tenancy which was a fixed term tenancy, a court shall make an order for possession of the dwelling-house if it is satisfied—
    (a) that the assured shorthold tenancy has come to an end and no further assured tenancy (whether shorthold or not) is for the time being in existence, other than [F103an assured shorthold periodic tenancy (whether statutory or not)]; and
    (b) the landlord or, in the case of joint landlords, at least one of them has given to the tenant not less than two months' notice [F104in writing] stating that he requires possession of the dwelling-house.
[F105. (1. A)Subsection (1. B) applies to an assured shorthold tenancy of a dwelling-house in England if—
    (a) it is a fixed term tenancy for a term certain of not less than two years, and
    (b) the landlord is a private registered provider of social housing.
(1. B)The court may not make an order for possession of the dwelling-house let on the tenancy unless the landlord has given to the tenant not less than six months' notice in writing—
    (a) stating that the landlord does not propose to grant another tenancy on the expiry of the fixed term tenancy, and
    (b) informing the tenant of how to obtain help or advice about the notice and, in particular, of any obligation of the landlord to provide help or advice.]
(2) A notice under paragraph (b) of subsection (1) above may be given before or on the day on which the tenancy comes to an end; and that subsection shall have effect notwithstanding that on the coming to an end of the fixed term tenancy a statutory periodic tenancy arises.
(3) Where a court makes an order for possession of a dwelling-house by virtue of subsection (1) above, any statutory periodic tenancy which has arisen on the coming to an end of the assured shorthold tenancy shall end (without further notice and regardless of the period) [F106in

accordance with section 5. (1. A)].

(4) Without prejudice to any such right as is referred to in subsection (1) above, a court shall make an order for possession of a dwelling-house let on an assured shorthold tenancy which is a periodic tenancy if the court is satisfied—

(a) that the landlord or, in the case of joint landlords, at least one of them has given to the tenant a notice [F107in writing] stating that, after a date specified in the notice, being the last day of a period of the tenancy and not earlier than two months after the date the notice was given, possession of the dwelling-house is required by virtue of this section; and

(b) that the date specified in the notice under paragraph (a) above is not earlier than the earliest day on which, apart from section 5. (1) above, the tenancy could be brought to an end by a notice to quit given by the landlord on the same date as the notice under paragraph (a) above.

[F108. (4. ZA)In the case of a dwelling-house in England, subsection (4)(a) above has effect with the omission of the requirement for the date specified in the notice to be the last day of a period of the tenancy.]

[F109. (4. A)Where a court makes an order for possession of a dwelling-house by virtue of subsection (4) above, the assured shorthold tenancy shall end in accordance with section 5. (1. A).]

[F110. (4. B)A notice under subsection (1) or (4) may not be given in relation to an assured shorthold tenancy of a dwelling-house in England—

(a) in the case of a tenancy which is not a replacement tenancy, within the period of four months beginning with the day on which the tenancy began, and

(b) in the case of a replacement tenancy, within the period of four months beginning with the day on which the original tenancy began.

(4. C)Subsection (4. B) does not apply where the tenancy has arisen due to section 5. (2).

(4. D)Subject to subsection (4. E), proceedings for an order for possession under this section in relation to a dwelling-house in England may not be begun after the end of the period of six months beginning with the date on which the notice was given under subsection (1) or (4).

(4. E)Where—

(a) a notice under subsection (4) has been given in relation to a dwelling-house in England, and

(b) paragraph (b) of that subsection requires the date specified in the notice to be more than two months after the date the notice was given,

proceedings for an order for possession under this section may not be begun after the end of the period of four months beginning with the date specified in the notice.]

[F111. (5)Where an order for possession under subsection (1) or (4) above is made in relation to a dwelling-house let on a tenancy to which section 19. A above applies, the order may not be made so as to take effect earlier than—

(a) in the case of a tenancy which is not a replacement tenancy, six months after the beginning of the tenancy, and

(b) in the case of a replacement tenancy, six months after the beginning of the original tenancy.

[F112. (5. A)Subsection (5) above does not apply to an assured shorthold tenancy to which section 20. B (demoted assured shorthold tenancies) applies.]

(6) In [F113subsections (4. B)(b) and] (5)(b) above, the reference to the original tenancy is—

(a) where the replacement tenancy came into being on the coming to an end of a tenancy which was not a replacement tenancy, to the immediately preceding tenancy, and

(b) where there have been successive replacement tenancies, to the tenancy immediately preceding the first in the succession of replacement tenancies.

(7) For the purposes of this section, a replacement tenancy is a tenancy—

(a) which comes into being on the coming to an end of an assured shorthold tenancy, and

(b) under which, on its coming into being—

(i) the landlord and tenant are the same as under the earlier tenancy as at its coming to an end, and
(ii) the premises let are the same or substantially the same as those let under the earlier tenancy as at that time.]

[F114. (8)The Secretary of State may by regulations made by statutory instrument prescribe the form of a notice under subsection (1) or (4) given in relation to an assured shorthold tenancy of a

dwelling-house in England.
(9) A statutory instrument containing regulations made under subsection (8) is subject to annulment in pursuance of a resolution of either House of Parliament.]

Amendments (Textual)

F103. Words inserted by Local Government and Housing Act 1989 (c. 42, SIF 75:1), s. 194, Sch. 11 para. 103

F104. Words in s. 21. (1)(b) inserted (28.2.1997) by 1996 c. 52, s. 98. (2); S.I. 1997/225, art. 2 (subject to saving in Sch. para. 2)

F105. S. 21. (1. A)(1. B) inserted (1.4.2012) by Localism Act 2011 (c. 20), ss. 164. (1), 240. (2) (with s. 164. (2)); S.I. 2012/628, art. 6. (c) (with arts. 9 11 14 15 17)

F106. Words in s. 21. (3) substituted (20.5.2009) by Housing and Regeneration Act 2008 (c. 17), ss. 299, 325, Sch. 11 para. 9. (2) (with Sch. 11 para. 14); S.I. 2009/1261, {arts. 2, 3}

F107. Words in s. 21. (4)(a) inserted (28.2.1997) by 1996 c. 52, s. 98. (3); S.I. 1997/225, art. 2 (subject to saving Sch. para. 2)

F108. S. 21. (4. ZA) inserted (1.10.2015) by Deregulation Act 2015 (c. 20), ss. 35, 115. (7) (with s. 41); S.I. 2015/994, art. 11. (i)

F109. S. 21. (4. A) inserted (20.5.2009) by Housing and Regeneration Act 2008 (c. 17), ss. 299, 325, Sch. 11 para. 9. (3) (with Sch. 11 para. 14); S.I. 2009/1261, {arts. 2, 3}

F110. S. 21. (4. B)-(4. E) inserted (1.10.2015) by Deregulation Act 2015 (c. 20), ss. 36. (2), 115. (7) (with s. 41); S.I. 2015/994, art. 11. (j)

F111. S. 21. (5)-(7) inserted (28.2.1997) by 1996 c. 52, s. 99; S.I. 1997/225, art. 2 (with Sch.)

F112. S. 21. (5. A) inserted (30.6.2004 for E. and 30.4.2005 for W.) by Anti-Social Behaviour Act 2003 (c. 38), ss. 15. (2), 93; S.I. 2004/1502, art. 2. (a)(iv) (with savings in Sch.); S.I. 2005/1225, art. 2. (c)

F113. Words in s. 21. (6) substituted (1.10.2015) by Deregulation Act 2015 (c. 20), ss. 36. (3), 115. (7) (with s. 41); S.I. 2015/994, art. 11. (j)

F114. S. 21. (8)(9) inserted (1.7.2015) by Deregulation Act 2015 (c. 20), ss. 37, 115. (7) (with s. 41); S.I. 2015/994, art. 10. (a)

[F11521. ACompliance with prescribed legal requirements

(1) A notice under subsection (1) or (4) of section 21 may not be given in relation to an assured shorthold tenancy of a dwelling-house in England at a time when the landlord is in breach of a prescribed requirement.

(2) The requirements that may be prescribed are requirements imposed on landlords by any enactment and which relate to—
    (a) the condition of dwelling-houses or their common parts,
    (b) the health and safety of occupiers of dwelling-houses, or
    (c) the energy performance of dwelling-houses.

(3) In subsection (2) " enactment " includes an enactment contained in subordinate legislation within the meaning of the Interpretation Act 1978.

(4) For the purposes of subsection (2)(a) " common parts " has the same meaning as in Ground 13 in Part 2 of Schedule 2.

(5) A statutory instrument containing regulations made under this section is subject to annulment in pursuance of a resolution of either House of Parliament.]

Amendments (Textual)

F115. S. 21. A inserted (1.7.2015 for specified purposes, 1.10.2015 in so far as not already in force) by Deregulation Act 2015 (c. 20), ss. 38, 115. (7) (with s. 41); S.I. 2015/994, arts. 10. (b), 11. (k)

[F11621. BRequirement for landlord to provide prescribed

information

(1) The Secretary of State may by regulations require information about the rights and responsibilities of a landlord and a tenant under an assured shorthold tenancy of a dwelling-house in England (or any related matters) to be given by a landlord under such a tenancy, or a person acting on behalf of such a landlord, to the tenant under such a tenancy.
(2) Regulations under subsection (1) may—
   (a) require the information to be given in the form of a document produced by the Secretary of State or another person,
   (b) provide that the document to be given is the version that has effect at the time the requirement applies, and
   (c) specify cases where the requirement does not apply.
(3) A notice under subsection (1) or (4) of section 21 may not be given in relation to an assured shorthold tenancy of a dwelling-house in England at a time when the landlord is in breach of a requirement imposed by regulations under subsection (1).
(4) A statutory instrument containing regulations made under subsection (1) is subject to annulment in pursuance of a resolution of either House of Parliament.]
Amendments (Textual)
F116. S. 21. B inserted (1.7.2015 for specified purposes, 1.10.2015 in so far as not already in force) by Deregulation Act 2015 (c. 20), ss. 39, 115. (7) (with s. 41); S.I. 2015/994, arts. 10. (c), 11. (l)

[F11721. CRepayment of rent where tenancy ends before end of a period

(1) A tenant under an assured shorthold tenancy of a dwelling-house in England is entitled to a repayment of rent from the landlord where—
   (a) as a result of the service of a notice under section 21 the tenancy is brought to an end before the end of a period of the tenancy,
   (b) the tenant has paid rent in advance for that period, and
   (c) the tenant was not in occupation of the dwelling-house for one or more whole days of that period.
(2) The amount of repayment to which a tenant is entitled under subsection (1) is to be calculated in accordance with the following formula—
where—
R is the rent paid for the final period;
D is the number of whole days of the final period for which the tenant was not in occupation of the dwelling-house; and
P is the number of whole days in that period.
(3) If the repayment of rent described in subsections (1) and (2) has not been made when the court makes an order for possession under section 21, the court must order the landlord to repay the amount of rent to which the tenant is entitled.
(4) Nothing in this section affects any other right of the tenant to a repayment of rent from the landlord.]
Amendments (Textual)
F117. S. 21. C inserted (1.10.2015) by Deregulation Act 2015 (c. 20), ss. 40, 115. (7) (with s. 41); S.I. 2015/994, art. 11. (m)

22 Reference of excessive rents to [F118appropriate tribunal].

(1) Subject to section 23 and subsection (2) below, the tenant under an assured shorthold tenancy

F119. . . . may make an application in the prescribed form to [F120the appropriate tribunal] for a determination of the rent which, in [F121the appropriate tribunal's] opinion, the landlord might reasonably be expected to obtain under the assured shorthold tenancy.

(2) No application may be made under this section if—

(a) the rent payable under the tenancy is a rent previously determined under this section; F122. . .

[F123. (aa)the tenancy is one to which section 19. A above applies and more than six months have elapsed since the beginning of the tenancy or, in the case of a replacement tenancy, since the beginning of the original tenancy; or]

(b) the tenancy is an assured shorthold tenancy falling within subsection (4) of section 20 above (and, accordingly, is one in respect of which notice need not have been served as mentioned in subsection (2) of that section).

(3) Where an application is made to [F124the appropriate tribunal] under subsection (1) above with respect to the rent under an assured shorthold tenancy, [F125the appropriate tribunal] shall not make such a determination as is referred to in that subsection unless they consider—

(a) that there is a sufficient number of similar dwelling-houses in the locality let on assured tenancies (whether shorthold or not); and

(b) that the rent payable under the assured shorthold tenancy in question is significantly higher than the rent which the landlord might reasonably be expected to be able to obtain under the tenancy, having regard to the level of rents payable under the tenancies referred to in paragraph (a) above.

(4) Where, on an application under this section, [F126the appropriate tribunal] make a determination of a rent for an assured shorthold tenancy—

(a) the determination shall have effect from such date as [F127the appropriate tribunal] may direct, not being earlier than the date of the application;

(b) if, at any time on or after the determination takes effect, the rent which, apart from this paragraph, would be payable under the tenancy exceeds the rent so determined, the excess shall be irrecoverable from the tenant; and

(c) no notice may be served under section 13. (2) above with respect to a tenancy of the dwelling-house in question until after the first anniversary of the date on which the determination takes effect.

(5) Subsections (4), (5) and (8) of section 14 above apply in relation to a determination of rent under this section as they apply in relation to a determination under that section and, accordingly, where subsection (5) of that section applies, any reference in subsection (4)(b) above to rent is a reference to rent exclusive of the amount attributable to rates.

[F128. (5. A)Where—

(a) an assured tenancy ceases to be an assured shorthold tenancy by virtue of falling within paragraph 2 of Schedule 2. A to this Act, and

(b) at the time when it so ceases to be an assured shorthold tenancy there is pending before [F129the appropriate tribunal] an application in relation to it under this section,

the fact that it so ceases to be an assured shorthold tenancy shall, in relation to that application, be disregarded for the purposes of this section.]

[F130. (6)In subsection (2)(aa) above, the references to the original tenancy and to a replacement tenancy shall be construed in accordance with subsections (6) and (7) respectively of section 21 above.]

Amendments (Textual)

F118. Words in s. 22 substituted (1.7.2013) by The Transfer of Tribunal Functions Order 2013 (S.I. 2013/1036), art. 1, Sch. 1 para. 86. (a) (with Sch. 3)

F119. Words in s. 22. (1) repealed (28.2.1997) by 1996 c. 52, ss. 104, 227, Sch. 8 para. 2. (5), Sch. 19 Pt. IV; S.I. 1997/225, art. 2 (with Sch.)

F120. Words in s. 22. (1) substituted (1.7.2013) by The Transfer of Tribunal Functions Order 2013 (S.I. 2013/1036), art. 1, Sch. 1 para. 86. (b)(i) (with Sch. 3)

F121. Words in s. 22. (1) substituted (1.7.2013) by The Transfer of Tribunal Functions Order 2013

(S.I. 2013/1036), art. 1, Sch. 1 para. 86. (b)(ii) (with Sch. 3)
F122. Word in s. 22. (2)(a) repealed (28.2.1997) by 1996 c. 52, s. 227, Sch. 19 Pt. IV; S.I. 1997/225, art. 2
F123. S. 22. (2)(aa) inserted (28.2.1997) by 1996 c. 52, s. 100. (2); S.I. 1997/225, art. 2 (with Sch.)
F124. Words in s. 22. (3) substituted (1.7.2013) by The Transfer of Tribunal Functions Order 2013 (S.I. 2013/1036), art. 1, Sch. 1 para. 86. (c)(i) (with Sch. 3)
F125. Words in s. 22. (3) substituted (1.7.2013) by The Transfer of Tribunal Functions Order 2013 (S.I. 2013/1036), art. 1, Sch. 1 para. 86. (c)(ii) (with Sch. 3)
F126. Words in s. 22. (4) substituted (1.7.2013) by The Transfer of Tribunal Functions Order 2013 (S.I. 2013/1036), art. 1, Sch. 1 para. 86. (d)(i) (with Sch. 3)
F127. Words in s. 22. (4) substituted (1.7.2013) by The Transfer of Tribunal Functions Order 2013 (S.I. 2013/1036), art. 1, Sch. 1 para. 86. (d)(ii) (with Sch. 3)
F128. S. 22. (5. A) inserted (28.2.1997) by 1996 c. 52, s. 104, Sch. 8 para. 2. (6); S.I. 1997/225, art. 2 (with Sch.)
F129. Words in s. 22. (5. A)(b) substituted (1.7.2013) by The Transfer of Tribunal Functions Order 2013 (S.I. 2013/1036), art. 1, Sch. 1 para. 86. (e) (with Sch. 3)
F130. S. 22. (6) inserted (28.2.1997) by 1996 c. 52, s. 100. (3); S.I. 1997/225, art. 2 (with Sch.)

23 Termination of [F131tribunal's] functions.

(1) If the Secretary of State by order made by statutory instrument so provides, section 22 above shall not apply in such cases or to tenancies of dwelling-houses in such areas or in such other circumstances as may be specified in the order.
(2) An order under this section may contain such transitional, incidental and supplementary provisions as appear to the Secretary of State to be desirable.
(3) No order shall be made under this section unless a draft of the order has been laid before, and approved by a resolution of, each House of Parliament.
Amendments (Textual)
F131. Words in s. 23 substituted (1.7.2013) by The Transfer of Tribunal Functions Order 2013 (S.I. 2013/1036), art. 1, Sch. 1 para. 87 (with Sch. 3)

chapter III Assured Agricultural Occupancies

Modifications etc. (not altering text)
C14. Pt. I Chapter III modified (1.10.1997) by 1996 c. 27, ss. 53, 63. (4), Sch. 7 Pt. II para. 7. (5)(6)(with Sch. 9 paras. 8-10); S.I. 1997/1892, art. 3 (with art. 4)

24 Assured agricultural occupancies.

(1) A tenancy or licence of a dwelling-house is for the purposes of this Part of this Act an "assured agricultural occupancy" if—
    (a) it is of a description specified in subsection (2) below; and
    (b) by virtue of any provision of Schedule 3 to this Act the agricultural worker condition is for the time being fulfilled with respect to the dwelling-house subject to the tenancy or licence.
(2) The following are the tenancies and licences referred to in subsection (1)(a) above—
    (a) an assured tenancy which is not an assured shorthold tenancy;
    (b) a tenancy which does not fall within paragraph (a) above by reason only of paragraph 3 [F132, 3. A, 3. B] or paragraph 7 of Schedule 1 to this Act ([F133or more than one of those paragraphs]) [F134and is not an excepted tenancy]; and
    (c) a licence under which a person has the exclusive occupation of a dwelling-house as a

separate dwelling and which, if it conferred a sufficient interest in land to be a tenancy, would be a tenancy falling within paragraph (a) or paragraph (b) above.
[F135. (2. A)For the purposes of subsection (2)(b) above, a tenancy is an excepted tenancy if it is—
   (a) a tenancy of an agricultural holding within the meaning of the Agricultural Holdings Act 1986 in relation to which that Act applies, or
   (b) a farm business tenancy within the meaning of the Agricultural Tenancies Act 1995]
(3) For the purposes of Chapter I above and the following provisions of this Chapter, every assured agricultural occupancy which is not an assured tenancy shall be treated as if it were such a tenancy and any reference to a tenant, a landlord or any other expression appropriate to a tenancy shall be construed accordingly; but the provisions of Chapter I above shall have effect in relation to every assured agricultural occupancy subject to the provisions of this Chapter.
(4) Section 14 above shall apply in relation to an assured agricultural occupancy as if in subsection (1) of that section the reference to an assured tenancy were a reference to an assured agricultural occupancy.
Amendments (Textual)
F132. Words inserted by S.I. 1990/434, reg. 2, Sch. para. 28
F133. Words substituted by S.I. 1990/434, reg. 2, Sch. para. 28
F134. Words in s. 24. (2)(b) inserted (28.2.1997) by 1996 c. 52, s. 103. (2); S.I. 1997/225, art. 2 (with Sch.)
F135. S. 24. (2. A) inserted (28.2.1997) by 1996 c. 52, s. 103. (3); S.I. 1997/225, art. 2 (with Sch.)

25 Security of tenure.

(1) If a statutory periodic tenancy arises on the coming to an end of an assured agricultural occupancy—
   (a) it shall be an assured agricultural occupancy as long as, by virtue of any provision of Schedule 3 to this Act, the agricultural worker condition is for the time being fulfilled with respect to the dwelling-house in question; and
   (b) if no rent was payable under the assured agricultural occupancy which constitutes the fixed term tenancy referred to in subsection (2) of section 5 above, subsection (3)(d) of that section shall apply as if for the words "the same as those for which rent was last payable under" there were substituted "monthly beginning on the day following the coming to an end of".
(2) In its application to an assured agricultural occupancy, Part II of Schedule 2 to this Act shall have effect with the omission of Ground 16.
(3) In its application to an assured agricultural occupancy, Part III of Schedule 2 to this Act shall have effect as if any reference in paragraph 2 to an assured tenancy included a reference to an assured agricultural occupancy.
(4) If the tenant under an assured agricultural occupancy gives notice to terminate his employment then, notwithstanding anything in any agreement or otherwise, that notice shall not constitute a notice to quit as respects the assured agricultural occupancy.
(5) Nothing in subsection (4) above affects the operation of an actual notice to quit given in respect of an assured agricultural occupancy.

26 Rehousing of agricultural workers etc.

In section 27 of the M5. Rent (Agriculture) Act 1976 (rehousing: applications to housing authority)—
   (a) in subsection (1)(a) after "statutory tenancy" there shall be inserted " "or an assured agricultural occupancy "; and
   (b) at the end of subsection (3) there shall be added " "and assured agricultural occupancy has the same meaning as in Chapter III of Part I of the Housing Act 1988 ".

Marginal Citations
M51976 c. 80.

chapter IV Protection from Eviction

27 Damages for unlawful eviction.

(1) This section applies if, at any time after 9th June 1988, a landlord (in this section referred to as "the landlord in default") or any person acting on behalf of the landlord in default unlawfully deprives the residential occupier of any premises of his occupation of the whole or part of the premises.
(2) This section also applies if, at any time after 9th June 1988, a landlord (in this section referred to as "the landlord in default") or any person acting on behalf of the landlord in default—
    (a) attempts unlawfully to deprive the residential occupier of any premises of his occupation of the whole or part of the premises, or
    (b) knowing or having reasonable cause to believe that the conduct is likely to cause the residential occupier of any premises—
(i) to give up his occupation of the premises or any part thereof, or
(ii) to refrain from exercising any right or pursuing any remedy in respect of the premises or any part thereof,
does acts likely to interfere with the peace or comfort of the residential occupier or members of his household, or persistently withdraws or withholds services reasonably required for the occupation of the premises as a residence,
and, as a result, the residential occupier gives up his occupation of the premises as a residence.
(3) Subject to the following provisions of this section, where this section applies, the landlord in default shall, by virtue of this section, be liable to pay to the former residential occupier, in respect of his loss of the right to occupy the premises in question as his residence, damages assessed on the basis set out in section 28 below.
(4) Any liability arising by virtue of subsection (3) above—
    (a) shall be in the nature of a liability in tort; and
    (b) subject to subsection (5) below, shall be in addition to any liability arising apart from this section (whether in tort, contract or otherwise).
(5) Nothing in this section affects the right of a residential occupier to enforce any liability which arises apart from this section in respect of his loss of the right to occupy premises as his residence; but damages shall not be awarded both in respect of such a liability and in respect of a liability arising by virtue of this section on account of the same loss.
(6) No liability shall arise by virtue of subsection (3) above if—
    (a) before the date on which proceedings to enforce the liability are finally disposed of, the former residential occupier is reinstated in the premises in question in such circumstances that he becomes again the residential occupier of them; or
    (b) at the request of the former residential occupier, a court makes an order (whether in the nature of an injunction or otherwise) as a result of which he is reinstated as mentioned in paragraph (a) above;
and, for the purposes of paragraph (a) above, proceedings to enforce a liability are finally disposed of on the earliest date by which the proceedings (including any proceedings on or in consequence of an appeal) have been determined and any time for appealing or further appealing has expired, except that if any appeal is abandoned, the proceedings shall be taken to be disposed of on the date of the abandonment.
(7) If, in proceedings to enforce a liability arising by virtue of subsection (3) above, it appears to the court—
    (a) that, prior to the event which gave rise to the liability, the conduct of the former residential

occupier or any person living with him in the premises concerned was such that it is reasonable to mitigate the damages for which the landlord in default would otherwise be liable, or

    (b) that, before the proceedings were begun, the landlord in default offered to reinstate the former residential occupier in the premises in question and either it was unreasonable of the former residential occupier to refuse that offer or, if he had obtained alternative accommodation before the offer was made, it would have been unreasonable of him to refuse that offer if he had not obtained that accommodation,

the court may reduce the amount of damages which would otherwise be payable to such amount as it thinks appropriate.

(8) In proceedings to enforce a liability arising by virtue of subsection (3) above, it shall be a defence for the defendant to prove that he believed, and had reasonable cause to believe—

    (a) that the residential occupier had ceased to reside in the premises in question at the time when he was deprived of occupation as mentioned in subsection (1) above or, as the case may be, when the attempt was made or the acts were done as a result of which he gave up his occupation of those premises; or

    (b) that, where the liability would otherwise arise by virtue only of the doing of acts or the withdrawal or withholding of services, he had reasonable grounds for doing the acts or withdrawing or withholding the services in question.

(9) In this section—

    (a) "residential occupier", in relation to any premises, has the same meaning as in section 1 of the 1977 Act;

    (b) "the right to occupy", in relation to a residential occupier, includes any restriction on the right of another person to recover possession of the premises in question;

    (c) "landlord", in relation to a residential occupier, means the person who, but for the occupier's right to occupy, would be entitled to occupation of the premises and any superior landlord under whom that person derives title;

    (d) "former residential occupier", in relation to any premises, means the person who was the residential occupier until he was deprived of or gave up his occupation as mentioned in subsection (1) or subsection (2) above (and, in relation to a former residential occupier, "the right to occupy" and "landlord" shall be construed accordingly).

28 The measure of damages.

(1) The basis for the assessment of damages referred to in section 27. (3) above is the difference in value, determined as at the time immediately before the residential occupier ceased to occupy the premises in question as his residence, between—

    (a) the value of the interest of the landlord in default determined on the assumption that the residential occupier continues to have the same right to occupy the premises as before that time; and

    (b) the value of that interest determined on the assumption that the residential occupier has ceased to have that right.

(2) In relation to any premises, any reference in this section to the interest of the landlord in default is a reference to his interest in the building in which the premises in question are comprised (whether or not that building contains any other premises) together with its curtilage.

(3) For the purposes of the valuations referred to in subsection (1) above, it shall be assumed—

    (a) that the landlord in default is selling his interest on the open market to a willing buyer;

    (b) that neither the residential occupier nor any member of his family wishes to buy; and

    (c) that it is unlawful to carry out any substantial development of any of the land in which the landlord's interest subsists or to demolish the whole or part of any building on that land.

(4) In this section "the landlord in default" has the same meaning as in section 27 above and subsection (9) of that section applies in relation to this section as it applies in relation to that.

(5) Section 113 of the M6. Housing Act 1985 (meaning of "members of a person's family")

applies for the purposes of subsection (3)(b) above.
(5) The reference in subsection (3)(c) above to substantial development of any of the land in which the landlord's interest subsists is a reference to any development other than—

(a) development for which planning permission is granted by a general development order for the time being in force and which is carried out so as to comply with any condition or limitation subject to which planning permission is so granted; or

(b) a change of use resulting in the building referred to in subsection (2) above or any part of it being used as, or as part of, one or more dwelling-houses;

and in this subsection "general development order"[F136has the meaning given in section 56. (6) of the Town and Country Planning Act 1990] and other expressions have the same meaning as in that Act.

Amendments (Textual)
F136. Words substituted by Planning (Consequential Provisions) Act 1990 (c. 11, SIF 123:1), s. 4, Sch. 2 para. 79. (1)
Marginal Citations
M61985 c. 68.

29 Offences of harassment.

(1) In section 1 of the 1977 Act (unlawful eviction and harassment of occupier), with respect to acts done after the commencement of this Act, subsection (3) shall have effect with the substitution, for the word "calculated", of the word "likely".

(2) After that subsection there shall be inserted the following subsections—

"(3. A)Subject to subsection (3. B) below, the landlord of a residential occupier or an agent of the landlord shall be guilty of an offence if—

(a) he does acts likely to interfere with the peace or comfort of the residential occupier or members of his household, or

(b) he persistently withdraws or withholds services reasonably required for the occupation of the premises in question as a residence,

and (in either case) he knows, or has reasonable cause to believe, that that conduct is likely to cause the residential occupier to give up the occupation of the whole or part of the premises or to refrain from exercising any right or pursuing any remedy in respect of the whole or part of the premises.

(3. B)A person shall not be guilty of an offence under subsection (3. A) above if he proves that he had reasonable grounds for doing the acts or withdrawing or withholding the services in question.

(3. C)In subsection (3. A) above "landlord", in relation to a residential occupier of any premises, means the person who, but for—

(a) the residential occupier's right to remain in occupation of the premises, or

(b) a restriction on the person's right to recover possession of the premises,

would be entitled to occupation of the premises and any superior landlord under whom that person derives title."

30 Variation of scope of 1977 ss. 3 and 4.

(1) In section 3 of the 1977 Act (prohibition of eviction without due process of law), in subsection (1) for the words "not a statutorily protected tenancy" there shall be substituted "neither a statutorily protected tenancy nor an excluded tenancy".

(2) After subsection (2. A) of that section there shall be inserted the following subsections—

"(2. B)Subsections (1) and (2) above apply in relation to any premises occupied as a dwelling under a licence, other than an excluded licence, as they apply in relation to premises let as a dwelling under a tenancy, and in those subsections the expressions "let" and "tenancy" shall be construed accordingly.

(2. C)References in the preceding provisions of this section and section 4. (2. A) below to an excluded tenancy do not apply to—
  (a) a tenancy entered into before the date on which the Housing Act 1988 came into force, or
  (b) a tenancy entered into on or after that date but pursuant to a contract made before that date,but, subject to that, "excluded tenancy" and "excluded licence" shall be construed in accordance with section 3. A below."
(3) In section 4 of the 1977 Act (special provisions for agricultural employees) after subsection (2) there shall be inserted the following subsection—
"(2. A)In accordance with section 3. (2. B) above, any reference in subsections (1) and (2) above to the tenant under the former tenancy includes a reference to the licensee under a licence (other than an excluded licence) which has come to an end (being a licence to occupy premises as a dwelling); and in the following provisions of this section the expressions "tenancy" and "rent" and any other expressions referable to a tenancy shall be construed accordingly."

31 Excluded tenancies and licences.

After section 3 of the 1977 Act there shall be inserted the following section—
"3. A Excluded tenancies and licences.
(1) Any reference in this Act to an excluded tenancy or an excluded licence is a reference to a tenancy or licence which is excluded by virtue of any of the following provisions of this section.
(2) A tenancy or licence is excluded if—
  (a) under its terms the occupier shares any accommodation with the landlord or licensor; and
  (b) immediately before the tenancy or licence was granted and also at the time it comes to an end, the landlord or licensor occupied as his only or principal home premises of which the whole or part of the shared accommodation formed part.
(3) A tenancy or licence is also excluded if—
  (a) under its terms the occupier shares any accommodation with a member of the family of the landlord or licensor;
  (b) immediately before the tenancy or licence was granted and also at the time it comes to an end, the member of the family of the landlord or licensor occupied as his only or principal home premises of which the whole or part of the shared accommodation formed part; and
  (c) immediately before the tenancy or licence was granted and also at the time it comes to an end, the landlord or licensor occupied as his only or principal home premises in the same building as the shared accommodation and that building is not a purpose-built block of flats.
(4) For the purposes of subsections (2) and (3) above, an occupier shares accommodation with another person if he has the use of it in common with that person (whether or not also in common with others) and any reference in those subsections to shared accommodation shall be construed accordingly, and if, in relation to any tenancy or licence, there is at any time more than one person who is the landlord or licensor, any reference in those subsections to the landlord or licensor shall be construed as a reference to any one of those persons.
(5) In subsections (2) to (4) above—
  (a) "accommodation" includes neither an area used for storage nor a staircase, passage, corridor or other means of access;
  (b) "occupier" means, in relation to a tenancy, the tenant and, in relation to a licence, the licensee; and
  (c) "purpose-built block of flats" has the same meaning as in Part III of Schedule 1 to the Housing Act 1988;
and section 113 of the Housing Act 1985 shall apply to determine whether a person is for the purposes of subsection (3) above a member of another's family as it applies for the purposes of Part IV of that Act.
(6) A tenancy or licence is excluded if it was granted as a temporary expedient to a person who entered the premises in question or any other premises as a trespasser (whether or not, before the

beginning of that tenancy or licence, another tenancy or licence to occupy the premises or any other premises had been granted to him).

(7) A tenancy or licence is excluded if—
   (a) it confers on the tenant or licensee the right to occupy the premises for a holiday only; or
   (b) it is granted otherwise than for money or money's worth.

(8) A licence is excluded if it confers rights of occupation in a hostel, within the meaning of the Housing Act 1985, which is provided by—
   (a) the council of a county, district or London Borough, the Common Council of the City of London, the Council of the Isles of Scilly, the Inner London Education Authority, a joint authority within the meaning of the Local Government Act 1985 or a residuary body within the meaning of that Act;
   (b) a development corporation within the meaning of the New Towns Act 1981;
   (c) the Commission for the New Towns;
   (d) an urban development corporation established by an order under section 135 of the Local Government, Planning and Land Act 1980;
   (e) a housing action trust established under Part III of the Housing Act 1988;
   (f) the Development Board for Rural Wales;
   (g) the Housing Corporation or Housing for Wales;
   (h) a housing trust which is a charity or a registered housing association, within the meaning of the Housing Associations Act 1985; or
   (i) any other person who is, or who belongs to a class of person which is, specified in an order made by the Secretary of State.

(9) The power to make an order under subsection (8)(i) above shall be exercisable by statutory instrument which shall be subject to annulment in pursuance of a resolution of either House of Parliament."

32 Notice to quit etc.

(1) In section 5 of the 1977 Act (validity of notices to quit) at the beginning of subsection (1) there shall be inserted the words "Subject to subsection (1. B) below".

(2) After subsection (1) of that section there shall be inserted the following subsections—
"(1. A)Subject to subsection (1. B) below, no notice by a licensor or a licensee to determine a periodic licence to occupy premises as a dwelling (whether the licence was granted before or after the passing of this Act) shall be valid unless—
   (a) it is in writing and contains such information as may be prescribed, and
   (b) it is given not less than 4 weeks before the date on which it is to take effect.

(1. B)Nothing in subsection (1) or subsection (1. A) above applies to—
   (a) premises let on an excluded tenancy which is entered into on or after the date on which the Housing Act 1988 came into force unless it is entered into pursuant to a contract made before that date; or
   (b) premises occupied under an excluded licence."

33 Interpretation of Chapter IV and the 1977 Act.

(1) In this Chapter "the 1977 Act" means the M7. Protection from Eviction Act 1977.
(2) In section 8 of the 1977 Act (interpretation) at the end of subsection (1) (statutory protected tenancy) there shall be inserted—
"(e)an assured tenancy or assured agricultural occupancy under Part I of the Housing Act 1988."
(3) At the end of that section there shall be added the following subsections—
"(4)In this Act "excluded tenancy" and "excluded licence" have the meaning assigned by section 3. A of this Act.

(5) If, on or after the date on which the Housing Act 1988 came into force, the terms of an excluded tenancy or excluded licence entered into before that date are varied, then—

(a) if the variation affects the amount of the rent which is payable under the tenancy or licence, the tenancy or licence shall be treated for the purposes of sections 3. (2. C) and 5. (1. B) above as a new tenancy or licence entered into at the time of the variation; and

(b) if the variation does not affect the amount of the rent which is so payable, nothing in this Act shall affect the determination of the question whether the variation is such as to give rise to a new tenancy or licence.

(6) Any reference in subsection (5) above to a variation affecting the amount of the rent which is payable under a tenancy or licence does not include a reference to—

(a) a reduction or increase effected under Part III or Part VI of the Rent Act 1977 (rents under regulated tenancies and housing association tenancies), section 78 of that Act (power of rent tribunal in relation to restricted contracts) or sections 11 to 14 of the Rent (Agriculture) Act 1976; or

(b) a variation which is made by the parties and has the effect of making the rent expressed to be payable under the tenancy or licence the same as a rent for the dwelling which is entered in the register under Part IV or section 79 of the Rent Act 1977."

Marginal Citations
M71977 c. 43.

Chapter V Phasing out of Rent Acts and other Transitional Provisions

34 New protected tenancies and agricultural occupancies restricted to special cases.

(1) A tenancy which is entered into on or after the commencement of this Act cannot be a protected tenancy, unless—

(a) it is entered into in pursuance of a contract made before the commencement of this Act; or

(b) it is granted to a person (alone or jointly with others) who, immediately before the tenancy was granted, was a protected or statutory tenant and is so granted by the person who at that time was the landlord (or one of the joint landlords) under the protected or statutory tenancy; or

(c) it is granted to a person (alone or jointly with others) in the following circumstances—
(i) prior to the grant of the tenancy, an order for possession of a dwelling-house was made against him (alone or jointly with others) on the court being satisfied as mentioned in section 98. (1)(a) of, or Case 1 in Schedule 16 to, the M8. Rent Act 1977 or Case 1 in Schedule 4 to the M9. Rent (Agriculture) Act 1976 (suitable alternative accommodation available); and
(ii) the tenancy is of the premises which constitute the suitable alternative accommodation as to which the court was so satisfied; and
(iii) in the proceedings for possession the court considered that, in the circumstances, the grant of an assured tenancy would not afford the required security and, accordingly, directed that the tenancy would be a protected tenancy; or

[F137. (d)it is a tenancy under which the interest of the landlord was at the time the tenancy was granted held by [F138the Commission for the New Towns or a development] corporation, within the meaning of section 80 of the Housing Act 1985, and, before the date which has effect by virtue of paragraph (a) or paragraph (b) of subsection (4) of section 38 below, ceased to be so held by virtue of a disposal by the Commission for the New Towns made pursuant to a direction under section 37 of the New Towns Act 1981]

(2) In subsection (1)(b) above "protected tenant" and "statutory tenant" do not include—

(a) a tenant under a protected shorthold tenancy;

(b) a protected or statutory tenant of a dwelling-house which was let under a protected shorthold tenancy which ended before the commencement of this Act and in respect of which at that commencement either there has been no grant of a further tenancy or any grant of a further tenancy has been to the person who, immediately before the grant, was in possession of the dwelling-house as a protected or statutory tenant;
and in this subsection "protected shorthold tenancy" includes a tenancy which, in proceedings for possession under Case 19 in Schedule 15 to the Rent Act 1977, is treated as a protected shorthold tenancy.
(3) In any case where—
(a) by virtue of subsections (1) and (2) above, a tenancy entered into on or after the commencement of this Act is an assured tenancy, but
(b) apart from subsection (2) above, the effect of subsection (1)(b) above would be that the tenancy would be a protected tenancy, and
(c) the landlord and the tenant under the tenancy are the same as at the coming to an end of the protected or statutory tenancy which, apart from subsection (2) above, would fall within subsection (1)(b) above,
the tenancy shall be an assured shorthold tenancy (whether or not [F139, in the case of a tenancy to which the provision applies,] it fulfils the conditions in section 20. (1) above) unless, before the tenancy is entered into, the landlord serves notice on the tenant that it is not to be a shorthold tenancy.
(4) A licence or tenancy which is entered into on or after the commencement of this Act cannot be a relevant licence or relevant tenancy for the purposes of the M10. Rent (Agriculture) Act 1976 (in this subsection referred to as "the 1976 Act") unless—
(a) it is entered into in pursuance of a contract made before the commencement of this Act; or
(b) it is granted to a person (alone or jointly with others) who, immediately before the licence or tenancy was granted, was a protected occupier or statutory tenant, within the meaning of the 1976 Act, and is so granted by the person who at that time was the landlord or licensor (or one of the joint landlords or licensors) under the protected occupancy or statutory tenancy in question.
(5) Except as provided in subsection (4) above, expressions used in this section have the same meaning as in the M11. Rent Act 1977.
Amendments (Textual)
F137. S. 34. (1)(d) substituted by Local Government and Housing Act 1989 (c. 42, SIF 75:1), s. 194, Sch. 11 para. 104
F138. Words in s. 34. (1)(d) substituted (1.12.2008) by The Housing and Regeneration Act 2008 (Consequential Provisions) Order 2008 (S.I. 2008/3002), arts. 1. (2), 4, Sch. 1 para. 37 (with Sch. 2); S.I. 2008/3068, art. 2. (1)(b) (with arts. 6-13)
F139. Words in s. 34. (3) inserted (28.2.1997) by 1996 c. 52, s. 104, Sch. 8 para. 2. (7); S.I. 1997/225, art. 2 (with Sch.)
Marginal Citations
M81977 c. 42.
M91976 c. 80.
M101976 c. 80.
M111977 c. 42.

35 Removal of special regimes for tenancies of housing associations etc.

(1) In this section "housing association tenancy" has the same meaning as in Part VI of the Rent Act 1977.
(2) A tenancy which is entered into on or after the commencement of this Act cannot be a housing association tenancy unless—
(a) it is entered into in pursuance of a contract made before the commencement of this Act; or

(b) it is granted to a person (alone or jointly with others) who, immediately before the tenancy was granted, was a tenant under a housing association tenancy and is so granted by the person who at that time was the landlord under that housing association tenancy; or

(c) it is granted to a person (alone or jointly with others) in the following circumstances—

(i) prior to the grant of the tenancy, an order for possession of a dwelling-house was made against him (alone or jointly with others) on the court being satisfied as mentioned in paragraph (b) or paragraph (c) of subsection (2) of section 84 of the M12. Housing Act 1985; and

(ii) the tenancy is of the premises which constitute the suitable accommodation as to which the court was so satisfied; and

(iii) in the proceedings for possession the court directed that the tenancy would be a housing association tenancy; or

[F140. (d)it is a tenancy under which the interest of the landlord was at the time the tenancy was granted held by [F141the Commission for the New Towns or a development] corporation, within the meaning of section 80 of the Housing Act 1985, and, before the date which has effect by virtue of paragraph (a) or paragraph (b) of subsection (4) of section 38 below, ceased to be so held by virtue of a disposal by the Commission for the New Towns made pursuant to a direction under section 37 of the New Towns Act 1981]

(3) Where, on or after the commencement of this Act, [F142a private registered provider of social housing or] a [F143registered social lanlord, within the meaning of the Housing Act 1985 (see section 5. (4) and (5) of the Act)], grants a secure tenancy pursuant to an obligation under section 554. (2. A) of the M13. Housing Act 1985 (as set out in Schedule 17 to this Act) then, in determining whether that tenancy is a housing association tenancy, it shall be assumed for the purposes only of section 86. (2)(b) of the M14. Rent Act 1977 (tenancy would be a protected tenancy but for section 15 or 16 of that Act) that the tenancy was granted before the commencement of this Act.

(4) [F144. Subject to section 38. (4. A) below] a tenancy or licence which is entered into on or after the commencement of this Act cannot be a secure tenancy unless—

(a) the interest of the landlord belongs to a local authority, a [F145development] corporation or an urban development corporation, all within the meaning of section 80 of the Housing Act 1985 [F146or a housing action trust established under Part III of this Act]; or

[F147. (aa)the interest of the landlord belongs to a Mayoral development corporation; or]

(b) the interest of the landlord belongs to a housing co-operative within the meaning of section 27. B of the Housing Act 1985 (agreements between local housing authorities and housing co-operatives) and the tenancy or licence is of a dwelling-house comprised in a housing co-operative agreement falling within that section; or

[F148. (ba)the interest of the landlord belongs to the Homes and Communities Agency[F149, the Greater London Authority] or the Welsh Ministers and the tenancy or licence falls within section 80. (2. A) to (2. E) of the Housing Act 1985; or]

(c) it is entered into in pursuance of a contract made before the commencement of this Act; or

(d) it is granted to a person (alone or jointly with others) who, immediately before it was entered into, was a secure tenant and is so granted by the body which at that time was the landlord or licensor under the secure tenancy; or

(e) it is granted to a person (alone or jointly with others) in the following circumstances—

(i) prior to the grant of the tenancy or licence, an order for possession of a dwelling-house was made against him (alone or jointly with others) on the court being satisfied as mentioned in paragraph (b) or paragraph (c) of subsection (2) of section 84 of the Housing Act 1985; and

(ii) the tenancy or licence is of the premises which constitute the suitable accommodation as to which the court was so satisfied; and

(iii) in the proceedings for possession the court considered that, in the circumstances, the grant of an assured tenancy would not afford the required security and, accordingly, directed that the tenancy or licence would be a secure tenancy; or

(f) it is granted pursuant to an obligation under section 554. (2. A) of the Housing Act 1985 (as set out in Schedule 17 to this Act).

(5) If, on or after the commencement of this Act, the interest of the landlord under a protected or statutory tenancy becomes held by a housing association, a housing trust [F150[F151or the Regulator of Social Housing]][F152or, where that interest becomes held by him as the result of the exercise by him of functions under Part III of the Housing Association Act 1985, the Secretary of State,] nothing in the preceding provisions of this section shall prevent the tenancy from being a housing association tenancy or a secure tenancy and, accordingly, in such a case section 80 of the Housing Act 1985 (and any enactment which refers to that section) shall have effect without regard to the repeal of provisions of that section effected by this Act.

(6) In subsection (5) above "housing association" and "housing trust" have the same meaning as in the M15. Housing Act 1985.

Amendments (Textual)

F140. S. 35. (2)(d) substituted by Local Government and Housing Act 1989 (c. 42, SIF 75:1), s. 194, Sch. 11 para. 105. (1)

F141. Words in s. 35. (2)(d) substituted (1.12.2008) by The Housing and Regeneration Act 2008 (Consequential Provisions) Order 2008 (S.I. 2008/3002), arts. 1. (2), 4, Sch. 1 para. 38. (2) (with Sch. 2); S.I. 2008/3068, art. 2. (1)(b) (with arts. 6-13)

F142. Words in s. 35. (3) inserted (1.4.2010) by The Housing and Regeneration Act 2008 (Consequential Provisions) Order 2010 (S.I. 2010/866), art. 1. (2), Sch. 2 para. 66. (2) (with art. 6, Sch. 3)

F143. Words in s. 35. (3) substituted (1.10.1996) by S.I. 1996/2325, art. 5. (1), Sch. 2 para. 18. (2)

F144. Words inserted by Local Government and Housing Act 1989 (c. 42, SIF 75:1), s. 194, Sch. 11 para. 105. (2)

F145. Word in s. 35. (4)(a) substituted (1.12.2008) by The Housing and Regeneration Act 2008 (Consequential Provisions) Order 2008 (S.I. 2008/3002), arts. 1. (2), 4, Sch. 1 para. 38. (3)(a) (with Sch. 2); S.I. 2008/3068, art. 2. (1)(b) (with arts. 6-13)

F146. Words in s. 35. (4)(a) substituted (1.10.1998) by 1998 c. 38, s. 129, Sch. 15 para. 15 (with ss. 139. (2), 141. (3), 143. (2)); S.I. 1998/2244, art. 4

F147. S. 35. (4)(aa) inserted (15.1.2012) by Localism Act 2011 (c. 20), s. 240. (1)(l), Sch. 22 para. 26

F148. S. 35. (4)(ba) inserted (1.12.2008) by The Housing and Regeneration Act 2008 (Consequential Provisions) Order 2008 (S.I. 2008/3002), arts. 1. (2), 4, Sch. 1 para. 38. (3)(b) (with Sch. 2); S.I. 2008/3068, art. 2. (1)(b) (with arts. 6-13)

F149. Words in s. 35. (4)(ba) inserted (1.4.2012) by Localism Act 2011 (c. 20), s. 240. (2), Sch. 19 para. 26; S.I. 2012/628, art. 6. (i) (with arts. 9 11 14 15 17)

F150. Words in s. 35. (5) substituted (1.11.1998) by 1998 c. 38, s. 140. (1), Sch. 16 para. 60; S.I. 1998/2244, art. 5

F151. Words in s. 35. (5) substituted (1.4.2010) by The Housing and Regeneration Act 2008 (Consequential Provisions) Order 2010 (S.I. 2010/866), art. 1. (2), Sch. 2 para. 66. (3) (with art. 6, Sch. 3)

F152. Words in s. 35. (5) inserted (15.1.1999) by S.I. 1999/61, art. 2, Sch. para. 3. (2)

Modifications etc. (not altering text)

C15. S. 35. (5) modified (1.12.2008) by The Transfer of Housing Corporation Functions (Modifications and Transitional Provisions) Order 2008 (S.I. 2008/2839), arts. 1. (1), 3, Sch. para. 1; S.I. 2008/3068, art. 2. (1)(b) (with arts. 6-11)

Marginal Citations

M121985 c. 68.
M131985 c. 68.
M141977 c. 42.
M151985 c. 68.

36 New restricted contracts limited to transitional cases.

(1) A tenancy or other contract entered into after the commencement of this Act cannot be a restricted contract for the purposes of the Rent Act 1977 unless it is entered into in pursuance of a contract made before the commencement of this Act.

(2) If the terms of a restricted contract are varied after this Act comes into force then, subject to subsection (3) below,—

(a) if the variation affects the amount of the rent which, under the contract, is payable for the dwelling in question, the contract shall be treated as a new contract entered into at the time of the variation (and subsection (1) above shall have effect accordingly); and

(b) if the variation does not affect the amount of the rent which, under the contract, is so payable, nothing in this section shall affect the determination of the question whether the variation is such as to give rise to a new contract.

(3) Any reference in subsection (2) above to a variation affecting the amount of the rent which, under a contract, is payable for a dwelling does not include a reference to—

(a) a reduction or increase effected under section 78 of the Rent Act 1977 (power of [F153appropriate] tribunal); or

(b) a variation which is made by the parties and has the effect of making the rent expressed to be payable under the contract the same as the rent for the dwelling which is entered in the register under section 79 of the Rent Act 1977.

(4) In subsection (1) of section 81. A of the Rent Act 1977 (cancellation of registration of rent relating to a restricted contract) paragraph (a) (no cancellation until two years have elapsed since the date of the entry) shall cease to have effect.

(5) In this section "rent" has the same meaning as in Part V of the Rent Act 1977.

Amendments (Textual)

F153. Word in s. 36. (3)(a) substituted (1.7.2013) by The Transfer of Tribunal Functions Order 2013 (S.I. 2013/1036), art. 1, Sch. 1 para. 88 (with Sch. 3)

37 No further assured tenancies under Housing Act 1980.

(1) A tenancy which is entered into on or after the commencement of this Act cannot be an assured tenancy for the purposes of sections 56 to 58 of the M16. Housing Act 1980 (in this section referred to as a "1980 Act tenancy").

(2) In any case where—

(a) before the commencement of this Act, a tenant under a 1980 Act tenancy made an application to the court under section 24 of the M17. Landlord and Tenant Act 1954 (for the grant of a new tenancy), and

(b) at the commencement of this Act the 1980 Act tenancy is continuing by virtue of that section or of any provision of Part IV of the said Act of 1954,

section 1. (3) of this Act shall not apply to the 1980 Act tenancy.

(3) If, in a case falling within subsection (2) above, the court makes an order for the grant of a new tenancy under section 29 of the M18. Landlord and Tenant Act 1954, that tenancy shall be an assured tenancy for the purposes of this Act.

(4) In any case where—

(a) before the commencement of this Act a contract was entered into for the grant of a 1980 Act tenancy, but

(b) at the commencement of this Act the tenancy had not been granted,

the contract shall have effect as a contract for the grant of an assured tenancy (within the meaning of this Act).

(5) In relation to an assured tenancy falling within subsection (3) above or granted pursuant to a contract falling within subsection (4) above, Part I of Schedule 1 to this Act shall have effect as if it consisted only of paragraphs 11 and 12; and, if the landlord granting the tenancy is a fully mutual housing association, then, so long as that association remains the landlord under that tenancy (and under any statutory periodic tenancy which arises on the coming to an end of that

tenancy), the said paragraph 12 shall have effect in relation to that tenancy with the omission of sub-paragraph (1)(h).

(6) Any reference in this section to a provision of the Landlord and Tenant Act 1954 is a reference only to that provision as applied by section 58 of the M19. Housing Act 1980.

Marginal Citations

M161980 c. 51.
M171954 c. 56.
M181954 c. 56.
M191980 c. 51.

38 Transfer of existing tenancies from public to private sector.

(1) The provisions of subsection (3) below apply in relation to a tenancy which was entered into before, or pursuant to a contract made before, the commencement of this Act if,—

(a) at that commencement or, if it is later, at the time it is entered into, the interest of the landlord is held by a public body (within the meaning of subsection (5) below); and

(b) at some time after that commencement, the interest of the landlord ceases to be so held.

(2) The provisions of subsection (3) below also apply in relation to a tenancy which was entered into before, or pursuant to a contract made before, the commencement of this Act if,—

(a) at the commencement of this Act or, if it is later, at the time it is entered into, it is a housing association tenancy; and

(b) at some time after that commencement, it ceases to be such a tenancy.

(3) [F154. Subject to subsections (4) [F155[F156. (4. ZA), (4. A), (4. BA)] and (4. B),] below] on and after the time referred to in subsection (1)(b) or, as the case may be, subsection (2)(b) above—

(a) the tenancy shall not be capable of being a protected tenancy, a protected occupancy or a housing association tenancy;

(b) the tenancy shall not be capable of being a secure tenancy unless (and only at a time when) the interest of the landlord under the tenancy is (or is again) held by a public body; and

(c) paragraph 1 of Schedule 1 to this Act shall not apply in relation to it, and the question whether at any time thereafter it becomes (or remains) an assured tenancy shall be determined accordingly.

(4) In relation to a tenancy under which, at the commencement of this Act or, if it is later, at the time the tenancy is entered into, the interest of the landlord is held by [F157the Commission for the New Towns or a development] corporation, within the meaning of section 80 of the M20. Housing Act 1985 [F158and which subsequently ceases to be so held by virtue of a disposal by the Commission for the New Towns made pursuant to a direction under section 37 of the New Towns Act 1981], subsections (1) and (3) above shall have effect as if any reference in subsection (1) above to the commencement of this Act were a reference to—

(a) the date on which expires the period of two years beginning on the day this Act is passed; or

(b) if the Secretary of State by order made by statutory instrument within that period so provides, such other date (whether earlier or later) as may be specified by the order for the purposes of this subsection.

[F159. (4. ZA)In relation to any time on or after the coming into force of this subsection, subsection (4) applies as if—

(a) the references to the Commission for the New Towns were references to the new towns residuary body;

(b) in the case of a disposal by the English new towns residuary body, the reference to section 37 of the New Towns Act 1981 were a reference to section 47 of the Housing and Regeneration Act 2008; and

(c) in the case of a disposal by the Welsh new towns residuary body, the words "made pursuant to a direction under section 37 of the New Towns Act 1981" were omitted.]

[F160. (4. A)Where, by virtue of a disposal falling within subsection (4) above and made before the date which has effect by virtue of paragraph (a) or paragraph (b) of that subsection, the interest of the landlord under a tenancy passes to [F161a private registered provider of social housing or] a [F162registered social landlord (within the meaning of the Housing Act 1985 (see section 5. (4) and (5) of that Act))], then, notwithstanding anything in subsection (3) above, so long as the tenancy continues to be held by a body which would have been specified in subsection (1) of section 80 of the Housing Act 1985 if the repeal of provisions of that section effected by this Act had not been made, the tenancy shall continue to be a secure tenancy and to be capable of being a housing association tenancy.]

[F163. (4. B)Where, by virtue of a disposal by the Secretary of State made in the exercise by him of functions under Part III of the Housing Associations Act 1985, the interest of the landlord under a secure tenancy passes to a registered social landlord (within the meaning of the Housing Act 1985) then, notwithstanding anything in subsection (3) above, so long as the tenancy continues to be held by a body which would have been specified in subsection (1) of section 80 of the Housing Act 1985 if the repeal of provisions of that section effected by this Act had not been made, the tenancy shall continue to be a secure tenancy and to be capable of being a housing association tenancy.]

[F164. (4. BA)The references in subsections (4. A) and (4. B) to a body which would have been specified in subsection (1) of section 80 of the Housing Act 1985 if the repeal of provisions of that section effected by this Act had not been made includes a reference to the new towns residuary body.]

(5) For the purposes of this section, the interest of a landlord under a tenancy is held by a public body at a time when—

(a) it belongs to a local authority, a [F165development] corporation or an urban development corporation, all within the meaning of section 80 of the Housing Act 1985 [F166or to the English new towns residuary body]; or

[F167. (aa)it belongs to a Mayoral development corporation; or]

(b) it belongs to a housing action trust established under Part III of this Act; or

F168. (c). . . . .

(d) it belongs to Her Majesty in right of the Crown or to a government department or is held in trust for Her Majesty for the purposes of a government department.

[F169. (5. A) In this section " new towns residuary body " means—

(a) in relation to times before the coming into force of this subsection, the Commission for the New Towns; and

(b) in relation to other times—

(i) in relation to England, the Homes and Communities Agency so far as exercising functions in relation to anything transferred (or to be transferred) to it as mentioned in section 52. (1)(a) to (d) of the Housing and Regeneration Act 2008 [F170or the Greater London Authority so far as exercising its new towns and urban development functions] (and any reference to the English new towns residuary body shall be construed accordingly); and

(ii) in relation to Wales, the Welsh Ministers so far as exercising functions in relation to anything transferred (or to be transferred) to them as mentioned in section 36. (1)(a)(i) to (iii) of the New Towns Act 1981 (and any reference to the Welsh new towns residuary body shall be construed accordingly).]

(6) In this section—

(a) "housing association tenancy" means a tenancy to which Part VI of the M21. Rent Act 1977 applies;

(b) "protected tenancy" has the same meaning as in that Act; and

(c) "protected occupancy" has the same meaning as in the M22. Rent (Agriculture) Act 1976.

Amendments (Textual)

F154. Words inserted by Local Government and Housing Act 1989 (c. 42, SIF 75:1), s. 194, Sch. 11 para. 106. (1)

F155. Words in s. 38. (3) substituted (15.1.1999) by S.I. 1999/61, art. 2, Sch. para. 3. (3)(a)

F156. Words in s. 38. (3) substituted (1.12.2008) by The Housing and Regeneration Act 2008

(Consequential Provisions) Order 2008 (S.I. 2008/3002), arts. 1. (2), 4, Sch. 1 para. 39. (2) (with Sch. 2); S.I. 2008/3068, art. 2. (1)(b) (with arts. 6-13)
F157. Words in s. 38. (4) substituted (1.12.2008) by The Housing and Regeneration Act 2008 (Consequential Provisions) Order 2008 (S.I. 2008/3002), arts. 1. (2), 4, Sch. 1 para. 39. (3) (with Sch. 2); S.I. 2008/3068, art. 2. (1)(b) (with arts. 6-13)
F158. Words inserted by Local Government and Housing Act 1989 (c. 42, SIF 75:1), s. 194, Sch. 11 para. 106. (2)
F159. S. 38. (4. ZA) inserted (1.12.2008) by The Housing and Regeneration Act 2008 (Consequential Provisions) Order 2008 (S.I. 2008/3002), arts. 1. (2), 4, Sch. 1 para. 39. (4) (with Sch. 2); S.I. 2008/3068, art. 2. (1)(b) (with arts. 6-13)
F160. S. 38. (4. A) inserted by Local Government and Housing Act 1989 (c. 42, SIF 75:1), s. 194, Sch. 11 para. 106. (3)
F161. Words in s. 38. (4. A) inserted (1.4.2010) by The Housing and Regeneration Act 2008 (Consequential Provisions) Order 2010 (S.I. 2010/866), art. 1. (2), Sch. 2 para. 67 (with art. 6, Sch. 3)
F162. Words in s. 38. (4. A) substituted (1.10.1996) by S.I. 1996/2325, art. 5. (1), Sch. 2 para. 18. (3)
F163. S. 38. (4. B) inserted (15.1.1999) by S.I. 1999/61, art. 2, Sch. para. 3. (3)(b)
F164. S. 38. (4. BA) inserted (1.12.2008) by The Housing and Regeneration Act 2008 (Consequential Provisions) Order 2008 (S.I. 2008/3002), arts. 1. (2), 4, Sch. 1 para. 39. (5) (with Sch. 2); S.I. 2008/3068, art. 2. (1)(b) (with arts. 6-13)
F165. Word in s. 38. (5)(a) substituted (1.12.2008) by The Housing and Regeneration Act 2008 (Consequential Provisions) Order 2008 (S.I. 2008/3002), arts. 1. (2), 4, Sch. 1 para. 39. (6)(a) (with Sch. 2); S.I. 2008/3068, art. 2. (1)(b) (with arts. 6-13)
F166. Words in s. 38. (5)(a) inserted (1.12.2008) by The Housing and Regeneration Act 2008 (Consequential Provisions) Order 2008 (S.I. 2008/3002), arts. 1. (2), 4, Sch. 1 para. 39. (6)(b) (with Sch. 2); S.I. 2008/3068, art. 2. (1)(b) (with arts. 6-13)
F167. S. 38. (5)(aa) inserted (15.1.2012) by Localism Act 2011 (c. 20), s. 240. (1)(l), Sch. 22 para. 27
F168. S. 38. (5)(c) repealed (1.10.1998) by 1998 c. 38, s. 152, Sch. 18 Pt. IV (with ss. 137. (1), 139. (2), 141. (1), 143. (2)); S.I. 1998/2244, art. 4
F169. S. 38. (5. A) inserted (1.12.2008) by The Housing and Regeneration Act 2008 (Consequential Provisions) Order 2008 (S.I. 2008/3002), arts. 1. (2), 4, Sch. 1 para. 39. (7) (with Sch. 2); S.I. 2008/3068, art. 2. (1)(b) (with arts. 6-13)
F170. Words in s. 38. (5. A)(b)(i) inserted (1.4.2012) by Localism Act 2011 (c. 20), s. 240. (2), Sch. 19 para. 27; S.I. 2012/628, art. 6. (i) (with arts. 9 11 14 15 17)
Marginal Citations
M201985 c. 68.
M211977 c. 42.
M221976 c. 80.

39 Statutory tenants: succession.

(1) In section 2. (1)(b) of the Rent Act 1977 (which introduces the provisions of Part I of Schedule 1 to that Act relating to statutory tenants by succession) after the words "statutory tenant of a dwelling-house" there shall be inserted "or, as the case may be, is entitled to an assured tenancy of a dwelling-house by succession".
(2) Where the person who is the original tenant, within the meaning of Part I of Schedule 1 to the Rent Act 1977, dies after the commencement of this Act, that Part shall have effect subject to the amendments in Part I of Schedule 4 to this Act.
(3) Where subsection (2) above does not apply but the person who is the first successor, within the meaning of Part I of Schedule 1 to the Rent Act 1977, dies after the commencement of this Act,

that Part shall have effect subject to the amendments in paragraphs 5 to 9 of Part I of Schedule 4 to this Act.

(4) In any case where the original occupier, within the meaning of section 4 of the Rent (Agriculture) Act 1976 (statutory tenants and tenancies) dies after the commencement of this Act, that section shall have effect subject to the amendments in Part II of Schedule 4 to this Act.

(5) In any case where, by virtue of any provision of—

(a) Part I of Schedule 1 to the M23. Rent Act 1977, as amended in accordance with subsection (2) or subsection (3) above, or

(b) section 4 of the M24. Rent (Agriculture) Act 1976, as amended in accordance with subsection (4) above,

a person (in the following provisions of this section referred to as "the successor") becomes entitled to an assured tenancy of a dwelling-house by succession, that tenancy shall be a periodic tenancy arising by virtue of this section.

(6) Where, by virtue of subsection (5) above, the successor becomes entitled to an assured periodic tenancy, that tenancy is one—

(a) taking effect in possession immediately after the death of the protected or statutory tenant or protected occupier (in the following provisions of this section referred to as "the predecessor") on whose death the successor became so entitled;

(b) deemed to have been granted to the successor by the person who, immediately before the death of the predecessor, was the landlord of the predecessor under his tenancy;

(c) under which the premises which are let are the same dwelling-house as, immediately before his death, the predecessor occupied under his tenancy;

(d) under which the periods of the tenancy are the same as those for which rent was last payable by the predecessor under his tenancy;

(e) under which, subject to sections 13 to 15 above, the other terms are the same as those on which, under his tenancy, the predecessor occupied the dwelling-house immediately before his death; and

(f) which, for the purposes of section 13. (2) above, is treated as a statutory periodic tenancy;

and in paragraphs (b) to (e) above "under his tenancy", in relation to the predecessor, means under his protected tenancy or protected occupancy or in his capacity as a statutory tenant.

(7) If, immediately before the death of the predecessor, the landlord might have recovered possession of the dwelling-house under Case 19 in Schedule 15 to the Rent Act 1977, the assured periodic tenancy to which the successor becomes entitled shall be an assured shorthold tenancy (whether or not [F171, in the case of a tenancy to which the provision applies] it fulfils the conditions in section 20. (1) above).

(8) If, immediately before his death, the predecessor was a protected occupier or statutory tenant within the meaning of the Rent (Agriculture) Act 1976, the assured periodic tenancy to which the successor becomes entitled shall be an assured agricultural occupancy (whether or not it fulfils the conditions in section 24. (1) above).

(9) Where, immediately before his death, the predecessor was a tenant under a fixed term tenancy, section 6 above shall apply in relation to the assured periodic tenancy to which the successor becomes entitled on the predecessor's death subject to the following modifications—

(a) for any reference to a statutory periodic tenancy there shall be substituted a reference to the assured periodic tenancy to which the successor becomes so entitled;

(b) in subsection (1) of that section, paragraph (a) shall be omitted and the reference in paragraph (b) to section 5. (3)(e) above shall be construed as a reference to subsection (6)(e) above; and

(c) for any reference to the coming to an end of the former tenancy there shall be substituted a reference to the date of the predecessor's death.

(10) If and so long as a dwelling-house is subject to an assured tenancy to which the successor has become entitled by succession, section 7 above and Schedule 2 to this Act shall have effect subject to the modifications in Part III of Schedule 4 to this Act; and in that Part "the predecessor" and "the successor" have the same meaning as in this section.

Amendments (Textual)
F171. Words in s. 39. (7) inserted (28.2.1997) by 1996 c. 52, s. 104, Sch. 8 para. 2. (8); S.I. 1997/225, art. 2 (with Sch.)
Marginal Citations
M23 1977 c. 42.
M24 1976 c. 80.

Chapter VI General Provisions

40 Jurisdiction of county courts.

(1) [F172. The county court] shall have jurisdiction to hear and determine any question arising under any provision of—
    (a) Chapters I to III and V above, or
    (b) sections 27 and 28 above,
other than a question falling within the jurisdiction of [F173the appropriate tribunal] by virtue of any such provision.
F174. (2). . . . .
(3) Where any proceedings under any provision mentioned in subsection (1) above are being taken in [F175the county court], the court shall have jurisdiction to hear and determine any other proceedings joined with those proceedings, notwithstanding that, apart from this subsection, those other proceedings would be outside the court's jurisdiction.
[F176. (4)If any person takes any proceedings under any provision mentioned in subsection (1) above in the High Court, he shall not be entitled to recover any more costs of those proceedings than those to which he would have been entitled if the proceedings had been taken in [F177the county court]: and in such a case the taxing master shall have the same power of directing on what county court scale costs are to be allowed, and of allowing any item of costs, as the judge would have had if the proceedings had been taken in [F177the county court].
(5) Subsection (4) above shall not apply where the purpose of taking the proceedings in the High Court was to enable them to be joined with any proceedings already pending before that court (not being proceedings taken under any provision mentioned in subsection (1) above).]
Amendments (Textual)
F172. Words in s. 40. (1) substituted (22.4.2014) by Crime and Courts Act 2013 (c. 22), s. 61. (3), Sch. 9 para. 52; S.I. 2014/954, art. 2. (c) (with art. 3) (with transitional provisions and savings in S.I. 2014/956, arts. 3-11)
F173. Words in s. 40. (1) substituted (1.7.2013) by The Transfer of Tribunal Functions Order 2013 (S.I. 2013/1036), art. 1, Sch. 1 para. 89 (with Sch. 3)
F174. S. 40. (2) omitted (1.7.1991) by virtue of S.I. 1991/724, art. 2. (8), Schedule Pt.I
F175. Words in s. 40. (3) substituted (22.4.2014) by Crime and Courts Act 2013 (c. 22), s. 61. (3), Sch. 9 para. 52; S.I. 2014/954, art. 2. (c) (with art. 3) (with transitional provisions and savings in S.I. 2014/956, arts. 3-11)
F176. S. 40. (4)(5) repealed (prosp.) by Courts and Legal Services Act 1990 (c. 41, SIF 76:1), ss. 124. (3), 125. (7), Sch. 20
F177. Words in s. 40. (4) substituted (22.4.2014) by Crime and Courts Act 2013 (c. 22), s. 61. (3), Sch. 9 para. 52; S.I. 2014/954, art. 2. (c) (with art. 3) (with transitional provisions and savings in S.I. 2014/956, arts. 3-11)
Modifications etc. (not altering text)
C16. S. 40 extended (1.7.1991) by S.I. 1991/724, art.2. (1)(o)

41 Rent assessment committees: procedure and information

powers.

F178. (1). . . . .
(2) The rent assessment committee to whom a matter is referred under Chapter I or Chapter II above may by notice in the prescribed form served on the landlord or the tenant require him to give to the committee, within such period of not less than fourteen days from the service of the notice as may be specified in the notice, such information as they may reasonably require for the purposes of their functions.
(3) If any person fails without reasonable excuse to comply with a notice served on him under subsection (2) above, he shall be liable on summary conviction to a fine not exceeding level 3 on the standard scale.
(4) Where an offence under subsection (3) above committed by a body corporate is proved to have been committed with the consent or connivance of, or to be attributable to any neglect on the part of, any director, manager or secretary or other similar officer of the body corporate or any person who was purporting to act in any such capacity, he as well as the body corporate shall be guilty of that offence and shall be liable to be proceeded against and punished accordingly.
Amendments (Textual)
F178. S. 41. (1) repealed (2.9.1993) by 1993 c. 28, s. 187. (2), Sch.22; S.I. 1993/2134, arts. 2,3
Modifications etc. (not altering text)
C17. S. 41. (2)–(4) applied by Local Government and Housing Act 1989 (c. 42, SIF 75:1), s. 186, Sch. 10 paras. 12. (1), 21, 22

[41. A F179 Amounts attributable to services.

In order to assist authorities to give effect to the housing benefit scheme under Part VII of the Social Security Contributions and Benefits Act 1992[F180 or to assist the Secretary of State in the administration of universal credit], where a rent is determined under section 14 or 22 above, the [F181appropriate tribunal] shall note in their determination the amount (if any) of the rent which, in the opinion of the [F182tribunal], is fairly attributable to the provision of services, except where that amount is in their opinion negligible; and the amount so noted may be included in the information specified in an order under section 42 [F183or 42. A] below.]
Amendments (Textual)
F179. S. 41. A added (1.7.1992) by Social Security (Consequential Provisions) Act 1992 (c. 6), ss. 4, 7. (2), Sch. 2 para. 103
F180. Words in s. 41. A inserted (29.4.2013) by The Universal Credit (Consequential, Supplementary, Incidental and Miscellaneous Provisions) Regulations 2013 (S.I. 2013/630), regs. 1. (2), 6
F181. Words in s. 41. A substituted (1.7.2013) by The Transfer of Tribunal Functions Order 2013 (S.I. 2013/1036), art. 1, Sch. 1 para. 90. (a) (with Sch. 3)
F182. Word in s. 41. A substituted (1.7.2013) by The Transfer of Tribunal Functions Order 2013 (S.I. 2013/1036), art. 1, Sch. 1 para. 90. (b) (with Sch. 3)
F183. Words in s. 41. A inserted (1.7.2013) by The Transfer of Tribunal Functions Order 2013 (S.I. 2013/1036), art. 1, Sch. 1 para. 90. (c) (with Sch. 3)

[41. B F184 Provision of information as to exemption from council tax

A billing authority within the meaning of Part I of the Local Government Finance Act 1992 shall, if so requested in writing by a rent officer or [F185the appropriate tribunal] in connection with his or their functions under any enactment, inform the rent officer or [F185the appropriate tribunal] in writing whether or not a particular dwelling (within the meaning of Part I of the Local

Government Finance Act 1992) is, or was at any time specified in the request, an exempt dwelling for the purposes of that Part of that Act.]
Amendments (Textual)
F184. S. 41. B inserted (23.4.1993) by S.I. 1993/651, art. 2. (1), Sch. 1 para.18 (as amended (23.4.1993) by S.I. 1993/1120, art.2).
F185. Words in s. 41. B substituted (1.7.2013) by The Transfer of Tribunal Functions Order 2013 (S.I. 2013/1036), art. 1, Sch. 1 para. 91 (with Sch. 3)

42 Information as to determinations of rents [F186in Wales].

(1) The President of [F187the] rent assessment panel shall keep and make publicly available, in such manner as is specified in an order made by the [F188. Welsh Ministers], such information as may be so specified with respect to rents under assured tenancies and assured agricultural occupancies which have been the subject of references or applications to, or determinations by, rent assessment committees [F189in areas in Wales].
(2) A copy of any information certified under the hand of an officer duly authorised by the President of the rent assessment panel F190... shall be receivable in evidence in any court and in any proceedings.
(3) An order under subsection (1) above—
   (a) may prescribe the fees to be charged for the supply of a copy, including a certified copy, of any of the information kept by virtue of that subsection; and
   (b) may make different provision with respect to different cases or descriptions of case, including different provision for different areas.
(4) The power to make an order under subsection (1) above shall be exercisable by statutory instrument which shall be subject to annulment in pursuance of a resolution of [F191the National Assembly for Wales].
Amendments (Textual)
F186. Words in s. 42 inserted (1.7.2013) by The Transfer of Tribunal Functions Order 2013 (S.I. 2013/1036), art. 1, Sch. 1 para. 92. (a) (with Sch. 3)
F187. Word in s. 42. (1) substituted (1.7.2013) by The Transfer of Tribunal Functions Order 2013 (S.I. 2013/1036), art. 1, Sch. 1 para. 92. (b)(i) (with Sch. 3)
F188. Words in s. 42. (1) substituted (1.7.2013) by The Transfer of Tribunal Functions Order 2013 (S.I. 2013/1036), art. 1, Sch. 1 para. 92. (b)(ii) (with Sch. 3)
F189. Words in s. 42. (1) inserted (1.7.2013) by The Transfer of Tribunal Functions Order 2013 (S.I. 2013/1036), art. 1, Sch. 1 para. 92. (b)(iii) (with Sch. 3)
F190. Word in s. 42. (2) omitted (1.7.2013) by virtue of The Transfer of Tribunal Functions Order 2013 (S.I. 2013/1036), art. 1, Sch. 1 para. 92. (c) (with Sch. 3)
F191. Words in s. 42. (4) substituted (1.7.2013) by The Transfer of Tribunal Functions Order 2013 (S.I. 2013/1036), art. 1, Sch. 1 para. 92. (d) (with Sch. 3)

[F19242. A.Information as to determination of rents in England

(1) The Chamber President of the Property Chamber of the First-tier Tribunal shall keep and make publicly available, in such manner as may be specified in an order made by the Lord Chancellor, such information as may be specified in an order made by the Secretary of State with respect to rents under assured tenancies and assured agricultural occupancies which have been the subject of references or applications to, or determinations by—
   (a) rent assessment committees in England,
   (b) the First-tier Tribunal, or
   (c) the Upper Tribunal.
(2) A copy of any information certified by a member of staff appointed by the Lord Chancellor and duly authorised by the Chamber President shall be receivable in evidence in any court and in

any proceedings.
(3) An order made by the Lord Chancellor under subsection (1) may prescribe the fees to be charged for the supply of a copy, including a certified copy, of any of the information kept by virtue that subsection.
(4) The power to make an order under subsection (1) shall be exercisable by statutory instrument which shall be subject to annulment in pursuance of a resolution of either House of Parliament.]
Amendments (Textual)
F192. S. 42. A inserted (1.7.2013) by The Transfer of Tribunal Functions Order 2013 (S.I. 2013/1036), art. 1, Sch. 1 para. 93 (with Sch. 3)

43 Powers of local authorities for purposes of giving information.

In section 149 of the M25. Rent Act 1977 (which, among other matters, authorises local authorities to publish information for the benefit of landlords and tenants with respect to their rights and duties under certain enactments), in subsection (1)(a) after sub-paragraph (iv) there shall be inserted—
    "(v)Chapters I to III of Part I of the Housing Act 1988".
Marginal Citations
M251977 c. 42.

44 Application to Crown Property.

(1) Subject to paragraph 11 of Schedule 1 to this Act and subsection (2) below, Chapters I to IV above apply in relation to premises in which there subsists, or at any material time subsisted, a Crown interest as they apply in relation to premises in relation to which no such interest subsists or ever subsisted.
(2) In Chapter IV above—
    (a) sections 27 and 28 do not bind the Crown; and
    (b) the remainder binds the Crown to the extent provided for in section 10 of the M26. Protection from Eviction Act 1977.
(3) In this section "Crown interest" means an interest which belongs to Her Majesty in right of the Crown or of the Duchy of Lancaster or to the Duchy of Cornwall, or to a government department, or which is held in trust for Her Majesty for the purposes of a government department.
(4) Where an interest belongs to Her Majesty in right of the Duchy of Lancaster, then, for the purposes of Chapters I to IV above, the Chancellor of the Duchy of Lancaster shall be deemed to be the owner of the interest.
Marginal Citations
M261977 c. 43.

45 Interpretation of Part I.

(1) In this Part of this Act, except where the context otherwise requires,—
[F193"appropriate tribunal" means—
    - in relation to a dwelling-house in England, the First-tier Tribunal or, where determined by or under Tribunal Procedure Rules, the Upper Tribunal;
    - in relation to a dwelling-house in Wales, a rent assessment committee;]
"dwelling-house" may be a house or part of a house;
"fixed term tenancy" means any tenancy other than a periodic tenancy;
"fully mutual housing association" has the same meaning as in Part I of the M27. Housing Associations Act 1985;
"landlord" includes any person from time to time deriving title under the original landlord and

also includes, in relation to a dwelling-house, any person other than a tenant who is, or but for the existence of an assured tenancy would be, entitled to possession of the dwelling-house;
"let" includes "sub-let";
"prescribed" means prescribed by regulations made by the Secretary of State by statutory instrument;
"rates" includes water rates and charges but does not include an owner's drainage rate, as defined in section 63. (2)(a) of the M28. Land Drainage Act 1976;
"secure tenancy" has the meaning assigned by section 79 of the M29. Housing Act 1985;
"statutory periodic tenancy" has the meaning assigned by section 5. (7) above;
"tenancy" includes a sub-tenancy and an agreement for a tenancy or sub-tenancy; and
"tenant" includes a sub-tenant and any person deriving title under the original tenant or sub-tenant.
(2) Subject to paragraph 11 of Schedule 2 to this Act, any reference in this Part of this Act to the beginning of a tenancy is a reference to the day on which the tenancy is entered into or, if it is later, the day on which, under the terms of any lease, agreement or other document, the tenant is entitled to possession under the tenancy.
(3) Where two or more persons jointly constitute either the landlord or the tenant in relation to a tenancy, then, except where this Part of this Act otherwise provides, any reference to the landlord or to the tenant is a reference to all the persons who jointly constitute the landlord or the tenant, as the case may require.
(4) For the avoidance of doubt, it is hereby declared that any reference in this Part of this Act (however expressed) to a power for a landlord to determine a tenancy does not include a reference to a power of re-entry or forfeiture for breach of any term or condition of the tenancy.
(5) Regulations under subsection (1) above may make different provision with respect to different cases or descriptions of case, including different provision for different areas.
Amendments (Textual)
F193. Words in s. 45. (1) inserted (1.7.2013) by The Transfer of Tribunal Functions Order 2013 (S.I. 2013/1036), art. 1, Sch. 1 para. 94 (with Sch. 3)
Marginal Citations
M271985 c. 69.
M281976 c. 70.
M291985 c. 68.

Interpretation of Part I.

45 Interpretation of Part I.

(1) In this Part of this Act, except where the context otherwise requires,—
[F1"appropriate tribunal" means—
 - in relation to a dwelling-house in England, the First-tier Tribunal or, where determined by or under Tribunal Procedure Rules, the Upper Tribunal;
 - in relation to a dwelling-house in Wales, a rent assessment committee;]
"dwelling-house" may be a house or part of a house;
"fixed term tenancy" means any tenancy other than a periodic tenancy;
"fully mutual housing association" has the same meaning as in Part I of the M1. Housing Associations Act 1985;
"landlord" includes any person from time to time deriving title under the original landlord and also includes, in relation to a dwelling-house, any person other than a tenant who is, or but for the existence of an assured tenancy would be, entitled to possession of the dwelling-house;
"let" includes "sub-let";

"prescribed" means prescribed by regulations made by the Secretary of State by statutory instrument;
"rates" includes water rates and charges but does not include an owner's drainage rate, as defined in section 63. (2)(a) of the M2. Land Drainage Act 1976;
"secure tenancy" has the meaning assigned by section 79 of the M3. Housing Act 1985;
"statutory periodic tenancy" has the meaning assigned by section 5. (7) above;
"tenancy" includes a sub-tenancy and an agreement for a tenancy or sub-tenancy; and
"tenant" includes a sub-tenant and any person deriving title under the original tenant or sub-tenant.
(2) Subject to paragraph 11 of Schedule 2 to this Act, any reference in this Part of this Act to the beginning of a tenancy is a reference to the day on which the tenancy is entered into or, if it is later, the day on which, under the terms of any lease, agreement or other document, the tenant is entitled to possession under the tenancy.
(3) Where two or more persons jointly constitute either the landlord or the tenant in relation to a tenancy, then, except where this Part of this Act otherwise provides, any reference to the landlord or to the tenant is a reference to all the persons who jointly constitute the landlord or the tenant, as the case may require.
(4) For the avoidance of doubt, it is hereby declared that any reference in this Part of this Act (however expressed) to a power for a landlord to determine a tenancy does not include a reference to a power of re-entry or forfeiture for breach of any term or condition of the tenancy.
(5) Regulations under subsection (1) above may make different provision with respect to different cases or descriptions of case, including different provision for different areas.
Amendments (Textual)
F1. Words in s. 45. (1) inserted (1.7.2013) by The Transfer of Tribunal Functions Order 2013 (S.I. 2013/1036), art. 1, Sch. 1 para. 94 (with Sch. 3)
Marginal Citations
M11985 c. 69.
M21976 c. 70.
M31985 c. 68.

Part II Housing Associations

Part II Housing Associations

F146. . . . .

Amendments (Textual)
F1. S. 46 repealed (1.11.1998) by 1998 c. 38, ss. 140, 152, Sch. 16 para. 62, Sch. 18 Pt. VI (with ss. 137. (1), 139. (2), 141. (1), 143. (2)); S.I. 1998/2244, art. 5

F247. . . . .

Amendments (Textual)
F2. S. 47 repealed (1.11.1998) by 1998 c. 38, ss. 140, 152, Sch. 16 para. 63, Sch. 18 Pt. VI (with ss. 137. (1), 139. (2), 141. (1), 143. (2)); S.I. 1998/2244, art. 5

Registration and issue of guidance

F3 48. . . . .

Amendments (Textual)
F3. S. 48 repealed (E.W.) (1.10.1996) by 1996 c. 52, ss. 227, 231. (4)(b), Sch. 19 Pt. I; S.I. 1996/2402, art. 3 (subject to transitional provisions in Sch.); and repealed (S.) (1.11.2001) by 2001 asp 10, s. 112, Sch. 10 para. 15. (2); S.S.I. 2001/336, art. 2. (3), Sch. Pt. II Table (with transitional provisions and savings in art. 3)

F4 49. . . . .

Amendments (Textual)
F4. S. 49 repealed (E.W.) (1.10.1996) by 1996 c. 52, ss. 227, 231. (4)(b), Sch. 19 Pt. I; S.I. 1996/2402, art. 3 (subject to transitional provisions in Sch.); and repealed (S.) (1.11.2001) by 2001 asp 10, s. 112, Sch. 10 para. 15. (2); S.S.I. 2001/336, art. 2. (3), Sch. Pt. II Table (with transitional provisions and savings in art. 3)

Grants F5...

Amendments (Textual)
F5. Words in s. 50 cross-heading repealed (1.4.2010) by Housing and Regeneration Act 2008 (c. 17), s. 325. (1), Sch. 8 para. 45, Sch. 16; S.I. 2010/862, arts. 2, 3 (with Sch.)

F6 50 Housing association grants.

. . . .
Extent Information
E1. This version of this provision extends to England and Wales only; a separate version has been created for Scotland only
Amendments (Textual)
F6. S. 50 repealed (1.4.2010) by Housing and Regeneration Act 2008 (c. 17), s. 325. (1), Sch. 8 para. 46, Sch. 16; S.I. 2010/862, arts. 2, 3 (with Sch.)
Modifications etc. (not altering text)
C1. S. 50 restricted (E.W.) (1.4.1997) by 1996 c. 52, ss. 28. (1), 251. (4)(b) (with s. 51. (4)); S.I. 1997/618, art. 2 (subject to transitional provisions and savings in Sch.)
S. 50 amended (E.W.) (1.4.1997) by 1996 c. 52, ss. 28. (6), 251. (4)(b) (with s. 51. (4)); S.I. 1997/618, art. 2 (subject to transitional provisions and savings in Sch.)
C2. S. 50 functions transferred (E.W.) (1.12.2008) by The Transfer of Housing Corporation Functions (Modifications and Transitional Provisions) Order 2008 (S.I. 2008/2839), arts. 1. (1), 2; S.I. 2008/3068, art. 2. (1)(b) (with arts. 6-12)
C3. S. 50 modified (E.W.) (1.12.2008) by The Transfer of Housing Corporation Functions (Modifications and Transitional Provisions) Order 2008 (S.I. 2008/2839), arts. 1. (1), 3, Sch. para. 4; S.I. 2008/3068, art. 2. (1)(b) (with arts. 6-12)

F6 50 Housing association grants.S

. . . .
Extent Information
E8. This version of this provision extends to Scotland only; a separate version has been created for England and Wales only
Amendments (Textual)

F6. S. 50 repealed (1.4.2010) by Housing and Regeneration Act 2008 (c. 17), s. 325. (1), Sch. 8 para. 46, Sch. 16; S.I. 2010/862, arts. 2, 3 (with Sch.)

F751 Revenue deficit grants.

. . . .
Extent Information
E2. This version of this provision extends to England and Wales only; a separate version has been created for Scotland only
Amendments (Textual)
F7. S. 51 repealed (1.4.2010) by Housing and Regeneration Act 2008 (c. 17), s. 325. (1), Sch. 8 para. 46, Sch. 16; S.I. 2010/862, arts. 2, 3 (with Sch.)
Modifications etc. (not altering text)
C4. S. 51 restricted (1.4.1997) by 1996 c. 52, ss. 28. (2), 251. (4)(b), (with s. 51. (4)); S.I. 1997/618, art. 2 (subject to transitional provisions and savings in Sch.)
S. 51 amended (1.4.1997) by 1996 c. 52, ss. 28. (6), 251. (4)(b); S.I. 1997/618, art. 2 (subject to transitional provisions and savings in Sch.)
C5. S. 51 functions transferred (E.W.) (1.12.2008) by The Transfer of Housing Corporation Functions (Modifications and Transitional Provisions) Order 2008 (S.I. 2008/2839), arts. 1. (1), 2; S.I. 2008/3068, art. 2. (1)(b) (with arts. 6-12)
C6. S. 51 modified (E.W.) (1.12.2008) by The Transfer of Housing Corporation Functions (Modifications and Transitional Provisions) Order 2008 (S.I. 2008/2839), arts. 1. (1), 3, Sch. para. 4; S.I. 2008/3068, art. 2. (1)(b) (with arts. 6-12)

F751 Revenue deficit grants.S

. . . .
Extent Information
E9. This version of this provision extends to Scotland only; a separate version has been created for England and Wales only
Amendments (Textual)
F7. S. 51 repealed (1.4.2010) by Housing and Regeneration Act 2008 (c. 17), s. 325. (1), Sch. 8 para. 46, Sch. 16; S.I. 2010/862, arts. 2, 3 (with Sch.)

52 Recovery etc. of grants.

(1) Where a grant to which this section applies, that is to say—
   (a) a grant under section 50 or 51 above, or
   (b) a grant under section 41 of the 1985 Act or any enactment replaced by that section, or
   (c) a grant under section 2. (2) of the M1. Housing (Scotland) Act 1988,
has been made to a [F8relevant housing association], the powers conferred by subsection (2) below are exercisable in such events (including the association not complying with any conditions) as the [F9appropriate authority] may from time to time determine (in this section referred to as "relevant events").
(2) The [F9appropriate authority]. . . may—
   (a) reduce the amount of, or of any payment in respect of, the grant;
   (b) suspend or cancel any instalment of the grant; or
   (c) direct the association [F10to apply or appropriate for such purposes as the [F9appropriate authority] may specify, or to pay to the [F9appropriate authority]] an amount equal to the whole, or such proportion as it may specify, of the amount of any payment made to the association in respect of the grant,

and a direction under paragraph (c) above [F11may require the application, appropriation or payment of an amount with interest] in accordance with subsections (7) to (9) below.

(3) Where, after a grant to which this section applies has been made to an association, a relevant event occurs, the association shall notify the [F9appropriate authority] and, if so required by written notice of the [F9appropriate authority], shall furnish it with such particulars of and information relating to the event as are specified in the notice.

(4) Where a grant to which this section applies (other than one falling within subsection (1)(c) above) has been made to an association, the Chief Land Registrar may furnish the [F9appropriate authority] with such particulars and information as it may reasonably require for the purpose of ascertaining whether a relevant event has occurred; but this subsection shall cease to have effect on the day appointed under section 3. (2) of the M2. Land Registration Act 1988 for the coming into force of that Act.

(5) Where—

   (a) a grant to which this section applies has been made to an association, and

   (b) at any time property to which the grant relates becomes vested in, or is leased for a term of years to, or reverts to, some other [F12relevant housing association], or trustees for some other such association,

this section (including this subsection) shall have effect after that time as if the grant, or such proportion of it as is specified or determined under subsection (6) below, had been made to that other association.

(6) The proportion referred to in subsection (5) above is that which, in the circumstances of the particular case,—

   (a) the [F9appropriate authority], acting in accordance with such principles as it may from time to time determine, may specify as being appropriate; or

   (b) the [F9appropriate authority] may determine to be appropriate.

(7) A direction under subsection (2)(c) above [F13requiring the application, appropriation or payment of an amount with interest] shall specify, in accordance with subsection (9) below,—

   (a) the rate or rates of interest (whether fixed or variable) which is or are applicable;

   (b) the date from which interest is payable, being not earlier than the date of the relevant event; and

   (c) any provision for suspended or reduced interest which is applicable.

(8) In subsection (7)(c) above—

   (a) the reference to a provision for suspended interest is a reference to a provision whereby, if [F14the principle amount is applied, appropriated or paid] before a date specified in the direction, no interest will be payable for any period after the date of the direction; and

   (b) the reference to a provision for reduced interest is a reference to a provision whereby, if [F15the principle amount is so applied, appropriated or paid], any interest payable will be payable at a rate or rates lower than the rate or rates which would otherwise be applicable.

(9) The matters specified in a direction as mentioned in paragraphs (a) to (c) of subsection (7) above shall be either—

   (a) such as the [F9appropriate authority], acting in accordance with such principles as it may from time to time determine, may specify as being appropriate, or

   (b) such as the [F9appropriate authority] may determine to be appropriate in the particular case.

[F16. (9. A)In this section and sections 53 and 54—

"the appropriate authority"—

   - in relation to an English relevant housing association [F17and property outside Greater London], means the Homes and Communities Agency,

   - [F18in relation to an English relevant housing association and property in Greater London, means the Greater London Authority, and]

   - in relation to a Welsh relevant housing association, means the Welsh Ministers,

" relevant housing association " means—

   - a housing association which is a registered provider of social housing ("an English relevant housing association"), and

- a housing association which is a registered social landlord ("a Welsh relevant housing association").

(9. B)In this section a reference to registration as a provider of social housing, so far as the context permits, is to be construed as including, in relation to times, circumstances and purposes before the commencement of section 111 of the Housing and Regeneration Act 2008, a reference to registration under—
  (a) Part 1 of the Housing Act 1996,
  (b) Part 1 of the 1985 Act, or
  (c) any corresponding earlier enactment.]

Extent Information
E3. This version of this provision extends to England and Wales only; a separate version has been created for Scotland only

Amendments (Textual)
F8. Words in s. 52. (1) substituted (1.4.2010) by Housing and Regeneration Act 2008 (c. 17), s. 325. (1), Sch. 8 para. 47. (3); S.I. 2010/862, art. 2 (with Sch.)
F9. Words in s. 52 substituted (1.4.2010) by Housing and Regeneration Act 2008 (c. 17), s. 325. (1), Sch. 8 para. 47. (2); S.I. 2010/862, art. 2 (with Sch.)
F10. Words in s. 52. (2)(c) substituted (E.W.) (1.10.1996 for specified purposes, otherwise 1.4.1997) by 1996 c. 52, ss. 28. (3)(a), 231. (4)(b) (with s. 51. (4)); S.I. 1996/2402, art. 5; S.I. 1997/618, art. 2 (subject to transitional provisions in Sch.)
F11. Words in s. 52. (2) substituted (E.W.) (1.10.1996 for specified purposes, otherwise 1.4.1997) by 1996 c. 52, ss. 28. (3)(b), 231. (4)(b); S.I. 1996/2402, art. 5; S.I. 1997/618, art. 2 (subject to transitional provisions in Sch.)
F12. Words in s. 52. (5)(b) substituted (1.4.2010) by Housing and Regeneration Act 2008 (c. 17), s. 325. (1), Sch. 8 para. 47. (3); S.I. 2010/862, art. 2 (with Sch.)
F13. Words in s. 52. (7) substituted (E.W.) (1.10.1996 for specified purposes, otherwise 1.4.1997) by 1996 c. 52, ss. 28. (3)(c), 231. (4)(b) (with s. 51. (4)); S.I. 1996/2402, art. 5; S.I. 1997/618, art. 2 (subject to transitional provisions in Sch.)
F14. Words in s. 52. (8)(a) substituted (E.W.) (1.10.1996 for specified purposes, otherwise 1.4.1997) by 1996 c. 52, ss. 28. (3)(d), 231. (4)(b) (with s. 51. (4)); S.I. 1996/2402, art. 5; S.I. 1997/618, art. 2 (subject to transitional provisions in Sch.)
F15. Words in s. 52. (8)(b) substituted (E.W.) (1.10.1996 for specified purposes, otherwise 1.4.1997) by 1996 c. 52, ss. 28. (3)(e), 231. (4)(b) (with s. 51. (4)); S.I. 1996/2402, art. 5; S.I. 1997/618, art. 2 (subject to transitional provisions in Sch.)
F16. S. 52. (9. A)(9. B) inserted (1.4.2010) by Housing and Regeneration Act 2008 (c. 17), s. 325. (1), Sch. 8 para. 47. (4); S.I. 2010/862, art. 2 (with Sch.)
F17. Words in s. 52. (9. A) inserted (1.4.2012) by Localism Act 2011 (c. 20), s. 240. (2), Sch. 19 para. 28. (a); S.I. 2012/628, art. 6. (i) (with arts. 9 11 14 15 17)
F18. Words in s. 52. (9. A) substituted (1.4.2012) by Localism Act 2011 (c. 20), s. 240. (2), Sch. 19 para. 28. (b); S.I. 2012/628, art. 6. (i) (with arts. 9 11 14 15 17)

Modifications etc. (not altering text)
C7. S. 52 excluded (E.W.) (1.8.1996 for specified purposes, otherwise 1.4.1997) by 1996 c. 52, ss. 24. (7), 231. (4)(b) (with s. 51. (4)); S.I. 1996/2048, art. 3; S.I. 1996/618, art. 2 (subject to transitional provisions in Sch.)
C8. Ss. 50-55 amended (1.4.1997) by 1996 c. 52, s. 28. (6) (with s. 51. (4)); S.I. 1997/618, art. 2 (subject to transitional provisions and savings in Sch.)
C9. S. 52 functions transferred (E.W.) (1.12.2008) by The Transfer of Housing Corporation Functions (Modifications and Transitional Provisions) Order 2008 (S.I. 2008/2839), arts. 1. (1), 2; S.I. 2008/3068, art. 2. (1)(b) (with arts. 6-12)
C10. S. 52 modified (E.W.) (1.12.2008) by The Transfer of Housing Corporation Functions (Modifications and Transitional Provisions) Order 2008 (S.I. 2008/2839), arts. 1. (1), 3, Sch. para. 4; S.I. 2008/3068, art. 2. (1)(b) (with arts. 6-12)
C11. S. 52 modified (E.W.) (1.12.2008) by The Transfer of Housing Corporation Functions

(Modifications and Transitional Provisions) Order 2008 (S.I. 2008/2839), arts. 1. (1), 3, Sch. para. 3. (10); S.I. 2008/3068, art. 2. (1)(b) (with arts. 6-12)
C12. S. 52 excluded (1.4.2010) by Housing and Regeneration Act 2008 (c. 17), ss. 177. (8), 325. (1) (with s. 189); S.I. 2010/862, art. 2 (with Sch.)
Marginal Citations
M11988 c. 43.
M21988 c. 3.

52 Recovery etc. of grants.S

(1) Where a grant to which this section applies, that is to say—
    (a) a grant under section 50 or 51 above, or
    (b) a grant under section 41 of the 1985 Act or any enactment replaced by that section, or
    (c) a grant under section 2. (2) of the M7. Housing (Scotland) Act 1988,
has been made to a registered [F42social landlord], the powers conferred by subsection (2) below are exercisable in such events (including the association not complying with any conditions) as the Corporation may from time to time determine (in this section referred to as "relevant events").
(2) The Corporation, acting in accordance with such principles as it may from time to time determine, may—
    (a) reduce the amount of, or of any payment in respect of, the grant;
    (b) suspend or cancel any instalment of the grant; or
    (c) direct the [F43landlord] to pay to it an amount equal to the whole, or such proportion as it may specify, of the amount of any payment made to the [F43landlord] in respect of the grant,
and a direction under paragraph (c) above requiring the payment of any interest on that amount in accordance with subsections (7) to (9) below.
(3) Where, after a grant to which this section applies has been made to [F44a registered social landlord], a relevant event occurs, the [F44landlord] shall notify the Corporation and, if so required by written notice of the Corporation, shall furnish it with such particulars of and information relating to the event as are specified in the notice.
(4) Where a grant to which this section applies (other than one falling within subsection (1)(c) above) has been made to [F44a registered social landlord], the Chief Land Registrar may furnish the Corporation with such particulars and information as it may reasonably require for the purpose of ascertaining whether a relevant event has occurred; but this subsection shall cease to have effect on the day appointed under section 3. (2) of the M8. Land Registration Act 1988 for the coming into force of that Act.
(5) Where—
    (a) a grant to which this section applies has been made to [F45a registered social landlord], and
    (b) at any time property to which the grant relates becomes vested in, or is leased for a term of years to, or reverts to, some other registered [F45social landlord], or trustees for some other such [F45landlord],
this section (including this subsection) shall have effect after that time as if the grant, or such proportion of it as is specified or determined under subsection (6) below, had been made to that other [F45landlord].
(6) The proportion referred to in subsection (5) above is that which, in the circumstances of the particular case,—
    (a) the Corporation, acting in accordance with such principles as it may from time to time determine, may specify as being appropriate; or
    (b) the Corporation may determine to be appropriate.
(7) A direction under subsection (2)(c) above requiring the payment of interest on the amount directed to be paid to the Corporation shall specify, in accordance with subsection (9) below,—
    (a) the rate or rates of interest (whether fixed or variable) which is or are applicable;
    (b) the date from which interest is payable, being not earlier than the date of the relevant event;

and

(c) any provision for suspended or reduced interest which is applicable.

(8) In subsection (7)(c) above—

(a) the reference to a provision for suspended interest is a reference to a provision whereby, if the amount which is directed to be paid to the Corporation is paid before a date specified in the direction, no interest will be payable for any period after the date of the direction; and

(b) the reference to a provision for reduced interest is a reference to a provision whereby, if that amount is so paid, any interest payable will be payable at a rate or rates lower than the rate or rates which would otherwise be applicable.

(9) The matters specified in a direction as mentioned in paragraphs (a) to (c) of subsection (7) above shall be either—

(a) such as the Corporation, acting in accordance with such principles as it may from time to time determine, may specify as being appropriate, or

(b) such as the Corporation may determine to be appropriate in the particular case.

[F16. (9. A)In this section and sections 53 and 54—
"the appropriate authority"—
- in relation to an English relevant housing association[F17and property outside Greater London], means the Homes and Communities Agency,
- [F18in relation to an English relevant housing association and property in Greater London, means the Greater London Authority, and]
- in relation to a Welsh relevant housing association, means the Welsh Ministers,
" relevant housing association " means—
- a housing association which is a registered provider of social housing ("an English relevant housing association"), and
- a housing association which is a registered social landlord ("a Welsh relevant housing association").

(9. B)In this section a reference to registration as a provider of social housing, so far as the context permits, is to be construed as including, in relation to times, circumstances and purposes before the commencement of section 111 of the Housing and Regeneration Act 2008, a reference to registration under—

(a) Part 1 of the Housing Act 1996,

(b) Part 1 of the 1985 Act, or

(c) any corresponding earlier enactment.]

[F46. (10)In this section and section 53, "registered social landlord" has the same meaning as in the [F47. Housing (Scotland) Act 2010 (asp 17).]]

Extent Information

E10. This version of this provision extends to Scotland only; a separate version has been created for England and Wales only

Amendments (Textual)

F16. S. 52. (9. A)(9. B) inserted (1.4.2010) by Housing and Regeneration Act 2008 (c. 17), s. 325. (1), Sch. 8 para. 47. (4); S.I. 2010/862, art. 2 (with Sch.)

F17. Words in s. 52. (9. A) inserted (1.4.2012) by Localism Act 2011 (c. 20), s. 240. (2), Sch. 19 para. 28. (a); S.I. 2012/628, art. 6. (i) (with arts. 9 11 14 15 17)

F18. Words in s. 52. (9. A) substituted (1.4.2012) by Localism Act 2011 (c. 20), s. 240. (2), Sch. 19 para. 28. (b); S.I. 2012/628, art. 6. (i) (with arts. 9 11 14 15 17)

F42. Words in s. 52. (1) substituted (S.) (1.11.2001) by 2001 asp 10, s. 112, Sch. 10 para. 15. (3)(a); S.S.I. 2001/397, art. 2. (2), Sch. Table (subject to transitional provisions and savings in arts. 3-6)

F43. Words in s. 52. (2)(c) substituted (S.) (1.11.2001) by 2001 asp 10, s. 112, Sch. 10 para. 15. (3)(b); S.S.I. 2001/397, art. 2. (2), Sch. Table (subject to transitional provisions and savings in arts. 3-6)

F44. Words in S. 52. (3)(4) substituted (S.) (1.11.2001) by 2001 asp 10, s. 112, Sch. 10 para 15. (3)(c)(d); S.S.I. 2001/397, art. 2. (2), Sch. Table (subject to transitional provisions and savings in

arts. 3-6)
F45. Words in s. 52. (5) substituted (S.) (1.11.2001) by 2001 asp 10, s. 112, Sch. 10 para. 15. (3)(e); S.S.I. 2001/397, art. 2. (2), Sch. Table (subject to transitional provisions and savings in arts. 3-6)
F46. S. 52. (10) inserted (S.) (1.11.2001) by 2001 asp 10, s. 112, Sch. 10 para. 15. (3)(f); S.S.I. 2001/397, art. 2. (2), Sch. Table (subject to transitional provisions and savings in arts. 3-6)
F47. Words in s. 52. (10) substituted (S.) (1.4.2012) by Housing (Scotland) Act 2010 (asp 17), s. 166. (2), sch. 2 para. 5; S.S.I. 2012/39, art. 2, sch. 1 (with sch. 2) (as amended (1.4.2012) by S.S.I. 2012/91, art. 4)
Modifications etc. (not altering text)
C12. S. 52 excluded (1.4.2010) by Housing and Regeneration Act 2008 (c. 17), ss. 177. (8), 325. (1) (with s. 189); S.I. 2010/862, art. 2 (with Sch.)
Marginal Citations
M71988 c. 43.
M81988 c. 3.

53 Determinations under Part II.

(1) A general determination may either—
   (a) make the same provision for all cases; or
   (b) make different provision for different cases or descriptions of cases, including different provision for different areas or for different descriptions of housing associations or housing activities;
and for the purposes of this subsection descriptions may be framed by reference to any matters whatever, including in particular, in the case of housing activities, the manner in which they are financed.
[F19. (2)The [F20[F21. Homes and Communities Agency]] shall not make a general determination under the foregoing provisions of this Part except with the approval of the Secretary of State]
(3) Before making a general determination, the [F22[F23appropriate authority]] shall consult such bodies appearing to it to be representative of housing associations as it considers appropriate; and after making such a determination, the [F22[F23appropriate authority]] shall publish the determination in such manner as it considers appropriate for bringing the determination to the notice of the associations concerned.
(4) In this section "general determination" means a determination under [F24section] 52 above, other than a determination relating solely to a particular case.
Extent Information
E4. This version of this provision extends to England and Wales only; a separate version has been created for Scotland only
Amendments (Textual)
F19. S. 53. (2) substituted (1.8.1996) by 1996 c. 52, ss. 28. (4), 231. (4)(b) (with s. 51. (4)); S.I. 1996/2048, art. 2
F20. Words in s. 53. (2) substituted (1.11.1998) by 1998 c. 38, s. 140, Sch. 16 para. 65 (with ss. 139. (2), 141. (1), 143. (2)); S.I. 1998/2244, art. 5
F21. Words in s. 53. (2) substituted (1.4.2010) by Housing and Regeneration Act 2008 (c. 17), s. 325. (1), Sch. 8 para. 48. (2); S.I. 2010/862, art. 2 (with Sch.)
F22. Words in s. 53 substituted (1.11.1998) by 1998 c. 38, s. 140, Sch. 16 para. 61. (1)(2) (with ss. 139. (2), 143. (2)); S.I. 1998/2244, art. 5
F23. Words in s. 53. (3) substituted (1.4.2010) by Housing and Regeneration Act 2008 (c. 17), s. 325. (1), Sch. 8 para. 48. (3); S.I. 2010/862, art. 2 (with Sch.)
F24. Words in s. 53. (4) substituted (1.4.2010) by Housing and Regeneration Act 2008 (c. 17), s. 325. (1), Sch. 8 para. 48. (4); S.I. 2010/862, art. 2 (with Sch.)

Modifications etc. (not altering text)
C13. S. 53 applied by section 87 of the Housing Associations Act 1985 (c. 69, SIF 61), as substituted by Local Government and Housing Act 1989 (c.42, SIF 61), s. 183
C14. Ss. 50-55 amended (1.4.1997) by 1996 c. 52, ss. 28. (6), 231. (4)(b) (with s. 51. (4)); S.I. 1997/618, art. 2 (subject to transitional provisions and savings in Sch.)
C15. S. 53 functions transferred (E.W.) (1.12.2008) by The Transfer of Housing Corporation Functions (Modifications and Transitional Provisions) Order 2008 (S.I. 2008/2839), arts. 1. (1), 2; S.I. 2008/3068, art. 2. (1)(b) (with arts. 6-12)
C16. S. 53 modified (E.W.) (1.12.2008) by The Transfer of Housing Corporation Functions (Modifications and Transitional Provisions) Order 2008 (S.I. 2008/2839), arts. 1. (1), 3, Sch. para. 4; S.I. 2008/3068, art. 2. (1)(b) (with arts. 6-12)

53 Determinations under Part II. S

(1) A general determination may either—
  (a) make the same provision for all cases; or
  (b) make different provision for different cases or descriptions of cases, including different provision for different areas or for different descriptions of [F48registered social landlords] or housing activities;
and for the purposes of this subsection descriptions may be framed by reference to any matters whatever, including in particular, in the case of housing activities, the manner in which they are financed.
(2) The Corporation shall not make a determination under the foregoing provisions of this Part except with the approval of the Secretary of State given, in the case of a general determination, with the consent of the Treasury.
(3) Before making a general determination, the Corporation shall consult such bodies appearing to it to be representative of [F49registered social landlords] as it considers appropriate; and after making such a determination, the Corporation shall publish the determination in such manner as it considers appropriate for bringing the determination to the notice of the [F49landlords] concerned.
(4) In this section "general determination" means a determination under [F24section] 52 above, other than a determination relating solely to a particular case.
Extent Information
E11. This version of this provision extends to Scotland only; a separate version has been created for England and Wales only
Amendments (Textual)
F24. Words in s. 53. (4) substituted (1.4.2010) by Housing and Regeneration Act 2008 (c. 17), s. 325. (1), Sch. 8 para. 48. (4); S.I. 2010/862, art. 2 (with Sch.)
F48. Words in s. 53. (1)(b) substituted (1.11.2001) by 2001 asp 10, s. 112, Sch. 10 para. 15. (4)(a); S.S.I. 2001/397, art. 2. (2), Sch. Table (subject to transitional provisions and savings in arts. 3-6)
F49. Words in s. 53. (3) substituted (1.11.2001) by 2001 asp 10, s. 112, Sch. 10 para. 15. (4)(b); S.S.I. 2001/397, art. 2. (2), Sch. Table (subject to transitional provisions and savings in arts. 3-6)
Modifications etc. (not altering text)
C18. S. 53 applied by section 87 of the Housing Associations Act 1985 (c. 69, SIF 61), as substituted by Local Government and Housing Act 1989 (c.42, SIF 61), s. 183

Grants: functions of Secretary of State

54 Tax relief grants.

(1) If a housing association makes a claim to the Secretary of State in respect of a period and

satisfies him that throughout the period it was a housing association to which this section applies and its functions either—

(a) consisted exclusively of the function of providing or maintaining housing accommodation for letting or hostels and activities incidental to that function, or

(b) included that function and activities incidental to that function,

the Secretary of State may make grants to the association for affording relief from tax chargeable on the association.

(2) This section applies to a housing association at any time if, at that time—

(a) it is [F25a relevant housing association];

(b) it does not trade for profit; and

(c) it is not approved for the purposes of [F26. Chapter 7 of Part 13 of the Corporation Tax Act 2010] (tax treatment of co-operative housing associations).

(3) References in this section to tax chargeable on an association are to income tax (other than income tax which the association is entitled to deduct on making any payment) and corporation tax.

(4) A grant under this section may be made—

(a) in a case falling within subsection (1)(a) above, for affording relief from any tax chargeable on the association for the period in respect of which the claim is made; and

(b) in a case falling within subsection (1)(b) above, for affording relief from such part of any tax so chargeable as the Secretary of State considers appropriate having regard to the other functions of the association;

and in any case shall be of such amount, shall be made at such times and shall be subject to such conditions as the Secretary of State thinks fit.

(5) The conditions may include conditions for securing the repayment in whole or in part of a grant made to an association—

(a) in the event of tax in respect of which it was made being found not to be chargeable; or

(b) in such other events (including the association beginning to trade for profit) as the Secretary of State may determine.

(6) A claim under this section shall be made in such manner and shall be supported by such evidence as the Secretary of State may direct.

(7) The Commissioners of Inland Revenue and their officers may disclose to the Secretary of State such particulars as he may reasonably require for determining whether a grant should be made on a claim or whether a grant should be repaid or the amount of such grant or repayment.

(8) In this section "letting" includes—

(a) in England and Wales, the grant of a shared ownership lease or a licence to occupy;

(b) in Scotland, disposal under a shared ownership agreement or the grant of a right or permission to occupy.

Extent Information

E5. This version of this provision extends to England and Wales only; a separate version has been created for Scotland only

Amendments (Textual)

F25. Words in s. 54. (2)(a) substituted (1.4.2010) by Housing and Regeneration Act 2008 (c. 17), s. 325. (1), Sch. 8 para. 49; S.I. 2010/862, art. 2 (with Sch.)

F26. Words in s. 54. (2)(c) substituted (1.4.2010) (with effect in accordance with s. 1184. (1) of the amending Act) by Corporation Tax Act 2010 (c. 4), s. 1184. (1), Sch. 1 para. 211 (with Sch. 2)

Modifications etc. (not altering text)

C17. Ss. 50-55 amended (1.4.1997) by 1996 c. 52, ss. 28. (6), 231. (4)(b) (with s. 51. (4)); S.I. 1997/618, art. 2 (subject to transitional provisions and savings in Sch.)

54 Tax relief grants.S

(1) If a housing association makes a claim to the Secretary of State in respect of a period and

satisfies him that throughout the period it was a housing association to which this section applies and its functions either—
    (a) consisted exclusively of the function of providing or maintaining housing accommodation for letting or hostels and activities incidental to that function, or
    (b) included that function and activities incidental to that function,
the Secretary of State may make grants to the association for affording relief from tax chargeable on the association.
(2) This section applies to a housing association at any time if, at that time—
    (a) it is registered;
    (b) it does not trade for profit; and
    (c) it is not approved for the purposes of [F26. Chapter 7 of Part 13 of the Corporation Tax Act 2010] (tax treatment of co-operative housing associations).
(3) References in this section to tax chargeable on an association are to income tax (other than income tax which the association is entitled to deduct on making any payment) and corporation tax.
(4) A grant under this section may be made—
    (a) in a case falling within subsection (1)(a) above, for affording relief from any tax chargeable on the association for the period in respect of which the claim is made; and
    (b) in a case falling within subsection (1)(b) above, for affording relief from such part of any tax so chargeable as the Secretary of State considers appropriate having regard to the other functions of the association;
and in any case shall be of such amount, shall be made at such times and shall be subject to such conditions as the Secretary of State thinks fit.
(5) The conditions may include conditions for securing the repayment in whole or in part of a grant made to an association—
    (a) in the event of tax in respect of which it was made being found not to be chargeable; or
    (b) in such other events (including the association beginning to trade for profit) as the Secretary of State may determine.
(6) A claim under this section shall be made in such manner and shall be supported by such evidence as the Secretary of State may direct.
(7) The Commissioners of Inland Revenue and their officers may disclose to the Secretary of State such particulars as he may reasonably require for determining whether a grant should be made on a claim or whether a grant should be repaid or the amount of such grant or repayment.
(8) In this section "letting" includes—
    (a) in England and Wales, the grant of a shared ownership lease or a licence to occupy;
    (b) in Scotland, disposal under a shared ownership agreement or the grant of a right or permission to occupy.
Extent Information
E12. This version of this provision extends to Scotland only; a separate version has been created for England and Wales only
Amendments (Textual)
F26. Words in s. 54. (2)(c) substituted (1.4.2010) (with effect in accordance with s. 1184. (1) of the amending Act) by Corporation Tax Act 2010 (c. 4), s. 1184. (1), Sch. 1 para. 211 (with Sch. 2)

55 Surplus rental income.

F27. . . . .
Amendments (Textual)
F27. S. 55 repealed (S.) (30.9.2002) by 2001 asp 10 para. 15. (5), s. 112, Sch. 10 para. 15. (5); S.I. 2002/321, art. 2 (with art. 3-5) and omitted (E.W.) (18.1.2005) by virtue of Housing Act 2004 (c. 34), ss. 218, 270, Sch. 11 para. 5 and repealed (6.4.2006 for E. and 16.6.2006 for W.) by Housing Act 2004 (c. 34), ss. 266, 270, Sch. 16; S.I. 2006/1060, art. 2. (1)(e)(ix) (with Sch.); S.I.

2006/1535, art. 2. (c)(ix) (with Sch.)

Miscellaneous and supplemental

F2856. . . . .

Amendments (Textual)
F28. S. 56 repealed (2.4.2001) by 2000 c. 34, s. 9. (2), Sch. 3; S.I. 2001/566, art. 2

57 Delegation of certain functions.

[F29. The Secretary of State may delegate to the [F30. Housing Corporation], to such extent and subject to such conditions as he may specify, any of his functions [F31, so far as they relate to English registered social landlords,] under—
    (a) section 54 F32 . . . above;
    (b) sections 53 (recoupment of surplus rental income), 54 to 57 (deficit grants) and 62 (grants for affording tax relief) of the 1985 Act, so far as continuing in force after the passing of this Act; and
    (c) Parts I and II of Schedule 5 to the 1985 Act (residual subsidies);
and where he does so, references to him in those provisions shall be construed accordingly.
[F33 In this section " English registered social landlords " means social landlords registered in the register maintained by the Housing Corporation under section 1 of the M3 Housing Act 1996.]]
Extent Information
E6. This version of this provision extends to England and Wales only; a separate version has been created for Scotland only
Amendments (Textual)
F29. S. 57 repealed (E.W.) (1.4.2010) by The Housing and Regeneration Act 2008 (Consequential Provisions) Order 2010 (S.I. 2010/866), art. 1. (2), Sch. 2 para. 68, Sch. 4 (with art. 6, Sch. 3)
F30. Words in s. 57 substituted (E.W.) (1.11.1998) by 1998 c. 38, s. 140, Sch. 16 para. 66. (a) (with ss. 139. (2), 141. (1), 143. (2)); S.I. 1998/2244, art. 5
F31. Words in s. 57 inserted (E.W.) (1.11.1998) by 1998 c. 38, s. 140, Sch. 16 para. 66. (b) (with ss. 139. (2), 141. (1). 143. (2)); S.I. 1998/2244, art. 5
F32. Words in s. 57. (a) repealed (6.4.2006 for E. and 16.6.2006 for W.) by Housing Act 2004 (c. 34), ss. 266, 270, Sch. 16; S.I. 2006/1060, art. 2. (1)(e)(ix) (with Sch.); S.I. 2006/1535, art. 2. (c)(ix) (with Sch.)
F33. Definition of "English registered social landlords" in s. 57 inserted (E.W.) (1.11.1998) by 1998 c. 38, s. 140, Sch. 16 para. 66. (c) (with ss. 139. (2), 141. (1), 143. (2)); S.I. 1998/2244, art. 5
Marginal Citations
M31996 c. 52.

57 Delegation of certain function.S

The Secretary of State may delegate to the Corporation, to such extent and subject to such conditions as he may specify, any of his functions under—
    (a) section 54 or 55 above;
    (b) sections 53 (recoupment of surplus rental income), 54 to 57 (deficit grants) and 62 (grants for affording tax relief) of the 1985 Act, so far as continuing in force after the passing of this Act; and
    (c) Parts I and II of Schedule 5 to the 1985 Act (residual subsidies);
and where he does so, references to him in those provisions shall be construed accordingly.

Extent Information
E13. This version of this provision extends to Scotland only; a separate version has been created for England and Wales only

F34 [58 Application of Housing Acts to certain transactions.S

(1) This section applies to any tenant of a publicly-funded house who, but for paragraph 1 of Schedule 5 to the M4 Housing Act 1985 (no right to buy where landlord a charitable housing trust or housing association), would have the right to buy under Part V of the Housing Act 1985.
(2) A house is publicly-funded for the purposes of subsection (1) above if a grant under section 50 above, or a grant under section 41 of the 1985 Act or any enactment replaced by that section, has been paid in respect of a project which included—
   (a) the acquisition of the house;
   (b) the acquisition of a building and the provision of the house by means of the conversion of the building; or
   (c) the acquisition of land and the construction of the house on the land.
(3) Where a registered housing association contracts for the acquisition of a house and, without taking the conveyance, grant or assignment, disposes of its interest at a discount to a tenant to whom this section applies, the provisions mentioned in subsection (4) below shall have effect as if the association first acquired the house and then disposed of it to the tenant.
(4) The said provisions are—
section 4 of the 1985 Act (eligibility for registration);
section 8 of that Act (disposal of land by registered housing associations);
section 9 of that Act (consent of Corporation to disposals);
section 79. (2) of that Act (power of Corporation to lend to person acquiring interest from registered housing association);
Schedule 2 to that Act (covenants for repayments of discount on early disposal and restricting disposal of houses in National Parks etc.); and
section 130 of the M5 Housing Act 1985 (reduction of discount on exercise of right to buy where previous discount given).]
Amendments (Textual)
F34. S. 58 repealed (E.W.) (1.10.1996) by 1996 c. 52, ss. 51. (4), 55, 227, 231. (4)(b), Sch. 3 para. 10, Sch. 19 Pt. I (with s. 51. (4)); S.I. 1996/2402, art. 3 (subject to transitional provisions in Sch.)
Marginal Citations
M41985 c. 68.
M51985 c. 68.

59 Interpretation of Part II and amendments of Housing Associations Act 1985.

(1) In this Part of this Act—
   (a) "the 1985 Act" means the M6. Housing Associations Act 1985; and
   (b) [F35subject to subsections (1. A) and (1. B) below] expressions used in this Part have the same meaning as in the 1985 Act.
[F36. (1. A)Expressions used in sections [F3752] to [F3854] F39... above have the same meaning as in Part I of the Housing Act 1996, subject as follows.
(1. B)In those sections "housing activities" and "shared ownership lease", in relation to times, circumstances and purposes before the commencement of section 1 of the Housing Act 1996 (the register of social landlords), have the same meaning as in the 1985 Act.]
(2) The 1985 Act shall have effect subject to the amendments in Schedule 6 to this Act, being amendments—

(a) extending the supervisory powers conferred by Part I of the 1985 Act;
(b) making provision incidental to and consequential upon F40. . . the establishment by the Housing (Scotland) Act 1988 of Scottish Homes;
(c) making provision incidental to and consequential upon [F41the] provisions of this Part of this Act and the provisions of Part IV of this Act; and
(d) varying the grounds on which the Secretary of State may remove a member of the Housing Corporation from office.
(3) In Schedule 6 to this Act,—
(a) Part I contains amendments of Part I of the 1985 Act, including amendments which reproduce the effect of amendments made by Schedule 3 to the Housing (Scotland) Act 1988 with respect to Scottish Homes; and
(b) Parts II and III contain amendments of Parts II and III respectively of the 1985 Act.
(4) Without prejudice to the operation of Schedule 3 to the Housing (Scotland) Act 1988 in relation to anything done before the day appointed for the coming into force of this section, for the purpose of giving effect to the amendments in Part I of Schedule 6 to this Act, the said Schedule 3 shall be deemed never to have come into force.
Extent Information
E7. This version of this provision extends to England and Wales only; a separate version has been created for Scotland only
Amendments (Textual)
F35. Words in s. 59. (1)(b) substituted (E.W.) (1.10.1996) by S.I. 1996/2325, art. 5. (1), Sch. 2 para. 18. (9)(b)
F36. S. 59. (1. A)(1. B) inserted (E.W.) (1.10.1996) by S.I. 1996/2325, art. 5. (1), Sch. 2 para. 18. (9)(c)
F37. Word in s. 59. (1. A) substituted (1.4.2010) by Housing and Regeneration Act 2008 (c. 17), s. 325. (1), Sch. 8 para. 50; S.I. 2010/862, art. 2 (with Sch.)
F38. Word in s. 59. (1. A) substituted (E.W.) (18.1.2005) by Housing Act 2004 (c. 34), ss. 218, 270, Sch. 11 para. 6
F39. Words in s. 59. (1. A) repealed (1.4.2010) by The Housing and Regeneration Act 2008 (Consequential Provisions) Order 2010 (S.I. 2010/866), art. 1. (2), Sch. 2 para. 69, Sch. 4 (with art. 6, Sch. 3)
F40. Words in s. 59. (2)(b) repealed (E.W.) (1.11.1998) by 1998 c. 38, ss. 140, 152, Sch. 16 para. 67. (a), Sch. 18 Pt. VI (with ss. 137. (1), 139. (2), 141. (1), 143. (2)); S.I. 1998/2244, art. 5
F41. Word in s. 59. (2)(c) substituted (E.W.) (1.11.1998) by 1998 c. 38, s. 140, Sch. 16 para. 67. (b) (with ss. 139. (2), 141. (1), 143. (2)); S.I. 1998/2244, art. 5
Marginal Citations
M61985 c. 69.

59. Interpretation of Part II and amendments of Housing Associations Act 1985.S

(1) In this Part of this Act—
(a) "the 1985 Act" means the M9. Housing Associations Act 1985; and
(b) except as provided in section 50. (1) above, "the Corporation"[F50means [F51the Scottish Ministers]] and other expressions used in this Part have the same meaning as in the 1985 Act.
(2) The 1985 Act shall have effect subject to the amendments in Schedule 6 to this Act, being amendments—
(a) extending the supervisory powers conferred by Part I of the 1985 Act;
F52. (b). . . . .
(c) making provision incidental to and consequential upon [F53the] provisions of this Part of this Act and the provisions of Part IV of this Act; and
(d) varying the grounds on which the Secretary of State may remove a member of the Housing

Corporation from office.

(3) In Schedule 6 to this Act,—

(a) Part I contains amendments of Part I of the 1985 Act, including amendments which reproduce the effect of amendments made by Schedule 3 to the Housing (Scotland) Act 1988 with respect to Scottish Homes; and

(b) Parts II and III contain amendments of Parts II and III respectively of the 1985 Act.

(4) Without prejudice to the operation of Schedule 3 to the Housing (Scotland) Act 1988 in relation to anything done before the day appointed for the coming into force of this section, for the purpose of giving effect to the amendments in Part I of Schedule 6 to this Act, the said Schedule 3 shall be deemed never to have come into force.

Extent Information

E14. This version of this provision extends to Scotland only; a separate version has been created for England and Wales only

Amendments (Textual)

F50. Words in s. 59. (1)(b) inserted (S.) (1.10.1996) by S.I. 1996/2325, art. 5. (1), Sch. 2 para. 19. (9)(a)

F51. Words in s. 59. (1)(b) substituted (S.) (1.11.2001) by 2001 asp 10, s. 112, Sch. 10 para. 15. (6)(a); S.S.I. 2001/397, art. 2. (2), Sch. Table (subject to transitional provisions and savings in arts. 3-6)

F52. S. 59. (2)(b) repealed (S.) (1.11.2001) by 2001 asp 10, s. 112, Sch. 10 para. 15. (6)(b); S.S.I. 2001/397, art. 2. (2), Sch. Table (subject to transitional provisions and savings in arts. 3-6)

F53. Word in s. 59. (2)(c) substituted (S.) (1.11.1998) by 1998 c. 38, s. 140, Sch. 16 para. 67. (b) (with ss. 139. (2), 141. (1), 143. (2)); S.I. 1998/2244, art. 5

Marginal Citations

M91985 c. 69.

Determinations under Part II.

53 Determinations under Part II.

(1) A general determination may either—

(a) make the same provision for all cases; or

(b) make different provision for different cases or descriptions of cases, including different provision for different areas or for different descriptions of housing associations or housing activities;

and for the purposes of this subsection descriptions may be framed by reference to any matters whatever, including in particular, in the case of housing activities, the manner in which they are financed.

[F2. (2)The [F3[F4. Homes and Communities Agency]] shall not make a general determination under the foregoing provisions of this Part except with the approval of the Secretary of State]

(3) Before making a general determination, the [F5[F6appropriate authority]] shall consult such bodies appearing to it to be representative of housing associations as it considers appropriate; and after making such a determination, the [F5[F6appropriate authority]] shall publish the determination in such manner as it considers appropriate for bringing the determination to the notice of the associations concerned.

(4) In this section "general determination" means a determination under [F7section] 52 above, other than a determination relating solely to a particular case.

Extent Information

E1. This version of this provision extends to England and Wales only; a separate version has been created for Scotland only

Amendments (Textual)
F2. S. 53. (2) substituted (1.8.1996) by 1996 c. 52, ss. 28. (4), 231. (4)(b) (with s. 51. (4)); S.I. 1996/2048, art. 2
F3. Words in s. 53. (2) substituted (1.11.1998) by 1998 c. 38, s. 140, Sch. 16 para. 65 (with ss. 139. (2), 141. (1), 143. (2)); S.I. 1998/2244, art. 5
F4. Words in s. 53. (2) substituted (1.4.2010) by Housing and Regeneration Act 2008 (c. 17), s. 325. (1), Sch. 8 para. 48. (2); S.I. 2010/862, art. 2 (with Sch.)
F5. Words in s. 53 substituted (1.11.1998) by 1998 c. 38, s. 140, Sch. 16 para. 61. (1)(2) (with ss. 139. (2), 143. (2)); S.I. 1998/2244, art. 5
F6. Words in s. 53. (3) substituted (1.4.2010) by Housing and Regeneration Act 2008 (c. 17), s. 325. (1), Sch. 8 para. 48. (3); S.I. 2010/862, art. 2 (with Sch.)
F7. Words in s. 53. (4) substituted (1.4.2010) by Housing and Regeneration Act 2008 (c. 17), s. 325. (1), Sch. 8 para. 48. (4); S.I. 2010/862, art. 2 (with Sch.)
Modifications etc. (not altering text)
C1. S. 53 applied by section 87 of the Housing Associations Act 1985 (c. 69, SIF 61), as substituted by Local Government and Housing Act 1989 (c.42, SIF 61), s. 183
C2. Ss. 50-55 amended (1.4.1997) by 1996 c. 52, ss. 28. (6), 231. (4)(b) (with s. 51. (4)); S.I. 1997/618, art. 2 (subject to transitional provisions and savings in Sch.)
C3. S. 53 functions transferred (E.W.) (1.12.2008) by The Transfer of Housing Corporation Functions (Modifications and Transitional Provisions) Order 2008 (S.I. 2008/2839), arts. 1. (1), 2; S.I. 2008/3068, art. 2. (1)(b) (with arts. 6-12)
C4. S. 53 modified (E.W.) (1.12.2008) by The Transfer of Housing Corporation Functions (Modifications and Transitional Provisions) Order 2008 (S.I. 2008/2839), arts. 1. (1), 3, Sch. para. 4; S.I. 2008/3068, art. 2. (1)(b) (with arts. 6-12)

53 Determinations under Part II. S

(1) A general determination may either—
   (a) make the same provision for all cases; or
   (b) make different provision for different cases or descriptions of cases, including different provision for different areas or for different descriptions of [F8registered social landlords] or housing activities;
and for the purposes of this subsection descriptions may be framed by reference to any matters whatever, including in particular, in the case of housing activities, the manner in which they are financed.
(2) The Corporation shall not make a determination under the foregoing provisions of this Part except with the approval of the Secretary of State given, in the case of a general determination, with the consent of the Treasury.
(3) Before making a general determination, the Corporation shall consult such bodies appearing to it to be representative of [F9registered social landlords] as it considers appropriate; and after making such a determination, the Corporation shall publish the determination in such manner as it considers appropriate for bringing the determination to the notice of the [F9landlords] concerned.
(4) In this section "general determination" means a determination under [F7section] 52 above, other than a determination relating solely to a particular case.
Extent Information
E2. This version of this provision extends to Scotland only; a separate version has been created for England and Wales only
Amendments (Textual)
F7. Words in s. 53. (4) substituted (1.4.2010) by Housing and Regeneration Act 2008 (c. 17), s. 325. (1), Sch. 8 para. 48. (4); S.I. 2010/862, art. 2 (with Sch.)
F8. Words in s. 53. (1)(b) substituted (1.11.2001) by 2001 asp 10, s. 112, Sch. 10 para. 15. (4)(a); S.S.I. 2001/397, art. 2. (2), Sch. Table (subject to transitional provisions and savings in arts. 3-6)

F9. Words in s. 53. (3) substituted (1.11.2001) by 2001 asp 10, s. 112, Sch. 10 para. 15. (4)(b); S.S.I. 2001/397, art. 2. (2), Sch. Table (subject to transitional provisions and savings in arts. 3-6)
Modifications etc. (not altering text)
C5. S. 53 applied by section 87 of the Housing Associations Act 1985 (c. 69, SIF 61), as substituted by Local Government and Housing Act 1989 (c.42, SIF 61), s. 183

Interpretation of Part II and amendments of Housing Associations Act 1985.

59 Interpretation of Part II and amendments of Housing Associations Act 1985.

(1) In this Part of this Act—
    (a) "the 1985 Act" means the M1. Housing Associations Act 1985; and
    (b) [F1subject to subsections (1. A) and (1. B) below] expressions used in this Part have the same meaning as in the 1985 Act.
[F2. (1. A)Expressions used in sections [F352] to [F454] F5... above have the same meaning as in Part I of the Housing Act 1996, subject as follows.
(1. B)In those sections "housing activities" and "shared ownership lease", in relation to times, circumstances and purposes before the commencement of section 1 of the Housing Act 1996 (the register of social landlords), have the same meaning as in the 1985 Act.]
(2) The 1985 Act shall have effect subject to the amendments in Schedule 6 to this Act, being amendments—
    (a) extending the supervisory powers conferred by Part I of the 1985 Act;
    (b) making provision incidental to and consequential upon F6. . . the establishment by the Housing (Scotland) Act 1988 of Scottish Homes;
    (c) making provision incidental to and consequential upon [F7the] provisions of this Part of this Act and the provisions of Part IV of this Act; and
    (d) varying the grounds on which the Secretary of State may remove a member of the Housing Corporation from office.
(3) In Schedule 6 to this Act,—
    (a) Part I contains amendments of Part I of the 1985 Act, including amendments which reproduce the effect of amendments made by Schedule 3 to the Housing (Scotland) Act 1988 with respect to Scottish Homes; and
    (b) Parts II and III contain amendments of Parts II and III respectively of the 1985 Act.
(4) Without prejudice to the operation of Schedule 3 to the Housing (Scotland) Act 1988 in relation to anything done before the day appointed for the coming into force of this section, for the purpose of giving effect to the amendments in Part I of Schedule 6 to this Act, the said Schedule 3 shall be deemed never to have come into force.
Extent Information
E1. This version of this provision extends to England and Wales only; a separate version has been created for Scotland only
Amendments (Textual)
F1. Words in s. 59. (1)(b) substituted (E.W.) (1.10.1996) by S.I. 1996/2325, art. 5. (1), Sch. 2 para. 18. (9)(b)
F2. S. 59. (1. A)(1. B) inserted (E.W.) (1.10.1996) by S.I. 1996/2325, art. 5. (1), Sch. 2 para. 18. (9)(c)
F3. Word in s. 59. (1. A) substituted (1.4.2010) by Housing and Regeneration Act 2008 (c. 17), s. 325. (1), Sch. 8 para. 50; S.I. 2010/862, art. 2 (with Sch.)

F4. Word in s. 59. (1. A) substituted (E.W.) (18.1.2005) by Housing Act 2004 (c. 34), ss. 218, 270, Sch. 11 para. 6
F5. Words in s. 59. (1. A) repealed (1.4.2010) by The Housing and Regeneration Act 2008 (Consequential Provisions) Order 2010 (S.I. 2010/866), art. 1. (2), Sch. 2 para. 69, Sch. 4 (with art. 6, Sch. 3)
F6. Words in s. 59. (2)(b) repealed (E.W.) (1.11.1998) by 1998 c. 38, ss. 140, 152, Sch. 16 para. 67. (a), Sch. 18 Pt. VI (with ss. 137. (1), 139. (2), 141. (1), 143. (2)); S.I. 1998/2244, art. 5
F7. Word in s. 59. (2)(c) substituted (E.W.) (1.11.1998) by 1998 c. 38, s. 140, Sch. 16 para. 67. (b) (with ss. 139. (2), 141. (1), 143. (2)); S.I. 1998/2244, art. 5
Marginal Citations
M11985 c. 69.

59. Interpretation of Part II and amendments of Housing Associations Act 1985.S

(1) In this Part of this Act—
  (a) "the 1985 Act" means the M2. Housing Associations Act 1985; and
  (b) except as provided in section 50. (1) above, "the Corporation"[F8means [F9the Scottish Ministers]] and other expressions used in this Part have the same meaning as in the 1985 Act.
(2) The 1985 Act shall have effect subject to the amendments in Schedule 6 to this Act, being amendments—
  (a) extending the supervisory powers conferred by Part I of the 1985 Act;
  F10. (b). . . . .
  (c) making provision incidental to and consequential upon [F11the] provisions of this Part of this Act and the provisions of Part IV of this Act; and
  (d) varying the grounds on which the Secretary of State may remove a member of the Housing Corporation from office.
(3) In Schedule 6 to this Act,—
  (a) Part I contains amendments of Part I of the 1985 Act, including amendments which reproduce the effect of amendments made by Schedule 3 to the Housing (Scotland) Act 1988 with respect to Scottish Homes; and
  (b) Parts II and III contain amendments of Parts II and III respectively of the 1985 Act.
(4) Without prejudice to the operation of Schedule 3 to the Housing (Scotland) Act 1988 in relation to anything done before the day appointed for the coming into force of this section, for the purpose of giving effect to the amendments in Part I of Schedule 6 to this Act, the said Schedule 3 shall be deemed never to have come into force.
Extent Information
E2. This version of this provision extends to Scotland only; a separate version has been created for England and Wales only
Amendments (Textual)
F8. Words in s. 59. (1)(b) inserted (S.) (1.10.1996) by S.I. 1996/2325, art. 5. (1), Sch. 2 para. 19. (9)(a)
F9. Words in s. 59. (1)(b) substituted (S.) (1.11.2001) by 2001 asp 10, s. 112, Sch. 10 para. 15. (6)(a); S.S.I. 2001/397, art. 2. (2), Sch. Table (subject to transitional provisions and savings in arts. 3-6)
F10. S. 59. (2)(b) repealed (S.) (1.11.2001) by 2001 asp 10, s. 112, Sch. 10 para. 15. (6)(b); S.S.I. 2001/397, art. 2. (2), Sch. Table (subject to transitional provisions and savings in arts. 3-6)
F11. Word in s. 59. (2)(c) substituted (S.) (1.11.1998) by 1998 c. 38, s. 140, Sch. 16 para. 67. (b) (with ss. 139. (2), 141. (1), 143. (2)); S.I. 1998/2244, art. 5
Marginal Citations
M21985 c. 69.

Part III Housing Action Trust Areas

Part III Housing Action Trust Areas

Modifications etc. (not altering text)
C1. Pt. III (ss. 60-92) amended (24.9.1996) by 1996 c. 52, ss. 221. (1)(c), 232. (2)

60 Housing action trust areas.

(1) Subject to section 61 below, the Secretary of State may by order designate an area of land for which, in his opinion, it is expedient that a corporation, to be known as a housing action trust, having the functions specified in this Part of this Act, should be established.
(2) The area designated by an order under this section may comprise two or more parcels of land which—
   (a) need not be contiguous; and
   (b) need not be in the district of the same local housing authority.
(3) An order under this section shall be made by statutory instrument but no such order shall be made unless a draft of it has been laid before, and approved by a resolution of, each House of Parliament.
(4) In deciding whether to make an order under this section designating any area of land, the Secretary of State shall have regard to such matters as he thinks fit.
(5) Without prejudice to the generality of subsection (4) above, among the matters to which the Secretary of State may have regard in deciding whether to include a particular area of land in an order under this section, are—
   (a) the extent to which the housing accommodation in the area as a whole is occupied by tenants or owner-occupiers and the extent to which it is local authority housing;
   (b) the physical state and design of the housing accommodation in the area and any need to repair or improve it;
   (c) the way in which the local authority housing in the area is being managed; and
   (d) the living conditions of those who live in the area and the social conditions and general environment of the area.
(6) An area designated by an order under this section shall be known as a housing action trust area and in the following provisions of this Part of this Act—
   (a) such an area is referred to as a "designated area"; and
   (b) an order under this section is referred to as a "designation order".

61 Consultation and publicity.

(1) Before making a designation order [F1 in relation to Wales], the Secretary of State shall consult every local housing authority any part of whose district is to be included in the proposed designated area.
(2) Where the Secretary of State is considering a proposal to make a designation order, he shall use his best endeavours to secure that notice of the proposal is given to all tenants of houses in the area proposed to be designated who are either secure tenants [F2 or introductory tenants] or tenants of such description as may be prescribed by regulations.
(3) After having taken the action required by subsection (2) above, the Secretary of State shall either—
   (a) make arrangements for such independent persons as appear to him to be appropriate to conduct, in such manner as seems best to them, a ballot or poll of the tenants who have been given notice of the proposal as mentioned in that subsection with a view to establishing their opinions

about the proposal to make a designation order; or

(b) if it seems appropriate to him to do so, arrange for the conduct of a ballot or poll of those tenants in such manner as appears to him best suited to establish their opinions about the proposal.

(4) If it appears from a ballot or poll conducted as mentioned in subsection (3) above that a majority of the tenants who, on that ballot or poll, express an opinion about the proposal to make the designation order are opposed to it, the Secretary of State shall not make the order proposed.

(5) The power to make regulations under subsection (2) above shall be exercisable by the Secretary of State by statutory instrument which shall be subject to annulment in pursuance of a resolution of either House of Parliament.

(6) Consultation undertaken before the passing of this Act shall constitute as effective compliance with subsection (1) above as if undertaken after that passing.

Amendments (Textual)

F1. Words in s. 61. (1) inserted (26.5.2015) by Deregulation Act 2015 (c. 20), s. 115. (3)(l), Sch. 22 para. 9

F2. Words in s. 61. (2) inserted (12.2.1997) by S.I. 1997/74, art. 2, Sch. para. 6. (a)

62 Housing action trusts.

(1) Subject to subsection (2) below, where the Secretary of State makes a designation order, he shall, in that order or by a separate order, either—
    (a) establish a housing action trust for the designated area; or
    (b) specify as the housing action trust for the designated area a housing action trust already established for another designated area.

(2) Such a separate order as is referred to in subsection (1) above shall be made by statutory instrument but no such order shall be made unless a draft of it has been laid before, and approved by a resolution of, each House of Parliament.

(3) Subject to subsection (4) below, a housing action trust shall be a body corporate by such name as may be prescribed by the order establishing it.

(4) Where the Secretary of State makes the provision referred to in subsection (1)(b) above,—
    (a) the housing action trust specified in the order shall, by virtue of the order, be treated as established for the new designated area (as well as for any designated area for which it is already established); and
    (b) the order may alter the name of the trust to take account of the addition of the new designated area.

(5) Schedule 7 to this Act shall have effect with respect to the constitution of housing action trusts and Schedule 8 to this Act shall have effect with respect to their finances.

(6) It is hereby declared that a housing action trust is not to be regarded as the servant or agent of the Crown or as enjoying any status, immunity or privilege of the Crown and that the trust's property is not to be regarded as the property of, or property held on behalf of, the Crown.

(7) At the end of section 4 of the M1. Housing Act 1985 (descriptions of authority) there shall be added—

"(f) "housing action trust" means a housing action trust established under Part III of the Housing Act 1988"; and at the end of section 14 of the M2. Rent Act 1977 (landlord's interest belonging to local authority etc.) there shall be added—

"(h)a housing action trust established under Part III of the Housing Act 1988".

Marginal Citations

M11985 c. 68.

M21977 c. 42.

63 Objects and general powers of housing action trusts.

(1) The primary objects of a housing action trust in relation to the designated area for which it is

established shall be—

(a) to secure the repair or improvement of housing accommodation for the time being held by the trust;

(b) to secure the proper and effective management and use of that housing accommodation;

(c) to encourage diversity in the interests by virtue of which housing accommodation in the area is occupied and, in the case of accommodation which is occupied under tenancies, diversity in the identity of the landlords; and

(d) generally to secure or facilitate the improvement of living conditions [F3of those living] in the area and the social conditions and general environment of the area.

(2) Without prejudice to subsection (1) above, a housing action trust may—

(a) provide and maintain housing accommodation; and

(b) facilitate the provision of shops, advice centres and other facilities for the benefit of the community or communities who live in the designated area.

[F4. (2. A)For the avoidance of doubt it is hereby declared that it is immaterial for the purposes of this section whether action taken by a housing action trust for achieving its objects or exercising the powers conferred on it by subsection (2) above also—

(a) benefits persons who do not live in the designated area; or

(b) improves the social conditions or general environment of an area outside the designated area.]

(3) For the purpose of achieving its objects and exercising the powers conferred on it by subsection (2) above, a housing action trust may—

(a) acquire, hold, manage, reclaim and dispose of land and other property;

(b) carry out building and other operations;

(c) seek to ensure the provision of water, electricity, gas, sewerage and other services; and

(d) carry on any business or undertaking;

and may generally do anything necessary or expedient for the purposes of those objects and powers or for purposes incidental thereto.

(4) For the avoidance of doubt it is hereby declared that subsection (3) above relates only to the capacity of a housing action trust as a statutory corporation; and nothing in this section authorises such a trust to disregard any enactment or rule of law.

F5. (5). . . . .

(6) A transaction between any person and a housing action trust shall not be invalidated by reason of any failure by the trust to observe the objects in subsection (1) above or the requirement that the trust shall exercise the powers conferred by subsections (2) and (3) above for the purpose referred to in that subsection.

Amendments (Textual)

F3. Words in s. 63. (1)(d) inserted (1.10.1996) by 1996 c. 52, s. 222, Sch. 18 Pt. IV para. 25. (1)(a); S.I. 1996/2402, art. 3 (subject to transitional provisions in Sch.)

F4. S. 63. (2. A) inserted (1.10.1996) by 1996 c. 52, s. 222, Sch. 18 Pt. IV para. 25. (1)(b); S.I. 1996/2402, art. 3 (subject to transitional provisions in Sch.)

F5. S. 63. (5) repealed (2.4.2001) by 2000 c. 34, s. 9. (2), Sch. 3; S.I. 2000/566, art. 2. (1)

64 The housing action trust's proposals for its area.

(1) As soon as practicable after a housing action trust has been established for a designated area, the trust shall prepare a statement of its proposals with regard to the exercise of its functions in [F6relation to] the area.

(2) The trust shall consult every local housing authority or county council, any part of whose area lies within the designated area, with regard to the proposals contained in the statement prepared under subsection (1) above.

(3) A housing action trust shall take such steps as it considers appropriate to secure—

(a) that adequate publicity is given in the designated area to the proposals contained in the statement prepared under subsection (1) above;

(b) that those who live in the designated area are made aware that they have an opportunity to make, within such time as the trust may specify, representations to the trust with respect to those proposals; and

(c) that those who live in the designated area are given an adequate opportunity of making such representations;

and the trust shall consider any such representations as may be made within the time specified.

(4) As soon as may be after a housing action trust has complied with the requirements of subsections (1) to (3) above it shall send to the Secretary of State a copy of the statement prepared under subsection (1) above together with a report of—

(a) the steps the trust has taken to consult as mentioned in subsection (2) above and to secure the matters referred to in subsection (3) above; and

(b) the consideration it has given to points raised in the course of consultation and to representations received.

(5) At such times as a housing action trust considers appropriate or as it may be directed by the Secretary of State, the trust shall prepare a further statement of its proposals with regard to the exercise of its functions in [F6relation to] its area; and subsections (2) to (4) above shall again apply as they applied in relation to the first statement.

Amendments (Textual)

F6. Words in s. 64. (1)(5) inserted (1.10.1996) by 1996 c. 52, s. 22, Sch. 18 Pt. IV para. 25. (2); S.I. 1996/2402, art. 3 (subject to transitional provisions in Sch.)

Functions

65 Housing action trust as housing authority etc.

(1) If the Secretary of State so provides by order, in a designated area or, as the case may be, in such part of the area as may be specified in the order, the housing action trust for the area shall have such of the functions described in subsection (2) below as may be so specified.

(2) The functions referred to in subsection (1) above are—

(a) the functions conferred on a local housing authority by Parts II, VI, VII and IX to [F7. XI] and XVI of the M3. Housing Act 1985 and section 3. (1) of the M4. Chronically Sick and Disabled Persons Act 1970;

(b) the functions conferred by Part II of the M5. Housing Associations Act 1985 on a local authority, within the meaning of that Act; and

(c) the functions conferred by sections 39 to 41 of the M6. Land Compensation Act 1973 on the authority which is "the relevant authority" for the purposes of section 39 of that Act.

(3) As respects the designated area or part thereof to which an order under this section applies, on the coming into force of the order, any function conferred on a housing action trust by the order shall, according to the terms of the order, be exercisable either—

(a) by the trust instead of by the authority by which, apart from the order, the function would be exercisable; or

(b) by the trust concurrently with that authority.

(4) Any enactment under which a housing action trust is to exercise a function by virtue of an order under this section shall have effect—

(a) in relation to the trust, and

(b) where the trust is to have the function concurrently with another authority, in relation to that authority,

subject to such modifications (if any) as may be specified in the order.

(5) Where a housing action trust is to exercise functions conferred on a local housing authority by any of Parts VI, VII, IX and XI of the Housing Act 1985, section 36 of the M7. Local Government

Act 1974 (recovery by local authorities of establishment charges) shall apply to the housing action trust as if it were a local authority within the meaning of that section.

(6) Such (if any) of the provisions of Parts XVII and XVIII of the Housing Act 1985 (compulsory purchase, land acquisition and general provisions) as may be specified in an order under this section shall have effect in relation to a housing action trust subject to such modifications as may be specified in the order.

(7) An order under this section—

(a) may contain such savings and transitional and supplementary provisions as appear to the Secretary of State to be appropriate; and

(b) shall be made by statutory instrument which shall be subject to annulment in pursuance of a resolution of either House of Parliament.

Amendments (Textual)

F7. Word in s. 65. (2)(a) substituted (3.5.1997) by 1996 c. 62, s. 80. (2)(b); S.I. 1997/350, art. 2

Marginal Citations

M31985 c. 68.

M41970 c. 44.

M51985 c. 69.

M61973 c. 26.

M71974 c. 7.

66 Planning control.

(1) A housing action trust may submit to the Secretary of State proposals for the development of land within its designated area and the Secretary of State, after consultation with the local planning authority within whose area the land is situated and with any other local authority which appears to him to be concerned, may approve any such proposals either with or without modification.

(2) Without prejudice to the generality of the powers conferred by [F8sections 59 to 61 of the 1990 Act], a special development order made by the Secretary of State under [F8section 59] with respect to a designated area may grant permission for any development of land in accordance with proposals approved under subsection (1) above, subject to such conditions, if any (including conditions requiring details of any proposed development to be submitted to the local planning authority), as may be specified in the order.

(3) The Secretary of State shall give to a housing action trust such directions with regard to the disposal of land held by it and with respect to the development by it of such land as appear to him to be necessary or expedient for securing, so far as practicable, the preservation of any features of special architectural or historical interest and, in particular, of any buildings included in any list compiled or approved or having effect as if compiled or approved under [F9section 1 of the Planning (Listed Buildings and Conservation Areas) Act 1990] (which relates to the compilation or approval by the Secretary of State of lists of buildings of special architectural or historical interest).

(4) Any reference in this section to the local planning authority,—

(a) in relation to land in [F10. Wales,] Greater London or a metropolitan county, is a reference to the authority which is the local planning authority as ascertained in accordance with [F11sections 1 and 2 of the 1990 Act]; and

(b) in relation to other land, is a reference to the district planning authority and also (in relation to proposals for any development which is a county matter, as defined in [F12paragraph 1 of Schedule 1 to the 1990 Act]) to the county planning authority.

Amendments (Textual)

F8. Words substituted by Planning (Consequential Provisions) Act 1990 (c. 11, SIF 123: 1, 2), s. 4, Sch. 2 para. 79. (2)(a)

F9. Words substituted by Planning (Consequential Provisions) Act 1990 (c. 11, SIF 123: 1, 2), s. 4, Sch. 2 para. 79. (2)(b)

F10. Word in s. 66. (4)(a) inserted (1.4.1996) by 1994 c. 19, s. 22. (2), Sch. 8 para. 9. (1) (with ss. 54. (7), 55. (5), Sch. 17 paras. 22. (1), 23. (2)); S.I. 1996/396, 3, Sch. 1

F11. Words substituted by Planning (Consequential Provisions) Act 1990 (c. 11, SIF 123: 1, 2), s. 4, Sch. 2 para. 79. (2)(c)

F12. Words substituted by Planning (Consequential Provisions) Act 1990 (c. 11, SIF 123: 1, 2), s. 4, Sch. 2 para. 79. (2)(d)

67 Housing action trust as planning authority.

(1) [F13. The Secretary of State may by order provide that, for such purposes of Part III of the 1990 Act and sections 67 and 73 of the Planning (Listed Buildings and Conservation Areas) Act 1990,] and in relation to such kinds of development as may be specified in the order, a housing action trust shall be the local planning authority for the whole or such part as may be so specified of its designated area . . . F14

(2) An order under subsection (1) above may provide—
   (a) that any enactment relating to local planning authorities shall not apply to the trust; and
   (b) that any such enactment which applies to the trust shall apply to it subject to such modifications as may be specified in the order.

(3) An order made by the Secretary of State may provide—
   (a) that, subject to any modifications specified in the order, a housing action trust specified in the order shall have, in the whole or any part of its designated area . . . F15, such of the functions conferred by [F16the provisions mentioned in subsection (3. A) below] as may be so specified; and
   (b) that such of the provisions of [F17. Part VI and sections 249 to 251 and 258 of the 1990 Act and sections 32 to 37 of the Planning (Listed Buildings and Conservation Areas) Act 1990] as are mentioned in the order shall have effect, in relation to the housing action trust specified in the order and to land in the trust's area, subject to the modifications there specified.

[F18. (3. A)The provisions referred to in subsection (3)(a) above are sections 96, 100, 104 [F19171. C, 171. D],172 to 185, 187 to 202, 206 to 222, 224, 225, 231 and 320 to 336 of and paragraph 11 of Schedule 9 to the 1990 Act, Chapters I, II and IV of Part I and sections 54 to 56, 59 to 61, 66, 68 to 72, 74 to 76 and 88 of the Planning (Listed Buildings and Conservation Areas) Act 1990 and sections 4 to 15, 17 to 21, 23 to [F2026. AA, 36 and 36. A] of the Planning (Hazardous Substances) Act 1990.]

(4) An order under subsection (3) above may provide that, for the purposes of any of the provisions specified in the order, any enactment relating to local planning authorities shall apply to the housing action trust specified in the order subject to such modifications as may be so specified.

(5) (6). F21

(7) Any power to make an order under this section shall be exercisable by statutory instrument which shall be subject to annulment in pursuance of a resolution of either House of Parliament; and any such order shall have effect subject to such savings and transitional provisions as may be specified in the order.

Amendments (Textual)

F13. Words substituted by Planning (Consequential Provisions) Act 1990 (c. 11, SIF 123: 1, 2), s. 4, Sch. 2 paras. 79. (3)(a)

F14. Words repealed by Planning (Consequential Provisions) Act 1990 (c. 11, SIF 123: 1, 2), ss. 3, 4, Sch. 1 Pt. I, Sch. 2 para. 79. (3)(a)

F15. Words repealed by Planning (Consequential Provisions) Act 1990 (c. 11, SIF 123: 1, 2), s. 3, Sch. 1 Pt. I

F16. Words substituted by Planning (Consequential Provisions) Act 1990 (c. 11, SIF 123: 1, 2), s. 4, Sch. 2 para. 79. (3)(b)(i)

F17. Words substituted by Planning (Consequential Provisions) Act 1990 (c. 11, SIF 123: 1, 2), s. 4, Sch. 2 para. 79. (3)(b)(ii)

F18. S. 67. (3. A) inserted by Planning (Consequential Provisions) Act 1990 (c. 11, SIF 123: 1, 2), s. 4, Sch. 2 para. 79. (3)(c)
F19. Words in s. 67. (3. A) inserted (2.1.1992) by Planning and Compensation Act 1991 (c. 34, SIF 123:1), s. 32, Sch. 7, para.7 (with s. 84. (5)); S.I. 1991/2905, art.3, Sch.
F20. Words in s. 67. (3. A) substituted (2.1.1992) by Planning and Compensation Act 1991 (c. 34, SIF 123:1), s. 25, Sch. 3, Pt. II, para.18 (with s. 84. (5)); S.I. 1991/2905, art.3
F21. S. 67. (5)(6) repealed by Planning (Consequential Provisions) Act 1990 (c. 11, SIF 123: 1, 2), ss. 3, 4, Sch. 1 Pt. I, Sch. 2 para. 79. (3)(d)

68 Public health.

(1) The Secretary of State may by order provide that, in relation to premises comprising or consisting of housing accommodation, a housing action trust shall have in its designated area (or in such part of its designated area as may be specified in the order) the functions conferred on a local authority—
    (a) by sections 83 and 84 of the M8. Public Health Act 1936 (the "1936 Act") and section 36 of the M9. Public Health Act 1961 (all of which relate to filthy or verminous premises or articles);
    (b) by any enactment contained in Part III (nuisances and offensive trades) of the 1936 Act;
    (c) by so much of Part XII of the 1936 Act as relates to any of the enactments mentioned in paragraphs (a) and (b) above; and
    (d) by Part I of the M10. Prevention of Damage by Pests Act 1949 (rats and mice).
(2) On the order coming into force, the trust shall have the functions conferred in relation to the designated area (or part) instead of or concurrently with any such authority, depending on the terms of the order.
(3) The order may provide that any enactment under which the trust is to exercise functions by virtue of the order shall have effect in relation to the trust and, where the trust is to have any function concurrently with another authority, in relation to that authority, as modified by the order.
(4) Where an order under this section provides that a housing action trust shall have the functions conferred upon a local authority by Part III of the 1936 Act, section 36 of the M11. Local Government Act 1974 (recovery by local authorities of establishment charges) shall apply to the housing action trust as if it were a local authority within the meaning of that section.
(5) The order shall have effect subject to such savings and transitional and supplementary provisions as may be specified in the order.
(6) The power to make an order under this section shall be exercisable by statutory instrument which shall be subject to annulment in pursuance of a resolution of either House of Parliament.
Marginal Citations
M81936 c. 49.
M91961 c. 64.
M101949 c. 55.
M111974 c. 7.

69 Highways.

(1) When any street works have been executed [F22on any land in a designated area which was then or has since become a private street (or part of a private street)], the housing action trust may serve a notice on the street works authority requiring it to declare the street (or part) to be a highway which for the purposes of the M12. Highways Act 1980 is a highway maintainable at the public expense.
(2) Within the period of two months beginning on the date of the service of a notice under subsection (1) above, the street works authority may appeal against the notice to the Secretary of State F23. . .
(3) After considering any representations made to him by the housing action trust and the street

works authority, the Secretary of State shall determine an appeal under subsection (2) above by setting aside or confirming the notice under subsection (1) above (with or without modifications).
(4) Where, under subsection (3) above, the Secretary of State confirms a notice,—
 (a) he may at the same time impose conditions (including financial conditions) upon the housing action trust with which the trust must comply in order for the notice to take effect, and
 (b) the highway (or part) shall become a highway maintainable at the public expense with effect from such date as the Secretary of State may specify.
(5) Where a street works authority neither complies with the notice under subsection (1) above, nor appeals under subsection (2) above, the street (or part) concerned shall become a highway maintainable at the public expense upon the expiry of the period of two months referred to in subsection (2) above.
(6) In this section "private street" and "street works authority" have the same meanings as in Part XI of the M13. Highways Act 1980.
Amendments (Textual)
F22. Words in s. 69. (1) substituted (11.10.1993) by 1993 c. 28, s. 182. (1); S.I. 1993/2134, arts. 2, 4
F23. Words in s. 69. (2) repealed (11.10.1993) by 1993 c. 28, ss. 182. (2), 187. (2), Sch. 22; S.I. 1993/2134, arts. 2, 4
Marginal Citations
M12 1980 c. 66.
M13 1980 c. 66.

F24 70. . . . .

Amendments (Textual)
F24. S. 70 repealed (20.1.1997) by 1996 c. 52, s. 227, Sch. 19 Pt. VIII; S.I. 1996/2959, art. 2 (subject to transitional provisions in Sch. para. 1)

71 Power to give financial assistance.

(1) For the purpose of achieving its objects a housing action trust may, with the consent of the Secretary of State, give financial assistance to any person.
(2) Financial assistance under subsection (1) above may be given in any form and, in particular, may be given by way of—
 (a) grants,
 (b) loans,
 (c) guarantees,
 (d) incurring expenditure for the benefit of the person assisted, or
 (e) purchasing loan or share capital in a company.
(3) Financial assistance under subsection (1) above may be given on such terms as the housing action trust, with the consent of the Secretary of State, considers appropriate.
(4) Any consent under this section—
 (a) may be given either unconditionally or subject to conditions; and
 (b) may be given in relation to a particular case or in relation to such description of cases as may be specified in the consent;
and the reference in subsection (3) above to the consent of the Secretary of State is a reference to his consent given with the approval of the Treasury.
(5) The terms referred to in subsection (3) above may, in particular, include provision as to—
 (a) the circumstances in which the assistance must be repaid or otherwise made good to the housing action trust and the manner in which that is to be done; or
 (b) the circumstances in which the housing action trust is entitled to recover the proceeds or part of the proceeds of any disposal of land or buildings in respect of which assistance was provided.

(6) Any person receiving assistance under subsection (1) above shall comply with the terms on which it is given and compliance may be enforced by the housing action trust.

72 Directions as to exercise of functions.

(1) In the exercise of its functions, a housing action trust shall comply with any directions given by the Secretary of State.
(2) Directions given by the Secretary of State may be of a general or particular character and may be varied or revoked by subsequent directions.
(3) The Secretary of State shall publish any direction given under this section.
(4) A transaction between any person and a housing action trust acting in purported exercise of its powers under this Part of this Act shall not be void by reason only that the transaction was carried out in contravention of a direction given under this section; and a person dealing with a housing action trust shall not be concerned to see or enquire whether a direction under this section has been given or complied with.

73 Transfer of functions.

(1) If, in the case of any designated area, it appears to the Secretary of State that it is expedient that the functions of a housing action trust established for the area should be transferred—
   (a) to the housing action trust established for another designated area, or
   (b) to a new housing action trust to be established for the area,
he may by order provide for the dissolution of the first-mentioned trust and for the transfer of its functions, property, rights and liabilities to the trust referred to in paragraph (a) above, or, as the case may be, to a new housing action trust established for the area by the order.
(2) Where an order under this section provides for the functions of a housing action trust established for a designated area to be transferred to the housing action trust established for another designated area—
   (a) the latter trust shall, by virtue of the order, be treated as established for the first-mentioned designated area (as well as the area referred to in subsection (1)(a) above); and
   (b) the order may alter the name of the latter trust in such manner as appears to the Secretary of State to be expedient.
(3) Before making an order under this section the Secretary of State shall consult the housing action trust whose functions are to be transferred and also, in a case falling within subsection (1)(a) above, the housing action trust to whom the functions are to be transferred.
(4) An order under this section shall be made by statutory instrument but no such order shall be made unless a draft of it has been laid before, and approved by a resolution of, each House of Parliament.

Transfer of housing accommodation etc.

74 Transfer of land and other property to housing action trusts.

(1) The Secretary of State may by order provide for the transfer from a local housing authority to a housing action trust of—
   (a) all or any of the authority's local authority housing situated in the designated area; and
   (b) any other land held or provided in connection with that local authority housing.
(2) Without prejudice to the powers under subsection (1) above, if in the opinion of the Secretary of State a housing action trust requires for the purposes of its functions any land which, though not falling within that subsection, is situated in the designated area and held (for whatever purpose) by

a local authority, the Secretary of State may by order provide for the transfer of that land to the trust.

(3) The Secretary of State may by order transfer from a local housing authority or other local authority to a housing action trust so much as appears to him to be appropriate of any property which is held or used by the authority in connection with any local authority housing or other land transferred to the trust under subsection (1) or subsection (2) above; and for this purpose "property" includes chattels of any description and rights and liabilities, whether arising by contract or otherwise.

(4) A transfer of any local authority housing or other land or property under the preceding provisions of this section shall be on such terms, including financial terms, as the Secretary of State thinks fit; and an order under this section may provide that, notwithstanding anything in section 141 of the M14. Law of Property Act 1925 (rent and benefit of lessee's covenants to run with the reversion), any rent or other sum which—

(a) arises under a tenancy of any local authority housing or other land transferred to the housing action trust under subsection (1) or subsection (2) above, and

(b) falls due before the date of the transfer,

shall continue to be recoverable by the local housing authority or, as the case may be, the local authority to the exclusion of the trust and of any other person in whom the reversion on the tenancy may become vested.

(5) Without prejudice to the generality of subsection (4) above, the financial terms referred to in that subsection may include provision for payments by a local authority (as well as or instead of payments to a local authority); and the transfer from a local housing authority or other local authority of any local authority housing or other land or property by virtue of this section shall not be taken to give rise to any right to compensation.

(6) Where an order is made under this section—

(a) payments made by a local authority as mentioned in subsection (5) above shall be [F25[F26capital expenditure for the purposes of Chapter 1 of Part 1 of the Local Government Act 2003 (capital finance)];]

(b) unless the order otherwise provides, payments made to a local authority as mentioned in subsection (5) above shall be regarded for the purposes of [F27section 9. (1) of that Act as sums received by the authority in respect of the disposal by it of an interest in a capital asset.]

(7) Any power to make an order under this section shall be exercisable by statutory instrument which shall be subject to annulment in pursuance of a resolution of either House of Parliament.

(8) In this section "local authority" means any of the following—

(a) a local housing authority;

(b) the council of a county;

(c) the Inner London Education Authority;

(d) an authority established by an order under section 10. (1) of the M15. Local Government Act 1985 (waste disposal);

(e) a joint authority established by Part IV of that Act; F28. . .

(f) a residuary body established by Part VII of that Act.

[F29. (fa)an economic prosperity board established under section 88 of the Local Democracy, Economic Development and Construction Act 2009;

(fb) a combined authority established under section 103 of that Act;]

[F30. (fc)a fire and rescue authority created by an order under section 4. A of the Fire and Rescue Services Act 2004;]

[F31. (g)the London Fire Commissioner.]

Amendments (Textual)

F25. Words substituted by S.I. 1990/778, art. 2, Sch. para. 1. (a)

F26. Words in s. 74. (6)(a) substituted (31.1.2008) by Local Government and Public Involvement in Health Act 2007 (c. 28), ss. 238. (1)(a), 245; S.I. 2008/172, art. 2. (1)(t) (as amended by S.I. 2008/337. art. 3)

F27. Words in s. 74. (6)(b) substituted (31.1.2008) by Local Government and Public Involvement

in Health Act 2007 (c. 28), ss. 238. (1)(b), 245; S.I. 2008/172, art. 2. (1)(t) (as amended by S.I. 2008/337. art. 3)
F28. Word in s. 74. (8)(e) repealed (3.7.2000) by 1999 c. 29, s. 423, Sch. 34 Pt. VIII (with Sch. 12 para. 9. (1)); S.I. 2000/1094, art. 4. (i)
F29. S. 74. (8)(fa)(fb) inserted (17.12.2009) by Local Democracy, Economic Development and Construction Act 2009 (c. 20), ss. 119, 148. (8), 149, Sch. 6 para. 79. (2); S.I. 2009/3318, art. 2
F30. S. 74. (8)(fc) inserted (31.1.2017 for specified purposes, 3.4.2017 in so far as not already in force) by Policing and Crime Act 2017 (c. 3), s. 183. (1)(5)(e), Sch. 1 para. 57; S.I. 2017/399, reg. 2, Sch. para. 38
F31. S. 74. (8)(g) substituted (31.1.2017 for specified purposes) by Policing and Crime Act 2017 (c. 3), s. 183. (1)(5)(e), Sch. 2 para. 82
Marginal Citations
M141925 c. 20.
M151985 c. 51.

75 Supplementary provisions as to transfer orders.

(1) In this section a "transfer order" means an order under any of subsections (1) to (3) of section 74 above and, in relation to a transfer order, "the transferor authority" means the local housing authority or other local authority from whom local authority housing or other land or property is or is to be transferred by the order.
(2) Before making a transfer order, the Secretary of State shall consult the transferor authority with respect to—
   (a) the local authority housing or other land or property which it is proposed should be transferred by the order; and
   (b) the terms of the proposed transfer.
(3) Before making a transfer order with respect to any local authority housing or other land, the Secretary of State shall take such steps as appear to him to be appropriate to bring the proposed transfer to the attention of any secure tenant [F32or introductory tenant] or other person (other than a local authority) having an interest in the property proposed to be transferred as lessor, lessee, mortgagor or mortgagee.
(4) In connection with any transfer made by it, a transfer order may contain such incidental, consequential, transitional or supplementary provisions as appear to the Secretary of State to be necessary or expedient and, in particular, may—
   (a) apply, with or without modification, any provision made by or under any enactment; and
   (b) modify the operation of any provision made by or under any enactment.
Amendments (Textual)
F32. Words in s. 75. (3) inserted (12.2.1997) by S.I. 1997/74, art. 2, Sch. para. 6. (b)

Vesting and acquisition of land

76 Vesting by order in housing action trust.

(1) Subject to subsections (2) and (3) below, the Secretary of State may by order provide that land specified in the order which is vested in statutory undertakers or any other public body or in a wholly-owned subsidiary of a public body shall vest in a housing action trust established or to be established for the designated area in which the land is situated.
(2) An order under this section may not specify land vested in statutory undertakers which is used for the purpose of carrying on their statutory undertakings or which is held for that purpose.
(3) In the case of land vested in statutory undertakers, the power to make an order under this

section shall be exercisable by the Secretary of State and the appropriate Minister.
(4) Part I of Schedule 9 to this Act shall have effect for supplementing the preceding provisions of this section.
(5) An order under this section shall have the same effect as a declaration under the M16. Compulsory Purchase (Vesting Declarations) Act 1981 except that, in relation to such an order, the enactments mentioned in Part II of Schedule 9 to this Act shall have effect subject to the modifications specified in that Part.
(6) Compensation under the M17. Land Compensation Act 1961, as applied by subsection (5) above and Part II of Schedule 9 to this Act, shall be assessed by reference to values current on the date the order under this section comes into force.
[(6. A)No order shall be made under this section in relation to a universal service provider (within the meaning of [F33. Part 3 of the Postal Services Act 2011]).]
(7) An order under this section shall be made by statutory instrument but no such order shall be made unless a draft of it has been laid before, and approved by a resolution of, each House of Parliament.
Amendments (Textual)
F33. Words in s. 76. (6. A) substituted (1.10.2011) by Postal Services Act 2011 (c. 5), s. 93. (2)(3), Sch. 12 para. 129; S.I. 2011/2329, art. 3
Modifications etc. (not altering text)
C2. S. 76. (6. A) inserted (26.3.2001) by S.I. 2001/1149, art. 3. (1), Sch. 1 para. 75. (2)
Marginal Citations
M161981 c. 66.
M171961 c. 33.

77 Acquisition by housing action trust.

(1) For the purposes of achieving its objects (and performing any of its functions), a housing action trust may acquire land within its designated area by agreement or, on being authorised to do so by the Secretary of State, compulsorily.
(2) A housing action trust may acquire (by agreement or, on being authorised to do so by the Secretary of State, compulsorily)—
   (a) land adjacent to the designated area which the trust requires for purposes connected with the discharge of its functions in the area; and
   (b) land outside the designated area (whether or not adjacent to it) which the trust requires for the provision of services in connection with the discharge of its functions in the area.
(3) Where a housing action trust exercises its powers under subsection (1) or subsection (2) above in relation to land which forms part of a common or open space or fuel or field garden allotment, the trust may acquire (by agreement or, on being authorised to do so by the Secretary of State, compulsorily) land for giving in exchange for the land acquired.
(4) Subject to section 78 below, the M18. Acquisition of Land Act 1981 shall apply in relation to the compulsory acquisition of land in pursuance of the preceding provisions of this section.
(5) A housing action trust may be authorised by the Secretary of State, by means of a compulsory purchase order, to purchase compulsorily such new rights as are specified in the order—
   (a) being rights over land in the designated area and which the trust requires for the purposes of its functions;
   (b) being rights over land adjacent to the designated area and which the trust requires for purposes connected with the discharge of its functions in the area; and
   (c) being rights over land outside the designated area (whether or not adjacent to it) and which the trust requires for the provision of services in connection with the discharge of its functions in the area.
(6) In subsection (5) above—
   (a) "new rights" means rights which are not in existence when the order specifying them is

made; and

(b) "compulsory purchase order" has the same meaning as in the Acquisition of Land Act 1981;

and Schedule 3 to that Act shall apply to a compulsory purchase of a right by virtue of subsection (5) above.

(7) The provisions of Part I of the M19. Compulsory Purchase Act 1965 (so far as applicable), other than section 31, shall apply in relation to the acquisition of land by agreement under this section; and in that Part as so applied "land" has the meaning given by the M20. Interpretation Act 1978.

Marginal Citations

M181981 c. 67.

M191965 c. 56.

M201978 c. 30.

78 Supplementary provisions as to vesting, acquisition and compensation.

(1) The M21. Acquisition of Land Act 1981, as applied by section 77 above, shall have effect subject to the modifications in Part I of Schedule 10 to this Act.

(2) The supplementary provisions in Parts II and III of that Schedule shall have effect, being,—

(a) as to those in Part II, provisions about land vested in or acquired by a housing action trust under this Part of this Act; and

(b) as to those in Part III, provisions about the acquisition by a housing action trust of rights over land under section 77. (5) above.

F34. (3). . . . .

F34. (4). . . . .

Amendments (Textual)

F34. S. 78. (3)(4) omitted (22.9.2017) by virtue of Neighbourhood Planning Act 2017 (c. 20), ss. 32. (6), 46. (1); S.I. 2017/936, reg. 3. (b) (with reg. 4)

Marginal Citations

M211981 c. 67.

Disposals of land

79 Disposal of land by housing action trusts.

(1) Subject to subsection (2) below and any directions given by the Secretary of State, a housing action trust may, with the consent of the Secretary of State, dispose of any land for the time being held by it to such persons, in such manner and on such terms as it considers expedient for the purpose of achieving its objects.

(2) A housing action trust may not dispose of a house which is for the time being subject to a secure tenancy [F35or an introductory tenant] except—

[F36. (za)to a non-profit registered provider of social housing,]

[F37. (a)to a registered social landlord (within the meaning of Part I of the Housing Act 1996), or]

(b) to a local housing authority or other local authority F38. . .;

but this subsection does not apply to a disposal under Part V of the M22. Housing Act 1985 (the right to buy).

(3) The reference in subsection (1) above to disposing of land includes a reference to granting an interest in or right over land and, in particular, the granting of an option to purchase the freehold

of, or any other interest in, land is a disposal for the purposes of that subsection; and a consent under that subsection given to such a disposal extends to a disposal made in pursuance of the option.

(4) The consent of the Secretary of State referred to in subsection (1) above may be given—
  (a) either generally to all housing action trusts or to a particular trust or description of trust;
  (b) either in relation to particular land or in relation to land of a particular description; and
  (c) subject to conditions.

(5) Without prejudice to the generality of subsection (4)(c) above, consent under subsection (1) above may, in particular, be given subject to conditions as to the price, premium or rent to be obtained by the housing action trust on the disposal, including conditions as to the amount by which, on the disposal of a house by way of sale or by the grant or assignment of a lease at a premium, the price or premium is to be, or may be, discounted by the housing action trust.

[F39. (5. A) Subsection (2) above has effect as if the saving effected by paragraph 9 of the Schedule to the Housing Act 1996 (Commencement No. 3 and Transitional Provisions) Order 1996 related also to disposals of houses subject to introductory tenancies.]

F40. (6). . . . .
F40. (7). . . . .
F40. (8). . . . .
F40. (9). . . . .
F40. (10). . . . .

(11) In section 45. (2)(b) of the M23. Housing Act 1985 (which defines "public sector authority" for the purposes of provisions of that Act restricting service charges payable after disposal of a house) after the entry "an urban development corporation" there shall be inserted "a housing action trust".

(12) A housing action trust shall be treated as a local authority for the purposes of sections 18 to 30 of the M24. Landlord and Tenant Act 1985 (service charges).

(13) The provisions of Schedule 11 to this Act shall have effect in the case of certain disposals of houses by a housing action trust.

Amendments (Textual)

F35. Words in s. 79. (2) inserted (12.2.1997) by S.I. 1997/74, art. 2, Sch. para. 6. (c)

F36. S. 79. (2)(za) inserted (1.4.2010) by The Housing and Regeneration Act 2008 (Consequential Provisions) Order 2010 (S.I. 2010/866), art. 1. (2), Sch. 2 para. 70 (with art. 6, Sch. 3)

F37. S. 79. (2): paragraph (a) and word "or" at the end of the paragraph substituted (1.10.1996) by 1996 c. 52, s. 55, Sch. 3 para. 11 (with s. 51. (4); S.I. 1996/2402, art. 3

F38. Words in s. 79. (2)(b) repealed (11.10.1993) by 1993 c. 28, ss. 124. (1), 187. (2), Sch. 22; S.I. 1993/2134, arts. 2, 4, Sch. 2 (with Sch. 1 para. 5).

F39. S. 79. (5. A) inserted (12.2.1997) by S.I. 1997/74, art. 2, Sch. para. 6. (d)

F40. S. 79. (6)-(10) repealed (1.10.1996) by 1996 c. 52, s. 227, Sch. 19 Pt. I; S.I. 1996/2402, art. 3

Modifications etc. (not altering text)

C3. S. 79. (1)(2) excluded (1.11.1993) by 1993 c. 28, ss. 37, 56. (7), Sch. 10 para. 1. (2)(c); S.I. 1993/2134, arts. 2, 5

Marginal Citations

M221985 c. 68.
M231985 c. 68.
M241985 c. 70.

80 Disposals made without consent.

(1) Any disposal of a house by a housing action trust which is made without the consent required by section 79. (1) above is void unless—
  (a) the disposal is to an individual (or to two or more individuals); and
  (b) the disposal does not extend to any other house.

(2) Subject to subsection (1) above,—

(a) a disposal of any land made by a housing action trust shall not be invalid by reason only that it is made without the consent required by section 79. (1) above; and

(b) a person dealing with a housing action trust or with a person claiming under such a trust shall not be concerned to see or enquire whether any consent required by section 79. (1) above has been obtained.

81 Consent required for certain subsequent disposals.

(1) If, by a material disposal, a housing action trust disposes of a house which is for the time being subject to a secure tenancy [F41or an introductory tenancy] to such a person as is mentioned in [F42 section 79. (2)(a)] above (in this section referred to as an "approved person"), the conveyance shall contain a statement that the requirement of this section as to consent applies to a subsequent disposal of the house by the approved person.

(2) For the purposes of this section a "material disposal" is—

(a) the transfer of the fee simple;

(b) the transfer of an existing lease; or

(c) the grant of a new lease; and "the conveyance" means the instrument by which such a disposal is effected.

(3) An approved person who acquires a house on a material disposal falling within subsection (1) above shall not dispose of it except with the consent of the [F43appropriate authority] which may be given either unconditionally or subject to conditions; but nothing in this subsection shall apply in relation to an exempt disposal as defined in subsection (8) below.

[F44. (3. A)In this section "the appropriate authority" means—

F45. (a)................................

(b) in relation to [F46 a] disposal of land in England, the Secretary of State, and

(c) in relation to a disposal of land in Wales, the Welsh Ministers.]

(4) Where an estate or interest in a house acquired by an approved person as mentioned in subsection (3) above has been mortgaged or charged, the prohibition in that subsection applies also to a disposal by the mortgagee or chargee in exercise of a power of sale or leasing, whether or not the disposal is in the name of the approved person; and in any case where—

(a) by operation of law or by virtue of an order of a court, property which has been acquired by an approved person passes or is transferred to another person, and

(b) that passing or transfer does not constitute a disposal for which consent is required under subsection (3) above,

this section (including, where there is more than one such passing or transfer, this subsection) shall apply as if the other person to whom the property passes or is transferred were the approved person.

(5) Before giving consent in respect of a disposal to which subsection (3) above applies, the [F47appropriate authority]—

(a) shall satisfy [F48itself] that the person who is seeking the consent has taken appropriate steps to consult every tenant of any house proposed to be disposed of; and

(b) shall have regard to the responses of any such tenants to that consultation.

F49. (6)................................

(7) No consent shall be required under F50... [F51section 9 or 42 of the Housing Act 1996 or section 9 of the Housing Associations Act 1985] for any disposal in respect of which consent is given [F52under this section].

(8) In this section an "exempt disposal" means—

(a) the disposal of a dwelling-house to a person having the right to buy it under Part V of the M25 Housing Act 1985 (whether the disposal is in fact made under that Part or otherwise);

[F53. (ab)the disposal of a dwelling-house to a person having the right to acquire it under [F54section 180 of the Housing and Regeneration Act 2008 or] Part I of the Housing Act 1996 (see sections 16 and 17 of that Act), whether or not the disposal is in fact made under provisions having effect by virtue of section 17 of that Act]

(b) a compulsory disposal, within the meaning of Part V of the Housing Act 1985;

(c) the disposal of an easement or rentcharge;

(d) the disposal of an interest by way of security for a loan;

(e) the grant of a secure tenancy or what would be a secure tenancy but for any of paragraphs 2 to 12 of Schedule I to the Housing Act 1985;

(f) the grant of an assured tenancy or an assured agricultural occupancy, within the meaning of Part I of this Act, or what would be such a tenancy or occupancy but for any of paragraphs 4 to 8 of Schedule I to this Act; and

(g) the transfer of an interest held on trust for any person where the disposal is made in connection with the appointment of a new trustee or in connection with the discharge of any trustee.

(9) Where the title of a housing action trust to a house which is disposed of by a material disposal falling within subsection (1) above is not registered—

F55. (a). . . . .

(b) the housing action trust shall give the approved person a certificate stating that it is entitled to make the disposal subject only to such encumbrances, rights and interests as are stated in the conveyance or summarised in the certificate; and

(c) for the purpose of registration of title, the Chief Land Registrar shall accept such a certificate as evidence of the facts stated in it, but if as a result he has to meet a claim against him under the [F56. Land Registration Act 2002] the housing action trust is liable to indemnify him.

[F57. (10) Where the Chief Land Registrar approves an application for registration of—

(a) a disposition of registered land, or

(b) the approved person's title under a disposition of unregistered land,

and the instrument effecting the disposition contains the statement required by subsection (1) above, he shall enter in the register a restriction reflecting the limitation under this section on subsequent disposal.]

(11) In this section references to disposing of a house include references to—

(a) granting or disposing of any interest in the house;

(b) entering into a contract to dispose of the house or to grant or dispose of any such interest; and

(c) granting an option to acquire the house or any such interest;

and any reference to a statement or certificate is a reference to a statement or, as the case may be, certificate in a form approved by the Chief Land Registrar.

Amendments (Textual)

F41. Words in s. 81. (1) inserted (12.2.1997) by S.I. 1997/74, art. 2, Sch. para. 6. (e)

F42. Words in s. 81. (1) substituted (6.4.2017) by Housing and Planning Act 2016 (c. 22), s. 216. (3), Sch. 4 para. 3. (2); S.I. 2017/75, reg. 4

F43. Words in s. 81. (3) substituted (1.4.2010) by Housing and Regeneration Act 2008 (c. 17), ss. 191. (2)(a), 325. (1) (with s. 189); S.I. 2010/862, art. 2 (with Sch.)

F44. S. 81. (3. A) inserted (1.4.2010) by Housing and Regeneration Act 2008 (c. 17), ss. 191. (2)(b), 325. (1) (with s. 189); S.I. 2010/862, art. 2 (with Sch.)

F45. S. 81. (3. A)(a) omitted (6.4.2017) by virtue of Housing and Planning Act 2016 (c. 22), s. 216. (3), Sch. 4 para. 3. (3)(a); S.I. 2017/75, reg. 4

F46. Word in s. 81. (3. A)(b) substituted (6.4.2017) by Housing and Planning Act 2016 (c. 22), s. 216. (3), Sch. 4 para. 3. (3)(b); S.I. 2017/75, reg. 4

F47. Words in s. 81. (5) substituted (1.4.2010) by Housing and Regeneration Act 2008 (c. 17), ss. 191. (2)(c), 325. (1) (with s. 189); S.I. 2010/862, art. 2 (with Sch.)

F48. Word in s. 81. (5)(a) substituted (1.4.2010) by Housing and Regeneration Act 2008 (c. 17), ss. 191. (2)(d), 325. (1) (with s. 189); S.I. 2010/862, art. 2 (with Sch.)

F49. S. 81. (6) repealed (1.4.2010) by Housing and Regeneration Act 2008 (c. 17), ss. 191. (2)(e), 325. (1), Sch. 16 (with s. 189); S.I. 2010/862, arts. 2, 3 (with Sch.)

F50. Words in s. 81. (7) omitted (6.4.2017) by virtue of Housing and Planning Act 2016 (c. 22), s. 216. (3), Sch. 4 para. 3. (4); S.I. 2017/75, reg. 4
F51. Words in s. 81. (7) substituted (1.10.1996) by S.I. 1996/2325, art. 5. (1), Sch. 2 para. 18. (10)(b)
F52. Words in s. 81. (7) substituted (1.11.1998) by 1998 c. 38, s. 140, Sch. 16 para. 68. (b)(with ss. 139. (2), 141. (1), 143. (2)); S.I. 1998/2244, art. 5
F53. S. 81. (8)(ab) inserted (1.4.1997) by S.I. 1997/627, art. 2, Sch. para. 6
F54. Words in s. 81. (8)(ab) inserted (1.4.2010) by The Housing and Regeneration Act 2008 (Consequential Provisions) Order 2010 (S.I. 2010/866), art. 1. (2), Sch. 2 para. 71. (4) (with art. 6, Sch. 3)
F55. S. 81. (9)(a) repealed (1.4.1998) by 1997 c. 2, s. 4, Sch. 2 Pt. I; S.I. 1997/3036, art. 2. (c)
F56. Words in s. 81. (9)(c) substituted (13.10.2003) by Land Registration Act 2002 (c. 9), ss. 133, 136. (2), Sch. 11 para. 23. (2) (with s. 129); S.I. 2003/1725, art. 2. (1)
F57. S. 81. (10) substituted (13.10.2003) by Land Registration Act 2002 (c. 9), ss. 133, 136. (2), Sch. 11 para. 23. (3) (with s. 129); S.I. 2003/1725, art. 2. (1)
Modifications etc. (not altering text)
C4. S. 81 excluded (1.11.1993) by 1993 c. 28, ss. 37, 56. (6), Sch. 10 para. 1. (2)(c); S.I. 1993/2134, arts. 2, 5
C5. S. 81: transfer of functions (1.4.2010) by Housing and Regeneration Act 2008 (c. 17), ss. 190. (b), 325. (1) (with s. 189); S.I. 2010/862, art. 2 (with Sch.)
C6. S. 81. (6) modified (1.12.2008) by The Transfer of Housing Corporation Functions (Modifications and Transitional Provisions) Order 2008 (S.I. 2008/2839), arts. 1. (1), 3, Sch. para. 1; S.I. 2008/3068, art. 2. (1)(b) (with arts. 6-11)
Marginal Citations
M251985 c. 68

82[F58. Provision of] legal assistance to tenants after disposal.

(1) This section applies where a house has been disposed of by a Corporation to disposal falling within section 79. (2) above and, in relation to a house provide legal which has been so disposed of, a "transferred tenant" means a tenant of it assistance to who either—

   (a) was the secure tenant [F59or the introductory tenant] of the house immediately before the disposal; or

   (b) is the widow [F60, widower or surviving civil partner] of the person who was then the secure tenant [F59or the introductory tenant] of it.

(2) On an application by a transferred tenant of a house who is a party or a prospective party to proceedings or prospective proceedings to determine any dispute between himself and the person who acquired the house on the disposal referred to in subsection (1) above, the [F61appropriate authority] may give assistance to the transferred tenant if it thinks fit to do so—

   (a) on the ground that the case raises a question of principle; or

   (b) on the ground that it is unreasonable, having regard to the complexity of the case, or to any other matter, to expect the transferred tenant to deal with it without assistance; or

   (c) by reason of any other special consideration.

(3) Assistance given by the [F61appropriate authority] under this section may include—

   (a) giving advice;

   (b) procuring or attempting to procure the settlement of the matter in dispute;

   (c) arranging for the giving of advice or assistance by a solicitor or counsel;

   (d) arranging for representation by a solicitor or counsel, including such assistance as is usually given by a solicitor or counsel in the steps preli*minary or incidental to any proceedings, or in arriving at or giving effect to a compromise to avoid or bring to an end any proceedings; and

   (e) any other form of assistance which the [F61appropriate authority] may consider appropriate; but paragraph (d) above does not affect the law and practice regulating the descriptions of persons

who may appear in, conduct, defend and address the court in any proceedings.
(4) In so far as expenses are incurred by the [F61appropriate authority] in providing a transferred tenant with assistance under this section, the recovery of those expenses (as taxed or assessed in such manner as may be prescribed by rules of court) shall constitute a first charge for the benefit of the [F61appropriate authority]—

(a) on any costs which (whether by virtue of a judgment or order of a court or an agreement or otherwise) are payable to the tenant by any other person in respect of the matter in connection with which the assistance was given, and

(b) so far as relates to any costs, on his rights under any compromise or settlement arrived at in connection with that matter to avoid or bring to an end any proceedings;

but subject to any charge [F62imposed by [F63section 25 of the Legal Aid, Sentencing and Punishment of Offenders Act 2012] and any provision in, or made under, Part I of that Act for the payment of any sum to the [F64. Lord Chancellor]].

[F65. (5)In this section "the appropriate authority" means—

(a) in a case where the disposal mentioned in subsection (1) was to a private registered provider of social housing, the Regulator of Social Housing, and

(b) in a case where the disposal mentioned in that subsection was to a registered social landlord, the Welsh Ministers.]

Amendments (Textual)

F58. Words in s. 82 heading substituted (1.4.2010) by The Housing and Regeneration Act 2008 (Consequential Provisions) Order 2010 (S.I. 2010/866), art. 1. (2), Sch. 2 para. 72. (4) (with art. 6, Sch. 3)

F59. Words in s. 82. (1)(a)(b) inserted (12.2.1997) by S.I. 1997/74, art. 2, Sch. para. 6. (f)

F60. Words in s. 82. (1)(b) substituted (5.12.2005) by Civil Partnership Act 2004 (c. 33), ss. 81, 263, Sch. 8 para. 42; S.I. 2005/3175, art. 2. (1), Sch. 1

F61. Words in s. 82 substituted (1.4.2010) by The Housing and Regeneration Act 2008 (Consequential Provisions) Order 2010 (S.I. 2010/866), art. 1. (2), Sch. 2 para. 72. (2) (with art. 6, Sch. 3)

F62. Words in s. 82. (4) substituted (1.4.2000) by 1999 c. 22, s. 24, Sch. 4 paras. 42, 43 (with s. 107, Sch. 14 para. 7. (2)); S.I. 2000/774, art. 2. (a)(ii)(iii) (with transitional provisions and savings in arts. 3-5)

F63. Words in s. 82. (4) substituted (1.4.2013) by Legal Aid, Sentencing and Punishment of Offenders Act 2012 (c. 10), s. 151. (1), Sch. 5 para. 37. (a); S.I. 2013/453, art. 3. (h) (with savings and transitional provisions in S.I. 2013/534, art. 6)

F64. Words in s. 82. (4) substituted (1.4.2013) by Legal Aid, Sentencing and Punishment of Offenders Act 2012 (c. 10), s. 151. (1), Sch. 5 para. 37. (b); S.I. 2013/453, art. 3. (h) (with savings and transitional provisions in S.I. 2013/534, art. 6)

F65. S. 82. (5) substituted (1.4.2010) by The Housing and Regeneration Act 2008 (Consequential Provisions) Order 2010 (S.I. 2010/866), art. 1. (2), Sch. 2 para. 72. (3) (with art. 6, Sch. 3)

Modifications etc. (not altering text)

C7. S. 82 functions transferred (1.12.2008) by The Transfer of Housing Corporation Functions (Modifications and Transitional Provisions) Order 2008 (S.I. 2008/2839), arts. 1. (1), 2; S.I. 2008/3068, art. 2. (1)(b) (with arts. 6-11)

C8. S. 82. (3)(c)(d) amended (1.1.1992) by S.I. 1991/2684, arts. 2. (1), 4, Sch. 1

C9. S. 82. (3)(c)(d) applied (with modifications) (23.12.2011) by The Legal Services Act 2007 (Designation as a Licensing Authority) (No. 2) Order 2011 (S.I. 2011/2866), art. 1. (2), Sch. 2

Secure tenancies and right to buy

83 Application of Parts IV and V of Housing Act 1985.

(1) Parts IV and V of the Housing Act 1985 (secure tenancies and the right to buy) shall be amended in accordance with this section.
(2) In section 80. (1) (which lists the landlords whose tenancies can qualify as secure tenancies), after the entry specifying a new town corporation there shall be inserted— " a housing action trust ".
(3) In section 108 (heating charges to secure tenants), in paragraph (a) of subsection (5) (the definition of "heating authority") after the words "housing authority" there shall be inserted "or housing action trust".
(4) In section 114 (meaning of "landlord authority" for the purposes of that Part), in each of subsections (1) and (2), after the entry specifying a development corporation, there shall be inserted— " a housing action trust ".
(5) In section 171 (power to extend right to buy where certain bodies hold an interest in a dwelling-house), in subsection (2), after the entry specifying a new town corporation there shall be inserted— " a housing action trust ".
(6) In each of the following provisions (all of which relate to cases where premises are or were let to a person in consequence of employment), namely—
    (a) paragraph 2. (1) of Schedule I (tenancies which are not secure tenancies),
    (b) Grounds 7 and 12 of Schedule 2 (grounds for possession of dwelling-houses let under secure tenancies),
    (c) Ground 5 of Schedule 3 (grounds for withholding consent to assignment by way of exchange), and
    (d) paragraph 5 of Schedule 5 (exceptions to the right to buy),
after the entry specifying a new town corporation there shall be inserted— " a housing action trust ".
(7) In Schedule 4 (qualifying period for right to buy and discount), inparagraph 7 (the landlord condition) after the entry specifying a new town corporation there shall be inserted— " a housing action trust ".

84 Provisions applicable to disposals of dwelling-houses subject to secure tenancies.

[F66. (1)The provisions of this section apply in any case where—
    (a) a housing action trust proposes to make a disposal of one or more houses let on secure tenancies [F67or introductory tenancies]which would result in a person who, before the disposal, is a secure tenant [F67or an introductory tenant] of the trust becoming, after the disposal, the tenant of another person, and
    (b) that other person is not a local housing authority or other local authority.]
[F68. (2)Before applying to the Secretary of State for consent to the proposed disposal or serving notice under subsection (4) below, the housing action trust shall serve notice in writing on any local housing authority in whose area any houses falling within subsection (1) above are situated—
    (a) informing the authority of the proposed disposal and specifying the houses concerned, and
    (b) requiring the authority within such period, being not less than 28 days, as may be specified in the notice, to serve on the trust a notice under subsection (3) below.
(3) A notice by a local housing authority under this subsection shall inform the housing action trust, with respect to each of the houses specified in the notice under subsection (2) above which is in the authority's area, of the likely consequences for the tenant if the house were to be acquired by the authority.]
(4) Before applying to the Secretary of State for consent to the proposed disposal, and after the expiry of the period specified in the notice under subsection (2) above, the housing action trust shall serve notice in writing on the secure tenant [F69or, as the case may be, introductory tenant]—

(a) informing him of the proposed disposal and of the name of the person to whom the disposal is to be made;

(b) containing such other details of the disposal as seem to the trust to be appropriate;

(c) informing him of the likely consequences of the disposal on his position as a secure tenant [F70or an introductory tenant] and, if appropriate, of the effect of sections 171. A to 171. H of the M26. Housing Act 1985 (preservation of right to buy on disposal to private sector landlord);

[F71. (d)if the local housing authority in whose area the house of which he is tenant is situated has served notice under subsection (3) above, informing him (in accordance with the information given in the notice) of the likely consequences for him if the house were to be acquired by that authority;

(e) informing him, if he wishes to become a tenant of that authority, of his right to make representations to that effect under paragraph (f) below and of the rights conferred by section 84. A below;]

(f) informing him of his right to make representations to the trust with respect to the proposed disposal within such period, being not less than 28 days, as may be specified in the notice.

[F72. (5)If, by virtue of any representations made to the housing action trust in accordance with subsection (4)(f) above, section 84. A below applies in relation to any house or block of flats, the trust shall—

(a) serve notice of that fact on the Secretary of State, on the local housing authority and on the tenant of the house or each of the tenants of the block, and

(b) so amend its proposals with respect to the disposal as to exclude the house or block;

and in this subsection " house " and " block of flats " have the same meanings as in that section.

(5. A)The housing action trust shall consider any other representations so made and, if it considers it appropriate to do so having regard to any of those representations—

(a) may amend (or further amend) its proposals with respect to the disposal, and

(b) in such a case, shall serve a further notice under subsection (4) above (in relation to which this subsection will again apply).]

(6) When applying to the Secretary of State for consent to the proposed disposal (as amended, where appropriate, by virtue of subsection (5) [F73or subsection (5. A)] above) the housing action trust shall furnish to him—

(a) a copy of any notice served on it under subsection (3) above or served by it under subsection (4) above;

(b) a copy of any representations received by the trust; and

(c) a statement of the consideration given by the trust to those representations.

(7) Without prejudice to the generality of section 72 above, where an application is made to the Secretary of State for consent to a disposal to which this section applies, [F74or a disposal which would be such a disposal if subsection (1)(b) above were omitted,] the Secretary of State may, by a direction under that section, require the housing action trust—

(a) to carry out such further consultation [F75or, as the case may be, such consultation] with respect to the proposed disposal as may be specified in the direction; and

(b) to furnish to him such information as may be so specified with respect to the results of that consultation.

[F76. (8)Notwithstanding the application to a housing action trust of Part IV of the M27 Housing Act 1985 (secure tenancies) of Chapter 1 of Part V of the Housing Act 1996 (introductory tenancies), a disposal falling within subsection (1) above shall be treated as not being a matter of housing management to which section 105 of the Act of 1985 applies (in the case of secure tenants) or section 137 of the Act of 1996 applies (in the case of introductory tenants).]

Amendments (Textual)

F66. S. 84. (1) substituted (11.10.1993) by 1993 c. 28, s. 124. (2); S.I. 1993/2134, arts. 2, 4 (with savings in Sch. 1 para. 5)

F67. Words in s. 84. (1)(a) inserted (12.2.1997) by S.I. 1997/74, art. 2, Sch. para. 6. (g)(i)(1)(2)

F68. S. 84. (2)(3) substituted (11.10.1993) by 1993 c. 28, s. 125. (1); S.I. 1993/2134, arts. 2, 4 (with savings in Sch. 1 para. 5)

F69. Words in s. 84. (4) inserted (12.2.1997) by S.I. 1997/74, art. 2, Sch. para. 6. (g)(ii)
F70. Words in s. 84. (4)(c) inserted (12.2.1997) by S.I. 1997/74, art. 2, Sch. para. 6. (g)(iii)
F71. S. 84. (4)(d)(e) substituted (11.10.1993) by 1993 c. 28, s. 125. (2); S.I. 1993/2134, arts. 2, 4 (with savings in Sch. 1 para. 5)
F72. S. 84. (5)(5. A) substituted (11.10.1993) for s. 84. (5) by 1993 c. 28, s. 125. (3); S.I. 1993/2134, arts. 2, 4 (with savings in Sch. 1 para. 5)
F73. Words in s. 84. (6) inserted (11.10.1993) by 1993 c. 28, s. 125. (4); S.I. 1993/2134, arts. 2, 4 (with savings in Sch. 1 para. 5)
F74. Words in s. 84. (7) inserted (11.10.1993) by 1993 c. 28, s. 124. (3)(a); S.I. 1993/2134, arts. 2, 4 (with savings in Sch. 1 para. 5)
F75. Words in s. 84. (7) inserted (11.10.1993) by 1993 c. 28, s. 124. (3)(b);S.I. 1993/2134, arts. 2, 4 (with savings in Sch. 1 para. 5)
F76. S. 84. (8) substituted (12.2.1997) by S.I. 1997/74, art. 2, Sch. para. 6. (g)(iv)
Modifications etc. (not altering text)
C10. S. 84 modified (11.10.1993) by 1993 c. 28, s. 124. (5); S.I. 1993/2134, arts. 2, 4 (with savings in Sch. 1 para. 5)
Marginal Citations
M261985 c. 68.
M271985 c. 68.

[F7784. A Transfer by order of certain dwelling-houses let on secure tenancies.

(1) This section applies in relation to any house or block of flats specified in a notice under subsection (2) of section 84 above if—
    (a) in the case of a house, the tenant makes representations in accordance with paragraph (f) of subsection (4) of that section to the effect that he wishes to become a tenant of the local housing authority in whose area the house is situated; or
    (b) in the case of a block of flats, the majority of the tenants who make representations in accordance with that paragraph make representations to the effect that they wish to become tenants of the local housing authority in whose area the block is situated.
(2) The Secretary of State shall by order provide for the transfer of the house or block of flats from the housing action trust to the local housing authority.
(3) The Secretary of State may also by order transfer from the housing action trust to the local housing authority so much as appears to the Secretary of State to be appropriate of any property belonging to or usually enjoyed with the house or, as the case may be, the block or any flat contained in it; and for this purpose " property " includes chattels of any description and rights and liabilities, whether arising by contract or otherwise.
(4) A transfer of any house, block of flats or other property under this section shall be on such terms, including financial terms, as the Secretary of State thinks fit; and an order under this section may provide that, notwithstanding anything in section 141 of the Law of Property Act 1925 (rent and benefit of lessee's covenants to run with the reversion), any rent or other sum which—
    (a) arises under the tenant's tenancy or any of the tenants' tenancies, and
    (b) falls due before the date of the transfer,
shall continue to be recoverable by the housing action trust to the exclusion of the authority.
(5) Without prejudice to the generality of subsection (4) above, the financial terms referred to in that subsection may include provision for payments to a local housing authority (as well as or instead of payments by a local housing authority); and the transfer from a housing action trust of any house, block of flats or other property by virtue of this section shall not be taken to give rise to any right to compensation.
(6) In this section—
" block of flats " means a building containing two or more flats;

" common parts ", in relation to a building containing two or more flats, means any parts of the building which the tenants of the flats are entitled under the terms of their tenancies to use in common with each other;

" flat " and " house " have the meanings given by section 183 of the Housing Act 1985;

and any reference to a block of flats specified in a notice under section 84. (2) above is a reference to a block in the case of which each flat which is let on a secure tenancy [F78or an introductory tenancy] is so specified.

(7) For the purposes of subsection (6) above, a building which contains—

(a) one or more flats which are let, or available for letting, on secure tenancies [F79or introductory tenancies] by the housing action trust concerned, and

(b) one or more flats which are not so let or so available,

shall be treated as if it were two separate buildings, the one containing the flat or flats mentioned in paragraph (a) above and the other containing the flat or flats mentioned in paragraph (b) above and any common parts.]

Amendments (Textual)

F77. S. 84. A inserted (11.10.1993) by 1993 c. 28, s. 125. (5); S.I. 1993/2134, arts. 2, 4 (with savings in Sch. 1 para. 5)

F78. Words in s. 84. A(6) inserted (12.2.1997) by S.I. 1997/74, art. 2, Sch. para. 6. (h)

F79. Words in s. 84. A(7)(a) inserted (12.2.1997) by S.I. 1997/74, art. 2, Sch. para. 6. (i)

Rents

85 Rents generally.

(1) A housing action trust may make such reasonable charges as it may determine for the tenancy or occupation of housing accommodation for the time being held by it.

(2) A housing action trust shall from time to time review rents and make such changes, either of rents generally or of particular rents, as circumstances may require.

86 Increase of rent where tenancy not secure.

(1) This section applies where a dwelling-house is let by a housing action trust on a periodic tenancy which is not a secure tenancy [F80or an introductory tenancy].

(2) The rent payable under the tenancy may, without the tenancy being terminated, be increased with effect from the beginning of a rental period by a written notice of increase given by the housing action trust to the tenant.

(3) A notice under subsection (2) above is not effective unless—

(a) it is given at least four weeks before the first day of the rental period, or any earlier day on which the payment of rent in respect of that period falls to be made;

(b) it tells the tenant of his right to terminate the tenancy and of the steps to be taken by him if he wishes to do so; and

(c) it gives him the, dates by which, if (by virtue of subsection (4) below) the increase is not to be effective, a notice to quit must be received by the trust and the tenancy be made to terminate.

(4) Where a notice is given under subsection (2) above specifying an increase in rent with effect from the beginning of a rental period and the tenancy continues into that period, the notice shall not have effect if—

(a) the tenancy is terminated by notice to quit given by the tenant in accordance with the provisions (express or implied) of the tenancy;

(b) the notice to quit is given before the expiry of the period of two weeks beginning on the day following the date on which the notice of increase is given, or before the expiry of such longer period as may be allowed by the notice of increase; and

(c) the date on which the tenancy is made to terminate is not later than the earliest day on which the tenancy could be terminated by a notice to quit given by the tenant on the last day of that rental period.

(5) In this section "rental period" means a period in respect of which a payment of rent falls to be made.

Amendments (Textual)

F80. Words in s. 86. (1) inserted (12.2.1997) by S.I. 1997/74, art. 2, Sch. para. 6. (j)

Agency and dissolution

87 Agency agreements.

(1) With the approval of the Secretary of State, a housing action trust may enter into an agreement with another person whereby, in relation to any housing accommodation or other land held by the trust which is specified in the agreement, that other person shall exercise, as agent of the trust, such of the functions of the trust as are so specified.

(2) An agreement under subsection (1) above shall set out the terms on which the functions of the housing action trust are exercisable by the person who, under the agreement, is the agent of the trust (in this Part of this Act referred to as "the agent").

(3) Where the agent is a body or association, an agreement under subsection (1) above may provide that the functions of the agent under the agreement may be performed by a committee or sub-committee, or by an officer, of the body or association.

(4) The approval of the Secretary of State under subsection (1) above may be given unconditionally or subject to conditions.

(5) References in this section to the functions of a housing action trust in relation to housing accommodation or other land include—

(a) functions conferred by any statutory provision, and

(b) the powers and duties of the trust as holder of an estate or interest in the housing accommodation or land in question.

88 Dissolution of housing action trust.

(1) A housing action trust shall use its best endeavours to secure that its objects are achieved as soon as practicable.

(2) Where it appears to a trust that its objects have been substantially achieved, it shall—

(a) so far as practicable, dispose or arrange to dispose of any remaining property, rights or liabilities of the trust in accordance with the preceding provisions of this Part of this Act; and

(b) submit proposals to the Secretary of State for—

(i) the dissolution of the trust;

(ii) the disposal to any person of any remaining property, rights or liabilities of the trust which it has not been able to dispose of or arrange to dispose of under paragraph (a) above;and

(iii) the transfer of any function exercisable by the trust to another person (including, where appropriate, a person with whom the trust has entered into an agreement under section 87 above).

(3) The Secretary of State may by order provide for the dissolution of a housing action trust and for any such disposal or transfer as is mentioned in subsection (2)(b) above, whether by way of giving effect (with or without modifications) to any proposals submitted to him under subsection (2) above or otherwise.

(4) Any order under this section—

(a) where it provides for any such disposal or transfer as is mentioned in subsection (2)(b) above, may be on such terms, including financial terms, as the Secretary of State thinks fit and may create or impose such new rights or liabilities in respect of what is transferred as appear to him to be necessary or expedient;

[F81. (aa)where it provides for any such disposal or transfer as is mentioned in subsection (2)(b) above, may contain provisions—
(i) establishing new bodies corporate to receive the disposal or transfer; or
(ii) amending, repealing or otherwise modifying any enactment for the purpose of enabling any body established under any enactment to receive the disposal or transfer;]

(b) may contain such supplementary and transitional provisions as the Secretary of State thinks necessary or expedient, including provisions amending [F82, repealing or otherwise modifying any enactment]; and

(c) shall be made by statutory instrument which shall be subject to annulment in pursuance of a resolution of either House of Parliament.

[F83. (5)In this section "enactment" includes any instrument made under any enactment.]
Amendments (Textual)
F81. S. 88. (4)(aa) inserted (24.9.1996) by 1996 c. 53, ss. 144. (2), 150. (2)
F82. Words in s. 88. (4)(b) substituted (24.9.1996) by 1996 c. 53, ss. 144. (3), 150. (2)
F83. S. 88. (5) inserted (24.9.1996) by 1996 c. 53, ss. 144. (4), 150. (2)

Miscellaneous and general

89 Supply of goods and services.

(1) A housing action trust and an urban development corporation established by an order under section 135 of the M28 Local Govemment, Planning and Land Act 1980, [F84or a housing action trust and a Mayoral development corporation,] may enter into any agreement with each other for all or any of the purposes set out in section 1. (1) of the M29 Local Authorities (Goods and Services) Act 1970, as if they were local authorities within the meaning of section I of that Act.
(2) Without prejudice to subsection (1) above, in section 1. (4) of the Local Authorities (Goods and Services) Act 1970 (supply of goods and services by local authorities to public bodies), after the words " "public body" means any local authority" there shall be inserted "housing action trust established under Part III of the Housing Act 1988".
Amendments (Textual)
F84. Words in s. 89. (1) inserted (15.1.2012) by Localism Act 2011 (c. 20), s. 240. (1)(l), Sch. 22 para. 28
Marginal Citations
M281980 c. 65.
M291970 c. 39.

90 Information

(1) If required to do so by notice in writing given by the Secretary of State for any of the purposes mentioned in subsection (3) below, a local authority,—
    (a) at such time and place as may be specified in the notice, shall produce any document; or
    (b) within such period as may be so specified, or such longer period as the Secretary of State may allow, shall furnish a copy of any document or supply any information;
being a document, copy or information of a description specified in the notice.
(2) Where notice is given to a local authority under subsection (1) above, any officer of the authority—
    (a) who has the custody or control of any document to which the notice relates, or

(b) who is in a position to give information to which the notice relates,
shall take all reasonable steps to ensure that the notice is complied with.
(3) The purposes referred to in subsection (1) above are—
(a) determining whether the Secretary of State should make a designation order in respect of any area;
(b) where a designation order is to be or has been made, detemining whether, and to what extent, he should exercise any of his other powers under this Part of this Act; and
(c) enabling him to provide information to a housing action trust the better to enable it to carry out its functions.
(4) Without prejudice to the generality of subsection (1) above, among the information which may be required by a notice under that subsection is information with respect to the interests in, and the occupation of, land held by a local authority and, in particular, information with respect to any matter entered in a register kept under the [F85. Land Registration Act 2002] or the M30 Land Charges Act 1972.
(5) To any extent to which, apart from this subsection, he would not be able to do so, the Secretary of State may use, for any of the purposes mentioned in subsection (3) above, any infor*mation obtained by him under, or in connection with his functions under, the M31. Housing Act 1985 or any other enactment.
(6) If the Secretary of State considers it necessary or desirable to do so in order the better to enable a housing action trust to carry out its functions, he may disclose to the trust any information originally obtained by him for a purpose falling within paragraph (a) or paragraph (b) of subsection (3) above as well as information obtained for the purpose referred to in paragraph (c) of that subsection.
(7) In this section "local authority" has the same meaning as in section 74 above.
Amendments (Textual)
F85. Words in s. 90. (4) substituted (13.10.2003) by Land Registration Act 2002 (c. 9), ss. 133, 136. (2), Sch. 11 para. 23. (4) (with s. 129); S.I. 2003/1725, art. 2. (1)
Marginal Citations
M301972 c. 61.
M311985 c. 68.

91

(1) This section has effect in relation to any notice required or notices. authorised by this Part of this Act to be served on any person by a housing action trust.
(2) Any such notice may be served on the person in question either by delivering it to him, or by leaving it at his proper address, or by sending it by post to him at that address.
(3) Any such notice may—
(a) in the case of a body corporate, be given to or served on the secretary or clerk of that body; and
(b) in the case of a partnership, be given to or served on a partner or a person having the control or management of the partnership business.
(4) For the purposes of this section and of section 7 of the M32 Interpretation Act 1978 (service of documents by post) in its application to this section, the proper address of any person to or on whom a notice is to be given or served shall be his last known address, except that—
(a) in the case of a body corporate or its secretary or clerk, it shall be the address of the registered or principal office of that body; and
(b) in the case of a partnership or a person having the control or management of the partnership business, it shall be that of the principal office of the partnership;
and for the purposes of this subsection the principal office of a company registered outside the United Kingdom or of a partnership carrying on business outside the United Kingdom shall be its principal office within the United Kingdom.

(5) If the person to be given or served with any notice mentioned in subsection (1) above has specified an address within the United Kingdom other than his proper address within the meaning of subsection (4) above as the one at which he or someone on his behalf will accept documents of the same description as that notice, that address shall also be treated for the purposes of this section and section 7 of the Interpretation Act 1978 as his proper address.

(6) If the name or address of any owner, lessee or occupier of land to or PART III on whom any notice mentioned in subsection (1) above is to be served cannot after reasonable inquiry be ascertained, the document may be served either by leaving it in the hands of a person who is or appears to be resident or employed on the land or by leaving it conspicuously affixed to some building or object on the land.

Marginal Citations
M321978 c. 30.

92 Interpretation of Part III.

(1) In this Part of this Act, except where the context otherwise requires,—
 (a) "designated area" and "designation order" have the meaning assigned by section 60. (6) above;
 (b) any reference to a "house" includes a reference to a flat and to any yard, garden, outhouses and appurtenances belonging to the house or flat or usually enjoyed with it;
 (c) "housing accommodation" includes flats, lodging-houses and hostels;
 [F86. (ca) "introductory tenancy" has the same meaning as in Chapter I of Part V of the Housing Act 1996 and "introductory tenant" shall be construed accordingly;]
 (d) "local housing authority" has the same meaning as in the M33. Housing Act 1985 and section 2 of that Act (the district of a local housing authority) has effect in relation to this Part of this Act as it has effect in relation to that Act;
 (e) "local authority housing" means housing accommodation provided by a local housing authority (whether in its own district or not);
 (f) "secure tenancy" has the meaning assigned by section 79 of the M34. Housing Act 1985 and "secure tenant" shall be construed accordingly; and
 [F87. (g) "the 1990 Act" means the Town and Country Planning Act 1990]
F88. (2). . . . .

Amendments (Textual)
F86. S. 92. (1)(ca) inserted (12.2.1997) by S.I 1997/74, art. 2, Sch. para. 6. (k)
F87. S. 92. (1)(g) substituted by Planning (Consequential Provisions) Act 1990 (c. 11, SIF 123: 1, 2), s. 4, Sch. 2 para. 79. (4)
F88. S. 92. (2) repealed (1.11.1998) by 1998 c. 38, ss. 140, 152, Sch. 16 para. 70, Sch. 18 Pt. VI (with ss. 137. (1), 139. (2), 141. (1), 143. (2)); S.I. 1998/2244, art. 5

Marginal Citations
M331985 c. 68.
M341985 c. 68.

Interpretation of Part III.

92 Interpretation of Part III.

(1) In this Part of this Act, except where the context otherwise requires,—
 (a) "designated area" and "designation order" have the meaning assigned by section 60. (6) above;
 (b) any reference to a "house" includes a reference to a flat and to any yard, garden, outhouses

and appurtenances belonging to the house or flat or usually enjoyed with it;

(c) "housing accommodation" includes flats, lodging-houses and hostels;

[F1. (ca) "introductory tenancy" has the same meaning as in Chapter I of Part V of the Housing Act 1996 and "introductory tenant" shall be construed accordingly;]

(d) "local housing authority" has the same meaning as in the M1. Housing Act 1985 and section 2 of that Act (the district of a local housing authority) has effect in relation to this Part of this Act as it has effect in relation to that Act;

(e) "local authority housing" means housing accommodation provided by a local housing authority (whether in its own district or not);

(f) "secure tenancy" has the meaning assigned by section 79 of the M2. Housing Act 1985 and "secure tenant" shall be construed accordingly; and

[F2. (g) "the 1990 Act" means the Town and Country Planning Act 1990]

F3. (2). . . . .

Amendments (Textual)

F1. S. 92. (1)(ca) inserted (12.2.1997) by S.I 1997/74, art. 2, Sch. para. 6. (k)

F2. S. 92. (1)(g) substituted by Planning (Consequential Provisions) Act 1990 (c. 11, SIF 123: 1, 2), s. 4, Sch. 2 para. 79. (4)

F3. S. 92. (2) repealed (1.11.1998) by 1998 c. 38, ss. 140, 152, Sch. 16 para. 70, Sch. 18 Pt. VI (with ss. 137. (1), 139. (2), 141. (1), 143. (2)); S.I. 1998/2244, art. 5

Marginal Citations

M11985 c. 68.

M21985 c. 68.

Part IV

F1. Part IV

. . . .

Amendments (Textual)

F1. Pt. IV (ss. 93-114) repealed (1.10.1996) by 1996 c. 52, ss. 222, 227, Sch. 18 Pt. I para. 1, Sch. 19 Pt. IX; S.I. 1996/2402, art. 3

Right conferred by Part IV.

93. . . . .

Associated Amendments (Textual)

F1. Pt. IV (ss. 93-114) repealed (1.10.1996) by 1996 c. 52, ss. 222, 227, Sch. 18 Pt. I para. 1, Sch. 19 Pt. IX; S.I. 1996/2402, art. 3

Interpretation of Part IV.

114 Interpretation of Part IV.

Marginal Citations

M11985 c.68.

Part V Miscellaneous and General

Part V Miscellaneous and General

115 Premiums on long leases.

(1) With respect to —
   (a) any premium received or required to be paid after the commencement of this Act, or
   (b) any loan required to be made after that commencement,
section 127 of the M1 Rent Act 1977 (allowable premiums in relation to certain long tenancies) shall have effect subject to the amendments in subsections (2) and (3) below.
(2) For subsections (2) and (3) there shall be substituted the following subsections—
"(2)The conditions mentioned in subsection (1)(a) above are—
   (a) that the landlord has no power to determine the tenancy at any time within twenty years beginning on the date when it was granted; and
   (b) that the terms of the tenancy do not inhibit both the assignment and the underletting of the whole of the premises comprised in the tenancy;
but for the purpose of paragraph (b) above there shall be disregarded any term of the tenancy which inhibits assignment and underletting only during a period which is or falls within the final seven years of the term for which the tenancy was granted.
(3) The reference in subsection (2) above to a power of the landlord to determine a tenancy does not include a reference to a power of re-entry or forfeiture for breach of any term or condition of the tenancy."
(3) Subsections (3. C) and (3. D) shall be omitted and in subsection (5) for "(2)(c)" there shall be substituted "(2)(b)".
(4) Expressions used in subsection (1) above have the same meaning as in Part IX of the Rent Act 1977.
Marginal Citations
M11977 c.42.

116 Repairing obligations in short leases.

(1) In section II of the M2 Landlord and Tenant Act 1985 (repairing obligations in short leases) after subsection (1) there shall be inserted the following subsections—
"(1. A)If a lease to which this section applies is a lease of a dwelling- house which forms part only of a building, then, subject to subsection (IB), the covenant implied by subsection (1) shall have effect as if—
   (a) the reference in paragraph (a) of that subsection to the dwelling-house included a reference to any part of the building in which the lessor has an estate or interest; and
   (b) any reference in paragraphs (b) and (c) of that subsection to an installation in the dwelling-house included a reference to an installation which, directly or indirectly, serves the dwelling-house and which either—
(i) forms part of any part of a building in which the lessor has an estate or interest; or
(ii) is owned by the lessor or under his control.
(1. B)Nothing in subsection (IA) shall be construed as requiring the lessor to carry out any works or repairs unless the disrepair (or failure to maintain in working order) is such as to affect the lessee's enjoyment of the dwelling-house or of any common parts, as defined in section 60. (1) of the Landlord and Tenant Act 1987, which the lessee, as such, is entitled to use."

(2) After subsection (3) of that section there shall be inserted the following subsection—
"(3. A)In any case where—
(a) the lessor's repairing covenant has effect as mentioned in subsection (IA), and
(b) in order to comply with the covenant the lessor needs to carry out works or repairs otherwise than in, or to an installation in, the dwelling-house, and
(c) the lessor does not have a sufficient right in the part of the building or the installation concerned to enable him to carry out the required works or repairs,
then, in any proceedings relating to a failure to comply with the lessor's repairing covenant, so far as it requires the lessor to carry out the works or repairs in question, it shall be a defence for the lessor to prove that he used all reasonable endeavours to obtain, but was unable to obtain, such rights as would be adequate to enable him to carry out the works or repairs."
(3) At the end of section 14. (4) of the said Act of 1985 (which excludes from section II certain leases granted to various bodies) there shall be added—
"a housing action trust established under Part 111 of the Housing Act 1988".
(4) The amendments made by this section do not have effect with respect to—-
(a) a lease entered into before the commencement of this Act; or
(b) a lease entered into pursuant to a contract made before the commencement of this Act.
Marginal Citations
M21985 c.70.

117 Certain tenancies excluded from bankrupt's estate

(1) In section 283 of the M3 Insolvency Act 1986 (definition of bankrupt's estate) at the end of subsection (3) (property excluded from the estate) there shall be inserted the following subsection—
"(3. A)Subject to section 308. A in Chapter IV, subsection (1) does not apply to—
(a) a tenancy which is an assured tenancy or an assured agricultural occupancy, within the meaning of Part I of the Housing Act 1988, and the terms of which inhibit an assignment as mentioned in section 127. (5) of the Rent Act 1977, or
(b) a protected tenancy, within the meaning of the Rent Act 1977, in respect of which, by virtue of any provision of Part IX of that Act, no premium can lawfully be required as a condition of assignment, or
(c) a tenancy of a dwelling-house by virtue of which the bankrupt is, within the meaning of the Rent (Agriculture) Act 1976, a protected occupier of the dwelling-house, and the terms of which inhibit an assignment as mentioned in section 127. (5) of the Rent Act 1977, or
(d) a secure tenancy, within the meaning of Part IV of the Housing Act 1985, which is not capable of being assigned, except in the cases mentioned in section 91. (3) of that Act."
(2) After section 308 of that Act there shall be inserted the following section—
"308. A Vesting in trustee of certain tenancies.
Upon the service on the bankrupt by the trustee of a notice in writing under this section, any tenancy—
(a) which is excluded by virtue of section 283. (3. A) from the bankrupt's estate, and
(b) to which the notice relates,
vests in the trustee as part of the bankrupt's estate; and, except against a purchaser in good faith, for value and without notice of the bankruptcy, the trustee's title to that tenancy has relation back to the commencement of the bankruptcy."
(3) In section 309 of that Act (time-limit for certain notices) in subsection (1)(b)—
(a) after the words "section 308" there shall be inserted "or section 308. A"; and
(b) after the words "the property" there shall be inserted "or tenancy".
(4) In section 315 of that Act (disclaimer (general power)), in subsection (4) after the words "reasonable replacement value)" there shall be inserted "or 308. A".
Marginal Citations

M31986 c.45.

F1118 Certain tenancies excluded from debtor's estate: Scotland.

. . . .
Amendments (Textual)
F1. S. 118 repealed (30.11.2016) by The Bankruptcy (Scotland) Act 2016 (Consequential Provisions and Modifications) Order 2016 (S.I. 2016/1034), art. 1, Sch. 2 Pt. 1

119 Amendment of Landlord and Tenant Act 1987.

The M4 Landlord and Tenant Act 1987 shall have effect subject to the amendments in Schedule 13 to this Act.
Marginal Citations
M41987 c.31.

Rent Officers

120 Appointment etc. of rent officers.

Section 63 of the M5 Rent Act 1977 (schemes for the appointment of rent officers) shall have effect subject to the amendments in Part I of Schedule 14 to this Act and after section 64 of that Act there shall be inserted the sections set out in Part II of that Schedule.
Marginal Citations
M51977 c.42.

F2121. . . . .

Amendments (Textual)
F2. S. 121 repealed (1.4.1997 subject to transitional provisions in the commencing S.I.) by 1996 c. 52, s. 227, Sch. 19 Pt. VI; S.I. 1997/618, art. 2. (1), Sch. paras. 4, 6)

Right to buy etc. and grants to obtain accommodation

122 Variation of cost floor for right to buy discount.

(1) Section 131 of the Housing Act 1985 (limits on amount of discount in relation to the right to buy) shall be amended in accordance with subsections (2) and (3) below.
(2) In subsection (1) (the cost floor provision) for paragraph (a) there shall be substituted the following paragraph—
  "(a)is to be treated as incurred at or after the beginning of that period of account of the landlord in which falls the date which is eight years, or such other period of time as may be specified in an order made by the Secretary of State, earlier than the relevant time, and".
(3) After subsection (1) there shall be inserted the following subsection—
"(1. A)In subsection (1)(a) above " period of account", in relation to any costs, means the period for which the landlord made up those of its accounts in which account is taken of those costs."
(4) This section has effect in relation to the determination of discount in any case where—
  (a) the relevant time falls on or after the date on which this section comes into force; or

(b) paragraph (a) above does not apply but the landlord has not before that date served on the tenant a notice complying with section 125 of the Housing Act 1985; or

(c) the tenant has before that date claimed to exercise the right to be granted a shared ownership lease but the landlord has not before that date served on the tenant a notice complying with section 147 of that Act; or

(d) the tenant has before that date served a notice under paragraph I of Schedule 8 to that Act (claiming to exercise the right to acquire an additional share under a shared ownership lease but the landlord has not before that date served a notice under sub- paragraph (3) of that paragraph; and, for the purposes of this subsection, no account shall be taken of any steps taken under section 177 of that Act (amendment or withdrawal and re-service of notice to correct mistakes).

(5) Expressions used in subsection (4) above have the same meaning as in Part V of the Housing Act 1985.

123 Amendment of Schedule 5 to Housing Act 1985.

(1) Schedule 5 of the Housing Act 1985 (exceptions to the right to buy) shall be amended in accordance with this section.

(2) Paragraphs 6 and 8 shall be omitted. Housing Act 1985.

(3) The repeal by this Act of paragraphs 6 and 8 of Schedule 5 shall not affect the operation of either of those paragraphs in any case where the tenant's notice claiming to exercise the right to buy was served before the repeal comes into force unless, at that time, no notice in response had been served under section 124 of the Housing Act 1985 (landlord's notice admitting or denying right to buy).

(4) For the purposes of subsection (3) above, no account shall be taken of any steps taken under section 177 of the M6 Housing Act 1985 (amendment or withdrawal and re-service of notice to correct mistakes).

Marginal Citations
M61985 c.68.

124 Right to buy: tenant's sanction for landlord's delays.

After section 153 of the Housing Act 1985 there shall be inserted the following sections—
"153. A Tenant's notices of delay.

(1) Where a secure tenant has claimed to exercise the right to buy, he may serve on his landlord a notice (in this section referred to as an "initial notice of delay") in any of the following cases, namely,—

(a) where the landlord has failed to serve a notice under section 124 within the period appropriate under subsection (2) of that section;

(b) where the tenant's right to buy has been established and the landlord has failed to serve a notice under section 125 within the period appropriate under subsection (1) of that section;

(c) where the tenant has claimed to exercise the right to be granted a shared ownership lease and the landlord has failed to serve a notice under section 146 within the period of the four weeks required by that section;

(d) where the tenant's right to a shared ownership lease has been established and the landlord has failed to serve a notice under section 147 within the period of the eight weeks required by that section; or

(e) where the tenant considers that delays on the part of the landlord are preventing him from exercising expeditiously his right to buy or his right to be granted a shared ownership lease; and where an initial notice of delay specifies any of the cases in paragraphs (a) to (d), any reference in this section or section 153. B to the default date is a reference to the end of the period referred to in the paragraph in question or, if it is later, the day appointed for the coming into force of section 124 of the Housing Act 1988.

(2) An initial notice of delay—
   (a) shall specify the most recent action of which the tenant is aware which has been taken by the landlord pursuant to this Part of this Act; and
   (b) shall specify a period (in this section referred to as "the response period"), not being less than one month, beginning on the date of service of the notice, within which the service by the landlord of a counter notice under subsection (3) will have the effect of cancelling the initial notice of delay.
(3) Within the response period specified in an initial notice of delay or at any time thereafter, the landlord may serve on the tenant a counter notice in either of the following circumstances—
   (a) if the initial notice specifies any of the cases in paragraphs (a) to (d) of subsection (1) and the landlord has served, or is serving together with the counter notice, the required notice under section 124, section 125, section 146 or section 147, as the case may be; or
   (b) if the initial notice specifies the case in subsection (1)(e) and there is no action under this Part which, at the beginning of the response period, it was for the landlord to take in order to allow the tenant expeditiously to exercise his right to buy or his right to be granted a shared ownership lease and which remains to be taken at the time of service of the counter notice.
(4) A counter notice under subsection (3) shall specify the circumstances by virtue of which it is served.
(5) At any time when—
   (a) the response period specified in an initial notice of delay has expired, and
   (b) the landlord has not served a counter notice under subsection (3),
the tenant may serve on the landlord a notice (in this section and section 153.B referred to as an "operative notice of delay") which shall state that section 153.B will apply to payments of rent made by the tenant on or after the default date or, if the initial notice of delay specified the case in subsection (1)(e), the date of the service of the notice.
(6) If, after a tenant has served an initial notice of delay, a counter notice has been served under subsection (3), then, whether or not the tenant has also served an operative notice of delay, if any of the cases in subsection (1) again arises, the tenant may serve a further initial notice of delay and the provisions of this section shall apply again accordingly.

153.B Payments of rent attributable to purchase price etc.
(1) Where a secure tenant has served on his landlord an operative notice of delay, this section applies to any payment of rent which is made on or after the default date or, as the case may be, the date of the service of the notice and before the occurrence of any of the following events (and, if more than one event occurs, before the earliest to occur—
   (a) the service by the landlord of a counter notice under section 153.A(3);
   (b) the date on which the landlord makes to the tenant the grant required by section 138 or, as the case may be, section 150;
   (c) the date on which the tenant serves notice under section 142.(2) (claiming to be entitled to defer completion);
   (d) the date on which the tenant withdraws or is deemed to have withdrawn the notice claiming to exercise the right to buy or, as the case may be, the notice claiming to exercise the right to be granted a shared ownership lease; and
   (e) the date on which the tenant ceases to be entitled to exercise the right to buy.
(2) Except where this section ceases to apply on a date determined under any of paragraphs (c) to (e) of subsection (1), so much of any payment of rent to which this section applies as does not consist of—
   (a) a sum due on account of rates, or
   (b) a service charge (as defined in section 62 1 A),
shall be treated not only as a payment of rent but also as a payment on account by the tenant which is to be taken into account in accordance with subsection (3).
(3) In a case where subsection (2) applies, the amount which, apart from this section, would be the purchase price or, as the case may be, the tenant's initial contribution for the grant of a shared ownership lease shall be reduced by an amount equal to the aggregate of—

(a) the total of any payments on account treated as having been paid by the tenant by virtue of subsection (2); and

(b) if those payments on account are derived from payments of rent referable to a period of more than twelve months, a sum equal to the appropriate percentage of the total referred to in paragraph (a).

(4) In subsection (3)(b) "the appropriate percentage" means 50 per cent. or such other percentage as may be prescribed."

125 Restriction on letting etc. of certain houses in National Parks etc.

(1) Section 37 of the M7 Housing Act 1985 (restriction on disposals of dwelling-houses in National Parks etc.) shall be amended in accordance with this section.

(2) In subsection (2) (the covenanted limitation) after the word "his" there shall be inserted " "(a) " and at the end there shall be added "and

(b) there will be no disposal by way of tenancy or licence without the written consent of the authority unless the disposal is to a person satisfying that condition or by a person whose only or principal home is and, throughout the duration of the tenancy or licence, remains the house".

(3) In subsection (3) (disposals limited to persons employed or living locally) after the words "application for consent" there shall be inserted the words " or, in the case of a disposal by way of tenancy or licence, preceding the disposal ".

(4) At the end of subsection (4) (disposals in breach of covenant to be void) there shall be added "and, so far as it relates to disposals by way of tenancy or licence, such a covenant may be enforced by the local authority as if—

(a) the authority were possessed of land adjacent to the house concerned; and

(b) the covenant were expressed to be made for the benefit of such adjacent land".

(5) After subsection (4) there shall be inserted the following subsection—

"(4. A)Any reference in the preceding provisions of this section to a disposal by way of tenancy or licence does not include a reference to a relevant disposal or an exempted disposal."

(6) This section has effect where the conveyance, grant or assignment referred to in subsection (1) of section 37 is executed on or after the commencement of this Act.

Marginal Citations

M71985 c. 68.

126 Restriction on disposal of dwelling-houses in National Parks etc. acquired under the right to buy.

(1) In Part V of the M8 Housing Act 1985 (the right to buy), section 157 (restriction on disposal of dwelling-houses in National Parks etc.) shall be amended in accordance with this section.

(2) In subsection (2) (the covenanted limitation) after the word "his" there shall be inserted " "(a) " and at the end there shall be added "and—

(b) there will be no disposal by way of tenancy or licence without the written consent of the landlord unless the disposal is to a person satisfying that condition or by a person whose only or principal home is and, throughout the duration of the tenancy or licence, remains the dwelling-house".

(3) In subsection (3) (disposals limited to persons employed or living locally) after the words "application for consent" there shall be inserted the words " "or, in the case of a disposal by way of tenancy or licence, preceding the disposal ".

(4) At the end of subsection (6) (disposals in breach of covenant to be void) there shall be added "and, so far as it relates to disposals by way of tenancy or licence, such a covenant may be enforced by the landlord as if—

(a) the landlord were possessed of land adjacent to the house concerned; and
(b) the covenant were expressed to be made for the benefit of such adjacent land".
(5) After subsection (6) there shall be inserted the following subsection—
"(6. A)Any reference in the preceding provisions of this section to a disposal by way of tenancy or licence does not include a reference to a relevant disposal or an exempted disposal."
(6) This section has effect where the conveyance or grant referred to in subsection (1) of section 157 is executed on or after the commencement of this Act.
Marginal Citations
M81985 c.68.

127 Preserved right to buy.

(1) In subsection (4) of section 171. B of the M9 Housing Act 1985 for paragraph (a) there shall be substituted the following paragraphs—
"(a)where the former secure tenancy was not a joint tenancy and, immediately before his death, the former secure tenant was tenant under an assured tenancy of a dwelling-house in relation to which he had the preserved right to buy, a member of the former secure tenant's family who acquired that assured tenancy under the will or intestacy of the former secure tenant;
(aa) where the former secure tenancy was not a joint tenancy, a member of the former secure tenant's family to whom the former secure tenant assigned his assured tenancy of a dwelling-house in relation to which, immediately before the assignment, he had the preserved right to buy".
(2) In subsection (2)(a) of section 171. C of that Act after the word "paragraphs" there shall be inserted " "1, 3 and ".
(3) After subsection (4) of that section there shall be added the following subsection—
"(5)The disapplication by the regulations of paragraph I of Schedule 5 shall not be taken to authorise any action on the part of a charity which would conflict with the trusts of the charity."
Marginal Citations
M91985 c. 68.

[F3128 Preservation of right to buy on disposal to private sector landlord: Scotland.

After section 81 of the M10. Housing (Scotland) Act 1987 there shall be inserted the following section—
" Preservation of right to buy on disposal to private sector landlord
81. A Preservation of right to buy on disposal to private sector landlord
(1) The right to buy provisions shall continue to right to buy on apply where a person ceases to be a secure tenant of a disposal to house by reason of the disposal by the landlord of an private sector interest in the house to a private sector landlord.
(2) The right to buy provisions shall not, however, continue to apply under subsection (1) in such circumstances as may be prescribed.
(3) The continued application under subsection (1) of the right to buy provisions shall be in accordance with and subject to such provision as is prescribed which may—
    (a) include—
(i) such additions and exceptions to, and adaptations and modifications of, the right to buy provisions in their continued application by virtue of this section; and
(ii) such incidental, supplementary and transitional provisions;
as the Secretary of State considers appropriate;
    (b) differ as between different cases or descriptions of case and as between different areas;
    (c) relate to a particular disposal.
(4) Without prejudice to the generality of subsection (3), provision may be made by virtue of it—

(a) specifying the persons entitled to the benefit of the right to buy provisions in their continued application by virtue of this section;

(b) preventing, except with the consent of the Secretary of State, the disposal by the private sector landlord of less than his whole interest in a house in relation to which the right to buy provisions continue to apply by virtue of this section;

(c) ensuring that where, under Ground 9 of Schedule 5 to the Housing (Scotland) Act 1988 (availability of suitable alternative accommodation), the sheriff makes an order for possession of a house in relation to which the right to buy provisions continue to apply by virtue of this section and the tenant would not have the right under this Part (other than this section) to buy the house which is or will be available by way of alternative accommodation, these provisions as so continued will apply in relation to the house which is or will be so available.

(5) In this section—

(a) "secure tenant" means a tenant under a secure tenancy;

(b) "private sector landlord" means a landlord other than one of those set out in sub-paragraphs (i) to (iv) and (viii) and (ix) of paragraph (a) of subsection (2) of section 61;

(c) the "right to buy provisions" means the provisions of this Act relating to the right of a tenant of a house to purchase it under this Part and to his rights in respect of a loan."]

Amendments (Textual)

F3. S. 128 repealed (30.9.2002) by 2001 asp 10, ss. 112, 113. (1), Sch. 10 para. 15. (7); S.S.I. 2002/321, art. 2, Sch. (with transitional provisions in arts. 3-5)

Commencement Information

I1. S. 128 wholly in force at 21.2.1992 see s. 141. (2) and S.I. 1992/324, art. 2

Marginal Citations

M101987 c.26.

129 Schemes for payments to assist local housing authority tenants to obtain other accomodation.

(1) In accordance with a scheme made by a local housing authority and [F4, where the authority is in Wales,] approved by the Secretary of State under this section, the authority may make grants to or for the benefit of qualifying tenants or licensees of the authority with a view to assisting each person to whom or for whose benefit a grant is made to obtain accommodation otherwise than as a tenant or licensee of the authority either—

(a) by acquiring an interest in a dwelling-house; or

(b) by carrying out works to a dwelling-house to provide additional accommodation; or

(c) by both of those means.

(2) A scheme under this section shall contain such provisions as the local housing authority considers appropriate together with [F5, where the authority is in Wales,] any which the Secretary of State may require as a condition of his approval and, without prejudice to the generality, a scheme may include provisions specifying, or providing for the determination of—

(a) the persons who are qualifying tenants or licensees for the purposes of the scheme;

(b) the interests which qualifying tenants or licensees may be assisted to acquire;

(c) the works for the carrying out of which grants may be made;

(d) the circumstances in which a grant may be made for the benefit of a qualifying tenant or licensee;

(e) the amount of the grant which may be made in any particular case and the terms on which it may be made;

(f) the limits on the total number and amount of grants which may be made; and

(g) the period within which the scheme is to apply.

(3) The Secretary of State may approve a scheme made by a local housing authority [F6in Wales] under this section with or without conditions and, where a scheme has been [F7made and, where the authority is in Wales, approved, a local housing authority] shall take such steps as it considers

appropriate to bring the scheme to the attention of persons likely to be able to benefit from it and shall take such other steps (if any) as the Secretary of State may direct in any particular case to secure publicity for the scheme.

(4) The Secretary of State may revoke an approval of a scheme under this section by a notice given to the local housing authority concerned; and, where such a notice is given, the revocation shall not affect the operation of the scheme in relation to any grants made or agreed before the date of the notice.

(5) Any grant made pursuant to a scheme under this section—

   (a) F8

   (b) F9

(6) Where a scheme [F10has been] made by a local housing authority under this section [F11and, where the authority is in Wales,] has been approved, a person dealing with the authority shall not be concerned to see or enquire whether the terms of the scheme have been or are being complied with; and any failure to comply with the terms of a scheme shall not invalidate any grant purporting to be made in accordance with the scheme unless the person to whom the grant is made has actual notice of the failure.

(7) In this section—

   (a) "local housing authority" has the meaning assigned by section 1 of the Housing Act 1985; of the Housing Act 1985;

   (b) "dwelling-house" has the meaning assigned by section 112 of that Act; and

   (c) "tenant" does not include a tenant under a long tenancy, as defined in section 115 of that Act.

Amendments (Textual)

F4. Words in s. 129. (1) inserted (1.4.2003) by The Regulatory Reform (Schemes under Section 129 of the Housing Act 1988) (England) Order 2003 (S.I. 2003/986), art. 2. (2)

F5. Words in s. 129. (2) inserted (1.4.2003) by The Regulatory Reform (Schemes under Section 129 of the Housing Act 1988) (England) Order 2003 (S.I. 2003/986), art. 2. (3)

F6. Words in s. 129. (3) inserted (1.4.2003) by The Regulatory Reform (Schemes under Section 129 of the Housing Act 1988) (England) Order 2003 (S.I. 2003/986), art. 2. (4)(a)

F7. Words in s. 129. (3) substituted (1.4.2003) by The Regulatory Reform (Schemes under Section 129 of the Housing Act 1988) (England) Order 2003 (S.I. 2003/986), art. 2. (4)(b)

F8. S. 129. (5)(a) repealed by Local Government and Housing Act 1989 (c. 42, SIF 61),s. 194. (2), Sch. 12 Pt. I

F9. S. 129. (5)(b) repealed by Local Government and Housing Act 1989 (c.42, SIF 61),s. 194. (4), Sch. 12 Pt. II note 2

F10. Words in s. 129. (6) inserted (1.4.2003) by The Regulatory Reform (Schemes under Section 129 of the Housing Act 1988) (England) Order 2003 (S.I. 2003/986), art. 2. (5)

F11. Words in s. 129. (6) inserted (1.4.2003) by The Regulatory Reform (Schemes under Section 129 of the Housing Act 1988) (England) Order 2003 (S.I. 2003/986), art. 2. (5)

Repair notices and improvement grants

130 Repair notices.

F12. . . . .

Amendments (Textual)

F12. S. 130 repealed (6.4.2006 for E. and 16.6.2006 for W.) by Housing Act 2004 (c. 34), ss. 266, 270, Sch. 16; S.I. 2006/1060, art. 2. (1)(e)(ix) (with Sch.); S.I. 2006/1535, art. 2. (c)(ix) (with Sch.)

[F13131 Letting conditions applicable to improvement grants etc.

(1) With respect to applications for grants approved after the commencement of this Act, Part XV of the M11. Housing Act 1985 (grants for works of improvement, repair and conversion) shall have effect subject to the following provisions of this section.

(2) In each of the following provisions—

(a) section 464 (preliminary condition: certificates as to future occupation), in subsection (5) (certificate of availability for letting), and

(b) section 501 (condition as to availability for letting), in subsection (2) (the terms of the condition),

in paragraph (a) after the word "holiday" there shall be inserted "on a tenancy which is not a long tenancy and".

(3) After the words "Rent (Agriculture) Act 1976", in each place where they occur in—

(a) section 464. (5),

(b) section 501. (2), and

(c) subsection (2)(d) of section 503 (restriction on imposition of further conditions in relation to certain grants),

there shall be inserted "or is occupied under an assured agricultural occupancy, within the meaning of Part I of the Housing Act 1988".

(4) In section 504 (further conditions as to letting of dwelling), at the beginning of subsection (1) there shall be inserted the words "Subject to subsection (1. A)"; in paragraph (a) of that subsection after the word "letting" there shall be inserted "on an assured tenancy which is not a long tenancy or"; and at the end of that subsection there shall be inserted the following subsection—

"(1. A)Paragraphs (d) to (f) of subsection (1) do not apply in the case of a dwelling which is or is to be let or available for letting on an assured tenancy."

(5) In subsection (2) of section 504 (definitions) after the words "subsection (1)" there shall be inserted "and subsection (1. A)" and before paragraph (a) there shall be inserted the following paragraph—

"(aa) "assured tenancy" means a tenancy which is an assured tenancy within the meaning of Part I of the Housing Act 1988 or would be such a tenancy if paragraphs 3, 6, 7 and 10 of Schedule 1 to that Act were omitted".

(6) In section 526 (index of defined expressions in Part XV), after the entry relating to "local housing authority" there shall be inserted—

"long tenancy section 115".

(7) Without prejudice to subsection (1) above, where an application for a grant—

(a) was made but not approved before the commencement of this Act, and

(b) was accompanied by a certificate of availability for letting in a form which does not take account of the amendments of section 464. (5) by subsections (2) and (3) above,

the certificate shall be treated as if it were in a form which takes account of the amendments made by those subsections.

(8) Without prejudice to subsection (1) above, where a grant has been approved before the commencement of this Act and—

(a) section 501. (2) applies to impose a condition of the grant, or

(b) conditions have been imposed in terms of section 504. (1),

the condition or conditions shall have effect as if it or they were in a form which takes account of the amendments made by subsection (3) or, as the case may be, subsections (4) and (5) above.]

Amendments (Textual)

F13. S. 131 repealed (prosp.) by Local Government and Housing Act 1989 (c. 42, SIF 61), ss. 194. (4), 195. (2), Sch. 12 Pt. II

Marginal Citations

M111985 c. 68.

Disposals of housing stock

132 Consents to disposals of housing stock and application of receipts.

(1) At the end of subsection (4) of section 34 of the M12. Housing Act 1985 (consent to disposals of land held for the purposes of Part II—provision of housing accommodation) and at the end of subsection (4) of section 43 of that Act (consent for certain disposals of other houses) there shall be inserted the subsections set out in subsection (2) below.
(2) The subsections referred to in subsection (1) above and subsection (3) below are as follows—
"(4. A)The matters to which the Secretary of State may have regard in determining whether to give consent and, if so, to what conditions consent should be subject shall include—
  (a) the extent (if any) to which the person to whom the proposed disposal is to be made (in this subsection referred to as "the intending purchaser") is, or is likely to be, dependent upon, controlled by or subject to influence from the local authority making the disposal or any members or officers of that authority;
  (b) the extent (if any) to which the proposed disposal would result in the intending purchaser becoming the predominant or a substantial owner in any area of housing accommodation let on tenancies or subject to licences;
  (c) the terms of the proposed disposal; and
  (d) any other matters whatsoever which he considers relevant.
(4. B)Where the Secretary of State gives consent to a disposal by a local authority, he may give directions as to the purpose for which any capital money received by the authority in respect of the disposal is to be applied and, where any such directions are given, nothing in any enactment shall require his consent to be given for the application of the capital money concerned in accordance with the directions."
(3) Section 13 of the M13. Housing (Scotland) Act 1987 (power of Secretary of State to impose conditions in sale of local authority houses) shall be renumbered as subsection (1) of that section and after that subsection there shall be inserted as subsections (2) and (3) the subsections which are set out in subsection (2) above and there numbered (4. A) and (4. B).
(4), (5). F14
(6) In section 208 of the Housing (Scotland) Act 1987 (application of receipts from disposal of certain land), in subsection (2) there shall be inserted at the end the words "or has made directions under section 13. (3)".
(7) In section 26 of the M14. Local Government Act 1988 (provisions as to consents under section 25 for provision of financial assistance etc.), in subsection (5) (which excludes consent under various enactments where consent is given to a disposal of land under section 25) after the words "such a consent" there shall be inserted "then, if the consent given for the purposes of section 25 above so provides".
(8) This section shall be deemed to have come into force on 9th June 1988.
Amendments (Textual)
F14. Ss. 132. (4)(5), 136 repealed by Local Government and Housing Act 1989 (c. 42, SIF 61),s. 194. (2), Sch. 12 Pt. I
Marginal Citations
M121985 c. 68.
M131987 c. 26.
M141988 c. 9.

133 Consent required for certain subsequent disposals.

(1) Where consent is required for a disposal (in this section referred to as "the original disposal") by virtue of section 32 or section 43 of the Housing Act 1985 and that consent does not provide otherwise, the person who acquires the land or house on the disposal shall not dispose of it except with the consent of the [F15appropriate authority]; but nothing in this section shall apply in relation to an exempt disposal as defined in section 81. (8) above.

[F16. (1. ZA)In this section "the appropriate authority" means—

F17. (a)............................

(b) in relation to [F18 a] disposal of land in England, the Secretary of State, and

(c) in relation to a disposal of land in Wales, the Welsh Ministers.]

[F19. (1. A)This section does not apply if the original disposal was made before the date on which this section comes into force.]

[F20. (1. B)This section does not apply if the original disposal was made to a private registered provider of social housing.]

(2) Where an estate or interest of the person who acquired the land or house on the original disposal has been mortgaged or charged, the prohibition in subsection (1) above applies also to a disposal by the mortgagee or chargee in exercise of a power of sale or leasing, whether or not the disposal is in the name of the person who so acquired the land or house; and in any case where—

(a) by operation of law or by virtue of an order of a court, the land or house which has been acquired passes or is transferred from the person who so acquired it to another person, and

(b) that passing or transfer does not constitute a disposal for which consent is required under this section,

this section (including, where there is more than one such passing or transfer, this subsection) shall apply as if the other person to whom the land or house passes or is transferred were the person who acquired it on the original disposal.

[F21. (2. A)Consent required for the purposes of this section may be given either generally to all persons who may require such consent or to any particular person or description of person who may require such consent.]

(3) Where subsection (1) above applies—

(a) if section 34 of the M15. Housing Act 1985 applies to the consent given to the original disposal, subsections (2)(b) [F22, (3), (4) and (4. A)(a) to (c) and (d)] of that section shall also apply to any consent required by virtue of this section;

(b) if the consent to the original disposal was given under section 43 of that Act, subsections (2)(b) and [F22, (3), (4) and (4. A)(a) to (c) and (d)] of that section shall also apply to any consent required by virtue of this section;

(c) in the application of subsection [F22. (4. A)(a) to (c) and (d)] of section 34 or section 43 to any consent required by virtue of this section, [F23 any reference to the appropriate national body shall be construed as a reference to the appropriate authority and]any reference to the local authority making the disposal shall be construed as a reference to the local authority making the original disposal; and

(d) the instrument by which the original disposal is effected shall contain a statement in a form approved by the Chief Land Registrar that the requirement of this section as to consent applies to a subsequent disposal of the land or house by the person to whom the original disposal was made.

(4) Subsection (4) of section 32 of the Housing Act 1985 or, as the case may be, subsection (5) of section 43 of that Act (options to purchase as disposals) applies for the purposes of this section.

(5) Before giving any consent required by virtue of this section, the [F24appropriate authority]—

(a) shall satisfy [F25itself] that the person who is seeking the consent has taken appropriate steps to consult every tenant of any land or house proposed to be disposed of; and

(b) shall have regard to the responses of any such tenants to that consultation.

F26[(5. A)A person seeking any consent required by virtue of this section is not required to consult a tenant of the land or house proposed to be disposed of if—

(a) consent is sought for the disposal of the land or house to that tenant or to persons including that tenant; or

(b) consent is sought subject to the condition that the land or house is vacant at the time of the disposal;

and, accordingly, subsection (5) does not apply in either case.]

F27. (6)............................

(7) No consent shall be required under F28... [F29section 9 or 42 of the Housing Act 1996 or section 9 of the Housing Associations Act 1985] for any disposal in respect of which consent is given [F30under this section].

(8) Where the title of the authority to the land or house which is disposed of by the original disposal is not registered, and the original disposal is a [F31transfer or grant] of a description mentioned in [F32section 4 of the Land Registration Act 2002] (compulsory registration of title)—

F33. (a).............................

(b) the authority shall give to the person to whom the original disposal is made a certificate in a form approved by the Chief Land Registrar stating that the authority is entitled to make the disposal subject only to such encumbrances, rights and interests as are stated in the instrument by which the original disposal is effected or summarised in the certificate; and

(c) for the purpose of registration of title, the Chief Land Registrar shall accept such a certificate as evidence of the facts stated in it, but if as a result he has to meet a claim against him under the [F34. Land Registration Act 2002] the authority by whom the original disposal was made is liable to indemnify him.

[F35. (9)Where the Chief Land Registrar approves an application for registration of—

(a) a disposition of registered land, or

(b) a person's title under a disposition of unregistered land,

and the instrument effecting the original disposal contains the statement required by subsection (3)(d) above, he shall enter in the register a restriction reflecting the limitation under this section on subsequent disposal.]

(10) In every case where the consent of the Secretary of State is required for the original disposal by virtue of section 32 or section 43 of the M16. Housing Act 1985 (whether or not consent is required under this section to a subsequent disposal), the authority by which the original disposal is made shall furnish to the person to whom it is made a copy of that consent.

Amendments (Textual)

F15. Words in s. 133. (1) substituted (1.4.2010) by Housing and Regeneration Act 2008 (c. 17), ss. 191. (3)(a), 325. (1) (with s. 189); S.I. 2010/862, art. 2 (with Sch.)

F16. S. 133. (1. ZA) inserted (1.4.2010) by Housing and Regeneration Act 2008 (c. 17), ss. 191. (3)(b), 325. (1) (with s. 189); S.I. 2010/862, art. 2 (with Sch.)

F17. S. 133. (1. ZA)(a) omitted (6.4.2017) by virtue of Housing and Planning Act 2016 (c. 22), s. 216. (3), Sch. 4 para. 4. (2)(a); S.I. 2017/75, reg. 4

F18. Word in s. 133. (1. ZA)(b) substituted (6.4.2017) by Housing and Planning Act 2016 (c. 22), s. 216. (3), Sch. 4 para. 4. (2)(b); S.I. 2017/75, reg. 4

F19. Words in s. 133. (1. A) inserted (1.10.1996) by 1996 c. 52, s. 222, Sch. 18 Pt. IV para. 21. (2); S.I. 1996/2402, art. 2

F20. S. 133. (1. B) substituted (6.4.2017) by Housing and Planning Act 2016 (c. 22), s. 216. (3), Sch. 4 para. 4. (3); S.I. 2017/75, reg. 4

F21. Words in s. 133. (2. A) inserted (1.10.1996) by 1996 c. 52, s. 222, Sch. 18 Pt. IV para. 21. (3); S.I. 1996/2402, art. 2

F22. Words in s. 133. (3) substituted (1.12.2008) by Housing and Regeneration Act 2008 (c. 17), ss. 311, 325, Sch. 14 para. 2; S.I. 2008/3068, art. 4. (1)(c) (with savings and transitional provisions in arts. 6-13)

F23. Words in s. 133. (3)(c) inserted (1.4.2010) by Housing and Regeneration Act 2008 (c. 17), ss. 191. (3)(d), 325. (1) (with s. 189); S.I. 2010/862, art. 2 (with Sch.)

F24. Words in s. 133. (5) substituted (1.4.2010) by Housing and Regeneration Act 2008 (c. 17), ss. 191. (3)(e), 325. (1) (with s. 189); S.I. 2010/862, art. 2 (with Sch.)

F25. Word in s. 133. (5)(a) substituted (1.4.2010) by Housing and Regeneration Act 2008 (c. 17), ss. 191. (3)(f), 325. (1) (with s. 189); S.I. 2010/862, art. 2 (with Sch.)

F26. Words in s. 133. (5. A) inserted (1.10.1996) by 1996 c. 52, s. 222, Sch. 18 Pt. IV para. 21.

(4); S.I. 1996/2402, art. 2

F27. S. 133. (6) repealed (1.4.2010) by Housing and Regeneration Act 2008 (c. 17), ss. 191. (3)(g), 325. (1), Sch. 16 (with s. 189); S.I. 2010/862, arts. 2, 3 (with Sch.)

F28. Words in s. 133. (7) omitted (6.4.2017) by virtue of Housing and Planning Act 2016 (c. 22), s. 216. (3), Sch. 4 para. 4. (4); S.I. 2017/75, reg. 4

F29. Words in s. 133. (7) substituted (1.10.1996) by S.I. 1996/2325, art. 5. (1), Sch. 2 para. 18. (12)(b)

F30. Words in s. 133. (7) substituted (1.11.1998) by 1998 c. 38, s. 140, Sch. 16 para. 71. (b)(with ss. 139. (2), 141. (1), 143. (2)); S.I. 1998/2244, art. 5

F31. Words in s. 133. (8) substituted (13.10.2003) by Land Registration Act 2002 (c. 9), ss. 133, 136. (2), Sch. 11 para. 23. (5)(a) (with s. 129); S.I. 2003/1725, art. 2. (1)

F32. Words in s. 133. (8) substituted (13.10.2003) by Land Registration Act 2002 (c. 9), ss. 133, 136, Sch. 11 para. 23. (5)(b) (with s. 129); S.I. 2003/1725, art. 2. (1)

F33. S. 133. (8)(a) repealed (1.4.1998) by 1997 c. 2, s. 4. (2), Sch. 2 Pt. I; S.I. 1997/3036, art. 2

F34. Words in s. 133. (8)(c) substituted (13.10.2003) by Land Registration Act 2002 (c. 9), ss. 133, 136. (2), Sch. 11 para. 23. (5)(c) (with s. 129); S.I. 2003/1725, art. 2. (1)

F35. S. 133. (9) substituted (13.10.2003) by Land Registration Act 2002 (c. 9), ss. 133, 136. (2), {Sch. 11 para. 23. (6)} (with s. 129); S.I. 2003/1725, art. 2. (1)

Modifications etc. (not altering text)

C1. S. 133 excluded (1.11.1993) by 1993 c. 28, ss. 37, 56. (6), Sch. 10 para. 1. (2)(a); S.I. 1993/2134, arts. 2, 5

C2. S. 133: transfer of functions (1.4.2010) by Housing and Regeneration Act 2008 (c. 17), ss. 190. (b), 325. (1) (with s. 189); S.I. 2010/862, art. 2 (with Sch.)

C3. S. 133. (6) modified (1.12.2008) by The Transfer of Housing Corporation Functions (Modifications and Transitional Provisions) Order 2008 (S.I. 2008/2839), arts. 1. (1), 3, Sch. para. 1; S.I. 2008/3068, art. 2. (1)(b) (with arts. 6-12)

Marginal Citations

M151985 c. 68.

M161985 c. 68.

[F36134 Consent required for certain subsequent disposals: Scotland.

In Part I of the M17. Housing (Scotland) Act 1987 (provision of housing) after section 12 there shall be inserted the following section—

12. A" Consent of Secretary of State required for certain subsequent disposals.

(1) Where a person acquires any land or house from a local authority under section 12. (1)(c) or (d) above and the consent of the Secretary of State is required under section 12. (7) above to the local authority's disposal of the land or house to that person, that person shall not dispose of the land or house without the consent in writing of the Secretary of State.

(2) Any consent for the purposes of subsection (1) above may be given either in respect of a particular disposal or in respect of disposals of any class or description (including disposals in particular areas) and either unconditionally or subject to conditions.

(3) Before giving any consent for the purposes of subsection (1) above, the Secretary of State—
  (a) shall satisfy himself that the person who is seeking the consent has taken appropriate steps to consult every tenant of any land or house proposed to be disposed of; and
  (b) shall have regard to the responses of any such tenants to that consultation.

(4) The consent of Scottish Homes under section 9 of the Housing Associations Act 1985 (control of dispositions) is not required for any disposal, or disposals of any class or description, in respect of which consent is given under subsection (1) above.

(5) In this section references to disposing of property include references to—
  (a) granting or disposing of any interest in property;

(b) entering into a contract to dispose of property or to grant or dispose of any such interest; and
(c) granting an option to acquire property or any such interest."]

Amendments (Textual)
F36. S. 134 repealed (30.9.2002) by 2001 asp 10, ss. 112, 113. (1), Sch. 10 para. 15. (7); S.S.I. 2002/321, art. 2, Sch. (with transitional provisions in arts. 3-5)
Marginal Citations
M171987 c. 26.

[F37135 Consultation before disposal: Scotland.

(1) In Part III of the M18. Housing (Scotland) Act 1987 (rights of public sector tenants) after section 81 there shall be inserted the following section—
" Consultation before disposal to private sector landlord
81. B Consultation before disposal to private sector landlord.
The provisions of Schedule 6. A have effect with respect to the duties of—
    (a) a local authority proposing to dispose of houses let on secure tenancies;
    (b) the Secretary of State in considering whether to give his consent under section 12. (7) to such a disposal,
to have regard to the views of tenants liable as a result of the disposal to cease to be secure tenants (that is to say, tenants under secure tenancies)."
(2) After Schedule 6 to the Housing (Scotland) Act 1987 there shall be inserted, as Schedule 6. A, the Schedule set out in Schedule 16 to this Act.
(3) The amendments made by this section apply to disposals after the coming into force of this section.]

Amendments (Textual)
F37. S. 135 repealed (30.9.2002) by 2001 asp 10, ss. 112, 113. (1), Sch. 10 para. 15. (7); S.S.I. 2002/321, art. 2, Sch. (with transitional provisions in arts. 3-5)
Commencement Information
I2. S. 135 wholly in force at 21.2.1992 see s. 141. (2) and S.I. 1992/324, art. 2
Marginal Citations
M181987 c. 26.

136. . . . . F38.

Amendments (Textual)
F38. Ss. 132. (4)(5), 136 repealed by Local Government and Housing Act 1989 (c. 42, SIF 61),s. 194. (2), Sch. 12 Pt. I

Codes of practice

137 Codes of practice in field of rented housing.

F39. . . . .
Amendments (Textual)
F39. S. 137 repealed (1.10.2007) by Equality Act 2006 (c. 3), ss. 91, 93, Sch. 4 (with s. 92); S.I. 2007/2603, art. 2. (c)(d) (subject to art. 3)

Supplementary

138 Financial provisions.

(1) There shall be paid out of money provided by Parliament—
    (a) any sums required for the payment by the Secretary of State of grants under this Act;
    (b) any sums required to enable the Secretary of State to make payments to housing action trusts established under Part III of this Act;
    (c) any other expenses of the Secretary of State under this Act; and
    (d) any increase attributable to this Act in the sums so payable under any other enactment.
(2) Any sums received by the Secretary of State under this Act, other than those required to be paid into the National Loans Fund, shall be paid into the Consolidated Fund.

139 Application to Isles of Scilly.

(1) This Act applies to the Isles of Scilly subject to such exceptions, adaptations and modifications as the Secretary of State may by order direct.
(2) The power to make an order under this section shall be exercisable by statutory instrument which shall be subject to annulment in pursuance of a resolution of either House of Parliament.

140 Amendments and repeals.

(1) Schedule 17 to this Act, which contains minor amendments and amendments consequential on the provisions of this Act and the M19. Housing (Scotland) Act 1988, shall have effect F40. . . .
(2) The enactments specified in Schedule 18 to this Act, which include some that are spent, are hereby repealed to the extent specified in the third column of that Schedule, but subject to any provision at the end of that Schedule and to any saving in Chapter V of Part I of or Schedule 17 to this Act.
Amendments (Textual)
F40. Words in s. 140. (1) repealed (1.11.1998) by 1998 c. 38, s. 140, 152, Sch. 16 para. 72, Sch. 18 Pt. VI (with 137. (1), 139. (2), 141. (1), 143. (2)); S.I. 1998/2244, art. 5
Commencement Information
I3. S. 140 partly in force; s. 140. (2) partly in force for certain purposes at 1.4.1991, see s. 141. (2)(3)(4) and S.I. 1991/954, art. 2
Marginal Citations
M191988 c. 43.

141 Short title, commencement and extent.

(1) This Act may be cited as the Housing Act 1988.
(2) The provisions of Parts II and IV of this Act and sections 119, 122, 124, 128, 129, 135 and 140 above shall come into force on such day as the Secretary of State may by order made by statutory instrument appoint, and different days may be so appointed for different provisions or for different purposes.
(3) Part I and this Part of this Act, other than sections 119, 122, 124, 128, 129, 132, 133, 134, 135 and 138 onwards, shall come into force at the expiry of the period of two months beginning on the day it is passed; and any reference in those provisions to the commencement of this Act shall be construed accordingly.
(4) An order under subsection (2) above may make such transitional provisions as appear to the Secretary of State necessary or expedient in connection with the provisions brought into force by the order.
(5) Parts I, III and IV of this Act and this Part, except sections 118, 128, 132, 134, 135 and 137 onwards, extend to England and Wales only.

(6) This Act does not extend to Northern Ireland.
Subordinate Legislation Made
P1. S. 141. (2)(4) power partly exercised; 1.4.1991 appointed for specified provisions by S.I.1991/954 (with saving and transitional provisions)
S. 141. (2) power partly exercised (20.2.1992): 21.2.1992 appointed for specified provisions by S.I. 1992/324, art. 2.
Modifications etc. (not altering text)
C4. Power of appointment conferred by s. 141. (2) partly exercised: S.I. 1988/2056, 2152, 1989/203, 404

Schedules

Schedule 1. Tenancies Which Cannot be Assured Tenancies

Section 1.
Modifications etc. (not altering text)
C1. Sch. 1 modified by Local Government and Housing Act 1989 (c. 42, SIF 75:1), s. 186, Sch. 10 paras. 1. (2), 21, 22

Part I The Tenancies

Tenancies entered into before commencement

1. A tenancy which is entered into before, or pursuant to a contract made before, the commencement of this Act.

Tenancies of dwelling-houses with high rateable values

[F12. (1)A tenancy—
(a) which is entered into on or after 1st April 1990 (otherwise than, where the dwelling-house had a rateable value on 31st March 1990, in pursuance of a contract made before 1st April 1990), and
(b) under which the rent payable for the time being is payable at a rate exceeding [F2£100,000] a year.
(2)In sub-paragraph (1) "rent" does not include any sum payable by the tenant as is expressed (in whatever terms) to be payable in respect of rates, [F3council tax,] services, management, repairs, maintenance or insurance, unless it could not have been regarded by the parties to the tenancy as a sum so payable.
2. A.A tenancy—
(a) which was entered into before the 1st April 1990, or on or after that date in pursuance of a contract made before that date, and
(b) under which the dwelling-house had a rateable value on the 31st March 1990 which, if it is in Greater London, exceeded £1,500 and, if it is elsewhere, exceeded £750.]
Amendments (Textual)
F1. Sch. 1 paras. 2, 2. A substituted for para 2 by S.I. 1990/434, reg. 2, Sch. para. 29
F2. Word in Sch. 1 para. 2. (1)(b) substituted (E.) (1.10.2010) by The Assured Tenancies

(Amendment)(England) Order 2010 (S.I. 2010/908), arts. 1, 3. (2) and word in Sch. 1 para. 2. (1)(b) substituted (W.) (1.12.2011) by The Assured Tenancies (Amendment of Rental Threshold) (Wales) Order 2011 (S.I. 2011/1409), arts. 1. (1), 2. (2)
F3. Words in Sch. 1 para. 2. (2) inserted (1.4.1993) by S.I. 1993/651, art. 2. (1), Sch. 1 para.19
Modifications etc. (not altering text)
C2. Sch. 1 para. 2. (2) applied by Local Government and Housing Act 1989 (c. 42, SIF 75:1), s. 186, Sch. 10 paras. 2. (5), 21, 22 (as amended by S.I. 1990/434, reg. 2, Sch. para. 34)

Tenancies at a low rent

[F43. A tenancy under which for the time being no rent is payable.]
Amendments (Textual)
F4. Sch. 1 paras. 3, 3. A, 3. B, 3. C substituted for para. 3 by S.I. 1990/434, reg. 2, Sch. para. 30
3. AA tenancy—
(a) which is entered into on or after 1st April 1990 (otherwise than, where the dwelling-house had a rateable value on 31st March 1990, in pursuance of a contract made before 1st April 1990), and
(b) under which the rent payable for the time being is payable at a rate of, if the dwelling-house is in Greater London, £1,000 or less a year and, if it is elsewhere, £250 or less a year.
3. BA tenancy—
(a) which was entered into before 1st April 1990 or, where the dwelling-house had a rateable value on the 31st March 1990, on or after 1st April 1990 in pursuance of a contract made before that date, and
(b) under which the rent for the time being payable is less than two-thirds of the rateable value of the dwelling-house on 31st March 1990.
3. CParagraph 2. (2) above applies for the purposes of paragraphs 3, 3. A and 3. B as it applies for the purposes of paragraph 2. (1).

Business tenancies

4. A tenancy to which Part II of the M1. Landlord and Tenant Act 1954 applies (business tenancies).
Marginal Citations
M11954 c.56.

Licensed premises

5. A tenancy under which the dwelling-house consists of or comprises [F5"premises which, by virtue of a premises licence under the Licensing Act 2003, may be used for the supply of alcohol (within the meaning of section 14 of that Act)"] for consumption on the premises.
Amendments (Textual)
F5. Words in Sch. 1 para. 5 substituted (24.11.2005) by Licensing Act 2003 (c. 17), ss. 198, 201. (2), Sch. 6 para. 108 (with ss. 2. (3), 15. (2), 195); S.I. 2005/3056, art. 2. (2)

Tenancies of agricultural land

6. (1)A tenancy under which agricultural land, exceeding two acres, is let together with the dwelling-house.
(2) In this paragraph "agricultural land" has the meaning set out in section 26. (3)(a) of the M2. General Rate Act 1967 (exclusion of agricultural land and premises from liability for rating).
Marginal Citations
M21967 c. 9.

[F6 Tenancies of agricultural holdings etc.]

Amendments (Textual)
F6. Sch. 1 para. 7 and cross-heading substituted (1.9.1995) by 1995 c. 8, ss. 40, 41. (2), Sch. para. 34 (with s. 37)
[F7 7. (1) A tenancy under which the dwelling-house—
(a) is comprised in an agricultural holding, and
(b) is occupied by the person responsible for the control (whether as tenant or as servant or agent of the tenant) of the farming of the holding.
(2) A tenancy under which the dwelling-house—
(a) is comprised in the holding held under a farm business tenancy, and
(b) is occupied by the person responsible for the control (whether as tenant or as servant or agent of the tenant) of the management of the holding.
(3) In this paragraph—
"agricultural holding" means any agricultural holding within the meaning of the Agricultural Holdings Act 1986 held under a tenancy in relation to which that Act applies, and
"farm business tenancy" and "holding", in relation to such a tenancy, have the same meaning as in the Agricultural Tenancies Act 1995.]
Amendments (Textual)
F7. Sch. 1 para. 7 and cross-heading substituted (1.9.1995) by 1995 c. 8, ss. 40, 41. (2), Sch. para. 34 (with s. 37)

Lettings to students

8. (1) A tenancy which is granted to a person who is pursuing, or intends to pursue, a course of study provided by a specified educational institution and is so granted either by that institution or by another specified institution or body of persons.
(2) In sub-paragraph (1) above "specified" means specified, or of a class specified, for the purposes of this paragraph by regulations made by the Secretary of State by statutory instrument.
(3) A statutory instrument made in the exercise of the power conferred by sub-paragraph (2) above shall be subject to annulment in pursuance of a resolution of either House of Parliament.

Holiday lettings

9. A tenancy the purpose of which is to confer on the tenant the right to occupy the dwelling-house for a holiday.

Resident landlords

10. (1) A tenancy in respect of which the following conditions are fulfilled—
(a) that the dwelling-house forms part only of a building and, except in a case where the dwelling-house also forms part of a flat, the building is not a purpose-built block of flats; and
(b) that, subject to Part III of this Schedule, the tenancy was granted by an individual who, at the time when the tenancy was granted, occupied as his only or principal home another dwelling-house which,—
(i) in the case mentioned in paragraph (a) above, also forms part of the flat; or
(ii) in any other case, also forms part of the building; and
(c) that, subject to Part III of this Schedule, at all times since the tenancy was granted the interest of the landlord under the tenancy has belonged to an individual who, at the time he owned that interest, occupied as his only or principal home another dwelling-house which,—

(i) in the case mentioned in paragraph (a) above, also formed part of the flat; or
(ii) in any other case, also formed part of the building; and
(d) that the tenancy is not one which is excluded from this sub-paragraph by sub-paragraph (3) below.
(2) If a tenancy was granted by two or more persons jointly, the reference in sub-paragraph (1)(b) above to an individual is a reference to any one of those persons and if the interest of the landlord is for the time being held by two or more persons jointly, the reference in sub-paragraph (1)(c) above to an individual is a reference to any one of those persons.
(3) A tenancy (in this sub-paragraph referred to as "the new tenancy") is excluded from sub-paragraph (1) above if—
(a) it is granted to a person (alone, or jointly with others) who, immediately before it was granted, was a tenant under an assured tenancy (in this sub-paragraph referred to as "the former tenancy") of the same dwelling-house or of another dwelling-house which forms part of the building in question; and
(b) the landlord under the new tenancy and under the former tenancy is the same person or, if either of those tenancies is or was granted by two or more persons jointly, the same person is the landlord or one of the landlords under each tenancy.

Crown tenancies

11. (1) A tenancy under which the interest of the landlord belongs to Her Majesty in right of the Crown or to a government department or is held in trust for Her Majesty for the purposes of a government department.
(2) The reference in sub-paragraph (1) above to the case where the interest of the landlord belongs to Her Majesty in right of the Crown does not include the case where that interest is under the management of the Crown Estate Commissioners [F8or it is held by the Secretary of State as the result of the exercise by him of functions under Part III of the Housing Associations Act 1985.]
Amendments (Textual)
F8. Words in Sch. 1 para. 11. (2) added (15.1.1999) by S.I. 1999/61, art. 2, Sch. 1 para. 3. (4)
Modifications etc. (not altering text)
C3. Sch. 1 para. 11 modified by National Health Service and Community Care Act 1990 (c. 19, SIF 113:2), s. 60. (2), Sch. 8 Pt. III para. 11

Local authority tenancies etc.

12. (1) A tenancy under which the interest of the landlord belongs to—
(a) a local authority, as defined in sub-paragraph (2) below;
[F9. (b) the Homes and Communities Agency but only if the tenancy falls within subsections (2. A) to (2. E) of section 80 of the Housing Act 1985;
(ba) the Welsh Ministers but only if the tenancy falls within subsections (2. A) to (2. E) of section 80 of the Housing Act 1985;]
F10. (c). . . . .
(d) an urban development corporation established by an order under section 135 of the M3. Local Government, Planning and Land Act 1980;
[F11. (da) a Mayoral development corporation;]
[F12. (da) a National Park authority;]
(e) a development corporation, within the meaning of the M4. New Towns Act 1981;
(f) an authority established under section 10 of the M5. Local Government Act 1985 (waste disposal authorities);
F13. (fa). . . . .
(g) a residuary body, within the meaning of the Local Government Act 1985;
[F14. (gg) The Residuary Body for Wales (Corff Gweddilliol Cymru);]

(h) a fully mutual housing association[F15, unless the tenancy is one which is excluded from this sub-paragraph by sub-paragraph (3) below;] or
(i) a housing action trust established under Part III of this Act.
(2) The following are local authorities for the purposes of sub-paragraph (1)(a) above—
(a) the council of a county, [F16county borough,] district or London borough;
(b) the Common Council of the City of London;
(c) the Council of the Isles of Scilly;
(d) the Broads Authority;
(e) the Inner London Education Authority; and
[F17. (ea)a fire and rescue authority created by an order under section 4. A of the Fire and Rescue Services Act 2004;]
[F18. (ee)the London Fire Commissioner;]
(f) a joint authority, within the meaning of the Local Government Act 1985;
[F19. (fa)an economic prosperity board established under section 88 of the Local Democracy, Economic Development and Construction Act 2009;
(fb) a combined authority established under section 103 of that Act;] and
[F20. (g)a police and crime commissioner.]
[F21. (3)A tenancy is excluded from sub-paragraph (1) if all of the following requirements are met—
(a) the interest of the landlord belongs to a fully mutual housing association;
(b) the dwelling-house is in Wales;
(c) the tenancy is granted on or after the date on which this sub-paragraph comes into force;
(d) the tenancy is in writing;
(e) before the tenancy is granted, the landlord has served on the person who is to be the tenant a notice stating that the tenancy is to be excluded from sub-paragraph (1);
(f) the tenancy states that it is excluded from sub-paragraph (1).]

Amendments (Textual)

F9. Sch. 1 para. 12. (b)(ba) substituted (1.12.2008) for Sch. 1 para. 12. (b) by The Housing and Regeneration Act 2008 (Consequential Provisions) Order 2008 (S.I. 2008/3002), arts. 1. (2), 4, Sch. 1 para. 40 (with Sch. 2); S.I. 2008/3038, art. 2. (1)(b) (with arts. 6-13)
F10. Sch. 1 para. 12. (1)(c) repealed (1.10.1998) by 1998 c. 38, s. 152, Sch. 18 Pt. IV (with ss. 137. (1), 139. (2), 141. (1), 143. (2)); S.I. 1998/2244, art. 4
F11. Sch. 1 para. 12. (1)(da) inserted (15.1.2012) by Localism Act 2011 (c. 20), s. 240. (1)(l), Sch. 22 para. 29
F12. Sch. 1 para. 12 (1)(da) inserted (23.11.1995) by 1995 c. 25, s. 78, Sch. 10 para. 28 (with ss. 7. (6), 115, 117, Sch. 8 para. 7); S.I. 1995/2950, art, 2. (1)
F13. Sch. 1 para. 12. (1)(fa) omitted (26.5.2015) by virtue of Deregulation Act 2015 (c. 20), s. 115. (7), Sch. 13 para. 6. (22); S.I. 2015/994, art. 6. (g)
F14. Sch. 1 para. 12. (1)(gg) inserted (5.7.1994) by 1994 c. 19, ss. 22. (2), 66. (2)(b), Sch. 13 para. 31 (with ss. 54. (7), 55. (5), Sch. 17 paras. 22. (1), 23. (2))
F15. Words in Sch. 1 para. 12. (1)(h) inserted (1.12.2014) by Housing (Wales) Act 2014 (anaw 7), ss. 137. (2), 145. (3); S.I. 2014/3127, art. 2. (a), Sch. Pt. 1
F16. Words in Sch. 1 para. 12. (2)(a) inserted (1.4.1996) by 1994 c. 19, s. 22. (2), Sch. 8 para. 9. (2) (with ss. 54. (7), 55. (5), Sch. 17 paras. 22. (1), 23. (2)); S.I. 1996/396, art. 3, Sch. 1
F17. Sch. 1 para. 12. (2)(ea) inserted (31.1.2017 for specified purposes, 3.4.2017 in so far as not already in force) by Policing and Crime Act 2017 (c. 3), s. 183. (1)(5)(e), Sch. 1 para. 58; S.I. 2017/399, reg. 2, Sch. para. 38
F18. Sch. 1 para. 12. (2)(ee) substituted (31.1.2017 for specified purposes) by Policing and Crime Act 2017 (c. 3), s. 183. (1)(5)(e), Sch. 2 para. 83
F19. Sch. 1 para. 12. (2)(fa)(fb) inserted (17.12.2009) by Local Democracy, Economic Development and Construction Act 2009 (c. 20), ss. 119, 148. (8), 149, Sch. 6 para. 79. (3); S.I. 2009/3318, art. 2
F20. Sch. 1 para. 12. (2)(g) substituted (22.11.2012) by Police Reform and Social Responsibility

Act 2011 (c. 13), s. 157. (1), Sch. 16 para. 178; S.I. 2012/2892, art. 2. (i)
F21. Sch. 1 para. 12. (3) inserted (1.12.2014) by Housing (Wales) Act 2014 (anaw 7), ss. 137. (3), 145. (3); S.I. 2014/3127, art. 2. (a), Sch. Pt. 1
Modifications etc. (not altering text)
C4. Sch.1 Pt.1 para.12 excluded (6.4.2006 for E.and 16.6.2006 for W.) by Housing Act 2004 (c. 34), ss.132,270,{Sch .7 para.18. (6)(b)};S.I.2006/1060,{art.2. (1)(a)}(with Sch.); S.I. 2006/1535, art.2. (a) (with Sch.)
C5. Sch.1 Pt.1 para.12 excluded (6.4.2006 for E. and 16.6.2006 for W.) by Housing Act 2004 (c. 34), ss.132,270, {Sch.7 para.12. (5)(b)(9)}; S.I.2006/1060, art.2. (1)(a) (with Sch.); S.I.2006/1535, art. 2. (a) (with Sch.)
C6. Sch. 1 Pt. 1 para.12 excluded (6.4.2006 for E. and 16.6.2006 for W.) by Housing Act 2004 (c. 34), ss.132,270,{Sch. 7 para.4. (5)(b)};S.I.2006/1060,{art.2. (1)(a)}(with Sch.);S.I.2006/1535,{art. 2. (a)}(with Sch.)
C7. Sch.1 Pt. 1 para. 12 excluded (6.4.2006 for E. and 16.6.2006 for W.) by Housing Act 2004 (c. 34), s. 124. (8) (with s. 124. (9)(10)); S.I.2006/1060,{art. 2. (1)(a)} (with Sch.); S.I. 2006/1535, art. 2. (a) (with Sch.)
C8. Sch. 1 para. 12. (2)(g) excluded (8.5.2017) by The Greater Manchester Combined Authority (Transfer of Police and Crime Commissioner Functions to the Mayor) Order 2017 (S.I. 2017/470), art. 1. (2), Sch. 2 para. 13
Marginal Citations
M31980 c. 65.
M41981 c. 64.
M51985 c. 51.

[F22. Family intervention tenancies

Amendments (Textual)
F22. Sch. 1 para. 12. ZA inserted (1.1.2009 for E., otherwise prosp.) by Housing and Regeneration Act 2008 (c. 17), ss. 297. (2), 325; S.I. 2008/3068, art. 4. (11) (with arts. 6-13)
12. ZA(1)A family intervention tenancy.
(2) But a family intervention tenancy becomes an assured tenancy if the landlord notifies the tenant that it is to be regarded as an assured tenancy.
(3) In this paragraph " a family intervention tenancy " means, subject to sub-paragraph (4), a tenancy granted by a [F23 private registered provider] of social housing or a registered social landlord (" the landlord ") in respect of a dwelling-house—
(a) to a person (" the new tenant ") against whom a possession order under section 7 in respect of another dwelling-house—
(i) has been made, in relation to an assured tenancy, on [F24ground 7. A of Part 1 of Schedule 2 or ground 14, 14. ZA] or 14. A of Part 2 of Schedule 2;
(ii) could, in the opinion of the landlord, have been so made in relation to such a tenancy; or
(iii) could, in the opinion of the landlord, have been so made if the person had had such a tenancy; and
(b) for the purposes of the provision of behaviour support services.
(4) A tenancy is not a family intervention tenancy for the purposes of this paragraph if the landlord has failed to serve a notice under sub-paragraph (5) on the new tenant before the new tenant entered into the tenancy.
(5) A notice under this sub-paragraph is a notice stating—
(a) the reasons for offering the tenancy to the new tenant;
(b) the dwelling-house in respect of which the tenancy is to be granted;
(c) the other main terms of the tenancy (including any requirements on the new tenant in respect of behaviour support services);
(d) the security of tenure available under the tenancy and any loss of security of tenure which is

likely to result from the new tenant agreeing to enter into the tenancy;
(e) that the new tenant is not obliged to enter into the tenancy or (unless otherwise required to do so) to surrender any existing tenancy or possession of a dwelling-house;
(f) any likely action by the landlord if the new tenant does not enter into the tenancy or surrender any existing tenancy or possession of a dwelling-house.
(6) The appropriate national authority may by regulations made by statutory instrument amend sub-paragraph (5).
(7) A notice under sub-paragraph (5) must contain advice to the new tenant as to how the new tenant may be able to obtain assistance in relation to the notice.
(8) The appropriate national authority may by regulations made by statutory instrument make provision about the type of advice to be provided in such notices.
(9) Regulations under this paragraph may contain such transitional, transitory or saving provision as the appropriate national authority considers appropriate.
(10) A statutory instrument containing (whether alone or with other provision) regulations under this paragraph which amend or repeal any of paragraphs (a) to (f) of sub-paragraph (5) may not be made—
(a) by the Secretary of State unless a draft of the instrument has been laid before, and approved by a resolution of, each House of Parliament; and
(b) by the Welsh Ministers unless a draft of the instrument has been laid before, and approved by a resolution of, the National Assembly for Wales.
(11) Subject to this, a statutory instrument containing regulations made under this paragraph—
(a) by the Secretary of State is subject to annulment in pursuance of a resolution of either House of Parliament; and
(b) by the Welsh Ministers is subject to annulment in pursuance of a resolution of the National Assembly for Wales.
(12) In this paragraph—
"appropriate national authority"—
- in relation to England, means the Secretary of State; and
- in relation to Wales, means the Welsh Ministers;
" behaviour support agreement " means an agreement in writing about behaviour and the provision of support services made between the new tenant, the landlord and the local housing authority for the district in which the dwelling-house which is to be subject to the new tenancy is situated (or between persons who include those persons);
" behaviour support services " means relevant support services to be provided by any person to—
- the new tenant; or
- any person who is to reside with the new tenant;
for the purpose of addressing the kind of behaviour which led to the new tenant falling within sub-paragraph (3)(a);
" family intervention tenancy " has the meaning given by sub-paragraph (3);
" landlord " has the meaning given by sub-paragraph (3);
"local housing authority" (and the reference to its district) has the same meaning as in the Housing Act 1985 (see sections 1 and 2. (1) of that Act);
" the new tenant " has the meaning given by sub-paragraph (3)(a);
" registered social landlord " has the same meaning as in Part 1 of the Housing Act 1996;
" relevant support services " means support services of a kind identified in a behaviour support agreement and designed to meet such needs of the recipient as are identified in the agreement.]
Amendments (Textual)
F23. Words in Sch. 1 para. 12. ZA(3) substituted (1.4.2010) by The Housing and Regeneration Act 2008 (Registration of Local Authorities) Order 2010 (S.I. 2010/844), art. 1. (2), Sch. 2 para. 21. (4)
F24. Words in Sch. 1 para. 12. ZA(3)(a)(i) substituted (13.5.2014 for E., 13.5.2014 for W.) by Anti-social Behaviour, Crime and Policing Act 2014 (c. 12), s. 185. (1)(2)(c)(3)(c), Sch. 11 para. 20 (with ss. 21, 33, 42, 58, 75, 93); S.I. 2014/949, art. 2. (d)(ii) (with art. 11. (1)(3)); S.I.

2014/1241, art. 2. (d)(ii) (with art. 3. (1)(3)); S.I. 2014/949, art. 2. (d)(ii) (with art. 11. (1)(3)); S.I. 2014/1241, art. 2. (d)(ii) (with art. 3. (1)(3))

[F25 Accommodation for asylum-seekers]

Amendments (Textual)
F25. Sch. 1 para. 12. A and cross-heading preceding it inserted (11.11.1999) by 1999 c. 33, ss. 169. (1), 170. (3)(s), Sch. 14 para. 88
[F2612. A(1)A tenancy granted by a private landlord under arrangements for the provision of support for asylum-seekers or dependants of asylum-seekers made [F27under section 4 or Part VI of the Immigration and Asylum Act 1999] .
(2) "Private landlord" means a landlord who is not within section 80. (1) of the M6. Housing Act 1985.]
Amendments (Textual)
F26. Sch. 1 para. 12. A and cross-heading preceding it inserted (11.11.1999) by 1999 c. 33, ss. 169. (1), 170. (3)(s), Sch. 14 para. 88
F27. Words in Sch. 1 para. 12. A(1) substituted (16.6.2006) by Immigration, Asylum and Nationality Act 2006 (c. 13), ss. 43. (4)(f), 62; S.I. 2006/1497, art. 3, Sch.
Marginal Citations
M61985 c. 68.

[F28. Accommodation for persons with Temporary Protection

Amendments (Textual)
F28. Sch. 1 para. 12. B and cross-heading inserted (15.6.2005) by The Displaced Persons (Temporary Protection) Regulations 2005 (S.I. 2005/1379), Sch. para. 6
12. B(1)A tenancy granted by a private landlord under arrangements for the provision of accommodation for persons with temporary protection made under the Displaced Persons (Temporary Protection) Regulations 2005.
(2) "Private landlord" means a landlord who is not within section 80. (1) of the Housing Act 1985.]

Transitional cases

13. (1)A protected tenancy, within the meaning of the M7. Rent Act 1977.
(2) A housing association tenancy, within the meaning of Part VI of that Act.
(3) A secure tenancy.
(4) Where a person is a protected occupier of a dwelling-house, within the meaning of the M8. Rent (Agriculture) Act 1976, the relevant tenancy, within the meaning of that Act, by virtue of which he occupies the dwelling-house.
Marginal Citations
M71977 c. 42.
M81976 c. 80.

Part II Rateable Values

Modifications etc. (not altering text)
C9. Pt. II (paras. 14–16) applied by Local Government and Housing Act 1989 (c. 42, SIF 75:1), s. 186, Sch. 10 paras. 2. (5), 21, 22
14. (1)The rateable value of a dwelling-house at any time shall be ascertained for the purposes of Part I of this Schedule as follows—

(a) if the dwelling-house is a hereditament for which a rateable value is then shown in the valuation list, it shall be that rateable value;
(b) if the dwelling-house forms part only of such a hereditament or consists of or forms part of more than one such hereditament, its rateable value shall be taken to be such value as is found by a proper apportionment or aggregation of the rateable value or values so shown.
(2) Any question arising under this Part of this Schedule as to the proper apportionment or aggregation of any value or values shall be determined by the county court and the decision of that court shall be final.
15 Where, after the time at which the rateable value of a dwelling-house is material for the purposes of any provision of Part I of this Schedule, the valuation list is altered so as to vary the rateable value of the hereditament of which the dwelling-house consists (in whole or in part) or forms part and the alteration has effect from that time or from an earlier time, the rateable value of the dwelling-house at the material time shall be ascertained as if the value shown in the valuation list at the material time had been the value shown in the list as altered.
16. Paragraphs 14 and 15 above apply in relation to any other land which, under section 2 of this Act, is treated as part of a dwelling-house as they apply in relation to the dwelling-house itself.

Part III Provisions for Determining Application of Paragraph 10 (Resident Landlords)

17. (1)In determining whether the condition in paragraph 10. (1)(c) above is at any time fulfilled with respect to a tenancy, there shall be disregarded—
(a) any period of not more than twenty-eight days, beginning with the date on which the interest of the landlord under the tenancy becomes vested at law and in equity in an individual who, during that period, does not occupy as his only or principal home another dwelling-house which forms part of the building or, as the case may be, flat concerned;
(b) if, within a period falling within paragraph (a) above, the individual concerned notifies the tenant in writing of his intention to occupy as his only or principal home another dwelling-house in the building or, as the case may be, flat concerned, the period beginning with the date on which the interest of the landlord under the tenancy becomes vested in that individual as mentioned in that paragraph and ending—
(i) at the expiry of the period of six months beginning on that date, or
(ii) on the date on which that interest ceases to be so vested, or
(iii) on the date on which that interest becomes again vested in such an individual as is mentioned in paragraph 10. (1)(c) or the condition in that paragraph becomes deemed to be fulfilled by virtue of paragraph 18. (1) or paragraph 20 below,
whichever is the earlier; and
(c) any period of not more than two years beginning with the date on which the interest of the landlord under the tenancy becomes, and during which it remains, vested—
(i) in trustees as such; or
(ii) by virtue of section 9 of the M9. Administration of Estates Act 1925, in [F29the Probate Judge or the Public trustee].
(2) Where the interest of the landlord under a tenancy becomes vested at law and in equity in two or more persons jointly, of whom at least one was an individual, sub-paragraph (1) above shall have effect subject to the following modifications—
(a) in paragraph (a) for the words from "an individual" to "occupy" there shall be substituted "the joint landlords if, during that period none of them occupies"; and
(b) in paragraph (b) for the words "the individual concerned" there shall be substituted "any of the joint landlords who is an individual" and for the words "that individual" there shall be substituted "the joint landlords".
Amendments (Textual)
F29. Words in Sch. 1 para. 17. (1)(c)(ii) substituted (1.7.1995) by 1994 c. 36, s. 21. (1), Sch. 1

para. 11 (with s. 20); S.I. 1995/1317, art. 2
Marginal Citations
M91925 c. 23.
18. (1) During any period when—
(a) the interest of the landlord under the tenancy referred to in paragraph 10 above is vested in trustees as such, and
(b) that interest is F30. . . held on trust for any person who or for two or more persons of whom at least one occupies as his only or principal home a dwelling-house which forms part of the building or, as the case may be, flat referred to in paragraph 10. (1)(a),
the condition in paragraph 10. (1)(c) shall be deemed to be fulfilled and accordingly, no part of that period shall be disregarded by virtue of paragraph 17 above.
(2) If a period during which the condition in paragraph 10. (1)(c) is deemed to be fulfilled by virtue of sub-paragraph (1) above comes to an end on the death of a person who was in occupation of a dwelling-house as mentioned in paragraph (b) of that sub-paragraph, then, in determining whether that condition is at any time thereafter fulfilled, there shall be disregarded any period—
(a) which begins on the date of the death;
(b) during which the interest of the landlord remains vested as mentioned in sub-paragraph (1)(a) above; and
(c) which ends at the expiry of the period of two years beginning on the date of the death or on any earlier date on which the condition in paragraph 10. (1)(c) becomes again deemed to be fulfilled by virtue of sub-paragraph (1) above.
Amendments (Textual)
F30. Words in Sch. 1 para. 18. (1)(b) repealed (1.1.1997) by 1996 c. 47, s. 25. (2), Sch. 4 (with ss. 24. (2), 25. (4)(5)); S.I. 1996/2974, art. 2
19. In any case where—
(a) immediately before a tenancy comes to an end the condition in paragraph 10. (1)(c) is deemed to be fulfilled by virtue of paragraph 18. (1) above, and
(b) on the coming to an end of that tenancy the trustees in whom the interest of the landlord is vested grant a new tenancy of the same or substantially the same dwelling-house to a person (alone or jointly with others) who was the tenant or one of the tenants under the previous tenancy, the condition in paragraph 10. (1)(b) above shall be deemed to be fulfilled with respect to the new tenancy.
20. (1)The tenancy referred to in paragraph 10 above falls within this paragraph if the interest of the landlord under the tenancy becomes vested in the personal representatives of a deceased person acting in that capacity.
(2) If the tenancy falls within this paragraph, the condition in paragraph 10. (1)(c) shall be deemed to be fulfilled for any period, beginning with the date on which the interest becomes vested in the personal representatives and not exceeding two years, during which the interest of the landlord remains so vested.
21. Throughout any period which, by virtue of paragraph 17 or paragraph 18. (2) above, falls to be disregarded for the purpose of determining whether the condition in paragraph 10. (1)(c) is fulfilled with respect to a tenancy, no order shall be made for possession of the dwelling-house subject to that tenancy, other than an order which might be made if that tenancy were or, as the case may be, had been an assured tenancy.
22. For the purposes of paragraph 10 above, a building is a purpose-built block of flats if as constructed it contained, and it contains, two or more flats; and for this purpose "flat" means a dwelling-house which—
(a) forms part only of a building; and
(b) is separated horizontally from another dwelling-house which forms part of the same building.

Schedule 2. Grounds for Possession of Dwelling-houses let on Assured Tenancies

Section 7.

Part I Grounds on which Court must order possession

Ground 1.

Not later than the beginning of the tenancy the landlord gave notice in writing to the tenant that possession might be recovered on this ground or the court is of the opinion that it is just and equitable to dispense with the requirement of notice and (in either case)—
(a) at some time before the beginning of the tenancy, the landlord who is seeking possession or, in the case of joint landlords seeking possession, at least one of them occupied the dwelling-house as his only or principal home; or
(b) the landlord who is seeking possession or, in the case of joint landlords seeking possession, at least one of them requires the dwelling-house as [F1his, his spouse's or his civil partner's] only or principal home and neither the landlord (or, in the case of joint landlords, any one of them) nor any other person who, as landlord, derived title under the landlord who gave the notice mentioned above acquired the reversion on the tenancy for money or money's worth.
Amendments (Textual)
F1. Words in Sch. 2 Pt. 1 Ground 1 substituted (5.12.2005) by Civil Partnership Act 2004 (c. 33), s. 81, 263, Sch. 8 para. 43. (2); S.I. 2005/ 3175, {art. 2. (1)}, Sch. 1

Ground 2.

The dwelling-house is subject to a mortgage granted before the beginning of the tenancy and—
(a) the mortgagee is entitled to exercise a power of sale conferred on him by the mortgage or by section 101 of the M1. Law of Property Act 1925; and
(b) the mortgagee requires possession of the dwelling-house for the purpose of disposing of it with vacant possession in exercise of that power; and
(c) either notice was given as mentioned in Ground 1 above or the court is satisfied that it is just and equitable to dispense with the requirement of notice;
and for the purposes of this ground "mortgage" includes a charge and "mortgagee" shall be construed accordingly.
Marginal Citations
M11925 c. 20.

Ground 3.

The tenancy is a fixed term tenancy for a term not exceeding eight months and—
(a) not later than the beginning of the tenancy the landlord gave notice in writing to the tenant that possession might be recovered on this ground; and
(b) at some time within the period of twelve months ending with the beginning of the tenancy, the dwelling-house was occupied under a right to occupy it for a holiday.

Ground 4.

The tenancy is a fixed term tenancy for a term not exceeding twelve months and—
(a) not later than the beginning of the tenancy the landlord gave notice in writing to the tenant that possession might be recovered on this ground; and
(b) at some time within the period of twelve months ending with the beginning of the tenancy, the dwelling-house was let on a tenancy falling within paragraph 8 of Schedule 1 to this Act.

Ground 5.

The dwelling-house is held for the purpose of being available for occupation by a minister of religion as a residence from which to perform the duties of his office and—
(a) not later than the beginning of the tenancy the landlord gave notice in writing to the tenant that possession might be recovered on this ground; and
(b) the court is satisfied that the dwelling-house is required for occupation by a minister of religion as such a residence.

Ground 6.

The landlord who is seeking possession or, if that landlord is a [F2non-profit registered provider of social housing,] [F3registered social landlord] or charitable housing trust, [F4or (where the dwelling-house is social housing within the meaning of Part 2 of the Housing and Regeneration Act 2008) a profit-making registered provider of social housing,] a superior landlord intends to demolish or reconstruct the whole or a substantial part of the dwelling-house or to carry out substantial works on the dwelling-house or any part thereof or any building of which it forms part and the following conditions are fulfilled—
(a) the intended work cannot reasonably be carried out without the tenant giving up possession of the dwelling-house because—
(i) the tenant is not willing to agree to such a variation of the terms of the tenancy as would give such access and other facilities as would permit the intended work to be carried out, or
(ii) the nature of the intended work is such that no such variation is practicable, or
(iii) the tenant is not willing to accept an assured tenancy of such part only of the dwelling-house (in this sub-paragraph referred to as "the reduced part") as would leave in the possession of his landlord so much of the dwelling-house as would be reasonable to enable the intended work to be carried out and, where appropriate, as would give such access and other facilities over the reduced part as would permit the intended work to be carried out, or
(iv) the nature of the intended work is such that such a tenancy is not practicable; and
(b) either the landlord seeking possession acquired his interest in the dwelling-house before the grant of the tenancy or that interest was in existence at the time of that grant and neither that landlord (or, in the case of joint landlords, any of them) nor any other person who, alone or jointly with others, has acquired that interest since that time acquired it for money or money's worth; and
(c) the assured tenancy on which the dwelling-house is let did not come into being by virtue of any provision of Schedule 1 to the M2. Rent Act 1977, as amended by Part I of Schedule 4 to this Act or, as the case may be, section 4 of the M3. Rent (Agriculture) Act 1976, as amended by Part II of that Schedule.
For the purposes of this ground, if, immediately before the grant of the tenancy, the tenant to whom it was granted or, if it was granted to joint tenants, any of them was the tenant or one of the joint tenants [F5of the dwelling-house concerned] under an earlier assured tenancy [F6or, as the case may be, under a tenancy to which Schedule 10 to the Local Government and Housing Act 1989 applied], any reference in paragraph (b) above to the grant of the tenancy is a reference to the grant of that earlier assured tenancy [F5or, as the case may be, to the grant of the tenancy to which the said Schedule 10 applied].
For the purposes of this ground [F7 "registered social landlord" has the same meaning as in the Housing Act 1985 (see section 5. (4) and (5) of that Act)] and "charitable housing trust" means a

housing trust, within the meaning of [F8the Housing Associations Act 1985], which is a charity, F9....
F10...

Amendments (Textual)
F2. Words in Sch. 2 Pt. I Ground 6 inserted (1.4.2010) by The Housing and Regeneration Act 2008 (Consequential Provisions) Order 2010 (S.I. 2010/866), art. 1. (2), Sch. 2 para. 74. (2)(a) (with art. 6, Sch. 3)
F3. Words in Sch. 2 Pt. I Ground 6 substituted (1.10.1996) by S.I. 1996/2325, art. 5. (1), Sch. 2 para. 18. (13)(a)
F4. Words in Sch. 2 Pt. I Ground 6 inserted (1.4.2010) by The Housing and Regeneration Act 2008 (Consequential Provisions) Order 2010 (S.I. 2010/866), art. 1. (2), Sch. 2 para. 74. (2)(b) (with art. 6, Sch. 3)
F5. Words in Sch. 2 Pt. I Ground 6 inserted by Local Government and Housing Act 1989 (c. 42, SIF 75:1), s. 194, Sch. 11 para. 108
F6. Words in Sch. 2 Pt. I Ground 6 substituted by Local Government and Housing Act 1989 (c. 42, SIF 75:1), s. 194, Sch. 11 para. 108
F7. Sch. 2 Pt. I Ground 6: definition of "registered social landlord" substituted (1.10.1996) for the definition of "registered housing association" by S.I. 1996/2325, art. 5. (1), Sch. 2 para. 18. (13)(b)
F8. Words in Sch. 2 Pt. I Ground 6 substituted (1.10.1996) by S.I. 1996/2325, art. 5. (1), Sch. 2 para. 18. (13)(c)
F9. Words in Sch. 2 Pt. I Ground 6 omitted (14.3.2012 immediately before the Charities Act 2011 (c. 25) comes into force) by virtue of The Charities (Pre-consolidation Amendments) Order 2011 (S.I. 2011/1396), art. 1. Sch. paras. 37. (1), (2)(d)
F10. Words in Sch. 2 Pt. I Ground 6 repealed (1.10.1996) by 1996 c. 52, s. 227, Sch. 19 Pt. IX; S.I. 1996/2402, art. 3 (subject to transitional provisions in Sch.)
Modifications etc. (not altering text)
C1. Sch. 2 Ground 6 applied with modifications by Local Government and Housing Act 1989 (c. 42, SIF 75:1), s. 186, Sch. 10 paras. 5, 21, 22
Marginal Citations
M21977 c. 42.
M31976 c. 80.

Ground 7.

The tenancy is a periodic tenancy (including a statutory periodic tenancy)[F11, or a fixed term tenancy of a dwelling-house in England,] which has devolved under the will or intestacy of the former tenant and the proceedings for the recovery of possession are begun not later than twelve months after the death of the former tenant or, if the court so directs, after the date on which, in the opinion of the court, the landlord or, in the case of joint landlords, any one of them became aware of the former tenant's death.
For the purposes of this ground, the acceptance by the landlord of rent from a new tenant after the death of the former tenant shall not be regarded as creating a new F12... tenancy, unless the landlord agrees in writing to a change (as compared with the tenancy before the death) in the amount of the rent, the period [F13 or length of term]of the tenancy, the premises which are let or any other term of the tenancy.
[F14. This ground does not apply to a fixed term tenancy that is a lease of a dwelling-house—
(a) granted on payment of a premium calculated by reference to a percentage of the value of the dwelling-house or of the cost of providing it, or
(b) under which the lessee (or the lessee's personal representatives) will or may be entitled to a sum calculated by reference, directly or indirectly, to the value of the dwelling-house.]
Amendments (Textual)

F11. Words in Sch. 2 Pt. I Ground 7 inserted (1.4.2012) by Localism Act 2011 (c. 20), ss. 162. (5)(a), 240. (2); S.I. 2012/628, art. 6. (b) (with arts. 9 11 14 15 17)
F12. Word in Sch. 2 Pt. I Ground 7 repealed (1.4.2012) by Localism Act 2011 (c. 20), ss. 162. (5)(b)(i), 240. (2), Sch. 25 Pt. 23; S.I. 2012/628, art. 6. (b) (with arts. 9 11 14 15 17)
F13. Words in Sch. 2 Pt. I Ground 7 inserted (1.4.2012) by Localism Act 2011 (c. 20), ss. 162. (5)(b)(ii), 240. (2); S.I. 2012/628, art. 6. (b) (with arts. 9 11 14 15 17)
F14. Words in Sch. 2 Pt. I Ground 7 inserted (1.4.2012) by Localism Act 2011 (c. 20), ss. 162. (5)(c), 240. (2); S.I. 2012/628, art. 6. (b) (with arts. 9 11 14 15 17)

[F15. Ground 7. A

Amendments (Textual)
F15. Sch. 2 Pt. I Ground 7. A inserted (20.10.2014 for E., 21.10.2014 for W.) by Anti-social Behaviour, Crime and Policing Act 2014 (c. 12), ss. 97. (1), 185. (1), (2)(c), (3)(a) (with ss. 21, 33, 42, 58, 75, 93); S.I. 2014/2590, art. 2. (d) (with art. 5); S.I. 2014/2830, art. 2. (d) (with art. 3)
Any of the following conditions is met.
Condition 1 is that—
(a) the tenant, or a person residing in or visiting the dwelling-house, has been convicted of a serious offence, and
(b) the serious offence—
(i) was committed (wholly or partly) in, or in the locality of, the dwelling-house,
(ii) was committed elsewhere against a person with a right (of whatever description) to reside in, or occupy housing accommodation in the locality of, the dwelling-house, or
(iii) was committed elsewhere against the landlord of the dwelling-house, or a person employed (whether or not by the landlord) in connection with the exercise of the landlord's housing management functions, and directly or indirectly related to or affected those functions.
Condition 2 is that a court has found in relevant proceedings that the tenant, or a person residing in or visiting the dwelling-house, has breached a provision of an injunction under section 1 of the Anti-social Behaviour, Crime and Policing Act 2014, other than a provision requiring a person to participate in a particular activity, and—
(a) the breach occurred in, or in the locality of, the dwelling-house, or
(b) the breach occurred elsewhere and the provision breached was a provision intended to prevent—
(i) conduct that is capable of causing nuisance or annoyance to a person with a right (of whatever description) to reside in, or occupy housing accommodation in the locality of, the dwelling-house, or
(ii) conduct that is capable of causing nuisance or annoyance to the landlord of the dwelling-house, or a person employed (whether or not by the landlord) in connection with the exercise of the landlord's housing management functions, and that is directly or indirectly related to or affects those functions.
Condition 3 is that the tenant, or a person residing in or visiting the dwelling-house, has been convicted of an offence under section 30 of the Anti-social Behaviour, Crime and Policing Act 2014 consisting of a breach of a provision of a criminal behaviour order prohibiting a person from doing anything described in the order, and the offence involved—
(a) a breach that occurred in, or in the locality of, the dwelling-house, or
(b) a breach that occurred elsewhere of a provision intended to prevent—
(i) behaviour that causes or is likely to cause harassment, alarm or distress to a person with a right (of whatever description) to reside in, or occupy housing accommodation in the locality of, the dwelling-house, or
(ii) behaviour that causes or is likely to cause harassment, alarm or distress to the landlord of the dwelling-house, or a person employed (whether or not by the landlord) in connection with the exercise of the landlord's housing management functions, and that is directly or indirectly related

to or affects those functions.
Condition 4 is that—
(a) the dwelling-house is or has been subject to a closure order under section 80 of the Anti-social Behaviour, Crime and Policing Act 2014, and
(b) access to the dwelling-house has been prohibited (under the closure order or under a closure notice issued under section 76 of that Act) for a continuous period of more than 48 hours.
Condition 5 is that—
(a) the tenant, or a person residing in or visiting the dwelling-house, has been convicted of an offence under—
(i) section 80. (4) of the Environmental Protection Act 1990 (breach of abatement notice in relation to statutory nuisance), or
(ii) section 82. (8) of that Act (breach of court order to abate statutory nuisance etc.), and
(b) the nuisance concerned was noise emitted from the dwelling-house which was a statutory nuisance for the purposes of Part 3 of that Act by virtue of section 79. (1)(g) of that Act (noise emitted from premises so as to be prejudicial to health or a nuisance).
Condition 1, 2, 3, 4 or 5 is not met if—
(a) there is an appeal against the conviction, finding or order concerned which has not been finally determined, abandoned or withdrawn, or
(b) the final determination of the appeal results in the conviction, finding or order being overturned.
In this ground—
"relevant proceedings" means proceedings for contempt of court or proceedings under Schedule 2 to the Anti-social Behaviour, Crime and Policing Act 2014;
"serious offence" means an offence which—
 - was committed on or after the day on which this ground comes into force,
 - is specified, or falls within a description specified, in Schedule 2. A to the Housing Act 1985 at the time the offence was committed and at the time the court is considering the matter, and
 - is not an offence that is triable only summarily by virtue of section 22 of the Magistrates' Courts Act 1980 (either-way offences where value involved is small).]

[F16. Ground 7. B

Amendments (Textual)
F16. Sch. 2 Pt. I Ground 7. B inserted (1.12.2016) by Immigration Act 2016 (c. 19), ss. 41. (2), 94. (1) (with s. 41. (7)); S.I. 2016/1037, reg. 5. (e)
Both of the following conditions are met in relation to a dwelling-house in England.
Condition 1 is that the Secretary of State has given a notice in writing to the landlord or, in the case of joint landlords, one or more of them which identifies—
(a) the tenant or, in the case of joint tenants, one or more of them, or
(b) one or more other persons aged 18 or over who are occupying the dwelling-house,
as a person or persons disqualified as a result of their immigration status from occupying the dwelling-house under the tenancy.
Condition 2 is that the person or persons named in the notice—
(a) fall within paragraph (a) or (b) of condition 1, and
(b) are disqualified as a result of their immigration status from occupying the dwelling-house under the tenancy.
For the purposes of this ground a person ("P") is disqualified as a result of their immigration status from occupying the dwelling-house under the tenancy if—
(a) P is not a relevant national, and
(b) P does not have a right to rent in relation to the dwelling-house.
P does not have a right to rent in relation to the dwelling-house if—
(a) P requires leave to enter or remain in the United Kingdom but does not have it, or

(b) P's leave to enter or remain in the United Kingdom is subject to a condition preventing P from occupying the dwelling-house.
But P is to be treated as having a right to rent in relation to a dwelling-house if the Secretary of State has granted P permission for the purposes of this ground to occupy a dwelling-house under an assured tenancy.
In this ground "relevant national" means—
(a) a British citizen,
(b) a national of an EEA State other than the United Kingdom, or
(c) a national of Switzerland.]

Ground 8.

Both at the date of the service of the notice under section 8 of this Act relating to the proceedings for possession and at the date of the hearing—
(a) if rent is payable weekly or fortnightly, at least [F17eight weeks'] rent is unpaid;
(b) if rent is payable monthly, at least [F18two months'] rent is unpaid;
(c) if rent is payable quarterly, at least one quarter's rent is more than three months in arrears; and
(d) if rent is payable yearly, at least three months' rent is more than three months in arrears;
and for the purpose of this ground "rent" means rent lawfully due from the tenant.
Amendments (Textual)
F17. Words in Sch. 2 Pt. I Ground 8 para. (a) substituted (28.2.1997) by 1996 c. 52, s. 101. (a); S.I. 1997/225, art. 2
F18. Words in Sch. 2 Pt. I Ground 8 para. (b) substituted (1.1.1997) by 1996 c. 52, s. 101. (b); S.I. 1997/225, art. 2

Part II Grounds on which Court may Order Possession

Modifications etc. (not altering text)
C2. Pt. II (Grounds 9–15) applied with modifications by Local Government and Housing Act 1989 (c. 42, SIF 75:1), s. 186, Sch. 10 paras. 5, 21, 22

Ground 9.

Suitable alternative accommodation is available for the tenant or will be available for him when the order for possession takes effect.

Ground 10.

Some rent lawfully due from the tenant—
(a) is unpaid on the date on which the proceedings for possession are begun; and
(b) except where subsection (1)(b) of section 8 of this Act applies, was in arrears at the date of the service of the notice under that section relating to those proceedings.

Ground 11.

Whether or not any rent is in arrears on the date on which proceedings for possession are begun, the tenant has persistently delayed paying rent which has become lawfully due.

Ground 12.

Any obligation of the tenancy (other than one related to the payment of rent) has been broken or not performed.

Ground 13.

The condition of the dwelling-house or any of the common parts has deteriorated owing to acts of waste by, or the neglect or default of, the tenant or any other person residing in the dwelling-house and, in the case of an act of waste by, or the neglect or default of, a person lodging with the tenant or a sub-tenant of his, the tenant has not taken such steps as he ought reasonably to have taken for the removal of the lodger or sub-tenant.

For the purposes of this ground, "common parts" means any part of a building comprising the dwelling-house and any other premises which the tenant is entitled under the terms of the tenancy to use in common with the occupiers of other dwelling-houses in which the landlord has an estate or interest.

Ground 14.

[F19. The tenant or a person residing in or visiting the dwelling-house—
(a) has been guilty of conduct causing or likely to cause a nuisance or annoyance to a person residing, visiting or otherwise engaging in a lawful activity in the locality,
[F20. (aa)has been guilty of conduct causing or likely to cause a nuisance or annoyance to the landlord of the dwelling-house, or a person employed (whether or not by the landlord) in connection with the exercise of the landlord's housing management functions, and that is directly or indirectly related to or affects those functions,] or
(b) has been convicted of—
(i) using the dwelling-house or allowing it to be used for immoral or illegal purposes, or
(ii) an [F21indictable] offence committed in, or in the locality of, the dwelling-house.]
Amendments (Textual)
F19. Sch. 2 Pt. II Ground 14 substituted (28.2.1997) by 1996 c. 52, s. 148; S.I. 1997/225, art. 2 (with Sch.)
F20. Sch. 2 Pt. II Ground 14. (aa) inserted (13.5.2014 for E., 13.5.2014 for W.) by Anti-social Behaviour, Crime and Policing Act 2014 (c. 12), ss. 98. (2), 185. (1), (2)(c), (3)(a) (with ss. 21, 33, 42, 58, 75, 93); S.I. 2014/949, art. 2. (a); S.I. 2014/1241, art. 2. (a); S.I. 2014/949, art. 2. (a); S.I. 2014/1241, art. 2. (a)
F21. Word in Sch. 2 Pt. 2 Ground 14 para.(b)(ii) substituted (1.1.2006) by Serious Organised Crime and Police Act 2005 (c. 15), ss. 111, 178 {Sch. 7 para. 46}; S.I.2005/3495, art. 2. (1)(m)

[F22. Ground 14. ZA

Amendments (Textual)
F22. Sch. 2 Pt. II Ground 14. ZA inserted (13.5.2014) by Anti-social Behaviour, Crime and Policing Act 2014 (c. 12), ss. 99. (2), 185. (1) (with ss. 21, 33, 42, 58, 75, 93); S.I. 2014/949, art. 3, Sch. para. 1 (with art. 7)
The tenant or an adult residing in the dwelling-house has been convicted of an indictable offence which took place during, and at the scene of, a riot in the United Kingdom.
In this Ground—
"adult" means a person aged 18 or over;
"indictable offence" does not include an offence that is triable only summarily by virtue of section 22 of the Magistrates' Courts Act 1980 (either way offences where value involved is small);
"riot" is to be construed in accordance with section 1 of the Public Order Act 1986.
This Ground applies only in relation to dwelling-houses in England.]

[F23. Ground 14. A

Amendments (Textual)
F23. Sch. 2 Pt. II Ground 14. A and cross-heading inserted (28.2.1997) by 1996 c. 52, s. 149; S.I. 1997/225, art. 2 (with Sch.)
F24 The dwelling-house was occupied (whether alone or with others) by [F25 a married couple, a couple who are civil partners of each other,] a couple living together as husband and wife [F26 or a couple living together as if they were civil partners] and—
(a) one or both of the partners is a tenant of the dwelling-house,
(b) the landlord who is seeking possession is [F27a non-profit registered provider of social housing,] a registered social landlord or a charitable housing trust [F28or, where the dwelling-house is social housing within the meaning of Part 2 of the Housing and Regeneration Act 2008, a profit-making registered provider of social housing],
(c) one partner has left the dwelling-house because of violence or threats of violence by the other towards—
(i) that partner, or
(ii) a member of the family of that partner who was residing with that partner immediately before the partner left, and
(d) the court is satisfied that the partner who has left is unlikely to return.
 For the purposes of this ground "registered social landlord" and "member of the family" have the same meaning as in Part I of the M4 Housing Act 1996 and " charitable housing trust " means a housing trust, within the meaning of the M5 Housing Associations Act 1985, which is a charity F29....]
Amendments (Textual)
F24. Sch. 2 Pt. II Ground 14. A and cross-heading inserted (28.2.1997) by 1996 c. 52, s. 149; S.I. 1997/225, art. 2 (with Sch.)
F25. Words in Sch. 2 Pt. 2 Ground 14. A substituted (5.12.2005) by Civil Partnership Act 2004 (c. 33), ss. 81, 263, Sch. 8 para. 43. (3)(a); S.I. 2005/3175, art. 2. (1),Sch. 1
F26. Words in Sch. 2 Pt. 2 Ground 14. A inserted (5.12.2005) by Civil Partnership Act 2004 (c. 33), ss. 81, 263, Sch. 8 para. 43. (3)(b); S.I. 2005/3175, art. 2. (1), Sch. 1
F27. Words in Sch. 2 Ground 14. A(b) inserted (1.4.2010) by The Housing and Regeneration Act 2008 (Consequential Provisions) Order 2010 (S.I. 2010/866), art. 1. (2), Sch. 2 para. 74. (3)(a) (with art. 6, Sch. 3)
F28. Words in Sch. 2 Ground 14. A(b) inserted (1.4.2010) by The Housing and Regeneration Act 2008 (Consequential Provisions) Order 2010 (S.I. 2010/866), art. 1. (2), Sch. 2 para. 74. (3)(b) (with art. 6, Sch. 3)
F29. Words in Sch. 2 omitted (Ground 14. A) (14.3.2012 immediately before the Charities Act 2011 (c. 25) comes into force) by virtue of The Charities (Pre-consolidation Amendments) Order 2011 (S.I. 2011/1396), art. 1, Sch. paras. 37. (1), (2)(d)
Marginal Citations
M41985 c. 69.
M51993 c. 10.

Ground 15.

The condition of any furniture provided for use under the tenancy has, in the opinion of the court, deteriorated owing to ill-treatment by the tenant or any other person residing in the dwelling-house and, in the case of ill-treatment by a person lodging with the tenant or by a sub-tenant of his, the tenant has not taken such steps as he ought reasonably to have taken for the removal of the lodger or sub-tenant.

Ground 16.

The dwelling-house was let to the tenant in consequence of his employment by the landlord seeking possession or a previous landlord under the tenancy and the tenant has ceased to be in that employment.
[F30. For the purposes of this ground, at a time when the landlord is or was the Secretary of State, employment by a health service body, as defined in section 60. (7) of the National Health Service and Community Care Act 1990, [F31or by a Local Health Board,] shall be regarded as employment by the Secretary of State.]
Amendments (Textual)
F30. Words added by National Health and Community Care Act 1990 (c. 19, SIF 113:2), s. 60. (2), Sch. 8 para. 10
F31. Sch. 2 Pt. II Ground 16: words inserted (10.10.2002 for W. and otherwise prosp.) by National Health Service Reform and Health Care Professions Act 2002 (c. 17), ss. 6. (2), 42. (3), Sch. 5 para. 28; S.I. 2002/2532, art. 2, Sch.
Modifications etc. (not altering text)
C3. Pt. II Ground 16 applied with modifications by Local Government and Housing Act 1989 (c. 42, SIF 75:1), s. 186, Sch. 10 paras. 5, 21, 22

[F32. Ground 17]

Amendments (Textual)
F32. Sch. 2 Pt. II Ground 17 and cross-heading inserted (28.2.1997) by 1996 c. 52, s. 102; S.I. 1997/225, art. 2 (with Sch.)
[F33. The tenant is the person, or one of the persons, to whom the tenancy was granted and the landlord was induced to grant the tenancy by a false statement made knowingly or recklessly by—
the tenant, or
a person acting at the tenant's instigation.]
Amendments (Textual)
F33. Sch. 2 Pt. II Ground 17 and cross-heading inserted (28.2.1997) by 1996 c. 52, s. 102; S.I. 1997/225, art. 2 (with Sch.)

Part III Suitable Alternative Accommodation

Modifications etc. (not altering text)
C4. Pt. III (paras. 1–6) applied with modifications by Local Government and Housing Act 1989 (c. 42, SIF 75:1), s. 186, Sch. 10 paras. 13. (5), 21, 22
1. For the purposes of Ground 9 above, a certificate of the local housing authority for the district in which the dwelling-house in question is situated, certifying that the authority will provide suitable alternative accommodation for the tenant by a date specified in the certificate, shall be conclusive evidence that suitable alternative accommodation will be available for him by that date.
2. Where no such certificate as is mentioned in paragraph 1 above is produced to the court, accommodation shall be deemed to be suitable for the purposes of Ground 9 above if it consists of either—
(a) premises which are to be let as a separate dwelling such that they will then be let on an assured tenancy, other than—
(i) a tenancy in respect of which notice is given not later than the beginning of the tenancy that possession might be recovered on any of Grounds 1 to 5 above, or
(ii) an assured shorthold tenancy, within the meaning of Chapter II of Part I of this Act, or
(b) premises to be let as a separate dwelling on terms which will, in the opinion of the court, afford to the tenant security of tenure reasonably equivalent to the security afforded by Chapter I of Part I

of this Act in the case of an assured tenancy of a kind mentioned in sub-paragraph (a) above, and, in the opinion of the court, the accommodation fulfils the relevant conditions as defined in paragraph 3 below.

3. (1)For the purposes of paragraph 2 above, the relevant conditions are that the accommodation is reasonably suitable to the needs of the tenant and his family as regards proximity to place of work, and either—

(a) similar as regards rental and extent to the accommodation afforded by dwelling-houses provided in the neighbourhood by any local housing authority for persons whose needs as regards extent are, in the opinion of the court, similar to those of the tenant and of his family; or

(b) reasonably suitable to the means of the tenant and to the needs of the tenant and his family as regards extent and character; and

that if any furniture was provided for use under the assured tenancy in question, furniture is provided for use in the accommodation which is either similar to that so provided or is reasonably suitable to the needs of the tenant and his family.

(2) For the purposes of sub-paragraph (1)(a) above, a certificate of a local housing authority stating—

(a) the extent of the accommodation afforded by dwelling-houses provided by the authority to meet the needs of tenants with families of such number as may be specified in the certificate, and

(b) the amount of the rent charged by the authority for dwelling-houses affording accommodation of that extent,

shall be conclusive evidence of the facts so stated.

4. Accommodation shall not be deemed to be suitable to the needs of the tenant and his family if the result of their occupation of the accommodation would be that it would be an overcrowded dwelling-house for the purposes of Part X of M6 the Housing Act 1985.

Marginal Citations

M61985 c.68.

5. Any document purporting to be a certificate of a local housing authority named therein issued for the purposes of this Part of this Schedule and to be signed by the proper officer of that authority shall be received in evidence and, unless the contrary is shown, shall be deemed to be such a certificate without further proof.

6. In this Part of this Schedule "local housing authority" and "district", in relation to such an authority, have the same meaning as in the Housing Act 1985.

Part IV Notices Relating to Recovery of Possession

7. Any reference in Grounds 1 to 5 in Part I of this Schedule or in the following provisions of this Part to the landlord giving a notice in writing to the tenant is, in the case of joint landlords, a reference to at least one of the joint landlords giving such a notice.

8. (1)If, not later than the beginning of a tenancy (in this paragraph referred to as "the earlier tenancy"), the landlord gives such a notice in writing to the tenant as is mentioned in any of Grounds 1 to 5 in Part I of this Schedule, then, for the purposes of the ground in question and any further application of this paragraph, that notice shall also have effect as if it had been given immediately before the beginning of any later tenancy falling within sub-paragraph (2) below.

(2) Subject to sub-paragraph (3) below, sub-paragraph (1) above applies to a later tenancy—

(a) which takes effect immediately on the coming to an end of the earlier tenancy; and

(b) which is granted (or deemed to be granted) to the person who was the tenant under the earlier tenancy immediately before it came to an end; and

(c) which is of substantially the same dwelling-house as the earlier tenancy.

(3) Sub-paragraph (1) above does not apply in relation to a later tenancy if, not later than the beginning of the tenancy, the landlord gave notice in writing to the tenant that the tenancy is not one in respect of which possession can be recovered on the ground in question.

9. Where paragraph 8. (1) above has effect in relation to a notice given as mentioned in Ground 1

in Part I of this Schedule, the reference in paragraph (b) of that ground to the reversion on the tenancy is a reference to the reversion on the earlier tenancy and on any later tenancy falling within paragraph 8. (2) above.

10. Where paragraph 8. (1) above has effect in relation to a notice given as mentioned in Ground 3 or Ground 4 in Part I of this Schedule, any second or subsequent tenancy in relation to which the notice has effect shall be treated for the purpose of that ground as beginning at the beginning of the tenancy in respect of which the notice was actually given.

11. Any reference in Grounds 1 to 5 in Part I of this Schedule to a notice being given not later than the beginning of the tenancy is a reference to its being given not later than the day on which the tenancy is entered into and, accordingly, section 45. (2) of this Act shall not apply to any such reference.

Schedule 3. Assured Tenancies: Non-Shortholds

Amendments (Textual)
F1. Sch. 2. A inserted (28.2.1997) by 1996 c. 52, s. 96. (2), Sch. 7; S.I. 1997/225, art. 2 (subject to savings in Sch.)

Tenancies excluded by notice

F21. (1)An assured tenancy in respect of which a notice is served as mentioned in sub-paragraph (2) below.
(2) The notice referred to in sub-paragraph (1) above is one which—
(a) is served before the assured tenancy is entered into,
(b) is served by the person who is to be the landlord under the assured tenancy on the person who is to be the tenant under that tenancy, and
(c) states that the assured tenancy to which it relates is not to be an assured shorthold tenancy.
Amendments (Textual)
F2. Sch. 2. A para. 1 inserted (28.2.1997) by 1996 c. 52, s. 96. (2), Sch. 7; S.I. 1997/225, art. 2 (subject to savings in Sch.)
F32. (1)An assured tenancy in respect of which a notice is served as mentioned in sub-paragraph (2) below.
(2) The notice referred to in sub-paragraph (1) above is one which—
(a) is served after the assured tenancy has been entered into,
(b) is served by the landlord under the assured tenancy on the tenant under that tenancy, and
(c) states that the assured tenancy to which it relates is no longer an assured shorthold tenancy.
Amendments (Textual)
F3. Sch. 2. A para. 2 inserted (28.2.1997) by 1996 c. 52, s. 96. (2), Sch. 7; S.I. 1997/225, art. 2 (subject to savings in Sch.)

Tenancies containing exclusionary provision

F43. An assured tenancy which contains a provision to the effect that the tenancy is not an assured shorthold tenancy.
Amendments (Textual)
F4. Sch. 2. A para. 3 inserted (28.2.1997) by 1996 c. 52, s. 96. (2), Sch. 7; S.I. 1997/225, art. 2 (subject to savings in Sch.)

Tenancies under section 39.

F5 4. An assured tenancy arising by virtue of section 39 above, other than one to which subsection (7) of that section applies.
Amendments (Textual)
F5. Sch. 2. A para. 4 inserted (28.2.1997) by 1996 c. 52, s. 96. (2), Sch. 7; S.I. 1997/225, art. 2 (subject to savings in Sch.)

Former secure tenancies

F6 5. An assured tenancy which became an assured tenancy on ceasing to be a secure tenancy.
Amendments (Textual)
F6. Sch. 2. A para. 5 inserted (28.2.1997) by 1996 c. 52, s. 96. (2), Sch. 7; S.I. 1997/225, art. 2 (subject to savings in Sch.)

[F7. Former demoted tenancies

Amendments (Textual)
F7. Sch. 2. A para. 5. A and cross-heading inserted (30.6.2004 for E. and 30.4.2005 for W.) by Anti-Social Behaviour Act 2003 (c. 38), ss. 15. (3), 93; S.I. 2004/1502, art. 2. (a)(iv); S.I. 2002/1225, art. 2. (c)
5. AAn assured tenancy which ceases to be an assured shorthold tenancy by virtue of section 20. B(2) or (4).]

Tenancies under Schedule 10 to the Local Government and Housing Act 1989.

F8 6. An assured tenancy arising by virtue of Schedule 10 to the M1. Local Government and Housing Act 1989 (security of tenure on ending of long residential tenancies).
Amendments (Textual)
F8. Sch. 2. A para. 6 inserted (28.2.1997) by 1996 c. 52, s. 96. (2), Sch. 7; S.I. 1997/225, art. 2 (subject to savings in Sch.)
Marginal Citations
M11989 c. 42.

Tenancies replacing non-shortholds

F9 7. (1)An assured tenancy which—
(a) is granted to a person (alone or jointly with others) who, immediately before the tenancy was granted, was the tenant (or, in the case of joint tenants, one of the tenants) under an assured tenancy other than a shorthold tenancy ("the old tenancy"),
(b) is granted (alone or jointly with others) by a person who was at that time the landlord (or one of the joint landlords) under the old tenancy, and
(c) is not one in respect of which a notice is served as mentioned in sub-paragraph (2) below.
(2) The notice referred to in sub-paragraph (1)(c) above is one which—
(a) is in such form as may be prescribed,
(b) is served before the assured tenancy is entered into,
(c) is served by the person who is to be the tenant under the assured tenancy on the person who is to be the landlord under that tenancy (or, in the case of joint landlords, on at least one of the persons who are to be joint landlords), and
(d) states that the assured tenancy to which it relates is to be a shorthold tenancy.
Amendments (Textual)
F9. Sch. 2. A para. 7 inserted (23.8.1996 for certain purposes and 28.2.1997 otherwise) by 1996 c.

52, s. 96. (2), Sch. 7; S.I. 1996/2212, art. 3 (subject to savings in Sch.); S.I. 1997/225, art. 2 (subject to savings in Sch.)
F108. An assured tenancy which comes into being by virtue of section 5 above on the coming to an end of an assured tenancy which is not a shorthold tenancy.
Amendments (Textual)
F10. Sch. 2. A para. 8 inserted (28.2.1997) by 1996 c. 52, s. 96. (2), Sch. 7; S.I. 1997/225, art. 2 (subject to savings in Sch.)

Assured agricultural occupancies

F119. (1) An assured tenancy—
(a) in the case of which the agricultural worker condition is, by virtue of any provision of Schedule 3 to this Act, for the time being fulfilled with respect to the dwelling-house subject to the tenancy, and
(b) which does not fall within sub-paragraph (2) or (4) below.
(2) An assured tenancy falls within this sub-paragraph if—
(a) before it is entered into, a notice—
(i) in such form as may be prescribed, and
(ii) stating that the tenancy is to be a shorthold tenancy,
is served by the person who is to be the landlord under the tenancy on the person who is to be the tenant under it, and
(b) it is not an excepted tenancy.
(3) For the purposes of sub-paragraph (2)(b) above, an assured tenancy is an excepted tenancy if—
(a) the person to whom it is granted or, as the case may be, at least one of the persons to whom it is granted was, immediately before it is granted, a tenant or licensee under an assured agricultural occupancy, and
(b) the person by whom it is granted or, as the case may be, at least one of the persons by whom it is granted was, immediately before it is granted, a landlord or licensor under the assured agricultural occupancy referred to in paragraph (a) above.
(4) An assured tenancy falls within this sub-paragraph if it comes into being by virtue of section 5 above on the coming to an end of a tenancy falling within sub-paragraph (2) above.]
Amendments (Textual)
F11. Sch. 2. A para. 9 inserted (23.8.1996 for certain purposes and 28.2.1997 otherwise) by 1996 c. 52, s. 96. (2), Sch. 7; S.I. 1996/2212, art. 3 (subject to savings in Sch.); S.I. 1997/225, art. 2 (subject to savings in Sch.)

Schedule 4. Agricultural Worker Conditions

Section 24.

Interpretation

1. (1) In this Schedule—
"the 1976 Act" means the M1. Rent (Agriculture) Act 1976;
"agriculture" has the same meaning as in the 1976 Act; and
"relevant tenancy or licence" means a tenancy or licence of a description specified in section 24. (2) of this Act.
(2) In relation to a relevant tenancy or licence—
(a) "the occupier" means the tenant or licensee; and
(b) "the dwelling-house" means the dwelling-house which is let under the tenancy or, as the case

may be, is occupied under the licence.
(3) Schedule 3 to the 1976 Act applies for the purposes of this Schedule as it applies for the purposes of that Act and, accordingly, shall have effect to determine—
(a) whether a person is a qualifying worker;
(b) whether a person is incapable of whole-time work in agriculture, or work in agriculture as a permit worker, in consequence of a qualifying injury or disease; and
(c) whether a dwelling-house is in qualifying ownership.
Marginal Citations
M11976 c. 80.

The conditions

2. The agricultural worker condition is fulfilled with respect to a dwelling-house subject to a relevant tenancy or licence if—
(a) the dwelling-house is or has been in qualifying ownership at any time during the subsistence of the tenancy or licence (whether or not it was at that time a relevant tenancy or licence); and
(b) the occupier or, where there are joint occupiers, at least one of them—
(i) is a qualifying worker or has been a qualifying worker at any time during the subsistence of the tenancy or licence (whether or not it was at that time a relevant tenancy or licence); or
(ii) is incapable of whole-time work in agriculture or work in agriculture as a permit worker in consequence of a qualifying injury or disease.
3. (1)The agricultural worker condition is also fulfilled with respect to a dwelling-house subject to a relevant tenancy or licence if—
(a) that condition was previously fulfilled with respect to the dwelling-house but the person who was then the occupier or, as the case may be, a person who was one of the joint occupiers (whether or not under the same relevant tenancy or licence) has died; and
(b) that condition ceased to be fulfilled on the death of the occupier referred to in paragraph (a) above (hereinafter referred to as "the previous qualifying occupier"); and
(c) the occupier is either—
(i) the qualifying [F1surviving partner] of the previous qualifying occupier; or
(ii) the qualifying member of the previous qualifying occupier's family.
[F2. (2)For the purposes of sub-paragraph (1)(c)(i) above and sub-paragraph (3) below—
(a) "surviving partner" means widow, widower or surviving civil partner; and
(b) a surviving partner of the previous qualifying occupier of the dwelling-house is a qualifying surviving partner if that surviving partner was residing in the dwelling-house immediately before the previous qualifying occupier's death.]
(3) Subject to sub-paragraph (4) below, for the purposes of sub-paragraph (1)(c)(ii) above, a member of the family of the previous qualifying occupier of the dwelling-house is the qualifying member of the family if—
(a) on the death of the previous qualifying occupier there was no qualifying [F3surviving partner] ; and
(b) the member of the family was residing in the dwelling-house with the previous qualifying occupier at the time of, and for the period of two years before, his death.
(4) Not more than one member of the previous qualifying occupier's family may be taken into account in determining whether the agricultural worker condition is fulfilled by virtue of this paragraph and, accordingly, if there is more than one member of the family—
(a) who is the occupier in relation to the relevant tenancy or licence, and
(b) who, apart from this sub-paragraph, would be the qualifying member of the family by virtue of sub-paragraph (3) above,
only that one of those members of the family who may be decided by agreement or, in default of agreement by the county court, shall be the qualifying member.
[F4. (5)For the purposes of sub-paragraph (2)(a) above—

(a) a person who, immediately before the previous qualifying occupier's death, was living with the previous occupier as his or her wife or husband shall be treated as the widow or widower of the previous occupier, and

(b) a person who, immediately before the previous qualifying occupier's death, was living with the previous occupier as if they were civil partners shall be treated as the surviving civil partner of the previous occupier.]

(6) If, immediately before the death of the previous qualifying occupier, there is, by virtue of sub-paragraph (5) above, more than one person who falls within sub-paragraph (1)(c)(i) above, such one of them as may be decided by agreement or, in default of agreement, by the county court shall be treated as the qualifying [F5surviving partner] for the purposes of this paragraph.

Amendments (Textual)

F1. Words in Sch. 3 para. 3. (1)(c)(i) substituted (5.12.2005) by Civil Partnership Act 2004 (c. 33), ss. 81, 263, Sch. 8 para. 44. (2); S.I. 2005/3175, art. 2. (1), Sch. 1

F2. Sch. 3 para. 3. (2) substituted (5.12.2005) by Civil Partnership Act 2004 (c. 33), ss. 81, 263, Sch. 8 para. 44. (3); S.I. 2005/3175, art. 2. (1), Sch. 1

F3. Words in Sch. 3 para. 3. (3)(a) substituted (5.12.2005) by Civil Partnership Act 2004 (c. 33), ss. 81, 263, Sch. 8 para. 44. (2); S.I. 2005/3175, art. 2. (1), Sch. 1

F4. Sch. 3 para. 3. (5) substituted (5.12.2005) by Civil Partnership Act 2004 (c. 33), ss. 81, 263, Sch. 8 para. 44. (4); S.I. 2005/3175, art. 2. (1), Sch. 1

F5. Words in Sch. 3 para. 3. (6) substituted (5.12.2005) by Civil Partnership Act 2004 (c. 33), ss. 81, 263, Sch. 8 para. 44. (2); S.I. 2005/3175, art. 2. (1), Sch. 1

4. The agricultural worker condition is also fulfilled with respect to a dwelling-house subject to a relevant tenancy or licence if—

(a) the tenancy or licence was granted to the occupier or, where there are joint occupiers, at least one of them in consideration of his giving up possession of another dwelling-house of which he was then occupier (or one of joint occupiers) under another relevant tenancy or licence; and

(b) immediately before he gave up possession of that dwelling-house, as a result of his occupation the agricultural worker condition was fulfilled with respect to it (whether by virtue of paragraph 2 or paragraph 3 above or this paragraph);

and the reference in paragraph (a) above to a tenancy or licence granted to the occupier or at least one of joint occupiers includes a reference to the case where the grant is to him together with one or more other persons.

5. (1)This paragraph applies where—

(a) by virtue of any of paragraphs 2 to 4 above, the agricultural worker condition is fulfilled with respect to a dwelling-house subject to a relevant tenancy or licence (in this paragraph referred to as "the earlier tenancy or licence"); and

(b) another relevant tenancy or licence of the same dwelling-house (in this paragraph referred to as "the later tenancy or licence") is granted to the person who, immediately before the grant, was the occupier or one of the joint occupiers under the earlier tenancy or licence and as a result of whose occupation the agricultural worker condition was fulfilled as mentioned in paragraph (a) above;

and the reference in paragraph (b) above to the grant of the later tenancy or licence to the person mentioned in that paragraph includes a reference to the case where the grant is to that person together with one or more other persons.

(2) So long as a person as a result of whose occupation of the dwelling-house the agricultural worker condition was fulfilled with respect to the earlier tenancy or licence continues to be the occupier, or one of the joint occupiers, under the later tenancy or licence, the agricultural worker condition shall be fulfilled with respect to the dwelling-house.

(3) For the purposes of paragraphs 3 and 4 above and any further application of this paragraph, where sub-paragraph (2) above has effect, the agricultural worker condition shall be treated as fulfilled so far as concerns the later tenancy or licence by virtue of the same paragraph of this Schedule as was applicable (or, as the case may be, last applicable) in the case of the earlier tenancy or licence.

Schedule 5. Statutory Tenants: Succession

Section 39.

Part I Amendments of Schedule 1 to M1. Rent Act 1977

Marginal Citations
M11977 c. 42.
1. In paragraph 1 the words "or, as the case may be, paragraph 3" shall be omitted.
2 At the end of paragraph 2 there shall be inserted the following sub-paragraphs—
"(2)For the purposes of this paragraph, a person who was living with the original tenant as his or her wife or husband shall be treated as the spouse of the original tenant.
(3) If, immediately after the death of the original tenant, there is, by virtue of sub-paragraph (2) above, more than one person who fulfils the conditions in sub-paragraph (1) above, such one of them as may be decided by agreement or, in default of agreement, by the county court shall be treated as the surviving spouse for the purposes of this paragraph."
3. In paragraph 3—
(a) after the words "residing with him" there shall be inserted " "in the dwelling-house ";
(b) for the words "period of 6 months" there shall be substituted " "period of 2 years ";
(c) for the words from "the statutory tenant" onwards there shall be substituted " "entitled to an assured tenancy of the dwelling-house by succession "; and
(d) at the end there shall be added the following sub-paragraph—
"(2)If the original tenant died within the period of 18 months beginning on the operative date, then, for the purposes of this paragraph, a person who was residing in the dwelling-house with the original tenant at the time of his death and for the period which began 6 months before the operative date and ended at the time of his death shall be taken to have been residing with the original tenant for the period of 2 years immediately before his death."
4. In paragraph 4 the words "or 3" shall be omitted.
5. In paragraph 5—
(a) for the words from "or, as the case may be" to "of this Act" there shall be substituted " "below shall have effect "; and
(b) for the words "the statutory tenant" there shall be substituted " "entitled to an assured tenancy of the dwelling-house by succession ".
6. For paragraph 6 there shall be substituted the following paragraph—
"6. (1)Where a person who—
(a) was a member of the original tenant's family immediately before that tenant's death, and
(b) was a member of the first successor's family immediately before the first successor's death, was residing in the dwelling-house with the first successor at the time of, and for the period of 2 years immediately before, the first successor's death, that person or, if there is more than one such person, such one of them as may be decided by agreement or, in default of agreement, by the county court shall be entitled to an assured tenancy of the dwelling-house by succession.
(2) If the first successor died within the period of 18 months beginning on the operative date, then, for the purposes of this paragraph, a person who was residing in the dwelling-house with the first successor at the time of his death and for the period which began 6 months before the operative date and ended at the time of his death shall be taken to have been residing with the first successor for the period of 2 years immediately before his death."
7. Paragraph 7 shall be omitted.
8. In paragraph 10. (1)(a) for the words "paragraphs 6 or 7" there shall be substituted " "paragraph 6 ".
9. At the end of paragraph 11 there shall be inserted the following paragraph—

"11. AIn this Part of this Schedule "the operative date" means the date on which Part I of the Housing Act 1988 came into force."

Part II Amendments of Section 4 of M2. Rent (Agriculture) Act 1976

Marginal Citations
M21976 c. 80.
10. In subsection (2) the words "or, as the case may be, subsection (4)" shall be omitted.
11. In subsection (4)—
(a) in paragraph (b) after the words "residing with him" there shall be inserted " "in the dwelling-house " and for the words "period of six months" there shall be substituted " "period of 2 years "; and
(b) for the words from "the statutory tenant" onwards there shall be substituted " "entitled to an assured tenancy of the dwelling-house by succession ".
12. In subsection (5) for the words "subsections (1), (3) and (4)" there shall be substituted " "subsections (1) and (3) " and after that subsection there shall be inserted the following subsections—
"(5. A)For the purposes of subsection (3) above, a person who was living with the original occupier as his or her wife or husband shall be treated as the spouse of the original occupier and, subject to subsection (5. B) below, the references in subsection (3) above to a widow and in subsection (4) above to a surviving spouse shall be construed accordingly.
(5. B)If, immediately after the death of the original occupier, there is, by virtue of subsection (5. A) above, more than one person who fulfils the conditions in subsection (3) above, such one of them as may be decided by agreement or, in default of agreement by the county court, shall be the statutory tenant by virtue of that subsection.
(5. C)If the original occupier died within the period of 18 months beginning on the operative date, then, for the purposes of subsection (3) above, a person who was residing in the dwelling-house with the original occupier at the time of his death and for the period which began 6 months before the operative date and ended at the time of his death shall be taken to have been residing with the original occupier for the period of 2 years immediately before his death; and in this subsection "the operative date" means the date on which Part I of the Housing Act 1988 came into force."

Part III Modifications of Section 7 and Schedule 2

13. (1)Subject to sub-paragraph (2) below, in relation to the assured tenancy to which the successor becomes entitled by succession, section 7 of this Act shall have effect as if in subsection (3) after the word "established" there were inserted the words " "or that the circumstances are as specified in any of Cases 11, 12, 16, 17, 18 and 20 in Schedule 15 to the Rent Act 1977 ".
(2) Sub-paragraph (1) above does not apply if, by virtue of section 39. (8) of this Act, the assured tenancy to which the successor becomes entitled is an assured agricultural occupancy.
14. If by virtue of section 39. (8) of this Act, the assured tenancy to which the successor becomes entitled is an assured agricultural occupancy, section 7 of this Act shall have effect in relation to that tenancy as if in subsection (3) after the word "established" there were inserted the words " "or that the circumstances are as specified in Case XI or Case XII of the Rent (Agriculture) Act 1976 ".
15. (1)In relation to the assured tenancy to which the successor becomes entitled by succession, any notice given to the predecessor for the purposes of Case 13, Case 14 or Case 15 in Schedule 15 to the M3. Rent Act 1977 shall be treated as having been given for the purposes of whichever of Grounds 3 to 5 in Schedule 2 to this Act corresponds to the Case in question.
(2) Where sub-paragraph (1) above applies, the regulated tenancy of the predecessor shall be

treated, in relation to the assured tenancy of the successor, as "the earlier tenancy" for the purposes of Part IV of Schedule 2 to this Act.
Marginal Citations
M31977 c. 42.

Schedule 6. Amendments of Housing Associations Act 1985

Section 59.
Marginal Citations
M11985 c. 69.

Part I Amendments of Part I with Respect to the Housing Corporation, Housing for Wales and Scottish Homes

F11. . . . .
Amendments (Textual)
F1. Sch. 6 Pt. I para. 1 repealed (1.10.1996) by S.I. 1996/2325, art. 4. (1)-(3), Sch. 1 Pts. I, II
F22. . . . .
Amendments (Textual)
F2. Sch. 6 para. 2 repealed (1.11.1998) by 1998 c. 38, s. 152, Sch. 18 Pt. VI (with ss. 137. (1), 139. (2), 143. (2)); S.I. 1998/2244, art. 5
F33. . . . .
Amendments (Textual)
F3. Sch. 6 para. 3 repealed (E.W.) (1.10.1996) by 1996 c. 52, ss. 227, 231. (4)(b), Sch. 19 Pt. I; S.I. 1996/2402, art. 3 (subject to transitional provisions and savings in Sch.); and repealed (S.) (1.11.2001) by 2001 asp 10, s. 112, Sch. 10 para. 15. (8); S.S.I. 2001/336, art. 2. (3), Sch. Pt. II Table (subject to transitional provisions and savings in art. 3)
F44. . . . .
Amendments (Textual)
F4. Sch. 6 para. 4 repealed (E.W.) (1.10.1996) by 1996 c. 52, ss. 227, 231. (4)(b), Sch. 19 Pt. I; S.I. 1996/2402, art. 3 (subject to transitional provisions and savings in Sch.); and repealed (S.) (1.11.2001) by 2001 asp 10, s. 112, Sch. 10 para. 15. (8); S.S.I. 2001/336, art. 2. (3), Sch. Pt. II Table (subject to transitional provisions and savings in art. 3)
F55. . . . .
Amendments (Textual)
F5. Sch. 6 para. 5 repealed (1.10.1996) (E.W.) by 1996 c. 52, ss. 227, 231. (4)(b), Sch. 19 Pt. I; S.I. 1996/2402, art. 3 (subject to transitional provisions and savings in Sch.); and repealed (S.) (1.11.2001) by 2001 asp 10, s. 112, Sch. 10 para. 15. (8); S.S.I. 2001/336, art. 2. (3), Sch. Pt. II Table (subject to transitional provisions and savings in art. 3)
F66. . . . .
Amendments (Textual)
F6. Sch. 6 para. 6 repealed (E.W.) (1.10.1996) by 1996 c. 52, ss. 227, 231. (4)(b), Sch. 19 Pt. I; S.I. 1996/2402, art. 3 (subject to transitional provisions and savings in Sch.); and repealed (S.) (1.11.2001) by 2001 asp 10, s. 112, Sch. 10 para. 15. (8); S.S.I. 2001/336, art. 2. (3), Sch. Pt. II Table (subject to transitional provisions and savings in art. 3)
[F77. (1)In section 9 (control by Corporation of disposition of land by housing associations) for subsection (1) there shall be substituted the following subsections—
"(1)Subject to section 10 and sections 81. (7), 105. (6) and 133. (7) of the Housing Act 1988, the

consent of the Corporation is required for any disposition of land by a registered housing association.

(1. A) Subject to section 10, the consent of the relevant Corporation is required for any disposition of grant-aided land (as defined in Schedule 1) by an unregistered housing association; and for this purpose " the relevant Corporation " means,—
- (a) if the land is in England, the Housing Corporation;
- (b) if the land is in Scotland, Scottish Homes, and
- (c) if the land is in Wales, Housing for Wales."

(2) In subsection (3) of that section—

(a) for the words "the consent of the Corporation", in the first place where they occur, there shall be substituted "consent"; and

(b) for the words "the consent of the Corporation", in the second place where they occur, there shall be substituted "that consent".

F8. (3)]. . . . .

Amendments (Textual)

F7. Sch. 6 para. 7 repealed (S.) (1.11.2001) by 2001 asp 10, s. 112, Sch. 10 para. 15. (8); S.S.I. 2001/336, art. 2. (3), Sch. Pt. II Table (subject to transitional provisions and savings in art. 3)

F8. Sch. 6 para. 7. (3) repealed (1.4.2010) by Housing and Regeneration Act 2008 (c. 17), s. 325. (1), Sch. 16; S.I. 2010/862, arts. 2, 3 (with Sch.)

[F98. (1)In section 10 (dispositions excepted from section 9), in subsection (1) for the words from "the Charity Commissioners", in the second place where they occur, onwards there shall be substituted "before making an order in such a case the Charity Commissioners shall consult,—
- (a) in the case of dispositions of land in England, the Housing Corporation;
- (b) in the case of dispositions of land in Scotland, Scottish Homes; and
- (c) in the case of dispositions of land in Wales, Housing for Wales."

(2) In subsection (2) of that section at the end of paragraph (b) there shall be inserted "or
- (c) a letting of land under an assured tenancy or an assured agricultural occupancy, or
- (d) a letting of land in England or Wales under what would be an assured tenancy or an assured agricultural occupancy but for any of paragraphs 4 to 8 of Schedule 1 to the Housing Act 1988, or
- (e) a letting of land in Scotland under what would be an assured tenancy but for any of paragraphs 3 to 8 and 12 of Schedule 4 to the Housing (Scotland) Act 1988."]

Amendments (Textual)

F9. Sch. 6 para. 8 repealed (S.) (1.11.2001) by 2001 asp 10, s. 112, Sch. 10 para. 15. (8); S.S.I. 2001/336, art. 2. (3), Sch. Pt. II Table (subject to transitional provisions and savings in art. 3) (subject to transitional provisions and savings in art. 3)

F109. . . . .

Amendments (Textual)

F10. Sch. 6 para. 9 repealed (E.W.) (1.10.1996) by 1996 c. 52, ss. 227, 231. (4)(b), Sch. 19 Pt. I; S.I. 1996/2402, art. 3 (subject to transitional provisions and savings in Sch.); and repealed (S.) (1.11.2001) by 2001 asp 10, s. 112, Sch. 10 para. 15. (8); S.S.I. 2001/336, art. 2. (3), Sch. Pt. II Table (subject to transitional provisions and savings in art. 3)

F1110. . . . .

Amendments (Textual)

F11. Sch. 6 para. 10 repealed (E.W.) (1.10.1996) by 1996 c. 52, ss. 227, 231. (4)(b), Sch. 19 Pt. I; S.I. 1996/2402, art. 3 (subject to transitional provisions and savings in Sch.); and repealed (S.) (1.11.2001) by 2001 asp 10, s. 112, Sch. 10 para. 15. (8); S.S.I. 2001/336, art. 2. (3), Sch. Pt. II Table (subject to transitional provisions and savings in art. 3)

F1211. . . . .

Amendments (Textual)

F12. Sch. 6 para. 11 repealed (E.W.) (1.10.1996) by 1996 c. 52, ss. 227, 231. (4)(b), Sch. 19 Pt. I; S.I. 1996/2402, art. 3 (subject to transitional provisions and savings in Sch.); and repealed (S.) (1.11.2001) by 2001 asp 10, s. 112, Sch. 10 para. 15. (8); S.S.I. 2001/336, art. 2. (3), Sch. Pt. II Table (subject to transitional provisions and savings in art. 3)

F13¹²......

Amendments (Textual)

F13. Sch. 6 para. 12 repealed (E.W.) (1.10.1996) by 1996 c. 52, ss. 227, 231. (4)(b), Sch. 19 Pt. I; S.I. 1996/2402, art. 3 (subject to transitional provisions and savings in Sch.); and repealed (S.) (1.11.2001) by 2001 asp 10, s. 112, Sch. 10 para. 15. (8); S.S.I. 2001/336, art. 2. (3), Sch. Pt. II Table (subject to transitional provisions and savings in art. 3)

F14¹³......

Amendments (Textual)

F14. Sch. 6 para. 13 repealed (E.W.) (1.10.1996) by 1996 c. 52, ss. 227, 231. (4)(b), Sch. 19 Pt. I; S.I. 1996/2402, art. 3 (subject to transitional provisions and savings in Sch.); and repealed (S.) (1.11.2001) by 2001 asp 10, s. 112, Sch. 10 para. 15. (8); S.S.I. 2001/336, art. 2. (3), Sch. Pt. II Table (subject to transitional provisions and savings in art. 3)

F15¹⁴......S

Amendments (Textual)

F15. Sch. 6 para. 14 repealed (E.W.) (1.10.1996) by 1996 c. 52, ss. 227, 231. (4)(b), Sch. 19 Pt. I; S.I. 1996/2402, art. 3 (subject to transitional provisions and savings in Sch.); and repealed (S.) (1.11.2001) by 2001 asp 10, s. 112, Sch. 10 para. 15. (8); S.S.I. 2001/336, art. 2. (3), Sch. Pt. II Table (subject to transitional provisions and savings in art. 3)

F16¹⁵......

Amendments (Textual)

F16. Sch. 6 para. 15 repealed (E.W.) (1.10.1996) by 1996 c. 52, ss. 227, 231. (4)(b), Sch. 19 Pt. I; S.I. 1996/2402, art. 3 (subject to transitional provisions and savings in Sch.); and repealed (S.) (1.11.2001) by 2001 asp 10, s. 112, Sch. 10 para. 15. (8); S.S.I. 2001/336, art. 2. (3), Sch. Pt. II Table (subject to transitional provisions and savings in art. 3)

F17¹⁶......

Amendments (Textual)

F17. Sch. 6 para. 16 repealed (E.W.) (1.10.1996) by 1996 c. 52, ss. 227, 231. (4)(b), Sch. 19 Pt. I; S.I. 1996/2402, art. 3 (subject to transitional provisions and savings in Sch.); and repealed (S.) (1.11.2001) by 2001 asp 10, s. 112, Sch. 10 para. 15. (8); S.S.I. 2001/336, art. 2. (3), Sch. Pt. II Table (subject to transitional provisions and savings in art. 3)

F18¹⁷......

Amendments (Textual)

F18. Sch. 6 para. 17 repealed (E.W.) (1.10.1996) by 1996 c. 52, ss. 227, 231. (4)(b), Sch. 19 Pt. I; S.I. 1996/2402, art. 3 (subject to transitional provisions and savings in Sch.); and repealed (S.) (1.11.2001) by 2001 asp 10, s. 112, Sch. 10 para. 15. (8); S.S.I. 2001/336, art. 2. (3), Sch. Pt. II Table (subject to transitional provisions and savings in art. 3)

F19¹⁸......S

Amendments (Textual)

F19. Sch. 6 paras. 3-6, 9-23 repealed (E.W.) (1.10.1996) by 1996 c. 52, ss. 227, 231. (4)(b), Sch. 19 Pt. I; S.I. 1996/2402, art. 3 (subject to transitional provisions and savings in Sch.); and repealed (S.) (1.11.2001) by 2001 asp 10, s. 112, Sch. 10 para. 15. (8); S.S.I. 2001/336, art. 2. (3), Sch. Pt. II Table (subject to transitional provisions and savings in art. 3)

F20¹⁹......

Amendments (Textual)

F20. Sch. 6 para. 19 repealed (E.W.) (1.10.1996) by 1996 c. 52, ss. 227, 231. (4)(b), Sch. 19 Pt. I; S.I. 1996/2402, art. 3 (subject to transitional provisions and savings in Sch.); and repealed (S.) (1.11.2001) by 2001 asp 10, s. 112, Sch. 10 para. 15. (8); S.S.I. 2001/336, art. 2. (3), Sch. Pt. II Table (subject to transitional provisions and savings in art. 3)

F21²⁰......

Amendments (Textual)

F21. Sch. 6 para. 20 repealed (E.W.) (1.10.1996) by 1996 c. 52, ss. 227, 231. (4)(b), Sch. 19 Pt. I; S.I. 1996/2402, art. 3 (subject to transitional provisions and savings in Sch.); and repealed (S.) (1.11.2001) by 2001 asp 10, s. 112, Sch. 10 para. 15. (8); S.S.I. 2001/336, art. 2. (3), Sch. Pt. II

Table (subject to transitional provisions and savings in art. 3)
F2221. . . . .

Amendments (Textual)

F22. Sch. 6 para. 21 repealed (E.W.) (1.10.1996) by 1996 c. 52, ss. 227, 231. (4)(b), Sch. 19 Pt. I; S.I. 1996/2402, art. 3 (subject to transitional provisions and savings in Sch.); and repealed (S.) (1.11.2001) by 2001 asp 10, s. 112, Sch. 10 para. 15. (8); S.S.I. 2001/336, art. 2. (3), Sch. Pt. II Table (subject to transitional provisions and savings in art. 3)
F2322. . . . .

Amendments (Textual)

F23. Sch. 6 paras. 3-6, 9-23 repealed (E.W.) (1.10.1996) by 1996 c. 52, ss. 227, 231. (4)(b), Sch. 19 Pt. I; S.I. 1996/2402, art. 3 (subject to transitional provisions and savings in Sch.); and repealed (S.) (1.11.2001) by 2001 asp 10, s. 112, Sch. 10 para. 15. (8); S.S.I. 2001/336, art. 2. (3), Sch. Pt. II Table (subject to transitional provisions and savings in art. 3)

[F2423. In section 33 (recognition of central association), in subsection (1) after "housing associations" there shall be inserted "in Great Britain or in any part of Great Britain".]S

Amendments (Textual)

F24. Sch. 6 paras. 3-6, 9-23 repealed (E.W.) (1.10.1996) by 1996 c. 52, ss. 227, 231. (4)(b), Sch. 19 Pt. I; S.I. 1996/2402, art. 3 (subject to transitional provisions and savings in Sch.)
F2524. . . . .

Amendments (Textual)

F25. Sch. 6 para. 24 repealed (1.4.2010) by Housing and Regeneration Act 2008 (c. 17), s. 325. (1), Sch. 16; S.I. 2010/862, arts. 2, 3 (with Sch.)

[F2625. In section 39 (minor definitions) before the definition of "mental disorder" there shall be inserted—

" "assured tenancy" has, in England and Wales, the same meaning as in Part I of the Housing Act 1988 and, in Scotland, the same meaning as in Part II of the Housing (Scotland) Act 1988;
"assured agricultural occupancy" has the same meaning as in Part I of the Housing Act 1988."]

Amendments (Textual)

F26. Sch. 6 para. 25 repealed (S.) (1.11.2001) by 2001 asp 10, s. 112, Sch. 10 para. 15. (8); S.S.I. 2001/336, art. 2. (3), Sch. Pt. II Table (subject to transitional provisions and savings in art. 3)

[F2726. In section 40 (index of defined expressions in Part I)—

(a) after the entry relating to "appropriate registrar" there shall be inserted—

" "assured agricultural occupancy" section 39

"assured tenancy" section 39";

F28. (b). . . . .
F29. (c). . . . .]

Amendments (Textual)

F27. Sch. 6 para. 26 repealed (S.) (1.11.2001) by 2001 asp 10, s. 112, Sch. 10 para. 15. (8); S.S.I. 2001/336, art. 2. (3), Sch. Pt. II Table (subject to transitional provisions and savings in art. 3)
F28. Sch. 6 para. 26. (b) repealed (1.10.1996) by S.I. 1996/2325, art. 4, Sch. 1 Pts. I, II
F29. Sch. 6 para. 26. (c) repealed (E.W.) (1.10.1996) by S.I. 1996/2325, art. 4, Sch. 1 Pt. I

Part II Amendments of Part II with Respect to the Housing Corporation and Housing for Wales

27. (1)In section 63 (building society advances) for the words "the Housing Corporation", in each place where they occur in subsections (1) and (2), there shall be substituted "one of the Corporations" and in subsection (1) (b) for the words "the Corporation" there shall be substituted "that one of the Corporations which is concerned".

(2) After subsection (2) of that section there shall be inserted the following subsection—

"(2. A)In this section "the Corporations" means the Housing Corporation and Housing for Wales".

28[F30. (1)In section 69 (power to vary or terminate certain agreements) at the end of subsection

(1)(a) there shall be added "(including such an agreement under which rights and obligations have been transferred to Housing for Wales)".
(2) After subsection (2) of that section there shall be inserted the following subsection—
"(2. A)In the case of an agreement under which rights and obligations have been transferred to Housing for Wales, the reference to a party to the agreement includes a reference to Housing for Wales."]
Amendments (Textual)
F30. Sch. 6 para. 28 repealed (E.W.) (1.4.2010) by The Housing and Regeneration Act 2008 (Consequential Provisions) Order 2010 (S.I. 2010/866), art. 1. (2), Sch. 4 (with art. 6, Sch. 3)
29[F31. In section 69. A (land subject to housing management agreement) for the words "housing association grant, revenue deficit grant or hostel deficit grant" there shall be substituted "grant under section 50 (housing association grant) or section 51 (revenue deficit grant) of the Housing Act 1988".]
Amendments (Textual)
F31. Sch. 6 para. 29 repealed (E.W.) (1.4.2010) by The Housing and Regeneration Act 2008 (Consequential Provisions) Order 2010 (S.I. 2010/866), art. 1. (2), Sch. 4 (with art. 6, Sch. 3)
30. (1)In Part I of Schedule 5 (residual subsidies)—
(a) in paragraph 5. (3) the words "at such times and in such places as the Treasury may direct" and "with the approval of the Treasury" shall be omitted; F32. . .
(b) . . . .
(2) In Part II of that Schedule, in paragraph 5. (3) the words "at such times and in such places as the Treasury may direct" and "with the approval of the Treasury" shall be omitted.
Amendments (Textual)
F32. Sch. 6 para. 30. (1)(b) and the word "and" immediately preceding it repealed (1.11.1998) by 1998 c. 38, s. 152, Sch. 18 Pt. VI (with ss. 137. (1), 139. (2), 143. (2)); S.I. 1998/2244, art. 5

Part III Amendments of Part III with Respect to the Housing Corporation and Housing for Wales

31. F33. (1). . . . .
(2) [F34. In subsection (2) of that section for the words "the Corporation" there shall be substituted "the Housing Corporation".]
(3) [F35. At the end of that section there shall be inserted the following subsections—
"(3)In this Part "registered housing association" in relation to the Corporation, means a housing association registered in the register maintained by the Corporation.
(4) In this Part,—
   (a) in relation to land in Wales held by an unregistered housing association, "the Corporation" means Housing for Wales; and
   (b) in relation to land outside Wales held by such an association, "the Corporation" means the Housing Corporation."]
Amendments (Textual)
F33. Sch. 6 para. 31. (1) repealed (1.11.1998) by 1998 c. 38, s. 152, Sch. 18 Pt. VI (with ss. 137. (1), 139. (2), 143. (2)); S.I. 1998/2244, art. 5
F34. Sch. 6 para. 31. (2) repealed (E.W.) (1.4.2009) by The Housing Corporation (Dissolution) Order 2009 (S.I. 2009/484), art. 6, Sch. 2
F35. Sch. 6 para. 31. (3) repealed (E.W.) (1.4.2010) by The Housing and Regeneration Act 2008 (Consequential Provisions) Order 2010 (S.I. 2010/866), art. 1. (2), Sch. 4 (with art. 6, Sch. 3)
[F3632. In section 75 (general functions), in subsection (1)(c) for the words "a register of housing associations" there shall be substituted "the register of housing associations referred to in section 3".]S
Amendments (Textual)
F36. Sch. 6 para. 32 repealed (E.W.) (1.10.1996) by S.I. 1996/2325, art. 4, Sch. 1 Pt. I

33[F37. At the end of section 77 (advisory service) there shall be added the following subsection—

"(3)The powers conferred on the Corporation by subsections (1) and (2) may be exercised by the Housing Corporation and Housing for Wales acting jointly".]

Amendments (Textual)

F37. Sch. 6 para. 33 repealed (E.W.) (1.4.2010) by The Housing and Regeneration Act 2008 (Consequential Provisions) Order 2010 (S.I. 2010/866), art. 1. (2), Sch. 4 (with art. 6, Sch. 3)

34. (1)In section 83 (power to guarantee loans), in subsection (3) (maximum amount outstanding in respect of loans etc.) for the words "the Corporation", in each place where they occur, there shall be substituted "the Housing Corporation".

(2) After subsection (3) of that section there shall be inserted the following subsection—

"(3. A)The aggregate amount outstanding in respect of—

(a) loans for which Housing for Wales has given a guarantee under this section, and

(b) payments made by Housing for Wales in meeting an obligation arising by virtue of such a guarantee and not repaid to Housing for Wales,

shall not exceed £30 million or such greater sum not exceeding £50 million as the Secretary of State may specify by order made with the approval of the Treasury".

(3) In subsection (4) of that section (procedure for orders of Secretary of State) after the words "subsection (3)" there shall be inserted "or subsection (3. A)".

35.

35[F38. (1)In section 93 (limit on borrowing), in subsection (2) for the words from "shall not exceed" onwards there shall be substituted "shall not exceed the limit appropriate to the Corporation under subsection (2. A)".

(2) At the end of subsection (2) of that section there shall be inserted the following subsection—

"(2. A)The limit referred to in subsection (2) is,—

(a) in the case of the Housing Corporation, £2,000 million or such greater sum not exceeding £3,000 million as the Secretary of State may specify by order made with the consent of the Treasury; and

(b) in the case of Housing for Wales, £250 million or such greater sum not exceeding £300 million as the Secretary of State may specify by order made with the consent of the Treasury."

(3) In subsections (3) to (5) of that section for "(2)", in each place where it occurs, there shall be substituted "(2. A)".]

Amendments (Textual)

F38. Sch. 6 para. 35 repealed (E.W.) (1.4.2009) by The Housing Corporation (Dissolution) Order 2009 (S.I. 2009/484), art. 6, Sch. 2

[F3936. In section 106. (1) (minor definitions: general) for the definition of "housing activities" there shall be substituted the following—S

" "housing activities", in relation to a registered housing association, means all its activities in pursuance of such of its purposes, objects or powers as are of a description mentioned in section 1. (1) (a) or subsections (2) to (4) of section 4."]

Amendments (Textual)

F39. Sch. 6 para. 36 repealed (E.W.) (1.1.1996) by S.I. 1996/2325, art. 4, Sch. 1 Pt. I

37. In Schedule 6, paragraph 3. (3)(b) shall be omitted.

Schedule 7. Housing Action Trusts: Constitution

Section 62. (5).

Members

1. A housing action trust (in this Schedule referred to as a "trust") shall consist of a chairman and such number of other members (not less than five but not exceeding eleven) as the Secretary of State may from time to time appoint.

2. (1) In appointing members of a trust the Secretary of State shall have regard to the desirability of securing the services of persons who live in or have special knowledge of the locality in which the designated area is situated and before appointing any such person as a member he shall consult every local housing authority any part of whose district is included in the designated area.

(2) Before appointing a person to be a member of a trust the Secretary of State shall satisfy himself that that person will have no financial or other interest likely to affect prejudicially the exercise of his functions as a member; and the Secretary of State may require a person whom he proposes to appoint to give him such information as he considers necessary for that purpose.

(3) For the purposes of sub-paragraph (2) above, the fact that a person is or may become a tenant of a trust shall not be regarded as giving to that person an interest likely to affect prejudicially the exercise of his functions as a member.

(4) The Secretary of State shall appoint one of the members to be chairman and, if he thinks fit, another to be deputy chairman of the trust.

3. Subject to the following provisions of this Schedule, each member of the trust as such and the chairman and deputy chairman as such shall hold and vacate office in accordance with his appointment.

4. If the chairman or deputy chairman ceases to be a member of the trust, he shall also cease to be chairman or deputy chairman, as the case may be.

5. Any member of the trust may, by notice in writing addressed to the Secretary of State, resign his membership; and the chairman or deputy chairman may, by like notice, resign his office as such.

6. If the Secretary of State is satisfied that a member of the trust (including the chairman or deputy chairman)—

(a) has become bankrupt or made an arrangement with his creditors [F1 or has had a debt relief order (under Part 7. A of the Insolvency Act 1986) made in respect of him], or

(b) has been absent from meetings of the trust for a period longer than three consecutive months without the permission of the trust, or

(c) is otherwise unable or unfit to discharge the functions of a member, or is unsuitable to continue as a member,

the Secretary of State may remove him from his office.

Amendments (Textual)

F1. Words in Sch. 7 para. 6. (a) inserted (1.10.2012) by The Tribunals, Courts and Enforcement Act 2007 (Consequential Amendments) Order 2012 (S.I. 2012/2404), art. 1, Sch. 2 para. 25 (with art. 5)

7. A member of the trust who ceases to be a member or ceases to be chairman or deputy chairman shall be eligible for reappointment.

Remuneration

8. The trust may pay to each member such remuneration and allowances as the Secretary of State may F2. . . determine.

Amendments (Textual)

F2. Words in Sch. 7 para. 8 repealed (1.10.1996) by 1996 c. 52, ss. 222, 227, Sch. 18 Pt. IV para. 22. (1)(e)(3), Sch. 19 Pt. XIII; S.I. 1996/2402, art. 3 (subject to transitional provisions in Sch.)

9. The trust may pay or make provision for paying, to or in respect of any member, such sums by way of pensions, allowances and gratuities as the Secretary of State may F3. . . determine and, F3. . ., the Secretary of State may undertake to meet any liabilities arising in respect of such pensions, allowances or gratuities after the dissolution of the trust.

Amendments (Textual)

F3. Words in Sch. 7 para. 9 repealed (1.10.1996) by 1996 c. 52, ss. 222, 227, Sch. 18 Pt. IV para.

22. (1)(e)(3), Sch. 19 Pt. XIII; S.I. 1996/2402, art. 3 (subject to transitional provisions in Sch.)
10. Where a person ceases to be a member of a trust and it appears to the Secretary of State that there are special circumstances which make it right for him to receive compensation, the trust may make to him payment of such amount as the Secretary of State may F4. . . determine.
Amendments (Textual)
F4. Words in Sch. 7 para. 10 repealed (1.10.1996) by 1996 c. 52, ss. 222, 227, Sch. 18 Pt. IV para. 22. (1)(e)(3), Sch. 19 Pt. XIII; S.I. 1996/2402, art. 3 (subject to transitional provisions in Sch.)

Staff

11. (1)There shall be a chief officer of the trust who shall be appointed by the trust with the approval of the Secretary of State.
(2) The chief officer shall be responsible to the trust for the general exercise of the trust's functions.
(3) The trust may appoint such number of other employees as may be approved by the Secretary of State.
(4) References in paragraph 12 below to employees of the trust include references to the chief officer as well as other employees.
12. (1)Employees of the trust shall be appointed at such remuneration and on such other terms and conditions as the trust may determine.
(2) The trust may pay such pensions, allowances or gratuities as it may determine to or in respect of any of its employees, make such payments as it may determine towards the provision of pensions, allowances or gratuities to or in respect of any of its employees or provide and maintain such schemes as it may determine (whether contributory or not) for the payment of pensions, allowances or gratuities to or in respect of any of its employees; and F5. . . the Secretary of State may undertake to meet any liabilities arising in respect of such pensions, allowances or gratuities after the dissolution of the trust.
(3) The reference in sub-paragraph (2) above to pensions, allowances or gratuities to or in respect of any of the trust's employees includes a reference to pensions, allowances or gratuities by way of compensation to or in respect of any of the trust's employees who suffer loss of office or employment or loss or diminution of emoluments.
(4) If an employee of the trust becomes a member and was by reference to his employment by the trust a participant in a pension scheme maintained by the trust for the benefit of any of its employees, the trust may determine that his service as a member shall be treated for the purposes of the scheme as service as an employee of the trust whether or not any benefits are to be payable to or in respect of him by virtue of paragraph 9 above.
(5) A determination of the trust for the purposes of this paragraph is ineffective unless made with the approval of the Secretary of State F5. . ..
Amendments (Textual)
F5. Words in Sch. 7 para. 12. (2)(5) repealed (1.10.1996) by 1996 c. 52, ss. 222, 227, Sch. 18 Pt. IV para. 22. (1)(e)(3); S.I. 1996/2402, art. 3 (subject to transitional provisions in Sch.)

Meetings and proceedings

13. The quorum of the trust and the arrangements relating to its meetings shall, subject to any directions given by the Secretary of State, be such as the trust may determine.
14. The validity of any proceedings of the trust shall not be affected by any vacancy among its members or by any defect in the appointment of any of its members.

Instruments, etc.

15. The fixing of the seal of the trust shall be authenticated by the signature of the chairman or of some other member authorised either generally or specially by the trust to act for that purpose.
16. Any document purporting to be a document duly executed under the seal of the trust shall be received in evidence and shall, unless the contrary is proved, be deemed to be so executed.
17. A document purporting to be signed on behalf of a trust shall be received in evidence and shall, unless the contrary is proved, be deemed to be so signed.

House of Commons disqualification

18. In Part III of Schedule 1 to the M1. House of Commons Disqualification Act 1975 (disqualifying offices), there shall be inserted at the appropriate place the following entry— " Any member, in receipt of remuneration, of a housing action trust (within the meaning of Part III of the Housing Act 1988). "
Marginal Citations
M11975 c. 24.

Schedule 8. Housing Action Trusts: Finance Etc.

Section 62. (5).

Part I Preliminary

1. (1)References in this Schedule to a trust are to a housing action trust.
(2) The financial year of a trust shall begin with 1 April and references to a financial year in relation to a trust shall be construed accordingly.

Part II Finance

Financial duties

2. (1)After consultation with a trust, the Secretary of State may, with the Treasury's approval, determine the financial duties of the trust, and different determinations may be made in relation to different trusts or for different functions and activities of the same trust.
(2) The Secretary of State shall give the trust notice of every determination, and a determination may—
(a) relate to a period beginning before the date on which it is made;
(b) contain incidental or supplementary provisions; and
(c) be varied by a subsequent determination.

Government grants

3. (1)The Secretary of State may (out of moneys provided by Parliament and with the consent of the Treasury) pay to a trust, in respect of the exercise of its functions and in respect of its administrative expenses, such sums as he may (with the approval of the Treasury) determine.
(2)
The payment may be made on such terms as the Secretary of State (with the approval of the Treasury) provides.

Borrowing

4. (1) A trust may borrow temporarily, by way of overdraft or otherwise, such sums as it may require for meeting its obligations and discharging its functions—
(a) in sterling from the Secretary of State; or
(b) with the consent of the Secretary of State, or in accordance with any general authority given by the Secretary of State, either in sterling or in currency other than sterling from a person other than the Secretary of State.
(2) A trust may borrow otherwise than by way of temporary loan such sums as the trust may require—
(a) in sterling from the Secretary of State; or
(b) with the consent of the Secretary of State, in a currency other than sterling from a person other than the Secretary of State.
(3) The Secretary of State may lend to a trust any sums it has power to borrow from him under sub-paragraph (1) or sub-paragraph (2) above.
(4)
The Treasury may issue to the Secretary of State out of the National Loans Fund any sums necessary to enable him to make loans under sub-paragraph (3) above.
(5) Loans made under sub-paragraph (3)
above shall be repaid to the Secretary of State at such times and by such methods, and interest on the loans shall be paid to him at such times and at such rates, as he may determine.
(6) All sums received by the Secretary of State under sub-paragraph (5)
above shall be paid into the National Loans Fund.
(7)
References in this paragraph to the Secretary of State are references to him acting with the approval of the Treasury.

Guarantees

5. (1) The Treasury may guarantee, in such manner and on such conditions as they think fit, the repayment of the principal of and the payment of interest on any sums which a trust borrows from a person or body other than the Secretary of State.
(2) Immediately after a guarantee is given under this paragraph, the Treasury shall lay a statement of the guarantee before each House of Parliament; and, where any sum is issued for fulfilling a guarantee so given, the Treasury shall lay before each House of Parliament a statement relating to that sum, as soon as possible after the end of each financial year, beginning with that in which the sum is issued and ending with that in which all liability in respect of the principal of the sum and in respect of interest on it is finally discharged.
[F1. (3) Any sums required for fulfilling a guarantee under this paragraph shall be charged on and issued out of—
(a) the Consolidated Fund, if required by the Treasury, or
(b) the Welsh Consolidated Fund, if required by the Welsh Ministers.]
(4) If any sums are issued in fulfilment of a guarantee given under this paragraph, the trust shall make to the Treasury, at such times and in such manner as the Treasury may from time to time direct, payments of such amounts as the Treasury so direct in or towards repayment of the sums so issued and payments of interest, at such rates as the Treasury so direct, on what is outstanding for the time being in respect of sums so issued.
(5) Any sums received by the Treasury in pursuance of sub-paragraph (4) above shall be paid into the Consolidated Fund.
Amendments (Textual)
F1. Sch. 8 para. 5. (3) substituted (1.4.2007) by Government of Wales Act. 2006 (c. 32), ss. 160, 161. (3), {Sch. 10 para. 33} (with savings and transitional provisions in Sch. 11 para. 22)

Modifications etc. (not altering text)
C1. Sch. 8 para. 5. (3) modified (temp) by Government of Wales Act 2006 (c. 32), ss. 160, 161. (3), Sch. 11 para. 59. (c) (with savings and transitional provisions in Sch. 11 para. 22)

Assumed debt

6. (1) On any acquisition to which this paragraph applies, a trust shall assume a debt to the Secretary of State of such amount as may be notified to the trust in writing by him, with the approval of the Treasury.
(2) This paragraph applies to any acquisition by the trust of property held—
(a) by or on behalf of the Crown; or
(b) by a company all of whose shares are held by or on behalf of the Crown or by a wholly owned subsidiary of such a company.
(3) Subject to sub-paragraph (4) below, the amount to be notified is the aggregate of the following—
(a) the consideration given when the property was first brought into public ownership; and
(b) the costs and expenses of and incidental to its being brought into public ownership.
(4) If it appears to the Secretary of State that there has been such a change in circumstances since the property was first brought into public ownership that its true value would not be reflected by reference to the consideration mentioned in sub-paragraph (3) above, the Secretary of State, with the approval of the Treasury, shall determine the amount to be notified.
(5) The rate of interest payable on the debt assumed by a trust under this paragraph, and the date from which interest is to begin to accrue, the arrangements for paying off the principal, and the other terms of the debt shall be such as the Secretary of State, with the approval of the Treasury, may from time to time determine.
(6) Different rates and dates may be determined under sub-paragraph (5) above with respect to different portions of the debt.
(7) Any sums received by the Secretary of State under sub-paragraph (5)
above shall be paid into the National Loans Fund.

Surplus funds

7. (1) Where it appears to the Secretary of State, after consultation with the Treasury and the trust, that a trust has a surplus, whether on capital or on revenue account, after making allowance by way of transfer to reserve or otherwise for its future requirements, the trust shall, if the Secretary of State with the approval of the Treasury and after consultation with the trust so directs, pay to the Secretary of State such sum not exceeding the amount of that surplus as may be specified in the direction.
(2)
Any sum received by the Secretary of State under this paragraph shall, subject to sub-paragraph (4) below, be paid into the Consolidated Fund.
(3)
The whole or part of any payment made to the Secretary of State by a trust under sub-paragraph (1) above shall, if the Secretary of State with the approval of the Treasury so determines, be treated as made by way of repayment of such part of the principal of loans under paragraph 4. (3) above, and as made in respect of the repayments due at such times, as may be so determined.
(4) Any sum treated under sub-paragraph (3)
above as a repayment of a loan shall be paid by the Secretary of State into the National Loans Fund.

Financial limits

8. (1)The aggregate amount of the sums mentioned in sub-paragraph (2) below shall not exceed such sum as the Secretary of State, with the consent of the Treasury, may by order made by statutory instrument specify.
(2) The sums are—
(a) sums borrowed by all trusts under paragraph 4 above minus repayments made in respect of the sums; and
(b) sums issued by the Treasury in fulfilment of guarantees under paragraph 5 above of debts of all trusts.
(3) No order shall be made under sub-paragraph (1) above unless a draft of it has been laid before, and approved by a resolution of, the House of Commons.

Grants and loans: accounts

9. (1)The Secretary of State shall prepare in respect of each financial year an account—
(a) of the sums paid to trusts under paragraph 3 above;
(b) of the sums issued to him under paragraph 4. (4) above and the sums received by him under paragraph 4. (5) above and of the disposal by him of those sums; and
(c) of the sums paid into the Consolidated Fund or National Loans Fund under paragraph 7 above.
(2) The Secretary of State shall send the account to the Comptroller and Auditor General before the end of the month of November next following the end of that year.
(3) The Comptroller and Auditor General shall examine, certify and report on the account and lay copies of it and of his report before each House of Parliament.
(4) The form of the account and the manner of preparing it shall be such as the Treasury may direct.

Part III General Accounts Etc.

Accounts

10. (1)A trust shall keep proper accounts and other records in relation to them.
(2) The accounts and records shall show, in respect of the financial year to which they relate, a true and fair view of the trust's activities.
(3) A trust shall prepare in respect of each financial year a statement of accounts complying with any requirement which the Secretary of State has (with the consent of the Treasury) notified in writing to the trust relating to—
(a) the information to be contained in the statement;
(b) the manner in which the information is to be presented; and
(c) the methods and principles according to which the statement is to be prepared.
(4) Subject to any requirement notified to the trust under sub-paragraph (3) above, in preparing any statement of accounts in accordance with that sub-paragraph the trust shall follow, with respect to each of the matters specified in paragraphs (a) to (c) of that sub-paragraph, such course as may for the time being be approved by the Secretary of State with the consent of the Treasury.
(5) Section 6 of the M1. National Audit Act 1983 (which enables the Comptroller and Auditor General to conduct examinations into the economy, efficiency and effectiveness with which certain departments, authorities and bodies have used their resources) shall apply to a trust.
Marginal Citations
M11983 c. 44.

Audit

11. (1)The trust's accounts and statements of accounts shall be audited by an auditor to be appointed annually by the Secretary of State in relation to the trust.
[F2. (2)A person shall not be appointed under sub-paragraph (1) above unless he is eligible for appointment as a [F3statutory auditor under Part 42 of the Companies Act 2006].]
(3) A person shall not be qualified for appointment under sub-paragraph (1) above if the person is—
(a) a member, officer or servant of the trust,
(b) a partner of, or employed by, a member, officer or servant of the trust, F4 . . .
F4. (c). . . . .
Amendments (Textual)
F2. Sch. 8 para. 11. (2) substituted by S.I. 1991/1997, reg. 2, Sch. para. 71. (a) (with reg. 4)
F3. Words in Sch. 8 para. 11. (2) substituted (6.4.2008) by The Companies Act 2006 (Consequential Amendments etc) Order 2008 (S.I. 2008/948), arts. 2. (2), 3. (1), Sch. 1 para. 1. (ll) (with arts. 6, 11, 12)
F4. Words in Sch. 8 para. 11. (3) omitted by virtue of S.I. 1991/1997, reg. 2, Sch. para. 71. (b) (with reg. 4)

Transmission to Secretary of State

12. As soon as the accounts and statement of accounts of the trust for any financial year have been audited, the trust shall send to the Secretary of State a copy of the statement, together with a copy of any report made by the auditor on the statement or on the accounts.

Reports

13. (1)As soon as possible after the end of each financial year, a trust shall make to the Secretary of State a report dealing generally with the trust's operations during the year, and shall include in the report a copy of its audited statement of accounts for that year.
(2) Without prejudice to the generality of sub-paragraph (1) above, a report shall give particulars of the name and address of every person who, in the financial year to which the report relates, has received financial assistance from the trust under section 71. (1) of this Act, together with particulars of the form of the assistance, the amount involved and the purpose for which the assistance was given.
(3) The Secretary of State shall lay a copy of the report before each House of Parliament.

Information

14. Without prejudice to paragraph 13 above, a trust shall provide the Secretary of State with such information relating to its activities as he may require, and for that purpose shall permit any person authorised by the Secretary of State to inspect and make copies of the accounts, books, documents or papers of the trust and shall afford such explanation of them as that person or the Secretary of State may reasonably require.

Schedule 9. Orders Vesting Land in Housing Action Trusts

Section 76.

Part I Provisions Supplementing Section 76(1)—(3)

1. In this Part of this Schedule "the principal section" means section 76 of this Act.
2. (1)In the principal section and paragraph 3 below, "statutory undertakers" and "statutory undertaking" shall be construed in accordance with paragraph 4 below.
(2) In the principal section and the following provisions of this Part of this Schedule, "wholly-owned subsidiary" has the meaning given by [F1section 1159 of the Companies Act 2006].
Amendments (Textual)
F1. Words in Sch. 9 para. 2. (2) substituted (1.10.2009) by The Companies Act 2006 (Consequential Amendments, Transitional Provisions and Savings) Order 2009 (S.I. 2009/1941), art. 2. (1), Sch. 1 para. 100 (with art. 10)
3. (1)In subsection (3) of the principal section the reference to the Secretary of State and the appropriate Minister—
(a) in relation to statutory undertakers who are also statutory undertakers for the purposes of any provision of Part XI of [F2the Town and Country Planning Act 1990], shall be construed as if contained in that Part; and
(b) in relation to any other statutory undertakers shall be construed in accordance with an order made by the Secretary of State.
(2) If, for the purposes of subsection (3) of the principal section, any question arises as to which Minister is the appropriate Minister in relation to any statutory undertakers, that question shall be determined by the Treasury.
Amendments (Textual)
F2. Words substituted by Planning (Consequential Provisions) Act 1990 (c. 11, SIF 123: 1, 2), s. 4, Sch. 2 para. 79. (5)(a)
4. In the principal section and, except where the context otherwise requires, in paragraph 3 above "statutory undertakers" means—
(a) persons authorised by any enactment to carry on any railway, light railway, tramway, road transport, water transport, canal, inland navigation, dock, harbour, pier or lighthouse undertaking, or any undertaking for the supply of electricity, hydraulic power or water;
(b) F3... the British Steel Corporation, the Civil Aviation Authority, F4. . ., F5 . . ., F6. . . and any other authority, body or undertakers which, by virtue of any enactment, are to be treated as statutory undertakers for any of the purposes of [F7the Town and Country Planning Act 1990, the Planning (Listed Buildings and Conservation Areas) Act 1990 or the Planning (Hazardous Substances) Act 1990];
(c) any other authority, body or undertakers specified in an order made by the Secretary of State; and
(d) any wholly-owned subsidiary of any person, authority, body or undertakers mentioned in sub-paragraphs (a) and (b) above or specified in an order made under sub-paragraph (c) above;
and "statutory undertaking" shall be construed accordingly.
Amendments (Textual)
F3. Words in Sch. 9 para. 4. (b) omitted (22.3.2013) by virtue of The Public Bodies (Abolition of British Shipbuilders) Order 2013 (S.I. 2013/687), art. 1. (2), Sch. 1 para. 11
F4. Words in Sch. 9 Pt. I para. 4. (b) repealed (31.10.1994) by 1994 c. 21, ss. 7, 67, Sch. 9 para. 76, Sch. 11 Pt. II (with s. 40. (7)); S.I. 1994/2553, art. 2
F5. Words in Sch. 9 Pt. I para. 4. (b) repealed (6.1.1992) by British Technology Group Act 1991 (c. 66, SIF 64), s. 17. (2), Sch. 2, Pt. I; S.I. 1991/2721, art. 2
F6. Words in Sch. 9 Pt. I para. 4. (b) repealed (26.3.2001) by S.I. 2001/1149, art. 3. (2), Sch. 2
F7. Words substituted by Planning (Consequential Provisions) Act 1990 (c. 11, SIF 123: 1, 2), s. 4, Sch. 2 para. 79. (5)(b)
5. An order under any provision of this Part of this Schedule shall be made by statutory instrument which shall be subject to annulment in pursuance of a resolution of either House of Parliament.

Part II Modifications of Enactments

Land Compensation Act 1961.

6. The M1 Land Compensation Act 1961 shall have effect in relation to orders under section 76 of this Act subject to the modifications in paragraphs 7 to 11 below.
Marginal Citations
M11961 c.33.
7. References to the date of service of a notice to treat shall be treated as references to the date on which an order under section 76 of this Act comes into force.
8. Section 17. (2) shall be treated as if for the words "the [F8acquiring authority] have served a notice to treat [F9in respect of the interest] or an agreement has been made for the [F10sale of the interest] to that authority" there were substituted the words "an order under section 76 of the Housing Act 1988 vesting the land in which the interest subsists in a housing action trust has come into force, or an agreement has been made for the sale of the interest to such a trust".
Amendments (Textual)
F8. Words in Sch. 9 para. 8 substituted (6.4.2012) by Localism Act 2011 (c. 20), ss. 232. (7)(a), 240. (2); S.I. 2012/628, art. 8. (d) (with arts. 9 12 13 16 18-20) (as amended (3.8.2012) by S.I. 2012/2029, arts. 2, 4)
F9. Words in Sch. 9 para. 8 substituted (6.4.2012) by Localism Act 2011 (c. 20), ss. 232. (7)(b), 240. (2); S.I. 2012/628, art. 8. (d) (with arts. 9 12 13 16 18-20) (as amended (3.8.2012) by S.I. 2012/2029, arts. 2, 4)
F10. Words in Sch. 9 para. 8 substituted (6.4.2012) by Localism Act 2011 (c. 20), ss. 232. (7)(c), 240. (2); S.I. 2012/628, art. 8. (d) (with arts. 9 12 13 16 18-20) (as amended (3.8.2012) by S.I. 2012/2029, arts. 2, 4)
9. In section 22—
(a) subsection (2) shall be treated as if at the end of paragraph (c) there were added the words "or
   (cc) where an order has been made under section 76 of the Housing Act 1988 vesting the land in which the interest subsists in a housing action trust"; and
(b) subsection (3) shall be treated as if, in paragraph (a), after the words "paragraph (b)" there were inserted "or paragraph (cc)".
10. Any reference to a notice to treat in section 39. (2) shall be treated as a reference to an order under section 76 of this Act.
11. In Schedule 2, paragraph 1. (2) shall be treated as if at the end there were added the following paragraph—
"(k)an acquisition by means of an order under section 76 of the Housing Act 1988 vesting land in a housing action trust."

Compulsory Purchase (Vesting Declarations) Act 1981.

12. (1)In Schedule 2 to the Compulsory Purchase (Vesting Declarations) Act 1981 (vesting of land in urban development corporation), in paragraph I after the word "declaration)" there shall be inserted " or under section 76 of the Housing Act 1988 (subsection (5) of which contains similar provision) ".
(2) At the end of sub-paragraph (a) of paragraph 3 of that Schedule there shall be added " or, as the case may be, the housing action trust ".

Schedule 10. Housing Action Trusts: Land

Section 78.

Part I Modifications of Acquisition of Land Act 1981

1. The M1. Acquisition of Land Act 1981 (in this Part referred to as "the 1981 Act") shall apply in relation to the compulsory acquisition of land under section 77 of this Act with the modifications made by this Part of this Schedule.
Marginal Citations
M11981 c. 67.
2. F1. . . . .
Amendments (Textual)
F1. Sch. 10 para. 2 repealed (31.10.2004) by Planning and Compulsory Purchase Act 2004 (c. 5), ss. 118, 120, 121, Sch. 7 para. 15, Sch. 9 (with s. 111 and Sch. 7 para. 15. (2)); S.I. 2004/2593, art. 2. (d)(e)(v)
3. The reference in section 17. (3) of the 1981 Act to statutory undertakers includes a reference to a housing action trust.

Part II Land: Supplementary

Extinguishment of rights over land

4. (1)Subject to this paragraph, on an order under section 76 of this Act coming into force or the completion by a housing action trust of a compulsory acquisition of land under Part III of this Act, all private rights of way and rights of laying down, erecting, continuing or maintaining any apparatus on, under or over the land shall be extinguished, and any such apparatus shall vest in the trust.
(2) Sub-paragraph (1) above does not apply—
(a) to any right vested in, or apparatus belonging to, statutory undertakers for the purpose of carrying on their undertaking; or
(b) to any right conferred by or in accordance with [F2the electronic communications code] on the operator of [F3an electronic communications code network] system or to any [F4electronic communications apparatus] kept installed for the purposes of any [F5such network] .
(3) In respect of any right or apparatus not falling within sub-paragraph (2) above, sub-paragraph (1) above shall have effect subject—
(a) to any direction given by the Secretary of State before the coming into force of the order (or, as the case may be, by the trust before the completion of the acquisition) that sub-paragraph (1) above shall not apply to any right or apparatus specified in the direction, and
(b) to any agreement which may be made (whether before or after the coming into force of the order or completion of the acquisition) between the Secretary of State (or trust) and the person in or to whom the right or apparatus in question is vested or belongs.
(4) Any person who suffers loss by the extinguishment of a right or the vesting of any apparatus under this paragraph shall be entitled to compensation from the trust.
(5) Any compensation payable under this paragraph shall be determined in accordance with the M2. Land Compensation Act 1961.
Amendments (Textual)
F2. Words in Sch. 10 Pt. 2 para. 4 substituted (25.7.2003 for specified purposes, 29.12.2003 for further specified purposes) by Communications Act 2003 (c. 21), ss. 406, 411, Sch. 17 para. 94. (2)(a) (with transitional provisions in Sch. 18); S.I. 2003/1900, art. 1. (2), 2. (1), 3. (1), Sch. 1 (with art. 3. (2) (as amended (8.12.2003) by S.I. 2003/3142, art. 1. (3))); S.I. 2003/3142, art. 3. (2) (with art. 11)

F3. Words in Sch. 10 Pt. 2 para. 4 substituted (25.7.2003 for specified purposes, 29.12.2003 for further specified purposes) by Communications Act 2003 (c. 21), ss. 406, 411, Sch. 17 para. 94. (2)(b) (with transitional provisions in Sch. 18); S.I. 2003/1900, art. 1. (2), 2. (1), 3. (1), Sch. 1 (with art. 3. (2) (as amended (8.12.2003) by S.I. 2003/3142, art. 1. (3))); S.I. 2003/3142, art. 3. (2) (with art. 11)

F4. Words in Sch. 10 Pt. 2 para. 4 substituted (25.7.2003 for specified purposes, 29.12.2003 for further specified purposes) by Communications Act 2003 (c. 21), ss. 406, 411, Sch. 17 para. 94. (2)(c) (with transitional provisions in Sch. 18); S.I. 2003/1900, art. 1. (2), 2. (1), 3. (1), Sch. 1 (with art. 3. (2) (as amended (8.12.2003) by S.I. 2003/3142, art. 1. (3))); S.I. 2003/3142, art. 3. (2) (with art. 11)

F5. Words in Sch. 10 Pt. 2 para. 4 substituted (25.7.2003 for specified purposes, 29.12.2003 for further specified purposes) by Communications Act 2003 (c. 21), ss. 406, 411, Sch. 17 para. 94. (2)(d) (with transitional provisions in Sch. 18); S.I. 2003/1900, art. 1. (2), 2. (1), 3. (1), Sch. 1 (with art. 3. (2) (as amended (8.12.2003) by S.I. 2003/3142, art. 1. (3))); S.I. 2003/3142, art. 3. (2) (with art. 11)

Marginal Citations
M21961 c. 33.

F6...

Amendments (Textual)
F6. Sch. 10 para. 5 and crossheading omitted (13.7.2016) by virtue of Housing and Planning Act 2016 (c. 22), s. 216. (3), Sch. 19 para. 7. (2); S.I. 2016/733, reg. 3. (m)
F65. . . . .

Consecrated land and burial grounds

6. (1)Any consecrated land, whether including a building or not, which has been vested in or acquired by a housing action trust for the purposes of Part III of this Act may (subject to the following provisions of this paragraph) be used by the trust, or by any other person, in any manner in accordance with planning permission, notwithstanding any obligation or restriction imposed under ecclesiastical law or otherwise in respect of consecrated land.
(2) Sub-paragraph (1) above does not apply to land which consists or forms part of a burial ground.
(3) Any use of consecrated land authorised by sub-paragraph (1) above, and the use of any land, not being consecrated land, vested or acquired as mentioned in that sub-paragraph which at the time of acquisition included a church or other building used or formerly used for religious worship or the site thereof, shall be subject to compliance with the prescribed requirements with respect to the removal and reinterment of any human remains, and the disposal of monuments and fixtures and furnishings; and, in the case of consecrated land, shall be subject to such provisions as may be prescribed for prohibiting or restricting the use of the land, either absolutely or until the prescribed consent has been obtained, so long as any church or other building used or formerly used for religious worship, or any part thereof, remains on the land.
(4) Any regulations made for the purposes of sub-paragraph (3) above—
(a) shall contain such provisions as appear to the Secretary of State to be requisite for securing that any use of land which is subject to compliance with the regulations shall, as nearly as may be, be subject to the like control as is imposed by law in the case of a similar use authorised by an enactment not contained in this Act or by a Measure, or as it would be proper to impose on a disposal of the land in question otherwise than in pursuance of an enactment or Measure;
(b) shall contain requirements relating to the disposal of any such land as is mentioned in sub-paragraph (3) above such as appear to the Secretary of State requisite for securing that the provisions of that sub-paragraph shall be complied with in relation to the use of the land; and

(c) may contain such incidental and consequential provisions (including provision as to the closing of registers) as appear to the Secretary of State to be expedient for the purposes of the regulations.

(5) Any land consisting of a burial ground or part of a burial ground which has been vested in or acquired by a housing action trust for the purposes of Part III of this Act may be used by the trust in any manner in accordance with planning permission, notwithstanding anything in any enactment relating to burial grounds or any obligation or restriction imposed under ecclesiastical law or otherwise in respect of burial grounds.

(6) Sub-paragraph (5) above shall not have effect in respect of any land which has been used for the burial of the dead until the prescribed requirements with respect to the removal and reinterment of human remains and the disposal of monuments in or upon the land have been complied with.

(7) Provision shall be made by any regulations made for the purposes of sub-paragraphs (3) and (6) above—

(a) for requiring the persons in whom the land is vested to publish notice of their intention to carry out the removal and reinterment of any human remains or the disposal of any monuments; and

(b) for enabling the personal representatives or relatives of any deceased person themselves to undertake the removal and reinterment of the remains of the deceased and the disposal of any monument commemorating the deceased, and for requiring the persons in whom the land is vested to defray the expenses of such removal, reinterment and disposal, not exceeding such amount as may be prescribed; and

(c) for requiring compliance with such reasonable conditions (if any) as may be imposed, in the case of consecrated land, by the bishop of the diocese, with respect to the manner of removal and the place and manner of reinterment of any human remains and the disposal of any monuments; and

(d) for requiring compliance with any directions given in any case by the Secretary of State with respect to the removal and reinterment of any human remains.

(8) Subject to the provisions of any such regulations as are referred to in sub-paragraph (7) above, no faculty shall be required for the removal and reinterment in accordance with the regulations of any human remains or for the removal or disposal of any monuments, and the provisions of section 25 of the M3. Burial Act 1857 (which prohibits the removal of human remains without the licence of the Secretary of State except in certain cases) shall not apply to a removal carried out in accordance with the regulations.

(9) Any power conferred by this paragraph to use land in a manner therein mentioned shall be construed as a power so to use the land, whether it involves the erection, construction or carrying out of any building or work, or the maintenance of any building or work, or not.

(10) Nothing in this paragraph shall be construed as authorising any act or omission on the part of any person which is actionable at the suit of any person on any grounds other than contravention of any such obligation, restriction or enactment as is mentioned in sub-paragraph (1) or sub-paragraph (5) above.

[F7. (11)Nothing in this paragraph shall be construed as authorising any act or omission on the part of a housing action trust, or of any body corporate, in contravention of any limitation imposed by law on its capacity by virtue of the constitution of the trust or body.]

(12) In this paragraph "burial ground" includes any churchyard, cemetery or other ground, whether consecrated or not, which has at any time been set apart for the purposes of interment, and "monument" includes a tombstone or other memorial.

(13) In this paragraph "prescribed" means prescribed by regulations made by the Secretary of State.

(14) The power to make regulations under this paragraph shall be exercisable by statutory instrument which shall be subject to annulment in pursuance of a resolution of either House of Parliament.

Amendments (Textual)
F7. Sch. 10 para. 6. (11) substituted (13.7.2016) by Housing and Planning Act 2016 (c. 22), s. 216. (3), Sch. 19 para. 7. (3); S.I. 2016/733, reg. 3. (m)

Marginal Citations
M31857 c. 81.

Open spaces

7. (1)Any land being, or forming part of, a common, open space or fuel or field garden allotment, which has been vested in or acquired by a housing action trust for the purposes of Part III of this Act may be used by the trust, or by any other person, in any manner in accordance with planning permission, notwithstanding anything in any enactment relating to land of that kind, or in any enactment by which the land is specially regulated.
(2) Nothing in this paragraph shall be construed as authorising any act or omission on the part of any person which is actionable at the suit of any person on any grounds other than contravention of any such enactment as is mentioned in sub-paragraph (1) above.
[F8. (3)Nothing in this paragraph shall be construed as authorising any act or omission on the part of a housing action trust, or of any body corporate, in contravention of any limitation imposed by law on its capacity by virtue of the constitution of the trust or body.]
Amendments (Textual)
F8. Sch. 10 para. 7. (3) substituted (13.7.2016) by Housing and Planning Act 2016 (c. 22), s. 216. (3), Sch. 19 para. 7. (4); S.I. 2016/733, reg. 3. (m)

Displacement of persons

8. If the Secretary of State certifies that possession of a house which has been vested in or acquired by a housing action trust for the purposes of Part III of this Act and is for the time being held by that trust for the purposes for which it was acquired, is immediately required for those purposes, nothing in the M4. Rent (Agriculture) Act 1976 or the M5. Rent Act 1977 or this Act shall prevent that trust from obtaining possession of the house.
Marginal Citations
M41976 c. 80.
M51977 c. 42.

Extinguishment of public rights of way

9. (1)Where any land has been vested in or acquired by a housing action trust for the purposes of Part III of this Act and is for the time being held by that trust for those purposes, the Secretary of State may by order extinguish any public right of way over the land.
(2) Where the Secretary of State proposes to make an order under this paragraph, he shall publish in such manner as appears to him to be requisite a notice—
(a) stating the effect of the order, and
(b) specifying the time (not being less than 28 days from the publication of the notice) within which, and the manner in which, objections to the proposal may be made,
and shall serve a like notice—
(i) on the local planning authority in whose area the land is situated; and
(ii) on the relevant highway authority.
(3) In sub-paragraph (2) above "the relevant highway authority" means any authority which is a highway authority in relation to the right of way proposed to be extinguished by the order under this paragraph.
(4) Where an objection to a proposal to make an order under this paragraph is duly made and is not withdrawn, the provisions of paragraph 10 below shall have effect in relation to the proposal.
(5) For the purposes of this paragraph an objection to such a proposal shall not be treated as duly made unless—

(a) it is made within the time and in the manner specified in the notice required by this paragraph; and

(b) a statement in writing of the grounds of the objection is comprised in or submitted with the objection.

(6) Where it is proposed to make an order under this paragraph extinguishing a public right of way over a road on land acquired for the purposes of this Act by a housing action trust and compensation in respect of restrictions imposed under section 1 or section 2 of the M6. Restriction of Ribbon Development Act 1935 in respect of that road has been paid by the highway authority (or, in the case of a trunk road, by the authority which, when the compensation was paid, was the authority for the purposes of section 4 of the M7. Trunk Roads Act 1936), the order may provide for the payment by the housing action trust to that authority, in respect of the compensation so paid, of such sums as the Secretary of State, with the consent of the Treasury, may determine.

(7) Where the Secretary of State makes an order under this paragraph on the application of a housing action trust, he shall send a copy of it to [the universal service provider (within the meaning of [F9. Part 3 of the Postal Services Act 2011]) who provides a universal postal service (within the meaning of [F10that Part]) for the area in which the land is situated].

Amendments (Textual)

F9. Words in Sch. 10 para. 9. (7) substituted (1.10.2011) by Postal Services Act 2011 (c. 5), s. 93. (2)(3), Sch. 12 para. 130. (a); S.I. 2011/2329, art. 3

F10. Words in Sch. 10 para. 9. (7) substituted (1.10.2011) by Postal Services Act 2011 (c. 5), s. 93. (2)(3), Sch. 12 para. 130. (b); S.I. 2011/2329, art. 3

Modifications etc. (not altering text)

C1. Words in Sch. 10 para. 9. (7) substituted (26.3.2001) by S.I. 2001/1149, art. 3. (1), Sch. 1 para. 75. (3)

Marginal Citations

M61935 c. 47.

M71936 c. 5 (1 Edw. 8 & Geo. 6.)

10. (1) In this paragraph any reference to making a final decision, in relation to an order, is a reference to deciding whether to make the order or what modification, if any, ought to be made.

(2) Unless the Secretary of State decides apart from the objection not to make the order, or decides to make a modification which is agreed to by the objector as meeting the objection, the Secretary of State shall, before making a final decision, consider the grounds of the objection as set out in the statement comprised in or submitted with the objection, and may, if he thinks fit, require the objector to submit within a specified period a further statement in writing as to any of the matters to which the objection relates.

(3) In so far as the Secretary of State, after considering the grounds of the objection as set out in the original statement and in any such further statement, is satisfied that the objection relates to a matter which can be dealt with in the assessment of compensation, the Secretary of State may treat the objection as irrelevant for the purpose of making a final decision.

(4) If, after considering the grounds of the objection as set out in the original statement and in any such further statement, the Secretary of State is satisfied that, for the purpose of making a final decision, he is sufficiently informed as to the matters to which the objection relates, or if, where a further statement has been required, it is not submitted within the specified period, the Secretary of State may make a final decision without further investigation as to those matters.

(5) Subject to sub-paragraphs (3) and (4) above, the Secretary of State, before making a final decision, shall afford to the objector an opportunity of appearing before, and being heard by, a person appointed for the purpose by the Secretary of State; and if the objector avails himself of that opportunity, the Secretary of State shall afford an opportunity of appearing and being heard on the same occasion to the housing action trust on whose representation the order is proposed to be made, and to any other persons to whom it appears to the Secretary of State to be expedient to afford such an opportunity.

(6) Notwithstanding anything in the preceding provisions of this paragraph, if it appears to the Secretary of State that the matters to which the objection relates are such as to require

investigation by public local inquiry before he makes a final decision, he shall cause such an inquiry to be held; and where he determines to cause such an inquiry to be held, any of the requirements of those provisions to which effect has not been given at the time of that determination shall be dispensed with.

Telegraphic lines

11. (1)Where an order under paragraph 9 above extinguishing a public right of way is made on the application of a housing action trust and at the time of the publication of the notice required by sub-paragraph (2) of that paragraph any [F11electronic communications apparatus] was kept installed for the purposes of [F12an electronic communications code network] under, in, on, over, along or across the land over which the right of way subsisted—
(a) the power of the operator of [F13the network] to remove the apparatus shall, notwithstanding the making of the order, be exercisable at any time not later than the end of the period of three months from the date on which the right of way is extinguished and shall be exercisable in respect of the whole or any part of the apparatus after the end of that period if before the end of that period the operator of [F13the network] has given notice to the trust of his intention to remove the apparatus or that part of it, as the case may be;
(b) the operator of [F13the network] may by notice given in that behalf to the trust not later than the end of the said period of three months abandon the [F14electronic communications apparatus] or any part of it;
(c) subject to paragraph (b) above, the operator of [F14the network] shall be deemed at the end of that period to have abandoned any part of the apparatus which he has then neither removed nor given notice of his intention to remove;
(d) the operator of [F15the network] shall be entitled to recover from the trust the expense of providing, in substitution for the apparatus and any other [F15electronic communications apparatus] connected with it which is rendered useless in consequence of the removal or abandonment of the first-mentioned apparatus, any telecommunication apparatus in such other place as the operator may require; and
(e) where under the preceding provisions of this sub-paragraph the operator of [F15the network] has abandoned the whole or any part of any [F15electronic communications apparatus] , that apparatus or that part of it shall vest in the trust and shall be deemed, with its abandonment, to cease to be kept installed for the purposes of [F16an electronic communications code network]
(2) As soon as practicable after the making of an order under paragraph 9 above extinguishing a public right of way in circumstances in which sub-paragraph (1) above applies in relation to the operator of [F16an electronic communications code network] , the Secretary of State shall give notice to the operator of the making of the order.
Amendments (Textual)
F11. Words in Sch. 10 Pt. 2 para. 11 substituted (25.7.2003 for specified purposes, 29.12.2003 for further specified purposes) by Communications Act 2003 (c. 21), ss. 406, 411, Sch. 17 para. 94. (2) (with transitional provisions in Sch. 18); S.I. 2003/1900, art. 1. (2), 2. (1), 3. (1), Sch. 1 (with art. 3. (2) (as amended (8.12.2003) by S.I. 2003/3142, art. 1. (3))); S.I. 2003/3142, art. 3. (2) (with art. 11)
F12. Words in Sch. 10 Pt. 2 para. 11 substituted (25.7.2003 for specified purposes, 29.12.2003 for further specified purposes) by Communications Act 2003 (c. 21), ss. 406, 411, Sch. 17 para. 94. (2) (with transitional provisions in Sch. 18); S.I. 2003/1900, art. 1. (2), 2. (1), 3. (1), Sch. 1 (with art. 3. (2) (as amended (8.12.2003) by S.I. 2003/3142, art. 1. (3))); S.I. 2003/3142, art. 3. (2) (with art. 11)
F13. Words in Sch. 10 Pt. 2 para. 11 substituted (25.7.2003 for specified purposes, 29.12.2003 for further specified purposes) by Communications Act 2003 (c. 21), ss. 406, 411, Sch. 17 para. 94. (2) (with transitional provisions in Sch. 18); S.I. 2003/1900, art. 1. (2), 2. (1), 3. (1), Sch. 1 (with art. 3. (2) (as amended (8.12.2003) by S.I. 2003/3142, art. 1. (3))); S.I. 2003/3142, art. 3. (2) (with

art. 11)

F14. Words in Sch. 10 Pt. 2 para. 11 substituted (25.7.2003 for specified purposes, 29.12.2003 for further specified purposes) by Communications Act 2003 (c. 21), ss. 406, 411, Sch. 17 para. 94. (2) (with transitional provisions in Sch. 18); S.I. 2003/1900, art. 1. (2), 2. (1), 3. (1), Sch. 1 (with art. 3. (2) (as amended (8.12.2003) by S.I. 2003/3142, art. 1. (3))); S.I. 2003/3142, art. 3. (2) (with art. 11)

F15. Words in Sch. 10 Pt. 2 para. 11 substituted (25.7.2003 for specified purposes, 29.12.2003 for further specified purposes) by Communications Act 2003 (c. 21), ss. 406, 411, Sch. 17 para. 94. (2) (with transitional provisions in Sch. 18); S.I. 2003/1900, art. 1. (2), 2. (1), 3. (1), Sch. 1 (with art. 3. (2) (as amended (8.12.2003) by S.I. 2003/3142, art. 1. (3))); S.I. 2003/3142, art. 3. (2) (with art. 11)

F16. Words in Sch. 10 Pt. 2 para. 11 substituted (25.7.2003 for specified purposes, 29.12.2003 for further specified purposes) by Communications Act 2003 (c. 21), ss. 406, 411, Sch. 17 para. 94. (2) (with transitional provisions in Sch. 18); S.I. 2003/1900, art. 1. (2), 2. (1), 3. (1), Sch. 1 (with art. 3. (2) (as amended (8.12.2003) by S.I. 2003/3142, art. 1. (3))); S.I. 2003/3142, art. 3. (2) (with art. 11)

Statutory undertakers

12. (1)Where any land has been acquired by a housing action trust under section 77 of this Act and—
(a) there subsists over that land a right vested in or belonging to statutory undertakers for the purpose of the carrying on of their undertaking, being a right of way or a right of laying down, erecting, continuing or maintaining apparatus on, under or over that land, or
(b) there is on, under or over the land apparatus vested in or belonging to statutory undertakers for the purpose of the carrying on of their undertaking,
the trust, if satisfied that the extinguishment of the right or, as the case may be, the removal of the apparatus, is necessary for the purpose of carrying out any development, may serve on the statutory undertakers a notice stating that, at the end of the period of 28 days from the date of service of the notice or such longer period as may be specified therein, the right will be extinguished or requiring that, before the end of that period, the apparatus shall be removed.
(2) The statutory undertakers on whom a notice is served under sub-paragraph (1) above may, before the end of the period of 28 days from the service of the notice, serve a counter-notice on the trust stating that they object to all or any provisions of the notice and specifying the grounds of their objection.
(3) If no counter-notice is served under sub-paragraph (2) above—
(a) any right to which the notice relates shall be extinguished at the end of the period specified in that behalf in the notice; and
(b) if, at the end of the period so specified in relation to any apparatus, any requirement of the notice as to the removal of the apparatus has not been complied with, the trust may remove the apparatus and dispose of it in any way it may think fit.
(4) If a counter-notice is served under sub-paragraph (2) above on a trust, the trust may either withdraw the notice (without prejudice to the service of a further notice) or may apply to the Secretary of State and the appropriate Minister for an order under this paragraph embodying the provisions of the notice with or without modification.
(5) Where by virtue of this paragraph any right vested in or belonging to statutory undertakers is extinguished, or any requirement is imposed on statutory undertakers, those undertakers shall be entitled to compensation from the trust.
(6) [F17. Sections 280 and 282 of the Town and Country Planning Act 1990] (measure of compensation to statutory undertakers) shall apply to compensation under sub-paragraph (5) above as they apply to compensation under [F17section 279. (2)] of that Act.
(7) Except in a case in which paragraph 11 above has effect—

(a) the reference in paragraph (a) of sub-paragraph (1) above to a right vested in or belonging to statutory undertakers for the purpose of the carrying on of their undertaking shall include a reference to a right conferred by or in accordance with [F18the electronic communications code] on the operator of [F19an electronic communications code network] ; and

(b) the reference in paragraph (b) of that sub-paragraph to apparatus vested in or belonging to statutory undertakers for the purpose of the carrying on of their undertaking shall include a reference to [F20electronic communications apparatus] kept installed for the purposes of any [F21such network] .

(8) Where paragraph (a) or paragraph (b) of sub-paragraph (1) above has effect as mentioned in sub-paragraph (7) above, in the rest of this paragraph and in paragraph 13 below,—

(a) any reference to statutory undertakers shall have effect as a reference to the operator of any [F22such network] as is referred to in sub-paragraph (7) above; and

(b) any reference to the appropriate Minister shall have effect as a reference to the Secretary of State for Trade and Industry.

Amendments (Textual)

F17. Words substituted by Planning (Consequential Provisions) Act 1990 (c. 11, SIF 123: 1, 2), s. 4, Sch. 2 para. 79. (6)(a)

F18. Words in Sch. 10 Pt. 2 para. 12 substituted (25.7.2003 for specified purposes, 29.12.2003 for further specified purposes) by Communications Act 2003 (c. 21), ss. 406, 411, Sch. 17 para. 94. (2) (with transitional provisions in Sch. 18); S.I. 2003/1900, art. 1. (2), 2. (1), 3. (1), Sch. 1 (with art. 3. (2) (as amended (8.12.2003) by S.I. 2003/3142, art. 1. (3))); S.I. 2003/3142, art. 3. (2) (with art. 11)

F19. Words in Sch. 10 Pt. 2 para. 12 substituted (25.7.2003 for specified purposes, 29.12.2003 for further specified purposes) by Communications Act 2003 (c. 21), ss. 406, 411, Sch. 17 para. 94. (2) (with transitional provisions in Sch. 18); S.I. 2003/1900, art. 1. (2), 2. (1), 3. (1), Sch. 1 (with art. 3. (2) (as amended (8.12.2003) by S.I. 2003/3142, art. 1. (3))); S.I. 2003/3142, art. 3. (2) (with art. 11)

F20. Words in Sch. 10 Pt. 2 para. 12 substituted (25.7.2003 for specified purposes, 29.12.2003 for further specified purposes) by Communications Act 2003 (c. 21), ss. 406, 411, Sch. 17 para. 94. (2) (with transitional provisions in Sch. 18); S.I. 2003/1900, art. 1. (2), 2. (1), 3. (1), Sch. 1 (with art. 3. (2) (as amended (8.12.2003) by S.I. 2003/3142, art. 1. (3))); S.I. 2003/3142, art. 3. (2) (with art. 11)

F21. Words in Sch. 10 Pt. 2 para. 12 substituted (25.7.2003 for specified purposes, 29.12.2003 for further specified purposes) by Communications Act 2003 (c. 21), ss. 406, 411, Sch. 17 para. 94. (2) (with transitional provisions in Sch. 18); S.I. 2003/1900, art. 1. (2), 2. (1), 3. (1), Sch. 1 (with art. 3. (2) (as amended (8.12.2003) by S.I. 2003/3142, art. 1. (3))); S.I. 2003/3142, art. 3. (2) (with art. 11)

F22. Words in Sch. 10 Pt. 2 para. 12 substituted (25.7.2003 for specified purposes, 29.12.2003 for further specified purposes) by Communications Act 2003 (c. 21), ss. 406, 411, Sch. 17 para. 94. (2) (with transitional provisions in Sch. 18); S.I. 2003/1900, art. 1. (2), 2. (1), 3. (1), Sch. 1 (with art. 3. (2) (as amended (8.12.2003) by S.I. 2003/3142, art. 1. (3))); S.I. 2003/3142, art. 3. (2) (with art. 11)

Modifications etc. (not altering text)

C2. Sch. 10 para. 12. (8)(b): transfer of functions (13.4.2011) by Transfer of Functions (Media and Telecommunications etc.) Order 2011 (S.I. 2011/741), arts. 1. (2), 3, Sch. 1 (with art. 5)

13. (1)Before making an order under paragraph 12. (4) above the Ministers proposing to make the order—

(a) shall afford to the statutory undertakers on whom notice was served under paragraph 12. (1) above an opportunity of objecting to the application for the order; and

(b) if any objection is made, shall consider the objection and afford to those statutory undertakers and to the trust on whom the counter-notice was served, an opportunity of appearing before and being heard by a person appointed by the Secretary of State and the appropriate Minister for the purpose;

and the Ministers may then, if they think fit, make the order in accordance with the application either with or without modification.

(2) Where an order is made under paragraph 12. (4) above—

(a) any right to which the order relates shall be extinguished at the end of the period specified in that behalf in the order; and

(b) if, at the end of the period so specified in relation to any apparatus, any requirement of the order as to the removal of the apparatus has not been complied with, the trust may remove the apparatus and dispose of it in any way it may think fit.

14. (1) Subject to this paragraph, where any land has been acquired by a housing action trust under section 77 of this Act and—

(a) there is on, under or over the land apparatus vested in or belonging to statutory undertakers, and

(b) the undertakers claim that development to be carried out on the land is such as to require, on technical or other grounds connected with the carrying on of their undertaking, the removal or re-siting of the apparatus affected by the development,

the undertakers may serve on the trust a notice claiming the right to enter on the land and carry out such works for the removal or re-siting of the apparatus or any part of it as may be specified in the notice.

(2) Where, after the land has been acquired as mentioned in sub-paragraph (1) above, development of the land is begun to be carried out, no notice under this paragraph shall be served later than 21 days after the beginning of the development.

(3) Where a notice is served under this paragraph the trust on which it is served may, before the end of the period of 28 days from the date of service, serve on the statutory undertakers a counter-notice stating that it objects to all or any of the provisions of the notice and specifying the grounds of its objection.

(4) If no counter-notice is served under sub-paragraph (3) above, the statutory undertakers shall, after the end of the said period of 28 days, have the rights claimed in their notice.

(5) If a counter-notice is served under sub-paragraph (3) above, the statutory undertakers who served the notice under this paragraph may either withdraw it or may apply to the Secretary of State and the appropriate Minister for an order under this paragraph conferring on the undertakers the rights claimed in the notice or such modified rights as the Secretary of State and the appropriate Minister think it expedient to confer on them.

(6) Where by virtue of this paragraph or an order of Ministers made under it, statutory undertakers have the right to execute works for the removal or re-siting of apparatus, they may arrange with the trust for the works to be carried out by the trust, under the superintendence of the undertakers, instead of by the undertakers themselves.

(7) Where works are carried out for the removal or re-siting of statutory undertakers' apparatus, being works which the undertakers have the right to carry out by virtue of this paragraph or an order of Ministers made under it, the undertakers shall be entitled to compensation from the trust.

(8) [F23. Sections 280 and 282 of the Town and Country Planning Act 1990] (measure of compensation to statutory undertakers) shall apply to compensation under sub-paragraph (7) above as they apply to compensation under [F23section 279. (4)] of that Act.

(9) In sub-paragraph (1)(a) above, the reference to apparatus vested in or belonging to statutory undertakers shall include a reference to [F24electronic communications apparatus] kept installed for the purposes of [F25an electronic communications code network].

(10) Where sub-paragraph (1)(a) above has effect as mentioned in sub-paragraph (9) above, in the rest of this paragraph—

(a) any reference to statutory undertakers shall have effect as a reference to the operator of any [F26such network] as is referred to in sub-paragraph (9) above; and

(b) any reference to the appropriate Minister shall have effect as a reference to the Secretary of State for Trade and Industry.

Amendments (Textual)

F23. Words substituted by Planning (Consequential Provisions) Act 1990 (c. 11, SIF 123: 1, 2), s.

4, Sch. 2 para. 79. (6)(b)
F24. Words in Sch. 10 Pt. 2 para. 14 substituted (25.7.2003 for specified purposes, 29.12.2003 for further specified purposes) by Communications Act 2003 (c. 21), ss. 406, 411, Sch. 17 para. 94. (2) (with transitional provisions in Sch. 18); S.I. 2003/1900, art. 1. (2), 2. (1), 3. (1), Sch. 1 (with art. 3. (2) (as amended (8.12.2003) by S.I. 2003/3142, art. 1. (3))); S.I. 2003/3142, art. 3. (2) (with art. 11)
F25. Words in Sch. 10 Pt. 2 para. 14 substituted (25.7.2003 for specified purposes, 29.12.2003 for further specified purposes) by Communications Act 2003 (c. 21), ss. 406, 411, Sch. 17 para. 94. (2) (with transitional provisions in Sch. 18); S.I. 2003/1900, art. 1. (2), 2. (1), 3. (1), Sch. 1 (with art. 3. (2) (as amended (8.12.2003) by S.I. 2003/3142, art. 1. (3))); S.I. 2003/3142, art. 3. (2) (with art. 11)
F26. Words in Sch. 10 Pt. 2 para. 14 substituted (25.7.2003 for specified purposes, 29.12.2003 for further specified purposes) by Communications Act 2003 (c. 21), ss. 406, 411, Sch. 17 para. 94. (2) (with transitional provisions in Sch. 18); S.I. 2003/1900, art. 1. (2), 2. (1), 3. (1), Sch. 1 (with art. 3. (2) (as amended (8.12.2003) by S.I. 2003/3142, art. 1. (3))); S.I. 2003/3142, art. 3. (2) (with art. 11)
Modifications etc. (not altering text)
C3. Sch. 10 para. 14. (10)(b): transfer of functions (13.4.2011) by Transfer of Functions (Media and Telecommunications etc.) Order 2011 (S.I. 2011/741), arts. 1. (2), 3, Sch. 1 (with art. 5)
15. (1)The powers conferred by this paragraph shall be exercisable where, on a representation made by statutory undertakers, it appears to the Secretary of State and the appropriate Minister to be expedient that the powers and duties of those undertakers should be extended or modified, in order—
(a) to secure the provision for a designated area of services which would not otherwise be provided, or which would not otherwise be satisfactorily provided; or
(b) to facilitate an adjustment of the carrying on of the undertaking necessitated by any of the acts and events mentioned in sub-paragraph (2) below.
(2) The said acts and events are—
(a) the acquisition under Part III of this Act of any land in which an interest was held, or which was used, for the purpose of the carrying on of the undertaking of the statutory undertakers in question; and
(b) the extinguishment of a right or the imposition of any requirements by virtue of paragraph 12 above.
(3) The powers conferred by this paragraph shall also be exercisable where, on a representation made by a housing action trust, it appears to the Secretary of State and the appropriate Minister to be expedient that the powers and duties of statutory undertakers should be extended or modified, in order to secure the provision of new services, or the extension of existing services, for the purposes of a designated area under Part III of this Act.
(4) Where the powers conferred by this paragraph are exercisable, the Secretary of State and the appropriate Minister may, if they think fit, by order provide for such extension or modification of the powers and duties of the statutory undertakers as appears to them to be requisite in order to secure the provision of the services in question, as mentioned in sub-paragraph (1)(a) or sub-paragraph (3) above, or to secure the adjustment in question, as mentioned in sub-paragraph (1)(b) above, as the case may be.
(5) Without prejudice to the generality of sub-paragraph (4) above, an order under this paragraph may make provision—
(a) for empowering the statutory undertakers to acquire (whether compulsorily or by agreement) any land specified in the order, and to erect or construct any buildings or works so specified;
(b) for applying, in relation to the acquisition of any such land or the construction of any such works, enactments relating to the acquisition of land and the construction of works;
(c) where it has been represented that the making of the order is expedient for the purposes mentioned in sub-paragraph (1)(a) or sub-paragraph (3) above, for giving effect to such financial arrangements between the housing action trust and the statutory undertakers as they may agree, or

as, in default of agreement, may be determined to be equitable in such manner and by such tribunal as may be specified in the order; and

(d) for such incidental and supplemental matters as appear to the Secretary of State and the appropriate Minister to be expedient for the purposes of the order.

16. (1) As soon as may be after making such a representation as is mentioned in sub-paragraph (1) or sub-paragraph (3) of paragraph 15 above—

(a) the statutory undertakers, in a case falling within sub-paragraph (1), or

(b) the housing action trust, in a case falling within sub-paragraph (3),

shall publish, in such form and manner as may be directed by the Secretary of State and the appropriate Minister, a notice giving such particulars as may be so directed of the matters to which representation relates, and specifying the time within which, and the manner in which, objections to the making of an order on the representation may be made, and shall also, if it is so directed by the Secretary of State and the appropriate Minister, serve a like notice on such persons, or persons of such classes, as may be so directed.

(2) Orders under paragraph 15 above shall be subject to special parliamentary procedure.

17. (1) Where, on a representation made by statutory undertakers, the appropriate Minister is satisfied that the fulfilment of any obligations incurred by those undertakers in connection with the carrying on of their undertaking has been rendered impracticable by an act or event to which this sub-paragraph applies, the appropriate Minister may, if he thinks fit, by order direct that the statutory undertakers shall be relieved of the fulfilment of that obligation, either absolutely or to such extent as may be specified in the order.

(2) Sub-paragraph (1) above applies to the following acts and events—

(a) the compulsory acquisition under this Part of this Act of any land in which an interest was held, or which was used, for the purpose of the carrying on of the undertaking of the statutory undertakers; and

(b) the extinguishment of a right or the imposition of any requirement by virtue of paragraph 12 above.

(3) As soon as may be after making a representation to the appropriate Minister under sub-paragraph (1) above, the appropriate statutory undertakers shall, as may be directed by the appropriate Minister, either publish (in such form and manner as may be so directed) a notice giving such particulars as may be so directed of the matters to which the representation relates, and specifying the time within which, and the manner in which, objections to the making of an order on the representation may be made, or serve such a notice on such persons, or persons of such classes, as may be so directed, or both publish and serve such notices.

(4) If any objection to the making of an order under this paragraph is duly made and is not withdrawn before the order is made, the order shall be subject to special parliamentary procedure.

(5) Immediately after an order is made under this paragraph by the appropriate Minister, he shall publish a notice stating that the order has been made and naming a place where a copy of it may be seen at all reasonable hours, and shall serve a like notice—

(a) on any person who duly made an objection to the order and has sent to the appropriate Minister a request in writing to serve him with the notice required by this sub-paragraph, specifying an address for service; and

(b) on such other persons (if any) as the appropriate Minister thinks fit.

(6) Subject to the following provisions of this paragraph, an order under this paragraph shall become operative on the date on which the notice required by sub-paragraph (5) above is first published.

(7) Where in accordance with sub-paragraph (4) above the order is subject to special parliamentary procedure, sub-paragraph (6) above shall not apply.

(8) If any person aggrieved by an order under this paragraph wishes to question the validity of the order on the ground that it is not within the powers conferred by this paragraph, or that any requirement of this paragraph has not been complied with in relation to the order, he may, within six weeks from the date on which the notice required by sub-paragraph (5) above is first published, make an application to the High Court under this paragraph.

(9) On any application under sub-paragraph (8) above the High Court—
(a) may by interim order wholly or in part suspend the operation of the order, either generally or in so far as it affects any property of the applicant, until the final determination of the proceedings; and
(b) if satisfied that the order is wholly or to any extent outside the powers conferred by this paragraph, or that the interests of the applicant have been substantially prejudiced by the failure to comply with any requirement of this paragraph, may wholly or in part quash the order, either generally or in so far as it affects any property of the applicant.
(10) Subject to sub-paragraph (8) above, the validity of an order under this paragraph shall not be questioned in any legal proceedings whatsoever, either before or after the order has been made.
18. (1) For the purposes of paragraphs 15 and 17 above, an objection to the making of an order thereunder shall not be treated as duly made unless—
(a) the objection is made within the time and in the manner specified in the notice required by paragraph 16 or (as the case may be) paragraph 17 above; and
(b) a statement in writing of the grounds of the objection is comprised in or submitted with the objection.
(2) Where an objection to the making of such an order is duly made in accordance with sub-paragraph (1) above and is not withdrawn, the following provisions of this paragraph shall have effect in relation thereto; but, in the application of those provisions to an order under paragraph 15 above, any reference to the appropriate Minister shall be construed as a reference to the Secretary of State and the appropriate Minister.
(3) Unless the appropriate Minister decides apart from the objection not to make the order, or decides to make a modification which is agreed to by the objector as meeting the objection, the appropriate Minister, before making a final decision, shall consider the grounds of the objection as set out in the statement, and may, if he thinks fit, require the objector to submit within a specified period a further statement in writing as to any of the matters to which the objection relates.
(4) In so far as the appropriate Minister after considering the grounds of the objection as set out in the original statement and in any such further statement, is satisfied that the objection relates to a matter which can be dealt with in the assessment of compensation, the appropriate Minister may treat the objection as irrelevant for the purpose of making a final decision.
(5) If, after considering the grounds of the objection as set out in the original statement and in any such further statement, the appropriate Minister is satisfied that, for the purpose of making a final decision, he is sufficiently informed as to the matters to which the objection relates, or if, where a further statement has been required it is not submitted within the specified period, the appropriate Minister may make a final decision without further investigation as to those matters.
(6) Subject to sub-paragraphs (4) and (5) above, the appropriate Minister, before making a final decision, shall afford to the objector an opportunity of appearing before, and being heard by, a person appointed for the purpose by the appropriate Minister; and if the objector avails himself of that opportunity, the appropriate Minister shall afford an opportunity of appearing and being heard on the same occasion to the statutory undertakers, local authority or Minister on whose representation the order is proposed to be made, and to any other persons to whom it appears to the appropriate Minister to be expedient to afford such an opportunity.
(7) Notwithstanding anything in the preceding provisions of this paragraph, if it appears to the appropriate Minister that the matters to which the objection relates are such as to require investigation by public local inquiry before he makes a final decision, he shall cause such an inquiry to be held; and where he determines to cause such an inquiry to be held, any of the requirements of those provisions to which effect has not been given at the time of that determination shall be dispensed with.
(8) In this paragraph any reference to making a final decision, in relation to an order, is a reference to deciding whether to make the order or what modification (if any) ought to be made.

Interpretation

19. F27. . . . .
Amendments (Textual)
F27. Sch. 10 Pt. 2 para. 19 repealed (25.7.2003 for specified purposes, 29.12.2003 for further specified purposes) by Communications Act 2003 (c. 21), ss. 406, 411, Sch. 19. (1) (with transitional provisions in Sch. 18); S.I. 2003/1900, art. 1. (2), 2. (1), 3. (1), Sch. 1 (with art. 3. (2) (as amended (8.12.2003) by S.I. 2003/3142, art. 1. (3))); S.I. 2003/3142, art. 3. (2) (with art. 11)

Part III Acquisition of Rights

20. (1)The M8. Compulsory Purchase Act 1965 (in this Part of the Schedule referred to as "the 1965 Act") shall have effect with the modifications necessary to make it apply to the compulsory purchase of rights by virtue of section 77. (5) of this Act as it applies to the compulsory purchase of land so that, in appropriate contexts, references in the 1965 Act to land are read as referring, or as including references, to the rights or to land over which the rights are or are to be exercisable, according to the requirements of the particular context.
(2) Without prejudice to the generality of sub-paragraph (1) above, in relation to the purchase of rights in pursuance of section 77. (5) of this Act—
(a) Part I of the 1965 Act (which relates to compulsory purchases under the M9. Acquisition of Land Act 1981) shall have effect with the modifications specified in paragraphs 21 to 23 below; and
(b) the enactments relating to compensation for the compulsory purchase of land shall apply with the necessary modifications as they apply to such compensation.
Marginal Citations
M81965 c. 56.
M91981 c. 58.
21. (1)For section 7 of the 1965 Act (which relates to compensation) there shall be substituted the following—
"7. (1)In assesssing the compensation to be paid by the acquiring authority under this Act regard shall be had not only to the extent, if any, to which the value of the land over which the right is purchased is depreciated by the purchase but also to the damage, if any, to be sustained by the owner of the land by reason of injurious affection of other land of the owner by the exercise of the right.
(2) The modifications subject to which subsection (1) of section 44 of the Land Compensation Act 1973 is to have effect, as applied by subsection (2) of that section to compensation for injurious affection under this section, are that for the words "land is acquired or taken" there shall be substituted the words "a right over land is purchased" and for the words "acquired or taken from him" there shall be substituted the words "over which the right is exercisable"."
[F2822. Section 8. (1) of the Compulsory Purchase Act 1965 has effect as if references to acquiring land were to acquiring a right in the land, and Schedule 2. A to that Act is to be read as if, for that Schedule, there were substituted—
Introduction
1. (1)This Schedule applies where an acquiring authority serve a notice to treat in respect of a right over the whole or part of a house, building or factory.
(2) But see section 2. A of the Acquisition of Land Act 1981 (under which a compulsory purchase order can exclude from this Schedule land that is 9 metres or more below the surface).
2. In this Schedule "house" includes any park or garden belonging to a house.
Counter-notice requiring purchase of land
3. A person who is able to sell the house, building or factory ("the owner") may serve a counter-notice requiring the authority to purchase the owner's interest in the house, building or factory.
4. A counter-notice under paragraph 3 must be served within the period of 28 days beginning with the day on which the notice to treat was served.

Response to counter-notice
5. On receiving a counter-notice the acquiring authority must decide whether to—
(a) withdraw the notice to treat,
(b) accept the counter-notice, or
(c) refer the counter-notice to the Upper Tribunal.
6. The authority must serve notice of their decision on the owner within the period of 3 months beginning with the day on which the counter-notice is served ("the decision period").
7. If the authority decide to refer the counter-notice to the Upper Tribunal they must do so within the decision period.
8. If the authority do not serve notice of a decision within the decision period they are to be treated as if they had served notice of a decision to withdraw the notice to treat at the end of that period.
9. If the authority serve notice of a decision to accept the counter-notice, the compulsory purchase order and the notice to treat are to have effect as if they included the owner's interest in the house, building or factory.

Determination by Upper Tribunal
10. On a referral under paragraph 7 the Upper Tribunal must determine whether the acquisition of the right would—
(a) in the case of a house, building or factory, cause material detriment to the house, building or factory, or
(b) in the case of a park or garden, seriously affect the amenity or convenience of the house to which the park or garden belongs.
11. In making its determination, the Upper Tribunal must take into account—
(a) the effect of the acquisition of the right,
(b) the proposed use of the right, and
(c) if the right is proposed to be acquired for works or other purposes extending to other land, the effect of the whole of the works and the use of the other land.
12. If the Upper Tribunal determines that the acquisition of the right would have either of the consequences described in paragraph 10 it must determine how much of the house, building or factory the authority ought to be required to take.
13. If the Upper Tribunal determines that the authority ought to be required to take some or all of the house, building or factory the compulsory purchase order and the notice to treat are to have effect as if they included the owner's interest in that land.
14. (1) If the Upper Tribunal determines that the authority ought to be required to take some or all of the house, building or factory, the authority may at any time within the period of 6 weeks beginning with the day on which the Upper Tribunal makes its determination withdraw the notice to treat in relation to that land.
(2) If the acquiring authority withdraws the notice to treat under this paragraph they must pay the person on whom the notice was served compensation for any loss or expense caused by the giving and withdrawal of the notice.
(3) Any dispute as to the compensation is to be determined by the Upper Tribunal."]

Amendments (Textual)
F28. Sch. 10 para. 22 substituted (3.2.2017) by Housing and Planning Act 2016 (c. 22), s. 216. (3), Sch. 17 paras. 6, 7; S.I. 2017/75, reg. 3. (g) (with reg. 5)

23. (1) The following provisions of the 1965 Act (which state the effect of a deed poll executed in various circumstances where there is no conveyance by persons with interests in the land), namely—
section 9. (4) (failure of owners to convey),
paragraph 10. (3) of Schedule 1 (owners under incapacity),
paragraph 2. (3) of Schedule 2 (absent and untraced owners), and
paragraphs 2. (3) and 7. (2) of Schedule 4 (common land),
shall be so modified as to secure that, as against persons with interests in the land which are expressed to be overridden by the deed, the right which is to be purchased compulsorily is vested absolutely in the acquiring authority.

(2) Section 11 of the 1965 Act (powers of entry) shall be so modified as to secure that, as from the date on which the acquiring authority has served notice to treat in respect of any right, it has power, exercisable in the like circumstances and subject to the like conditions, to enter for the purpose of exercising that right (which shall be deemed for this purpose to have been created on the date of service of the notice); and sections 12 (penalty for unauthorised entry) and 13 (entry on [F29enforcement officer's or sheriff's warrant] in the event of obstruction) of the Act shall be modified correspondingly.

(3) Section 20 of the 1965 Act (compensation for short-term tenants) shall apply with the modifications necessary to secure that persons with such interests as are mentioned in that section are compensated in a manner corresponding to that in which they would be compensated on a compulsory acquisition of the interests but taking into account only the extent (if any) of such interference with such interests as is actually caused, or likely to be caused, by the exercise of the right in question.

(4) Section 22 of the 1965 Act (protection of acquiring authority's possession of land where by inadvertence an interest in the land has not been purchased) shall be so modified as to enable the acquiring authority, in circumstances corresponding to those referred to in that section, to continue to be entitled to exercise the right in question, subject to compliance with that section as respects compensation.

Amendments (Textual)

F29. Words in Sch. 10 para. 23. (2) substituted (1.4.2008) by Tribunals, Courts and Enforcement Act 2007 (c. 15), ss. 139, 148, Sch. 22 para. 6; S.I. 2007/2709, art. 5

Schedule 11. Provisions Applicable to Certain Disposals of Houses

Section 79. (13).

Repayment of discount on early disposal

1. (1)This paragraph applies where, on the disposal of a house under section 79 of this Act, a discount is given to the purchaser by the housing action trust in accordance with a consent given by the Secretary of State under subsection (1) of that section and that consent does not exclude the application of this paragraph.

(2) On the disposal, the conveyance, grant or assignment shall contain a covenant binding on the purchaser and his successors in title [F1to the following effect.]

[F2. (3)The covenant shall be to pay to the housing action trust such sum (if any) as the trust may demand in accordance with sub-paragraph (4) on the occasion of the first relevant disposal (other than an exempted disposal) which takes place within the period of five years beginning with the conveyance, grant or assignment.]

[F3. (4)The trust may demand such sum as it considers appropriate, up to and including the maximum amount specified in this paragraph.]

[F4. (5)The maximum amount which may be demanded by the trust is a percentage of the price or premium paid for the first relevant disposal which is equal to the percentage discount given to the purchaser in respect of the disposal of the house under section 79.]

[F5. (6)But for each complete year which has elapsed after the conveyance, grant or assignment and before the first relevant disposal the maximum amount which may be demanded by the trust is reduced by one-fifth.]

[F6. (7)Sub-paragraphs (4) to (6) are subject to paragraph 1. A.]

Amendments (Textual)

F1. Words in Sch. 11 para. 1. (2) substituted (18.1.2005) by Housing Act, 2004 (c. 34), ss. 203.

(2), 270 (with s. 203. (4))
F2. Sch. 11 para. 1. (3) inserted (18.1.2005) by Housing Act 2004 (c. 34), ss. 203. (3), 270 (with s. 203. (4))
F3. Sch. 11 para. 1. (4) inserted (18.1.2005) by Housing Act 2004 (c. 34), ss. 203. (3), 270 (with s. 203. (4))
F4. Sch. 11 para. 1. (5) inserted (18.1.2005) by Housing Act 2004 (c. 34), ss. 203. (3), 270 (with s. 203. (4))
F5. Sch. 11 para. 1. (6) inserted (18.1.2005) by Housing Act 2004 (c. 34), ss. 203. (3), 270 (with s. 203. (4))
F6. Sch. 11 para. 1. (7) inserted (18.1.2005) by Housing Act 2004 (c. 34), ss. 203. (3), 270 (with s. 203. (4))
Modifications etc. (not altering text)
C1. Sch. 11 para. 1. (2) modified (18.1.2005) by Housing Act 2004 (c. 34), ss. 203. (6), 270 (with s. 203. (4)(5)(7))

[F7. Increase in value of house attributable to home improvements

Amendments (Textual)
F7. Sch. 11 para. 1. A and cross-heading inserted (18.1.2005) by Housing Act (c. 34), {ss. 203}, 270 (with s. 203. (4))
1. A(1)In calculating the maximum amount which may be demanded by the housing action trust under paragraph 1, such amount (if any) of the price or premium paid for the first relevant disposal which is attributable to improvements made to the house—
(a) by the person by whom the disposal is, or is to be, made, and
(b) after the conveyance, grant or assignment and before the disposal,
shall be disregarded.
(2) The amount to be disregarded under this paragraph shall be such amount as may be agreed between the parties or determined by the district valuer.
(3) The district valuer shall not be required by virtue of this paragraph to make a determination for the purposes of this paragraph unless—
(a) it is reasonably practicable for him to do so; and
(b) his reasonable costs in making the determination are paid by the person by whom the disposal is, or is to be, made.
(4) If the district valuer does not make a determination for the purposes of this paragraph (and in default of an agreement), no amount is required to be disregarded under this paragraph.]

Obligation to repay a charge on the house

2. (1)The liability that may arise under the covenant required by paragraph 1 above is a charge on the house, taking effect as if it had been created by deed expressed to be by way of legal mortgage.
(2) The charge has priority immediately after any legal charge securing an amount—
(a) left outstanding by the purchaser; or
(b) advanced to him by an approved lending institution for the purpose of enabling him to acquire the interest disposed of on the first disposal; or
(c) further advanced to him by that institution;
but the housing action trust may at any time by written notice served on an approved lending institution postpone the charge taking effect by virtue of this paragraph to a legal charge securing an amount advanced or further advanced to the purchaser by that institution.
(3) F8. . . . .
(4) The covenant required by paragraph 1 above does not, by virtue of its binding successors in

title of the purchaser, bind a person exercising rights under a charge having priority over the charge taking effect by virtue of this paragraph, or a person deriving title under him; and a provision of the conveyance, grant or assignment, or of a collateral agreement, is void in so far as it purports to authorise a forfeiture, or to impose a penalty or disability, in the event of any such person failing to comply with the covenant.

(5) The approved lending institutions for the purposes of this paragraph are—

(a) a building society;

(b) a bank;

(c) an insurance company;

(d) a friendly society; and

[F9. (e)an authorised mortgage lender (within the meaning of the Housing Act 1985 (see section 622 of that Act)).]

Amendments (Textual)

F8. Sch. 11 para. 2. (3) repealed (13.10.2003) by Land Registration Act 2002 (c. 9), ss. 135, 136. (2), Sch. 13 (with s. 129); S.I. 2003/1725, art. 2. (1)

F9. Sch. 11 para. 2. (5)(e) substituted (22.9.2008) by Housing and Regeneration Act 2008 (c. 17), ss. 307. (6), 325

[F10. Right of first refusal for housing action trust

Amendments (Textual)

F10. Sch. 11 paras. 2. A, 2. B and cross-headings inserted (18.1.2005) by Housing Act 2004 (c. 34), ss. 204, 270 (with s. 204. (3))

2. A(1)This paragraph applies where, on the disposal of a house under section 79 of this Act, a discount is given to the purchaser by the housing action trust in accordance with a consent given by the Secretary of State under subsection (1) of that section and that consent does not exclude the application of this paragraph.

(2) On the disposal, the conveyance, grant or assignment shall contain the following covenant, which shall be binding on the purchaser and his successors in title.

(3) The covenant shall be to the effect that, until the end of the period of ten years beginning with the conveyance, grant or assignment, there will be no relevant disposal which is not an exempted disposal, unless the prescribed conditions have been satisfied in relation to that or a previous such disposal.

(4) In sub-paragraph (3) "the prescribed conditions" means such conditions as are prescribed by regulations under this section at the time when the conveyance, grant or assignment is made.

(5) The Secretary of State may by regulations prescribe such conditions as he considers appropriate for and in connection with conferring on—

(a) a housing action trust which has made a disposal as mentioned in sub-paragraph (1), or

(b) such other person as is determined in accordance with the regulations,

a right of first refusal to have a disposal within sub-paragraph (6) made to him for such consideration as is mentioned in paragraph 2. B.

(6) The disposals within this sub-paragraph are—

(a) a reconveyance or conveyance of the house; and

(b) a surrender or assignment of the lease.

(7) Regulations under this paragraph may, in particular, make provision—

(a) for the purchaser to offer to make such a disposal to such person or persons as may be prescribed;

(b) for a prescribed recipient of such an offer to be able either to accept the offer or to nominate some other person as the person by whom the offer may be accepted;

(c) for the person who may be so nominated to be either a person of a prescribed description or a person whom the prescribed recipient considers, having regard to any prescribed matters, to be a more appropriate person to accept the offer;

(d) for a prescribed recipient making such a nomination to give a notification of the nomination to the person nominated, the purchaser and any other prescribed person;
(e) for authorising a nominated person to accept the offer and for determining which acceptance is to be effective where the offer is accepted by more than one person;
(f) for the period within which the offer may be accepted or within which any other prescribed step is to be, or may be, taken;
(g) for the circumstances in which the right of first refusal lapses (whether following the service of a notice to complete or otherwise) with the result that the purchaser is able to make a disposal on the open market;
(h) for the manner in which any offer, acceptance or notification is to be communicated.
(8) In sub-paragraph (7) any reference to the purchaser is a reference to the purchaser or his successor in title.
Nothing in that sub-paragraph affects the generality of sub-paragraph (5).
(9) Regulations under this paragraph—
(a) may make different provision with respect to different cases or descriptions of case; and
(b) shall be made by statutory instrument which shall be subject to annulment in pursuance of a resolution of either House of Parliament.
(10) The limitation imposed by a covenant within sub-paragraph (3) is a local land charge.
(11) The Chief Land Registrar must enter in the register of title a restriction reflecting the limitation imposed by any such covenant.

Consideration payable for disposal under paragraph 2. A

2. B(1)The consideration for a disposal made in respect of a right of first refusal as mentioned in paragraph 2. A(5) shall be such amount as may be agreed between the parties, or determined by the district valuer, as being the amount which is to be taken to be the value of the house at the time when the offer is made (as determined in accordance with regulations under that paragraph).
(2) That value shall be taken to be the price which, at that time, the interest to be reconveyed, conveyed, surrendered or assigned would realise if sold on the open market by a willing vendor, on the assumption that any liability under the covenant required by paragraph 1 (repayment of discount on early disposal) would be discharged by the vendor.
(3) If the offer is accepted in accordance with regulations under paragraph 2. A, no payment shall be required in pursuance of any such covenant as is mentioned in sub-paragraph (2), but the consideration shall be reduced, subject to sub-paragraph (4), by such amount (if any) as, on a disposal made at the time the offer was made, being a relevant disposal which is not an exempted disposal, would fall to be paid under that covenant.
(4) Where there is a charge on the house having priority over the charge to secure payment of the sum due under the covenant mentioned in sub-paragraph (2), the consideration shall not be reduced under sub-paragraph (3) below the amount necessary to discharge the outstanding sum secured by the first-mentioned charge at the date of the offer (as determined in accordance with regulations under paragraph 2. A).]

Relevant disposals

3. (1)A disposal, whether of the whole or part of the house, is a relevant disposal for the purpose of this Schedule if it is—
(a) a conveyance of the freehold or an assignment of the lease; or
(b) the grant of a lease or sub-lease (other than a mortgage term) for a term of more than 21 years otherwise than at a rack rent.
(2) For the purposes of sub-paragraph (1)(b) above it shall be assumed—
(a) that any option to renew or extend a lease or sub-lease, whether or not forming part of a series of options, is exercised; and

(b) that any option to terminate a lease or sub-lease is not exercised.

Exempted disposals

4. (1)A disposal is an exempted disposal for the purposes of this Schedule if—
(a) it is a disposal of the whole of the house and a conveyance of the freehold or an assignment of the lease and the person or each of the persons to whom it is made is a qualifying person (as defined in sub-paragraph (2) below);
(b) it is a vesting of the whole of the house in a person taking under a will or on an intestacy;
[F11. (c)it is a disposal of the whole of the house in pursuance of an such order as is mentioned in sub-paragraph (4) below;]
(d) it is a compulsory disposal; or
(e) the property disposed of is property included with the house as being such a yard, garden, outhouse or appurtenance as is referred to in section 92. (1)(b) of this Act.
(2) For the purposes of sub-paragraph (1)(a) above, a person is a qualifying person in relation to a disposal if—
(a) he is the person or one of the persons by whom the disposal is made;
(b) he is the spouse or a former spouse [F12, or the civil partner or a former civil partner,] of that person or one of those persons; or
(c) he is a member of the family of that person or one of those persons and has resided with him throughout the period of twelve months ending with the disposal.
(3) Section 186 of the M1. Housing Act 1985 applies to determine whether a person is a member of another person's family for the purposes of sub-paragraph (2)(c) above.
[F13. (4)The orders referred to in sub-paragraph (1)(c) above are orders under—
(a) section 24 or 24. A of the Matrimonial Causes Act 1973 (property adjustment orders or orders for the sale of property in connection with matrimonial proceedings),
(b) section 2 of the Inheritance (Provision for Family and Dependants) Act 1975 (orders as to financial provision to be made from estate),
(c) section 17 of the Matrimonial and Family Proceedings Act 1984 (property adjustment orders or orders for the sale of property after overseas divorce, &c.),F14. . .
(d) paragraph 1 of Schedule 1 to the Children Act 1989 (orders for financial relief against parents) [F15, or]
[F15. (e)Part 2 or 3 of Schedule 5, or paragraph 9 of Schedule 7, to the Civil Partnership Act 2004 (property adjustment orders, or orders for the sale of property, in connection with civil partnership proceedings or after overseas dissolution of civil partnership, etc.).]]
Amendments (Textual)
F11. Sch. 11 para. 4. (1)(c) substituted (1.10.1996) by 1996 c. 52, s. 222, Sch. 18 Pt. III para. 19. (2); S.I. 1996/2402, art. 3 (subject to transitional provisions in Sch.)
F12. Words in Sch. 11 para. 4. (2)(b) inserted (5.12.2005) by Civil Partnership Act 2004 (c. 33), ss. 81, 263, {Sch. 8 para. 45. (1)(2)}; S.I. 2005/3175, art. 2. (1), Sch.1
F13. Sch 11 para. 4. (4) added (1.10.1996) by 1996 c. 52, s. 222, Sch. 18 Pt. III para. 19. (3); S.I. 1996/2402, art. 3 (subject to transitional provisions in Sch.)
F14. Words in Sch. 11 para. 4. (4) repealed (5.12.2005) by Civil Partnership Act 2004 (c. 33), ss. 81, 261. (4), Sch. 30; S.I. 2005/3175, art. 2. (1), Sch. 1
F15. Sch. 11 para. 4. (4)(e) and word inserted (5.12.2005) by Civil Partnership Act 2004 (c. 33), ss. 81, 263, Sch. 8 para. 45. (1)(3); S.I. 2005/3175, art. 2. (1), Sch.1
Marginal Citations
M11985 c. 68.

Compulsory disposal

5. In this Schedule a "compulsory disposal" means a disposal of property which is acquired

compulsorily, or is acquired by a person who has made or would have made, or for whom another person has made or would have made, a compulsory purchase order authorising its compulsory purchase for the purposes for which it is acquired.

Exempted disposals ending obligation under covenants

6. Where there is a relevant disposal which is an exempted disposal by virtue of paragraph 4. (1)(d) or paragraph 4. (1)(e) above—
(a) the covenant required by paragraph 1 above is not binding on the person to whom the disposal is made or any successor in title of his; and
(b) that covenant and the charge taking effect by virtue of paragraph 2 above cease to apply in relation to the property disposed of.
[F16and
(c) the covenant required by paragraph 2. A above is not binding on the person to whom the disposal is made or any successor in title of his; and
(d) that covenant ceases to apply in relation to the property disposed of.]
Amendments (Textual)
F16. Sch. 11 para. 6. (c)(d) and word inserted (18.1.2005) by Housing Act 2004 (c. 34), ss. 204. (2), 270 (with s. 204. (3))

Treatment of options

7. For the purpose of this Schedule, the grant of an option enabling a person to call for a relevant disposal which is not an exempted disposal shall be treated as such a disposal made to him.

[F17. Treatment of deferred resale agreements

Amendments (Textual)
F17. Sch. 11 para. 8 and cross-heading inserted (18.11.2004 for certain purposes and otherwise 18.1.2005) by Housing 2004 (c. 34), {ss. 205. (1)}, 270 (with 205. (2))
8. (1)If a purchaser or his successor in title enters into an agreement within sub-paragraph (3), any liability arising under the covenant required by paragraph 1 shall be determined as if a relevant disposal which is not an exempted disposal had occurred at the appropriate time.
(2) In sub-paragraph (1) "the appropriate time" means—
(a) the time when the agreement is entered into, or
(b) if it was made before the beginning of the discount repayment period, immediately after the beginning of that period.
(3) An agreement is within this sub-paragraph if it is an agreement between the purchaser or his successor in title and any other person—
(a) which is made (expressly or impliedly) in contemplation of, or in connection with, a disposal to be made, or made, under section 79,
(b) which is made before the end of the discount repayment period, and
(c) under which a relevant disposal (other than an exempted disposal) is or may be required to be made to any person after the end of that period.
(4) Such an agreement is within sub-paragraph (3)—
(a) whether or not the date on which the relevant disposal is to take place is specified in the agreement, and
(b) whether or not any requirement to make that disposal is or may be made subject to the fulfilment of any condition.
(5) The Secretary of State may by order provide—
(a) for sub-paragraph (1) to apply to agreements of any description specified in the order in

addition to those within sub-paragraph (3);
(b) for sub-paragraph (1) not to apply to agreements of any description so specified to which it would otherwise apply.
(6) An order under sub-paragraph (5)—
(a) may make different provision with respect to different cases or descriptions of case; and
(b) shall be made by statutory instrument which shall be subject to annulment in pursuance of a resolution of either House of Parliament.
(7) In this paragraph—
"agreement" includes arrangement;
"the discount repayment period" means the period of 3 years that applies for the purposes of paragraph 1. (2) or the period of five years that applies for the purposes of paragraph 1. (3)(depending on whether an offer such as is mentioned in section 203. (4) of the Housing Act 2004 was made before or on or after the coming into force of that section).]

Schedule 12. Amendments of Landlord and Tenant Act 1987

Section 119.
1. In Part I of the M1. Landlord and Tenant Act 1987 (tenants' rights of first refusal), in section 2 (landlords for the purposes of Part I), in subsection (1) after "(2)" there shall be inserted " and section 4. (1. A) ".
Marginal Citations
M11987 c. 31.
2. (1)In section 3 of that Act (qualifying tenants), in subsection (1) (paragraphs (a) to (c) of which exclude certain tenants) the word "or" immediately preceding paragraph (c) shall be omitted and at the end of that paragraph there shall be added "or
    (d) an assured tenancy or assured agricultural occupancy within the meaning of Part I of the Housing Act 1988".
(2) In subsection (2) of that section (which excludes persons having interests going beyond a particular flat), for paragraphs (a) and (b) there shall be substituted the words " by virtue of one or more tenancies none of which falls within paragraphs (a) to (d) of subsection (1), he is the tenant not only of the flat in question but also of at least two other flats contained in those premises "; and in subsection (3) of that section for "(2)(b)" there shall be substituted " (2) ".
3. (1)In section 4 of that Act (relevant disposals) after subsection (1) there shall be inserted the following subsection—
"(1. A)Where an estate or interest of the landlord has been mortgaged, the reference in subsection (1) above to the disposal of an estate or interest by the landlord includes a reference to its disposal by the mortgagee in exercise of a power of sale or leasing, whether or not the disposal is made in the name of the landlord; and, in relation to such a proposed disposal by the mortgagee, any reference in the following provisions of this Part to the landlord shall be construed as a reference to the mortgagee."
(2) In subsection (2) of that section, in paragraph (a), at the end of sub-paragraph (i) there shall be inserted "or", sub-paragraph (ii) shall be omitted and at the end of that paragraph there shall be inserted—
   "(aa)a disposal consisting of the creation of an estate or interest by way of security for a loan".
4. (1)In Part III of that Act (compulsory acquisition by tenants of their landlord's interest), in section 26 (qualifying tenants), in subsection (2) (which excludes persons having interests going beyond a particular flat) for the words following "if" there shall be substituted " by virtue of one or more long leases none of which constitutes a tenancy to which Part II of the Landlord and Tenant Act 1954 applies, he is the tenant not only of the flat in question but also of at least two

other flats contained in those premises ".
(2) At the end of the said section 26 there shall be added the following subsection—
"(4)For the purposes of subsection (2) any tenant of a flat contained in the premises in question who is a body corporate shall be treated as the tenant of any other flat so contained and let to an associated company, as defined in section 20. (1)."
5. In Part IV of that Act (variation of leases), for subsections (6) and (7) of section 35 (which make provision about long leases) there shall be substituted the following subsection—
"(6)For the purposes of this Part a long lease shall not be regarded as a long lease of a flat if—
　(a) the demised premises consist of or include three or more flats contained in the same building; or
　(b) the lease constitutes a tenancy to which Part II of the Landlord and Tenant Act 1954 applies."
6. In section 40 (application for variation of insurance provisions of lease of dwelling other than a flat) for subsection (4) (which makes provision about long leases) there shall be substituted the following subsections—
"(4)For the purpose of this section, a long lease shall not be regarded as a long lease of a dwelling if—
　(a) the demised premises consist of three or more dwellings; or
　(b) the lease constitutes a tenancy to which Part II of the Landlord and Tenant Act 1954 applies.
(4. A)Without prejudice to subsection (4), an application under subsection (1) may not be made by a person who is a tenant under a long lease of a dwelling if, by virtue of that lease and one or more other long leases of dwellings, he is also a tenant from the same landlord of at least two other dwellings.
(4. B)For the purposes of subsection (4. A), any tenant of a dwelling who is a body corporate shall be treated as a tenant of any other dwelling held from the same landlord which is let under a long lease to an associated company, as defined in section 20. (1)."
7. In Part VII of that Act (general), in section 58 (exempt landlords), in subsection (1) after paragraph (c) there shall be inserted the following paragraph—
　"(ca)a housing action trust established under Part III of the Housing Act 1988."

Schedule 13. Appointment etc. of Rent Officers

Section 120.

Part I Amendments of Section 63 of M1. Rent Act 1977

Marginal Citations
M11977 c. 42.
1. In subsection (1), paragraph (b) and the word "and" immediately preceding it shall be omitted.
2. In subsection (2)—
(a) in paragraph (a) the words "and deputy rent officers" shall be omitted;
(b) in paragraph (b) the words "or deputy rent officer" shall be omitted;
(c) in paragraph (d) the words "and deputy rent officers" and the word "and" at the end of the paragraph shall be omitted; and
(d) paragraph (e) shall be omitted.
3. After subsection (2) there shall be inserted the following subsection—
"(2. A)A scheme under this section may make all or any of the following provisions—
　(a) provision requiring the consent of the Secretary of State to the appointment of rent officers;
　(b) provision with respect to the appointment of rent officers for fixed periods;
　(c) provision for the proper officer of the local authority, in such circumstances and subject to

such conditions (as to consent or otherwise) as may be specified in the scheme,—
  (i) to designate a person appointed or to be appointed a rent officer as chief rent officer and to designate one or more such persons as senior rent officers;
(ii) to delegate to a person so designated as chief rent officer such functions as may be specified in the scheme; and
(iii) to revoke a designation under sub-paragraph (i) above and to revoke or vary a delegation under sub-paragraph (ii) above;
  (d) provision with respect to the delegation of functions by a chief rent officer to other rent officers (whether designated as senior rent officers or not);
  (e) provision as to the circumstances in which and the terms on which a rent officer appointed by the scheme may undertake functions outside the area to which the scheme relates in accordance with paragraph (f) below;
  (f) provision under which a rent officer appointed for an area other than that to which the scheme relates may undertake functions in the area to which the scheme relates and for such a rent officer to be treated for such purposes as may be specified in the scheme (which may include the purposes of paragraphs (c) and (d) above and paragraphs (c) and (d) of subsection (2) above) as if he were a rent officer appointed under the scheme; and
  (g) provision conferring functions on the proper officer of a local authority with respect to the matters referred to in paragraphs (d) to (f) above."
4. In subsection (3) the words "and deputy rent officers" shall be omitted.
5. In subsection (7)—
(a) in paragraph (b) the words "and deputy rent officers" shall be omitted, after the words "section 7" there shall be inserted " "or section 24 " and for the words following "1972" there shall be substituted " "or "; and
(b) at the end of paragraph (b) there shall be inserted the following paragraph—
  "(c)incurred in respect of increases of pensions payable to or in respect of rent officers (so appointed) by virtue of the Pensions (Increase) Act 1971".

Part II Sections to be Inserted in M2. Rent Act 1977 after Section 64

Marginal Citations
M21977 c. 42.

" Amalgamation schemes
64. A(1)If the Secretary of State is of the opinion—
(a) that there is at any time insufficient work in two or more registration areas to justify the existence of a separate service of rent officers for each area, or
(b) that it would at any time be beneficial for the efficient administration of the service provided by rent officers in two or more registration areas,
he may, after consultation with the local authorities concerned, make a scheme under section 63 above designating as an amalgamated registration area the areas of those authorities and making provision accordingly for that amalgamated area.
(2) Any reference in the following provisions of this Chapter to a registration area includes a reference to an amalgamated registration area and, in relation to such an area, "the constituent authorities" means the local authorities whose areas make up the amalgamated area.
(3) A scheme under section 63 above made for an amalgamated registration area—
(a) shall confer on the proper officer of one of the constituent authorities all or any of the functions which, in accordance with section 63 above, fall to be exercisable by the proper officer of the local authority for the registration area;

(b) may provide that any rent officer previously appointed for the area of any one of the constituent authorities shall be treated for such purposes as may be specified in the scheme as a rent officer appointed for the amalgamated registration area; and
(c) shall make such provision as appears to the Secretary of State to be appropriate for the payment by one or more of the constituent authorities of the remunerations, allowances and other expenditure which under section 63 above is to be paid by the local authority for the area.
(4) A scheme under section 63 above made for an amalgamated registration area may contain such incidental, transitional and supplementary provisions as appear to the Secretary of State to be necessary or expedient.

New basis for administration of rent officer service
64. B(1)If, with respect to registration areas generally or any particular registration area or areas, it appears to the Secretary of State that it is no longer appropriate for the appointment, remuneration and administration of rent officers to be a function of local authorities, he may by order—
(a) provide that no scheme under section 63 above shall be made for the area or areas specified in the order; and
(b) make, with respect to the area or areas so specified, such provision as appears to him to be appropriate with respect to the appointment, remuneration and administration of rent officers and the payment of pensions, allowances or gratuities to or in respect of them.
(2) An order under this section shall make provision for any expenditure attributable to the provisions of the order to be met by the Secretary of State in such manner as may be specified in the order (whether by way of grant, reimbursement or otherwise); and any expenditure incurred by the Secretary of State by virtue of this subsection shall be paid out of money provided by Parliament.
(3) An order under this section—
(a) may contain such incidental, transitional and supplementary provisions as appear to the Secretary of State to be appropriate, including provisions amending this Part of this Act; and
(b) shall be made by statutory instrument which shall be subject to annulment in pursuance of a resolution of either House of Parliament."

Schedule 14. Repair Notices: Amendments of Housing Act 1985, Part VI

Section 130.
Amendments (Textual)
F1. Sch. 15 repealed (6.4.2006 for E. and 16.6.2006 for W.) by Housing Act 2004 (c. 34), ss. 266, 270, Sch. 16; S.I. 2006/1060, art. 2. (1)(e)(ix) (with Sch.); S.I. 2006/1535, art. 2. (c)(ix) (with Sch.)
1. F2. . . . .
Amendments (Textual)
F2. Sch. 15 para. 1 repealed (6.4.2006 for E. and otherwise prosp.) by Housing Act 2004 (c. 34), s. 266, 270, Sch. 16; S.I. 2006/1060. {art. 2. (1)(e)(ix)}(with Sch.)
2. F3. . . . .
Amendments (Textual)
F3. Sch. 15 para. 2 repealed (6.4.2006 for E. and otherwise prosp.) by Housing Act 2004 (c. 34), ss. 266, 270,{Sch. 16}; S.I. 2006/1060, art. 2. (1)(e)(ix) (with Sch.)
3. F4. . . . .
Amendments (Textual)
F4. Sch. 15 para. 3 repealed (6.4.2006 for E. and otherwise prosp.) by Housing Act 2004 (c. 34), ss. 266, 270, Sch. 16; S.I. 2006/1060, art. 2. (1)(e)(ix) (with Sch.)
4. F5. . . . .

Amendments (Textual)
F5. Sch. 15 para. 4 repealed (6.4.2006 for E. and otherwise prosp.) by Housing Act 2004 (c,. 34), ss. 266, 270, {Sch. 16}; S.I. 2006/1060,{art. 2. (1)(e)(ix)} (with Sch.)
5. F6. . . . .
Amendments (Textual)
F6. Sch, 15 para. 5 repealed (6.4.2006 for E. and otherwise prosp.) by Housing Act 2004 (c. 34), ss. 266, 270, Sch. 16; S.I. 2006/1060, art. 2. (1)(e)(ix) (with Sch.)
6. F7. . . . .
Amendments (Textual)
F7. Sch. 15 para. 6 repealed (6.4,2006 for E. and otherwise prosp.) by Housing Act 2004 (c. 34), ss. 266, 270,{Sch. 16}; S.I. 2006/1060, art. 2. (1)(e)(ix) (with Sch.)
7. F8. . . . .
Amendments (Textual)
F8. Sch. 15 para. 7 repealed (6.4.2006 for E. and otherwise prosp.) by Housing Act 2004 (c. 34), ss. 266, 270, Sch. 16; S.I. 2006/1060, art. 2. (1)(e)(ix) (with Sch.)
8. F9. . . . .
Amendments (Textual)
F9. Sch. 15 para. 8 repealed (6.4.2006 and otherwise prosp.) by Housing Act 2004 (c. 34), ss.266,270, {Sch. 16}:S.I. 2006/1060, art. 2. (1)(e)(ix) (with Sch.)
9. F10. . . . .
Amendments (Textual)
F10. Sch. 15 para. 9 repealed (6.4.2006 for E. and otherwise prosp.) by Housing Act 2004 (c. 34), ss.266, 270, Sch. 16; S.I. 2006/1060, art. 2. (1)(e)(ix) (with Sch.)
10. F11. . . . .
Amendments (Textual)
F11. Sch. 15 para. 10 repealed (6.4.2006 for E. and otherwise prosp.) by Housing Act 2004 (c. 34), ss. 266, 270, Sch. 16; S.I. 2006/1060, art. 2. (1)(e)(ix) (with Sch.)
11. F12. . . . .
Amendments (Textual)
F12. Sch. 15 para. 11 repealed (6.4.2006 for E. and otherwise prosp.) by Housing Act 2004 (c. 34), ss. 266, 270, Sch. 16; S.I, 2006/1060, {art. 2. (1)(e)(ix)} (with Sch.)
12. F13. . . . .
Amendments (Textual)
F13. Sch. 15 para. 12 repealed (6.4.2006 for E and otherwise prosp.) by Housing Act (c. 34), ss. 266,270, {Sch. 16}; S.I. 2006/1060, art. 2. (1)(e)(ix) (with Sch.)
13. F14. . . . .
Amendments (Textual)
F14. Sch. 15 para. 13 repealed (6.4.2006 for E. and otherwise prosp.) by Housing Act (c. 34), ss. 266, 270, {Sch. 16}; S.I. 2006/1060, art. 2. (1)(e)(ix) (with Sch.)

Schedule 15. Schedule to be Inserted in the Housing (Scotland) Act 1987

Section 135.
Commencement Information
I1. Sch. 16 wholly in force at 21.2.1992 see s. 141. (2) and S.I. 1992/324, art. 2
Marginal Citations
M11987 c. 26.

Disposals to which this Schedule applies

1. (1)This Schedule applies to the disposal by a local authority of an interest in land as a result of which a secure tenant of the local authority will become the tenant of a private sector landlord.
(2) For the purposes of this Schedule the grant of an option which if exercised would result in a secure tenant of a local authority becoming the tenant of a private sector landlord shall be treated as a disposal of the interest which is the subject of the option.
(3) Where a disposal of land by a local authority is in part a disposal to which this Schedule applies, the provisions of this Schedule apply to that part as to a separate disposal.
(4) In this paragraph "private sector landlord" means a person other than one of those set out in sub-paragraphs (i) to (iv) and (viii) and (ix) of paragraph (a) of subsection (2) of section 61.

Application for Secretary of State's consent

2. (1)The Secretary of State shall not entertain an application for his consent under section 12. (7) to a disposal to which this Schedule applies unless the local authority certify either—
(a) that the requirements of paragraph 3 as to consultation have been complied with, or
(b) that the requirements of that paragraph as to consultation have been complied with except in relation to tenants expected to have vacated the house in question before the disposal;
and the certificate shall be accompanied by a copy of the notices given by the local authority in accordance with that paragraph.
(2) Where the certificate is in the latter form, the Secretary of State shall not determine the application until the local authority certify as regards the tenants not originally consulted—
(a) that they have vacated the house in question, or
(b) that the requirements of paragraph 3 as to consultation have been complied with;
and a certificate under sub-paragraph (b) shall be accompanied by a copy of the notices given by the local authority in accordance with paragraph 3.

Requirements as to consultation

3. (1)The requirements as to consultation referred to above are as follows.
(2) The local authority shall serve notice in writing on the tenant informing him of—
(a) such details of their proposal as the local authority consider appropriate, but including the identity of the person to whom the disposal is to be made,
(b) the likely consequences of the disposal for the tenant, and
(c) the effect of section 81. A and the provision made under it (preservation of right to buy on disposal to private sector landlord) and of this Schedule,
and informing him that he may, within such reasonable period as may be specified in the notice, which must be at least 28 days after the service of the notice, make representations to the local authority.
(3) The local authority shall consider any representations made to them within that period and shall serve a further written notice on the tenant informing him—
(a) of any significant changes in their proposal, and
(b) that he may within such period as is specified (which must be at least 28 days after the service of the notice) communicate to the Secretary of State his objection to the proposal,
and informing him of the effect of paragraph 5 (consent to be withheld if majority of tenants are opposed).

Power to require further consultation

4. The Secretary of State may require the local authority to carry out such further consultation with their tenants, and to give him such information as to the results of that consultation, as he may

direct.

Consent to be withheld if majority of tenants are opposed

5. (1)The Secretary of State shall not give his consent if it appears to him that a majority of the tenants of the houses to which the application relates do not wish the disposal to proceed; but this does not affect his general discretion to refuse consent on grounds relating to whether a disposal has the support of the tenants or on any other ground.
(2) In making his decision the Secretary of State may have regard to any information available to him; and the local authority shall give him such information as to the representations made to them by tenants and others, and other relevant matters, as he may require.

Protection of purchasers

6. The Secretary of State's consent to a disposal is not invalidated by a failure on his part or that of the local authority to comply with the requirements of this Schedule."

Schedule 16. Minor and Consequential Amendments

Section 140.

Part I General Amendments

The Reserve and Auxiliary Forces (Protection of Civil Interests) Act 1951.

1. In section 4 of the M1. Reserve and Auxiliary Forces (Protection of Civil Interests) Act 1951 (recovery of possession of dwelling-houses in default of payment of rent precluded in certain cases) after subsection (2) there shall be inserted the following subsection—
"(2. A)For the purposes of the foregoing provisions of this Act, a judgment or order for the recovery of possession of a dwelling-house let on an assured tenancy within the meaning of Part I of the Housing Act 1988 shall be regarded as a judgment or order for the recovery of possession in default of payment of rent if the judgment or order was made on any of Grounds 8, 10 and 11 in Schedule 2 to that Act and not on any other ground."
Marginal Citations
M11951 c. 65.
2. For section 16 of that Act (protection of tenure of rented premises by extension of Rent Acts), as it applies otherwise than to Scotland, there shall be substituted the following section—
"16 Protection of tenure of certain rented premises by extension of Housing Act 1988.
(1) Subject to subsection (2) of section 14 of this Act and subsection (3) below, if at any time during a service man's period of residence protection—
　(a) a tenancy qualifying for protection which is a fixed term tenancy ends without being continued or renewed by agreement (whether on the same or different terms and conditions), and
　(b) by reason only of such circumstances as are mentioned in subsection (4) below, on the ending of that tenancy no statutory periodic tenancy of the rented family residence would arise, apart from the provisions of this section,

Chapter I of Part I of the Housing Act 1988 shall, during the remainder of the period of protection, apply in relation to the rented family residence as if those circumstances did not exist and had not existed immediately before the ending of that tenancy and, accordingly, as if on the ending of that tenancy there arose a statutory periodic tenancy which is an assured tenancy during the remainder of that period.

(2) Subject to subsection (2) of section 14 of this Act and subsection (3) below, if at any time during a service man's period of residence protection—

(a) a tenancy qualifying for protection which is a periodic tenancy would come to an end, apart from the provisions of this section, and

(b) by reason only of such circumstances as are mentioned in subsection (4) below that tenancy is not an assured tenancy, and

(c) if that tenancy had been an assured tenancy, it would not have come to an end at that time, Chapter I of Part I of the Housing Act 1988 shall, during the remainder of the period of protection, apply in relation to the rented family residence as if those circumstances did not exist and, accordingly, as if the tenancy had become an assured tenancy immediately before it would otherwise have come to an end.

(3) Neither subsection (1) nor subsection (2) above applies if, on the ending of the tenancy qualifying for protection, a statutory tenancy arises.

(4) The circumstances referred to in subsections (1) and (2) above are any one or more of the following, that is to say,—

(a) that the tenancy was entered into before, or pursuant to a contract made before, Part I of the Housing Act 1988 came into force;

(b) that the rateable value (as defined for the purposes of that Act) of the premises which are the rented family residence, or of a property of which those premises form part, exceeded the relevant limit specified in paragraph 2 of Schedule 1 to that Act;

(c) that the circumstances mentioned in paragraph 3 or paragraph 6 of that Schedule applied with respect to the tenancy qualifying for protection; and

(d) that the reversion immediately expectant on the tenancy qualifying for protection belongs to any of the bodies specified in paragraph 12 of that Schedule."

3. For the said section 16, as it applies to Scotland, there shall be substituted the following section—

"16 Protection of tenure of certain rented premises by extension of Housing (Scotland) Act 1988.

(1) Subject to subsection (2) of section 14 of this Act and subsection (3) below, if at any time during a service man's period of residence protection—

(a) a tenancy qualifying for protection ends without being continued or renewed by agreement (whether on the same or different terms and conditions), and

(b) by reason only of such circumstances as are mentioned in subsection (4) below, on the ending of that tenancy no statutory tenancy of the rented family residence would arise, apart from the provisions of this section,

sections 12 to 31 of the Housing (Scotland) Act 1988 shall, during the remainder of the period of protection, apply in relation to the rented family residence as if those circumstances did not exist and had not existed immediately before the ending of that tenancy and, accordingly, as if on the ending of that tenancy there arose a statutory assured tenancy during the remainder of that period.

(2) Subject to subsection (2) of section 14 of this Act and subsection (3) below, if at any time during a service man's period of residence protection—

(a) a tenancy qualifying for protection would come to an end, apart from the provisions of this section,

(b) by reason only of such circumstances as are mentioned in subsection (4) below that tenancy is not an assured tenancy, and

(c) if that tenancy had been an assured tenancy, it would not have come to an end at that time, sections 12 to 31 of the Housing (Scotland) Act 1988 shall, during the remainder of the period of protection, apply in relation to the rented family residence as if those circumstances did not exist and, accordingly, as if the tenancy had become an assured tenancy immediately before it would otherwise have come to an end.

(3) Neither subsection (1) nor subsection (2) above applies if, on the ending of the tenancy qualifying for protection, a statutory tenancy arises.

(4) The circumstances referred to in subsections (1) and (2) above are one or more of the following, that is to say—

    (a) that the circumstances mentioned in paragraph 2 of Schedule 4 to the Housing (Scotland) Act 1988 applied with respect to the tenancy qualifying for protection;

    (b) that the circumstances mentioned in paragraph 5 of that Schedule applied with respect to the tenancy qualifying for protection; and

    (c) that the reversion immediately expectant on the tenancy qualifying for protection belongs to any of the bodies specified in paragraph 11 of that Schedule."

4. (1) Section 17 of that Act (provisions in case of rented premises which include accommodation shared otherwise than with landlord), as it applies otherwise than to Scotland, shall be amended in accordance with this paragraph.

(2) In subsection (1)—

(a) after the words "qualifying for protection" there shall be inserted " which is a fixed term tenancy ";

(b) in paragraph (b) for the words from "subsection (2)" to "1977" there shall be substituted " section 16. (4) above, subsection (1) of section 3 of the Housing Act 1988 ";

(c) for the words "said section 22" there shall be substituted " "said section 3 "; and

(d) at the end there shall be added " "and, accordingly, as if on the ending of the tenancy there arose a statutory periodic tenancy which is an assured tenancy during the remainder of that period ".

(3) For subsection (2) there shall be substituted the following subsections—

"(2) Where, at any time during a service man's period of residence protection—

    (a) a tenancy qualifying for protection which is a periodic tenancy would come to an end, apart from the provisions of this section and section 16 above, and

    (b) paragraphs (a) and (b) of subsection (1) above apply,

section 3 of the Housing Act 1988 shall, during the remainder of the period of protection, apply in relation to the separate accommodation as if the circumstances referred to in subsection (1)(b) above did not exist and, accordingly, as if the tenancy had become an assured tenancy immediately before it would otherwise have come to an end.

(3) Neither subsection (1) nor subsection (2) above applies if, on the ending of the tenancy qualifying for protection, a statutory tenancy arises."

5. (1) The said section 17, as it applies to Scotland, shall be amended in accordance with this paragraph.

(2) In subsection (1)—

(a) in paragraph (b) for the words from "subsection (2)" to "1977" there shall be substituted the words " "section 16. (4) above, subsection (1) of section 14 of the Housing (Scotland) Act 1988 ";

(b) for the words "said section 97" there shall be substituted the words " "said section 14 "; and

(c) at the end there shall be added the words " "and, accordingly, as if on the ending of the tenancy there arose a statutory assured tenancy during the remainder of that period ".

(3) For subsection (2) there shall be substituted the following subsections—

"(2) Where, at any time during a service man's period of residence protection—

    (a) a tenancy qualifying for protection would come to an end, apart from the provisions of this section and section 16 above, and

    (b) paragraphs (a) and (b) of subsection (1) above apply,

section 14 of the Housing (Scotland) Act 1988 shall, during the remainder of the period of protection, apply in relation to the separate accommodation as if the circumstances in subsection (1)(b) above did not exist and, accordingly, as if the tenancy had become an assured tenancy immediately before it would otherwise come to an end.

(3) Neither subsection (1) nor subsection (2) above applies if, on the ending of the tenancy qualifying for protection, a statutory tenancy arises."

6. (1) In section 18 of that Act (protection of tenure, in connection with employment, under a licence or rent-free letting), in subsection (1), as it applies otherwise than to Scotland,—
(a) for the words "Part VII of the Rent Act 1977" there shall be substituted " "Chapter I of Part I of the Housing Act 1988 "; and
(b) for the words "subject to a statutory tenancy within the meaning of the Rent Act 1977" there shall be substituted " "let on a statutory periodic tenancy which is an assured tenancy ".
(2) In that subsection, as it applies to Scotland,—
(a) for the words "the Rent (Scotland) Act 1971" there shall be substituted the words " "sections 12 to 31 of the Housing (Scotland) Act 1988 ", and
(b) for the words "subject to a statutory tenancy within the meaning of the Rent (Scotland) Act 1971" there shall be substituted the words " "let on a statutory assured tenancy ".
(3) Subsection (2) of that section shall be omitted.
(4) In subsection (3) of that section, as it applies otherwise than to Scotland, at the end of paragraph (c) there shall be added "or
  (d) is a dwelling-house which is let on or subject to an assured agricultural occupancy within the meaning of Part I of the Housing Act 1988 which is not an assured tenancy."
7. For section 19 of that Act (limitation on application of Rent Acts by virtue of sections 16 to 18), as it applies otherwise than to Scotland, there shall be substituted the following section—
"19 Limitation on application of Housing Act 1988 by virtue of sections 16 to 18.
Where by virtue of sections 16 to 18 above, the operation of Chapter I of Part I of the Housing Act 1988 in relation to any premises is extended or modified, the extension or modification shall not affect—
  (a) any tenancy of those premises other than the statutory periodic tenancy which is deemed to arise or, as the case may be, the tenancy which is for any period deemed to be an assured tenancy by virtue of any of those provisions; or
  (b) any rent payable in respect of a period beginning before the time when that statutory periodic tenancy was deemed to arise or, as the case may be, before that tenancy became deemed to be an assured tenancy; or
  (c) anything done or omitted to be done before the time referred to in paragraph (b) above."
8. For the said section 19, as it applies to Scotland, there shall be substituted the following section—
"19 Limitation on application of Housing (Scotland) Act 1988 by virtue of sections 16 to 18.
Where by virtue of sections 16 to 18 above, the operation of sections 12 to 31 of the Housing (Scotland) Act 1988 in relation to any premises is extended or modified, the extension or modification shall not affect—
  (a) any tenancy of those premises other than the statutory assured tenancy which is deemed to arise or, as the case may be, the tenancy which is for any period deemed to be an assured tenancy by virtue of any of those provisions; or
  (b) any rent payable in respect of a period beginning before the time when that statutory assured tenancy was deemed to arise or, as the case may be, before that tenancy became deemed to be an assured tenancy; or
  (c) anything done or omitted to be done before the time referred to in paragraph (b) above."
9. (1) Section 20 of that Act (modification of Rent Acts as respects occupation by employees), as it applies otherwise than to Scotland, shall be amended in accordance with this paragraph.
(2) In subsection (1) after the words "Case I in Schedule 15 to the Rent Act 1977" there shall be inserted " "or Ground 12 in Schedule 2 to the Housing Act 1988 ".
(3) In subsection (2) after the words "Case 8 in the said Schedule 15" there shall be inserted " "or, as the case may be, Ground 16 in the said Schedule 2 " and for paragraph (b) there shall be substituted the following paragraph—
  "(b) Chapter I of Part I of the Housing Act 1988 applies in relation to the premises as mentioned in section 18. (1) of this Act and a dependant or dependants of the service man is or are living in the premises or in part thereof in right of the statutory periodic tenancy or assured tenancy referred to in section 19. (a) of this Act".

(4) In subsection (3)—
(a) after the words "the Cases in Part I of the said Schedule 15" there shall be inserted " "or, as the case may be, Grounds 10 to 16 in Part II of the said Schedule 2 "; and
(b) after the words "section 98. (1) of the Rent Act 1977" there shall be inserted " "or, as the case may be, section 7. (4) of the Housing Act 1988 ".
10. (1)The said section 20, as it applies to Scotland, shall be amended in accordance with this paragraph.
(2) In subsection (1) after the words "Case 1 in Schedule 2 to the Rent (Scotland) Act 1984" there shall be inserted the words " "or Ground 13 in Schedule 5 to the Housing (Scotland) Act 1988 ".
(3) In subsection (2) after the words "Case 7 in the said Schedule 2" there shall be inserted the words " "or, as the case may be, Ground 17 in the said Schedule 5 " and for paragraph (b) there shall be substituted the following paragraph—
   "(b)sections 12 to 31 of the Housing (Scotland) Act 1988 apply in relation to the premises as mentioned in section 18. (1) of this Act and a dependant or dependants of the service man is or are living in the premises or in part thereof in right of the statutory assured tenancy or assured tenancy referred to in paragraph (a) of section 19 of this Act".
(4) In subsection (3)—
(a) after the words "the Cases in Part I of the said Schedule 2" there shall be inserted the words " "or, as the case may be, Grounds 10 to 17 in Part II of the said Schedule 5 "; and
(b) after the words "section 11 of the Rent (Scotland) Act 1984" there shall be inserted the words " "or, as the case may be, section 18. (4) of the Housing (Scotland) Act 1988 ".
11. In section 22 of that Act (facilities for action on behalf of men serving abroad in proceedings as to tenancies), as it applies otherwise than to Scotland, in subsection (1)—
(a) after the words "Rent Act 1977" there shall be inserted " "or under Part I of the Housing Act 1988 ";
(b) for the words "Part V of that Act" there shall be substituted " "Part V of the Rent Act 1977 or Part I of the Housing Act 1988 "; and
(c) in paragraph (a) after the word "tenancy" there shall be inserted " "or licence ".
12. In the said section 22, as it applies to Scotland, in subsection (1),—
(a) for the words "Part III of the Rent Act 1965 or under the Rent (Scotland) Act 1971" there shall be substituted the words " "the Rent (Scotland) Act 1984 or under Part II of the Housing (Scotland) Act 1988 ";
(b) for the words "rent tribunal" there shall be substituted the words " "rent assessment committee " and for the words "or tribunal" there shall be substituted the words " "or committee ";
(c) for the words "Part VII of that Act" there shall be substituted the words " "Part VII of the said Act of 1984 or under Part II of the Housing (Scotland) Act 1988 "; and
(d) in paragraph (a) after the word "tenancy" there shall be inserted the words " "or licence ".
13. (1)Section 23 of that Act (interpretation of Part II), as it applies otherwise than to Scotland, shall be amended in accordance with this paragraph.
(2) In subsection (1)—
(a) after the definition of "agricultural land" there shall be inserted—
" "assured tenancy" has the same meaning as in Part I of the Housing Act 1988";
(b) after the definition of "dependant" there shall be inserted—
" "fixed term tenancy" means any tenancy other than a periodic tenancy";
(c) for the definition of "landlord" and "tenant" there shall be substituted—
"in relation to a statutory tenancy or to a provision of the Rent Act 1977 "landlord" and "tenant" have the same meaning as in that Act but, subject to that, those expressions have the same meaning as in Part I of the Housing Act 1988"; and
(d) after the definition of "relevant police authority" there shall be inserted—
" "statutory periodic tenancy" has the same meaning as in Part I of the Housing Act 1988".
(3) At the end of subsection (1) there shall be inserted the following subsection—
"(1. A)Any reference in this Part of this Act to Chapter I of Part I of the Housing Act 1988 includes a reference to the General Provisions of Chapter VI of that Part, so far as applicable to

Chapter I."
(4) In subsection (3) after the words "Rent Act 1977" there shall be inserted " "or Chapter I of Part I of the Housing Act 1988 ".
14. (1)The said section 23, as it applies to Scotland, shall be amended in accordance with this paragraph.
(2) In subsection (1)—
(a) after the definition of "agricultural land" there shall be inserted—
" "assured tenancy" and "statutory assured tenancy" have the same meaning as in Part II of the Housing (Scotland) Act 1988";
(b) for the definition of "landlord" and "tenant" there shall be substituted—
"in relation to a statutory tenancy or to a provision of the Rent (Scotland) Act 1984 "landlord" and "tenant" have the same meaning as in that Act but, subject to that, those expressions have the same meaning as in Part II of the Housing (Scotland) Act 1988".
(3) At the end of subsection (1) there shall be inserted the following subsection—
"(1. A)Any reference in this Part of this Act to sections 12 to 31 of the Housing (Scotland) Act 1988 includes a reference to sections 47 to 55 of that Act so far as applicable to those sections."
(4) In subsection (3) after the words "Rent (Scotland) Act 1984" there shall be inserted the words " "or sections 12 to 31 of the Housing (Scotland) Act 1988 ".

The Leasehold Reform Act 1967.

15. In section 28 of the M2. Leasehold Reform Act 1967 (retention or resumption of land required for public purposes) at the end of subsection (5) (bodies to whom that section applies) there shall be added "and
   (g) a housing action trust established under Part III of the Housing Act 1988."
Marginal Citations
M21967 c. 88.
16. In section 29 of that Act (reservation of future right to develop) after subsection (6. B) there shall be inserted the following subsection—
"(6. C)Subsections (1) to (4) above shall have effect in relation to a housing action trust as if any reference in those subsections or in Part I of Schedule 4 to this Act to a local authority were a reference to the trust."
17. (1)In Schedule 4. A to that Act (which is set out in Schedule 4 to the M3. Housing and Planning Act 1986 and excludes certain shared ownership leases from Part I of the 1967 Act) at the end of paragraph 2. (1) there shall be added " "or to a person who acquired that interest in exercise of the right conferred by Part IV of the Housing Act 1988 ".
(2) In paragraph 2. (2) of that Schedule, at the end of paragraph (e) there shall be added the following paragraph—
"(f)a housing action trust established under Part III of the Housing Act 1988".
Marginal Citations
M31986 c. 63.

18. . . . . F1.
Amendments (Textual)
F1. Sch. 17 para. 18 repealed by Planning (Consequential Provisions) Act 1990 (c. 11, SIF 123:1, 2), s. 3. (1), Sch. 1 Pt. I

The Local Government Act 1974.

19. In section 25 of the M4. Local Government Act 1974 (local government administration:

authorities subject to investigation), in subsection (1) after paragraph (bd) there shall be inserted the following paragraph—
"(be)any housing action trust established under Part III of the Housing Act 1988".
Marginal Citations
M41974 c. 7.

The Consumer Credit Act 1974.

20[F2. In section 16 of the M5. Consumer Credit Act 1974 (exempt agreements), in subsection (6. B), in paragraph (a) after the words "England and Wales," there shall be inserted " "the Housing Corporation, Housing for Wales and ".]
Amendments (Textual)
F2. Sch. 17 para. 20 repealed (E.W.) (1.4.2010) by The Housing and Regeneration Act 2008 (Consequential Provisions) Order 2010 (S.I. 2010/866), art. 1. (2), Sch. 4 (with art. 6, Sch. 3)
Marginal Citations
M51974 c. 39.

The Rent (Agriculture) Act 1976.

21. In section 28 of the M6. Rent (Agriculture) Act 1976 (rehousing: duty of housing authority concerned), the following subsection shall be inserted after subsection (14) of that section—
"(14. A)Notwithstanding anything in section 127. (1) of the Magistrates' Courts Act 1980, an information relating to an offence under this section may be tried if it is laid at any time within two years after the commission of the offence and within six months after the date on which evidence sufficient in the opinion of the housing authority concerned to justify the proceedings comes to its knowledge."
Marginal Citations
M61976 c. 80.

The Rent Act 1977.

22. In the M7. Rent Act 1977, sections 68 and 69, Part II of Schedule 11 and Schedule 12 (which provide for applications by a local authority for the determination of a fair rent and make provision about certificates of fair rent) shall cease to have effect except as respects applications made before the commencement of this Act.
Marginal Citations
M71977 c. 42.
23. In section 77 of that Act (which provides for the reference of restricted contracts to rent tribunals by the lessor, the lessee or the local authority) the words "or the local authority" shall be omitted.
24. Section 89 of the Rent Act 1977 (which provides for the phasing of progression to a registered rent in the case of housing association tenancies) and Schedule 8 to that Act (phasing of rent increases: general provisions) shall cease to have effect except with respect to an increase in rent up to, or towards, a registered rent in relation to which the relevant date for the purposes of the said Schedule 8 falls before this Act comes into force.
25. In section 137 of the Rent Act 1977 (effect on sub-tenancy of determination of superior tenancy), in subsection (1) the words "this Part of" shall be omitted.

The Protection from Eviction Act 1977.

26. In section 7 of the M8. Protection from Eviction Act 1977 (service of notices), in subsection

(3)(c) (certain licensors treated as landlords for the purposes of the section) the words "under a restricted contract (within the meaning of the Rent Act 1977)" shall be omitted.
Marginal Citations
M81977 c. 43.

The Justices of the Peace Act 1979.

F327. . . . .
Amendments (Textual)
F3. Sch. 17 para. 27 repealed (19.6.1997) by 1997 c. 25, ss. 73. (3), 74. (1)(2), Sch. 6 Pt. I (with Sch. 4 para. 27)

The Local Government, Planning and Land Act 1980.

28. In Schedule 16 to the M9. Local Government, Planning and Land Act 1980 (bodies to whom Part X applies) after paragraph 8 there shall be inserted the following paragraph—
"8. AA housing action trust established under Part III of the Housing Act 1988."
Marginal Citations
M91980 c. 65.
29. In Schedule 28 to the Local Government, Planning and Land Act 1980, in paragraph 10 after the words "Rent Act 1977" there shall be inserted " "or the Housing Act 1988. "

The Highways Act 1980.

30. In Schedule 6 to the M10. Highways Act 1980, in Part I, in paragraph 1. (3)(b)(i) after the words "Rent Act 1977" there shall be inserted " "and licensees under an assured agricultural occupancy within the meaning of Part I of the Housing Act 1988 ".
Marginal Citations
M101980 c. 66.

The New Towns Act 1981.

31. In section 22 of the M11. New Towns Act 1981 (possession of houses) after the words "Rent Act 1977" there shall be inserted " "or Part I of the Housing Act 1988 ".
Marginal Citations
M111981 c. 64.

The Acquisition of Land Act 1981.

32. (1)In section 12. (2) of the M12. Acquisition of Land Act 1981 after the words "Rent (Agriculture) Act 1976" there shall be inserted " "or a licensee under an assured agricultural occupancy within the meaning of Part I of the Housing Act 1988 ".
(2) In Schedule 1 to that Act, in paragraph 3. (2) after the words "Rent (Agriculture) Act 1976" there shall be inserted " "or a licensee under an assured agricultural occupancy within the meaning of Part I of the Housing Act 1988 ".
Marginal Citations
M121981 c. 67.

The Matrimonial Homes Act 1983.

F4 33. . . . .
Amendments (Textual)
F4. Sch. 17 para. 33 repealed (E.W.) (1.10.1997) by 1996 c. 27, s. 66. (3), Sch. 10 Pt. I (with Sch. 9 para. 5); S.I. 1997/1892, art. 3. (d)(vi)
F5 34. . . . .
Amendments (Textual)
F5. Sch. 17 para. 34 repealed (E.W.) (1.10.1997) by 1996 c. 27, s. 66. (3), Sch. 10 (with Sch. 9 para. 5); S.I. 1997/1892, art. 3. (d)(vi)

The County Courts Act 1984.

35. (1)In section 66 of the M13. County Courts Act 1984 (trial by jury: exceptions), in subsection (1) at the end of paragraph (b)(iii) there shall be inserted "or
(iv) under Part I of the Housing Act 1988".
(2) In section 77. (6) of that Act (appeals: possession proceedings) after paragraph (e) there shall be inserted the following paragraph—
"(ee)section 7 of the Housing Act 1988, as it applies to the grounds in Part II of Schedule 2 to that Act; or".
Marginal Citations
M131984 c. 28.

The Matrimonial and Family Proceedings Act 1984.

36. In section 22 of the M14. Matrimonial and Family Proceedings Act 1984 (powers of the court in relation to certain tenancies of dwelling-houses), in paragraph (a) after the word "tenancy" there shall be inserted " "or assured agricultural occupancy ".
Marginal Citations
M141984 c. 42.

The Local Government Act 1985.

37. In section 101 of the M15. Local Government Act 1985 (power by order to make incidental, consequential, etc. provisions) in subsection (1)(b) after second "Act" insert " "or the Housing Act 1988 ".
Marginal Citations
M151985 c. 51.

The Housing Act 1985.

F6 38. . . . .
Amendments (Textual)
F6. Sch. 17 Pt. I para. 38 repealed (1.10.1996) by 1996 c. 52, ss. 227, 231. (4)(b), Sch. 19 Pt. IX; S.I. 1996/2402, art. 3 (subject to transitional provisions in Sch.)
F7 39. . . . .
Amendments (Textual)
F7. Sch. 17 Pt. I para. 39 repealed (1.10.1996) by 1996 c. 52, ss. 227, 231. (4)(b), Sch. 19 Pt. IX; S.I. 1996/2402, art. 3 (subject to transitional provisions in Sch.)
40. In section 115 of that Act (meaning of "long tenancy"), in subsection (2)(c) after "1980" there shall be inserted " "or paragraph 4. (2)(b) of Schedule 4. A to the Leasehold Reform Act 1967 ".
41. In section 155 of that Act (repayment of discount on early disposal) after subsection (3) there shall be inserted the following subsection—

"(3. A)Where a secure tenant has served on his landlord an operative notice of delay, as defined in section 153. A,—

(a) the three years referred to in subsection (2) shall begin from a date which precedes the date of the conveyance of the freehold or grant of the lease by a period equal to the time (or, if there is more than one such notice, the aggregate of the times) during which, by virtue of section 153. B, any payment of rent falls to be taken into account in accordance with subsection (3) of that section; and

(b) any reference in subsection (3) (other than paragraph (a) thereof) to the acquisition of the tenant's initial share shall be construed as a reference to a date which precedes that acquisition by the period referred to in paragraph (a) of this subsection."

42. In section 171. F of that Act (subsequent dealings after disposal of dwelling-house to private sector landlord: possession on grounds of suitable alternative accommodation) after "Rent Act 1977" there shall be inserted " "or on Ground 9 in Schedule 2 to the Housing Act 1988 ".

43. In section 236 of that Act at the end of subsection (2) (meaning of "occupying tenant") there shall be added the words "or

(e) is a licensee under an assured agricultural occupancy."

44. In section 238 of that Act (index of defined expressions in Part VII) before the entry relating to "clearance area" there shall be inserted— " assured agricultural occupancysection 622 ".

45. In section 247 of that Act (notification of certain disposals of land to the local housing authority), in subsection (5) (provision not to apply to certain disposals) after paragraph (c) there shall be inserted the following paragraph—

"(ca)the grant of an assured tenancy or assured agricultural occupancy, or of a tenancy which is not such a tenancy or occupancy by reason only of paragraph 10 of Schedule 1 to the Housing Act 1988 (resident landlords) or of that paragraph and the fact that the accommodation which is let is not let as a separate dwelling".

46. In section 263 of that Act (index of defined expressions in Part VIII) before the entry relating to "clearance area" there shall be inserted—

"assured agricultural occupancysection 622

assured tenancysection 622".

47. In Part IX of that Act (slum clearance) in the following provisions relating to the recovery of possession, namely, sections 264. (5), 270. (3), 276 and 286. (3), after the words "Rent Acts" there shall be inserted " "or Part I of the Housing Act 1988 ".

47. In Part IX of that Act (slum clearance) in the following provisions relating to the recovery of possession, namely, [F21section 270. (3)] , after the words "Rent Acts" there shall be inserted " "or Part I of the Housing Act 1988 ".

Amendments (Textual)

F21. Words in Sch. 17 para. 47 substituted (6.4.2006 for E. and 16.6.2006 for W) by Housing Act 2004 (c. 34), ss. 265. (1), 270, {Sch. 15 para, 33}; S.I. 2006/1060, art. 2. (1)(d) (with Sch.); S.I.2006/1535, art. 2. (b) (with Sch.)

48. In section 309 of that Act (recovery of possession of premises for purposes of approved redevelopment), in paragraph (a) of subsection (1) after the words "the Rent Act 1977)" the following words shall be inserted " "or let on or subject to an assured tenancy or assured agricultural occupancy "; and in the words following paragraph (b) of that subsection after the words "section 98. (1)(a) of the Rent Act 1977" there shall be inserted " "or section 7 of the Housing Act 1988 ".

49. In section 323 of that Act (index of defined expressions in Part IX) before the entry relating to "clearance area" there shall be inserted—

"assured agricultural occupancysection 622

assured tenancysection 622".

50. In section 368 of that Act (means of escape from fire: power to secure that part of house not used for human habitation), in subsection (6) after the words "Rent Acts" there shall be inserted " "or Part I of the Housing Act 1988 ".

51. In section 381 of that Act (general effect of control order), in subsection (3) after the words

"Rent Acts" there shall be inserted " "and Part I of the Housing Act 1988 ".

52. (1)In section 382 of that Act (effect of control order on persons occupying house) after subsection (3) there shall be inserted the following subsection—

"(3. A)Section 1. (2) of and paragraph 12 of Part I of Schedule 1 to the Housing Act 1988 (which exclude local authority lettings from Part I of that Act) do not apply to a lease or agreement under which a person to whom this section applies is occupying part of the house."

(2) In subsection (4) of that section after paragraph (b) there shall be inserted "or

(c) an assured tenancy or assured agricultural occupancy within the meaning of Part I of the Housing Act 1988"; and for the words "either of those Acts" there shall be substituted " "any of those Acts ".

53. In section 400 of that Act (index of defined expressions for Part XI) after the entry relating to "appropriate multiplier" there shall be inserted—

"assured tenancysection 622

assured agricultural occupancysection 622".

54. In section 429. A of that Act (housing management: financial assistance etc.) in subsection (2), in paragraph (a) after the words "secure tenancies)" there shall be inserted " "or subsection (2. A) " and at the end of that subsection there shall be inserted the following subsection—

"(2. A)Subsection (2)(a) applies to the following bodies—

(a) the Housing Corporation;
(b) Housing for Wales;
(c) a housing trust which is a charity;
(d) a registered housing association other than a co-operative housing association; and
(e) an unregistered housing association which is a co-operative housing association."

55. In section 434 of that Act (index of defined expressions for Part XIII) there shall be inserted, in the appropriate places in alphabetical order, the following entries—

"charitysection 622"

"co-operative housing associationsection 5. (2)"

"housing associationsection 5. (1)"

"housing trust"section 6".

F856. . . . .

Amendments (Textual)

F8. Sch. 17 Pt. I para. 56 repealed (with savings) (1.10.1996) by S.I. 1996/2325, art. 4. (1)-(3), Sch. 1 Pt. I

F957. . . . .

Amendments (Textual)

F9. Sch. 17 Pt. I para. 57 repealed (with savings) (1.10.1996) by S.I. 1996/2325, art. 4. (1)-(3), Sch. 1 Pt. I

58. In section 459 of that Act (index of defined expressions for Part XIV) after the entry relating to "building society" there shall be inserted—

"co-operative housing associationsection 5. (2)".

59. In section 533 of that Act (assistance for owners of defective housing: exceptions to eligibility) after the words "Rent (Agriculture) Act 1976" there shall be inserted " "or who occupies the dwelling under an assured agricultural occupancy which is not an assured tenancy ".

60. In section 553 of that Act (effect of repurchase of defective dwellings on certain existing tenancies) in subsection (2)—

(a) in paragraph (a) after the words "protected tenancy" there shall be inserted " "or an assured tenancy ";

(b) at the end of paragraph (b) there shall be added the words " "or in accordance with any of Grounds 1, 3, 4 and 5 in Schedule 2 to the Housing Act 1988 (notice that possession might be recovered under that ground) or under section 20. (1)(c) of that Act (notice served in respect of assured shorthold tenancies); and "; and

[F10. (c)after paragraph (b) there shall be added—

"(c)the tenancy is not an assured periodic tenancy which, by virtue of section 39. (7) of the

Housing Act 1988 (successors under the Rent Act 1977), is an assured shorthold tenancy".]
Amendments (Textual)
F10. Sch. 17 Pt. I para. 60. (c) repealed (28.2.1997) by 1996 c. 52, ss. 227, 231. (4)(b), Sch. 19 Pt. IV; S.I. 1997/225, art. 2 (subject to transitional provisions in Sch.)

61. (1)In section 554 of that Act (grant of tenancy of defective dwelling to former owner-occupier) at the end of subsection (2) there shall be inserted the following subsection—

"(2. A)If the authority is a registered housing association, other than a housing co-operative, within the meaning of section 27. B, their obligation is to grant a secure tenancy if the individual to whom a tenancy is to be granted—

(a) is a person who, immediately before he acquired his interest in the dwelling-house, was a secure tenant of it; or

(b) is the spouse or former spouse or widow or widower of a person falling within paragraph (a); or

(c) is a member of the family, within the meaning of section 186, of a person falling within paragraph (a) who has died, and was residing with that person in the dwelling-house at the time of and for the period of twelve months before his death."

(2) In subsection (3) of that section, at the end of paragraph (b) there shall be inserted "or

(c) an assured tenancy which is neither an assured shorthold tenancy, within the meaning of Part I of the Housing Act 1988, nor a tenancy under which the landlord might recover possession on any of Grounds 1 to 5 in Schedule 2 to that Act."

62. In section 577 of that Act (index of defined expressions for Part XVI) after the entry relating to "associated arrangement" there shall be inserted—

"assured agricultural occupancysection 622

 assured tenancysection 622".

63. In section 612 of that Act (exclusion of Rent Act protection) after the words "the Rent Acts" there shall be inserted " "or Part I of the Housing Act 1988 ".

64. In section 622 of that Act (definitions: general) before the definition of "bank" there shall be inserted—

" "assured tenancy" has the same meaning as in Part I of the Housing Act 1988;

 "assured agricultural occupancy" has the same meaning as in Part I of the Housing Act 1988".

65. In Schedule 2 to that Act, in Part IV (grounds for possession: suitability of alternative accommodation) in paragraph 1, at the end of sub-paragraph (b) there shall be added "or
(c) which are to be let as a separate dwelling under an assured tenancy which is neither an assured shorthold tenancy, within the meaning of Part I of the Housing Act 1988, nor a tenancy under which the landlord might recover possession under any of Grounds 1 to 5 in Schedule 2 to that Act".

66. In Schedule 5 to that Act, in paragraph 3, after the entry for section 58. (2) of the M16. Housing Associations Act 1985 there shall be inserted the following entries—

"section 50 of the Housing Act 1988 (housing association grants), or

section 51 of that Act (revenue deficit grants)."

Marginal Citations
M161985 c. 69.

The Landlord and Tenant Act 1985.

67. (1)In section 5 of the M17. Landlord and Tenant Act 1985 (information to be contained in rent books), in subsection (1)(b) after the word "tenancy" there shall be inserted " "or let on an assured tenancy within the meaning of Part I of the Housing Act 1988 ".

(2) In subsection (2) of that section after the word "tenancy" there shall be added " "or let on an assured tenancy within the meaning of Part I of the Housing Act 1988 ".

Marginal Citations
M171985 c. 70.

68. In section 26 of that Act (tenants of certain public authorities excepted from provisions about service charges etc.) in subsection (3)(c) after the words "Housing Act 1980" there shall be inserted " "or paragraph 4. (2)(b) of Schedule 4. A to the Leasehold Reform Act 1967 ".

The Agricultural Holdings Act 1986.

69. (1)In Schedule 3 to the M18. Agricultural Holdings Act 1986 (cases where consent of Tribunal to operation of notice to quit is not required), in Part II (provisions applicable to Case A: suitable alternative accommodation), in paragraph 3 after paragraph (b) there shall be inserted "or
(c) premises which are to be let as a separate dwelling such that they will then be let on an assured tenancy which is not an assured shorthold tenancy (construing those terms in accordance with Part I of the Housing Act 1988), or
(d) premises to be let as a separate dwelling on terms which will afford to the tenant security of tenure reasonably equivalent to the security afforded by Chapter I of Part I of that Act in the case of an assured tenancy which is not an assured shorthold tenancy."
(2) At the end of the said paragraph 3 there shall be added the following sub-paragraph—
"(2)Any reference in sub-paragraph (1) above to an assured tenancy does not include a reference to a tenancy in respect of which possession might be recovered on any of Grounds 1 to 5 in Schedule 2 to the Housing Act 1988."
Marginal Citations
M181986 c. 5.
70. In Schedule 5 to that Act (notice to quit where tenant is a service man), in paragraph 2. (2)(a) after the words "Rent Act 1977" there shall be inserted " "or paragraph 7 of Schedule 1 to the Housing Act 1988 ".

The Drug Trafficking Offences Act 1986.

F1171. . . . .
Amendments (Textual)
F11. Sch. 17 Pt. I para. 71 repealed (3.2.1995) by 1994 c. 37, ss. 67, 69. (2), Sch. 3
F1272. . . . .
Amendments (Textual)
F12. Sch. 17 Pt. I para. 72 repealed (3.2.1995) by 1994 c. 37, ss. 67, 69. (2), Sch. 3

The Insolvency Act 1986.

73. In section 308 of the M19. Insolvency Act 1986 (vesting in trustee of certain items of excess value), in subsection (1), for the words "the next section" there shall be substituted " "section 309 ".
Marginal Citations
M191986 c. 45.
74. In section 335 of that Act (adjustment between earlier and later bankruptcy estates), in subsection (4) after the words "replacement value)" there shall be inserted the words " "or section 308. A (vesting in trustee of certain tenancies) ".
75. In section 351 of that Act (definitions), in paragraph (a), for the words "or 308" there shall be substituted " ", section 308 " and after the words "replacement value)" there shall be inserted " "or section 308. A (vesting in trustee of certain tenancies) ".

The Social Security Act 1986.

76. In section 31 of the M20. Social Security Act 1986 (information relating to housing benefit), in

subsection (5) (information as to registered rents), after the words "housing benefit scheme" there shall be inserted " "(a) ", and at the end there shall be added "and

(b) where a rent is determined under section 14 or section 22 of the Housing Act 1988 or section 25 or section 34 of the Housing (Scotland) Act 1988 (determination of rents by rent assessment committee), the committee shall note in their determination the amount (if any) of the rent which, in the opinion of the committee, is fairly attributable to the provision of services, except where that amount is in their opinion negligible; and the amounts so noted may be included in the information specified in an order under section 42 of the Housing Act 1988 or, as the case may be, section 49 of the Housing (Scotland) Act 1988 (information to be publicly available)".
Marginal Citations
M20 1986 c. 50.

The Housing (Scotland) Act 1987.

77. In section 12 of the M21. Housing (Scotland) Act 1987 (which relates, amongst other things, to the disposal by local authorities of land acquired or appropriated for housing purposes and of houses)—
(a) in subsection (1)(c), for the words "subsection (5)" there shall be substituted the words " "subsections (5) and (7) ";
(b) in subsection (7)—
(i) for "(1)(d)" there shall be substituted " "(1)(c) or (d) ";
(ii) for the words "house or any part share thereof" there shall be substituted the words " "land, house or part share thereof ";
(iii) for the words "it is a house" there shall be substituted the words " ", in the case of a house, it is one ";
(c) in subsection (8) after the word "apply" there shall be inserted the words " ", in the case of a house, ".
Marginal Citations
M21 1987 c. 26.
78. In section 13 of that Act (power of Secretary of State in certain cases to impose conditions on sale of local authority's houses etc.) for the words "land or dwelling" there shall be substituted the words " "or land ".
79. F13. . . . .
Amendments (Textual)
F13. Sch. 17 para. 79 repealed (22.7.2004) by Statute Law (Repeals) Act 2004 (c. 14), ss. 1. (1), 2. (1), {Sch. 1 Pt. 10 Group. 3}

The Access to Personal Files Act 1987.

F14 80. . . . .
Amendments (Textual)
F14. Sch. 17 Pt. I para. 80 repealed (1.3.2000) by 1998 c. 29, s. 74. (2), Sch. 16 Pt. I; S.I. 2000/183, art. 2

The Criminal Justice (Scotland) Act 1987.

81. In section 33 of the M22. Criminal Justice (Scotland) Act 1987 (sequestration of person holding realisable property), in subsection (2)(b) for the words "under subsection (6) of that section" there shall be substituted the words " "under subsection (10) of section 31 of that Act or subsection (6) of the said section 32 of that Act ".
Marginal Citations

M221987 c. 41.
82. In section 34 of that Act (bankruptcy in England and Wales of person holding realisable property), in subsection (2)(b) for the words "or 308" there shall be substituted " "308 or 308. A " and after the word "replacement" there shall be inserted " "and certain tenancies ".

The Criminal Justice Act 1988.

83. F15. . . . .
Amendments (Textual)
F15. Sch. 17 para. 83 repealed (24.3.2003) by Proceeds of Crime Act 2000 (c. 29), ss. 457, 458. (1)(3), Sch. 12; S.I. 2003/333, art. 2, Sch. (with transitional provisions and savings in arts. 10, 12)
84. F16. . . . .
Amendments (Textual)
F16. Sch. 17 para. 84 repealed (24.3.2003) by Proceeds of Crime Act 2002 (c. 29), ss. 457, 458. (1)(3), Sch. 12; S.I. 2003/333, art. 2, Sch. (with transitional provisions and savings in arts. 10, 12)

The Housing (Scotland) Act 1988.

85. In section 19 of the M23. Housing (Scotland) Act 1988 (notice of proceedings for possession)—
(a) in subsection (2) for the word "is" there shall be substituted the words " "and particulars of it are ";
(b) in subsection (3) after the word "one" where it first occurs there shall be inserted the words " "in the prescribed form ".
Marginal Citations
M231988 c. 43.
86. In section 36 of that Act (damages for unlawful eviction)—
(a) in subsection (2) for the word "calculated" there shall be substituted the word " "likely ";
(b) in subsection (7)(b)—
(i) after the word "of" where it first occurs there shall be inserted the words " "the doing of acts or ";
(ii) after the word "for" there shall be inserted the words " "doing the acts or ".
87. In section 38 of that Act (further offence of harassment)—
(a) for the words from "In section 22" to "after subsection (2)" there shall be substituted the words—
"(1)Subsection (2) of section 22 of the Rent (Scotland) Act 1984 (unlawful eviction and harassment of occupier) shall, as respects acts done after the commencement of this section, have effect with the substitution of the word "likely" for the word " "calculated ".
(2) After that subsection";
(b) after "(2. A)" there shall be inserted the words " "Subject to subsection (2. B) below ";
(c) for the word "calculated" there shall be substituted the word " "likely ";
(d) the words "subject to subsection (2. B) below" and "by reason only of conduct falling within paragraph (b) of that subsection" shall cease to have effect;
(e) after the word "for" where it second occurs there shall be inserted the words " "doing the acts or ".
88. In section 36 of that Act (damages for unlawful eviction)—
(a) in subsection (6), for the words "proceedings are begun to enforce the liability" there shall be substituted the words " "the date on which the proceedings to enforce the liability are finally decided "; and
(b) after subsection (6) there shall be inserted the following subsections—
"(6. A)For the purposes of subsection (6)(a) above, proceedings to enforce a liability are finally decided—

(a) if no appeal may be made against the decision in these proceedings;

(b) if an appeal may be made against the decision with leave and the time limit for applications for leave expires and either no application has been made or leave has been refused;

(c) if leave to appeal against the decision is granted or is not required and no appeal is made within the time limit for appeals; or

(d) if an appeal is made but is abandoned before it is determined.

(6. B)If, in proceedings to enforce a liability arising by virtue of subsection (3) above, it appears to the court—

(a) that, prior to the event which gave rise to the liability, the conduct of the former residential occupier or any person living with him in the premises concerned was such that it is reasonable to mitigate the damages for which the landlord would otherwise be liable, or

(b) that, before the proceedings were begun, the landlord offered to reinstate the former residential occupier in the premises in question and either it was unreasonable of the former residential occupier to refuse that offer or, if he had obtained alternative accommodation before the offer was made, it would have been unreasonable of him to refuse that offer if he had not obtained that accommodation,

the court may reduce the amount of damages which would otherwise be payable to such amount as it thinks appropriate.".

89. In section 63 of that Act (consent for subsequent disposals) after subsection (2) there shall be inserted the following subsection—

"(2. A)Before giving any consent for the purposes of subsection (1) above, Scottish Homes—

(a) shall satisfy itself that the person who is seeking the consent has taken appropriate steps to consult the tenant of the house (or, as the case may be, each house) of which the property proposed to be disposed of consists; and

(b) shall have regard to the response of such tenant to that consultation."

90. In Schedule 4 to that Act (tenancies which cannot be assured tenancies) after paragraph 11 there shall be inserted the following paragraph—

" Accommodation for homeless persons

11. AA tenancy granted expressly on a temporary basis in the fulfilment of a duty imposed on a local authority by Part II of the Housing (Scotland) Act 1987."

Part II Amendments Consequential on the Establishment of Housing for Wales

The Land Commission Act 1967.

F1791. . . . .
Amendments (Textual)
F17. Sch. 17 Pt. II para. 91 repealed (19.11.1998) by 1998 c. 43, s. 1. (1), Sch. 1 Pt. IV Group 2

The Parliamentary Commissioner Act 1967.

92. In Schedule 2 to the M24. Parliamentary Commissioner Act 1967 (departments etc. subject to investigation) after the entry "Housing Corporation" there shall be inserted—
"Housing for Wales".
Marginal Citations
M241967 c. 13.

The Income and Corporation Taxes Act 1970.

[F18 93. In section 342 of the M25. Income and Corporation Taxes Act 1970 (disposals of land between Housing Corporation and housing societies) and in section 342. A of that Act (disposals by certain housing associations) after the words "Housing Corporation" in each place where they occur there shall be inserted "or Housing for Wales".]
Amendments (Textual)
F18. Sch. 17 Pt. II para. 93 repealed (retrospectively) by Finance Act 1991 (c. 31, SIF 63:2), s. 123, Sch. 19 Pt. VI, Note 1
Marginal Citations
M25 1970 c. 10.

The Land Compensation Act 1973.

94. In section 32. (7. B)(b) of the M26. Land Compensation Act 1973 (supplementary provisions about home loss payments) after the words "Housing Corporation" there shall be inserted "or Housing for Wales".
Marginal Citations
M26 1973 c. 26.

The House of Commons Disqualification Act 1975.

95. In Schedule 1 to the M27. House of Commons Disqualification Act 1975, in Part II (bodies of which all members are disqualified) there shall be inserted at the appropriate place the following entry—
"Housing for Wales".
Marginal Citations
M27 1975 c. 24.

The Statutory Corporations (Financial Provisions) Act 1975.

96. In Schedule 2 to the M28. Statutory Corporations (Financial Provisions) Act 1975 (bodies corporate affected by section 5 of that Act as to their power to borrow in currencies other than sterling) after the entry "The Housing Corporation" there shall be inserted—
"Housing for Wales".
Marginal Citations
M28 1975 c. 55.

The Development of Rural Wales Act 1976.

F19 97. . . . .
Amendments (Textual)
F19. Sch. 17 Pt. II para. 97 repealed (1.10.1998) by 1998 c. 38, s. 152, Sch. 18 Pt. IV; S.I. 1998/2244, art. 4

The Rent (Agriculture) Act 1976.

98. In section 5. (3) of the M29. Rent (Agriculture) Act 1976 (no statutory tenancy where landlord's interest belongs to Crown or to local authority etc.) after paragraph (d) there shall be inserted the following paragraph—
"(da) Housing for Wales".
Marginal Citations
M29 1976 c. 80.

The Rent Act 1977.

99. In section 15. (2)(a) of the M30. Rent Act 1977 (landlord's interest belonging to housing association etc.) after the words "Housing Corporation" there shall be inserted—
"(aa)Housing for Wales".
Marginal Citations
M301977 c. 42.
100. In each of the following provisions of that Act, that is to say, sections 86. (2)(a) (tenancies to which Part VI applies), 93. (1) (increase of rent without notice to quit) and Schedule 12 (certificates of fair rent), in paragraph 12 (meaning of "secure tenancy"), after the words "Housing Corporation" there shall be inserted "or Housing for Wales".

The Criminal Law Act 1977.

101. In section 7. (5) of the M31. Criminal Law Act 1977 (authorities who may authorise occupation by protected intending occupier for purposes of offence of adverse occupation of residential premises) after the words "Housing Corporation" there shall be inserted—
"(ba)Housing for Wales".
Marginal Citations
M311977 c. 45.

The National Health Service Act 1977.

102. In section 28. A(2)(e) of the M32. National Health Service Act 1977 (power to make payments towards expenditure on community services) at the end there shall be added the following sub-paragraph "and
(vii) Housing for Wales."
Marginal Citations
M321977 c. 49.
103. In section 28. B(1)(b)(v) of that Act (power of Secretary of State to make payments towards expenditure on community services in Wales) for the words "the Housing Corporation" there shall be substituted "Housing for Wales".

The Local Government, Planning and Land Act 1980.

104. In Schedule 16 to the M33. Local Government, Planning and Land Act 1980 (bodies to whom Part X of that Act applies) after paragraph 9 there shall be inserted the following paragraph—
"9a. Housing for Wales."
Marginal Citations
M331980 c. 65.

The Finance Act 1981.

105. In section 107. (3) of the M34. Finance Act 1981 (exemption from stamp duty in case of sale of houses at discount by local authorities etc.) after paragraph (c) there shall be inserted the following paragraph—
"(ca)Housing for Wales."
Marginal Citations
M341981 c. 35.

The Housing Act 1985.

106. In the M35. Housing Act 1985 for the words "Housing Corporation" in each place where they occur there shall be substituted "Corporation".
Marginal Citations
M351985 c. 68.
F20107. . . . .
Amendments (Textual)
F20. Sch. 17 Pt. II para. 107 repealed (with savings) (1.10.1996) by S.I. 1996/2325, art. 4. (1)-(3), Sch. 1 Pt. I
108. In section 57 of that Act (index of defined expressions: Part II) after the entry relating to "compulsory disposal" there shall be inserted—
"the Corporation»section 6. A".
109. In section 117 of that Act (index of defined expressions: Part IV) after the entry relating to "co-operative housing association" there shall be inserted—
"the Corporation» section 6. A".
110. In section 188 of that Act (index of defined expressions: Part V) after the entry relating to "co-operative housing association" there shall be inserted—
"the Corporation» section 6. A".
111. In section 238 of that Act (index of defined expressions: Part VII) after the entry relating to "clearance area" there shall be inserted—
"the Corporation» section 6. A".
112. In section 459 of that Act (index of defined expressions: Part XIV) after the entry relating to "building society" there shall be inserted—
"the Corporation section» 6. A".
113. In section 577 of that Act (index of defined expressions: Part XVI) after the entry relating to "co-operative housing association" there shall be inserted—
"the Corporation» section 6. A".

The Landlord and Tenant Act 1987.

114. In section 58. (1) of the M36. Landlord and Tenant Act 1987 (exempt landlords) after paragraph (e) there shall be inserted the following paragraph—
"(ea)Housing for Wales".
Marginal Citations
M361987 c. 31.

The Income and Corporation Taxes Act 1988.

115. In section 376. (4) of the M37. Income and Corporation Taxes Act 1988 (qualifying borrowers and lenders) after paragraph (k) there shall be inserted the following paragraph—
"(ka)Housing for Wales."
Marginal Citations
M371988 c. 1.
116. In section 560. (2)(e) of that Act (persons who are sub-contractors or contractors for the purposes of Chapter IV of Part XIII of that Act) after the words "Housing Corporation" there shall be inserted "Housing for Wales".

Schedule 17. Enactments Repealed

Section 140.

Chapter | Short title | Extend of repeal |
14 & 15 Geo. VI c. 65. | The Reserve and Auxiliary Forces (Protection of Civil Interests) Act 1951. | Section 18(2). |
1976 c.80. | The Rent (Agriculture) Act 1976. | In section 4(2) the words "or, as the case may be, subsection (4)".In section 13(3) the words "68, 69" and "or Part II of Schedule 11 or Schedule 12 to that Act".In Schedule 4, in Part I, paragraph 2(2). |
1977 c.42. | The Rent Act 1977. | Section 16A.Sections 19 to 21.In section 63, in subsection (1), paragraph (b) and the word "and" immediately preceding it; in subsection (2) in paragraph (a), the words "and deputy rent officers", in paragraph (b), the words "or deputy rent officer", in paragraph (d) the words "and deputy rent officers" and the word "and" at the endof the paragraph, andparagraph (e); in sub-section (3), the words "and deputy rent officers";and in subsection (7)(b), the words "and deputy rent officers".In section 67, in subsection (5), the words "and sections 68 and 69 of this Act" and in subsection (7), the words "Subject to section 69(4) of this Act."Sections 68 and 69.In section 74, in subsection (2), in paragraph (a) "69", in paragraph (b) the words "or II" and paragraph (c).In section 77(1) the words "or the local authority".In section 80(1) the words "or the local authority".Section 81A(1)(a).In section 87, in subsection (2), in paragraph (a) "69" and in paragraph (c) the words "and 12".In section 88(2) the words "then, subject to section 89 of this Act".Section 89.In section 103(1) the words "or the local authority".In section 137 the words "this Part of".In Schedule 1, in paragraph 1 the words "or, as the case may be, paragraph 3", in paragraph 4, the words "or 3", and paragraph 7.In Schedule 2, paragraph 6(3).Schedule 8.In Schedule 11, Part II.Schedule 12.In Schedule 14, paragraph 4.In Schedule 15, in Part IV, paragraph 4(2).In Schedule 20, paragraph 2(2).In Schedule 24, paragraph 8(3). |
1977 c. 43. | The Protection from Eviction Act 1977. | In section 7(3)(c) the words from "under" to "1977)". |
1980 c.51. | The Housing Act 1980. | Section 52.Sections 56 to 58.Section 59(1).Section 60.Section 73(2).Section 76(2).In Schedule 9, paragraph 2.In Schedule 10, paragraph 2.In Schedule 25, paragraph 36, in paragraph 40 "68 (4)" and paragraphs 46 and 63. |
1985 c. 51. | The Local Government Act 1985. | In Schedule 13, in paragraph 21, the words from "and section 19(5)(aa)" onwards. |
1985 c.68. | The Housing Act 1985. | In section 80, in subsection (1) the words from "the Housing Corporation" to "charity or", the words "housing association or" and subsection (2).Sections 199 to 201.In Schedule 5, in paragraph 3 the word "or" immediately following the entry for section 55 of the Housing Associations Act 1985; paragraphs 6 and 8. |
1985 c.69. | The Housing Associations Act 1985. | In section 3(2) the words "of housing associations maintained under this section".In section 18(3) the words from "and the Corporation" onwards.In section 40, the entries relating to housing association grant and revenue deficit grant.Sections 41 to 57.Section 62.In section 73, the entries relating to approved de-velopment programme,hostel deficit grant, housing association grant, housing project, revenue deficit grant, shared ownership agreement and shared ownership lease.Section 75(1)(d).In section 87(1) the words "registered housing asso-ciations and other".In section 107, in subsection (3) the entries relating to sections 4, 44 and 45 and 52, and in subsection (4) the words "section 4(3)(h)".In Schedule 5, in paragraph 5(3) of Part I and in paragraph 5(3) of Part II, the words "at such times and in such places as the Treasury may direct, and" and the words "withthe approval of the Treasury".In Schedule 6, paragraph 3(3)(b). |
1986 c.63. | The Housing and Planning Act 1986. | Section 7.Section 12.In section 13, subsections (1) to (3) and (5).Section 19.In Schedule 4, paragraphs 1(3) and 10.In Schedule 5, paragraph 8. |
1986 c.65. | The Housing (Scotland) Act 1986. | Section 13(1).Sections 14 to 16.In Schedule 2, in paragraph 4(8), sub-paragraph (a) and, in sub-paragraph (b), the words "section 4(3)(h)". |
1987 c.26. | The Housing (Scotland) Act 1987. | In section 61(4)(b) the word "or" at the end of

sub-paragraph (v) and at the end of sub-paragraph (vi). |
1987 c.31. | The Landlord and Tenant Act 1987. | In section 3(1)(b) the word "or".Section 4(2)(a)(ii).Section 45.Section 60(2).In Schedule 4, paragraph 7. |
1988 c.9. | The Local Government Act 1988. | Section 24(5)(b). |
1988 c.43. | The Housing (Scotland) Act 1988. | Section 4(4).In section 38, the words "subject to subsection (2B) below" and "by reason only of conduct falling within paragraph (b) of that subsection".Schedule 3.In Schedule 9, paragraphs 6(b) and 7.In Schedule 10, the entry relating to the Housing Associations Act 1985. |

1. The repeal of sections 19 to 21 of the Rent Act 1977 does not apply with respect to any tenancy or contract entered into before the coming into force of Part I of this Act nor to any other tenancy or contract which, having regard to section 36 of this Act, can be a restricted contract.

2. The repeal of section 52 of the Housing Act 1980 (protected shorthold tenancies) does not apply with respect to any tenancy entered into before the coming into force of Part I of this Act nor to any other tenancy which, having regard to section 34 of this Act, can be a protected shorthold tenancy.

3[F1. The repeal of sections 56 to 58 of the Housing Act 1980 does not have effect in relation to any tenancy [F2of a dwelling-house in Wales] to which, by virtue of section 37. (2) of this Act, section 1. (3) of this Act does not apply.]

Amendments (Textual)

F1. Sch. 18 para. 3 ceases to have effect (26.5.2015) by virtue of Deregulation Act 2015 (c. 20), s. 115. (3)(r), Sch. 23 para. 46. (1)

F2. Words in Sch. 18 para. 3 inserted (26.5.2015) by Deregulation Act 2015 (c. 20), s. 115. (3)(r), Sch. 23 para. 46. (2)

4. The repeals in section 80 of the Housing Act 1985—

(a) have effect (subject to section 35. (5) of this Act) in relation to any tenancy or licence entered into before the coming into force of Part I of this Act unless, immediately before that time, the landlord or, as the case may be, the licensor is a body which, in accordance with the repeals, would cease to be within the said section 80; and

(b) do not have effect in relation to a tenancy or licence entered into on or after the coming into force of Part I of this Act if the tenancy or licence falls within any of paragraphs (c) to (f) of subsection (4) of section 35 of this Act [F3and

(c) do not have effect in relation to a tenancy while it is a housing association tenancy.]

Amendments (Textual)

F3. Word and Sch. 18 para. 4. (c) added by Local Government and Housing Act 1989 (c. 42, SIF 61), s. 194. (1), Sch. 11 para. 112

Open Government Licence v3.0

Contains public sector information licensed under the Open Government Licence v3.0.
The full licence if available at the following address:
http://www.nationalarchives.gov.uk/doc/open-government-licence/version/3/

Printed in Great Britain
by Amazon